An Overview of Quantum Computing

" The State of the Art in Computers "

Edited by Paul F. Kisak

Contents

Chapter 1

Quantum computing

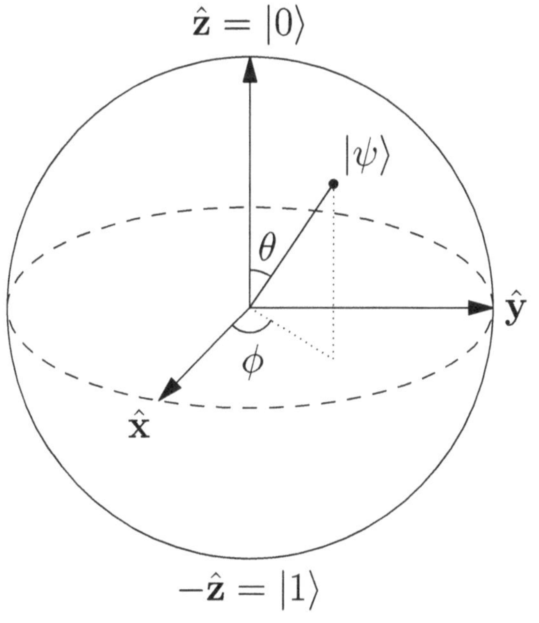

The Bloch sphere is a representation of a qubit, the fundamental building block of quantum computers.

Quantum computing studies theoretical computation systems (**quantum computers**) that make direct use of quantum-mechanical phenomena, such as superposition and entanglement, to perform operations on data.[1] Quantum computers are different from digital electronic computers based on transistors. Whereas digital computers require data to be encoded into binary digits (bits), each of which is always in one of two definite states (0 or 1), quantum computation uses quantum bits (qubits), which can be in superpositions of states. A quantum Turing machine is a theoretical model of such a computer, and is also known as the universal quantum computer. Quantum computers share theoretical similarities with non-deterministic and probabilistic computers. The field of quantum computing was initiated by the work of Paul Benioff[2] and Yuri Manin in 1980,[3] Richard Feynman in 1982,[4] and David Deutsch in 1985.[5] A quantum computer with spins as quantum bits was also formulated for use as a quantum space–time in 1968.[6]

As of 2016, the development of actual quantum computers is still in its infancy, but experiments have been carried out in which quantum computational operations were executed on a very small number of quantum bits.[7] Both practical and theoretical research continues, and many national governments and military agencies are funding quantum computing research in an effort to develop quantum computers for civilian, business, trade, environmental and national security purposes, such as cryptanalysis.[8]

Large-scale quantum computers would be able to solve certain problems much more quickly than any classical computers that use even the best currently known algorithms, like integer factorization using Shor's algorithm or the simulation of quantum many-body systems. There exist quantum algorithms, such as Simon's algorithm, that run faster than any possible probabilistic classical algorithm.[9] Given sufficient computational resources, a classical computer could in theory be made to simulate any quantum algorithm, as quantum computation does not violate the Church–Turing thesis.[10] On the other hand, quantum computers may be able to efficiently solve problems that no classical computer would be able to solve within a reasonable amount of time.

1.1 Basis

A classical computer has a memory made up of bits, where each bit is represented by either a one or a zero. A quantum computer maintains a sequence of qubits. A single qubit can represent a one, a zero, or any quantum superposition of those two qubit states; a pair of qubits can be in any quantum superposition of 4 states, and three qubits in any superposition of 8 states. In general, a quantum computer with n qubits can be in an arbitrary superposition of up to 2^n different states simultaneously (this compares to a normal computer that can only be in *one* of these 2^n states at any one time). A quantum computer operates by setting the qubits in a controlled initial state that represents the problem at hand and by manipulating those qubits with a fixed sequence of quantum logic gates. The sequence of gates to be applied is called a quantum algorithm. The calculation ends with a measurement, collapsing the system of qubits into one of the 2^n pure states, where each qubit is zero or one, decomposing into a classical state. The outcome can therefore be at most n classical bits of information. Quantum algorithms are often non-deterministic, in that they provide the correct solution only with a certain known probability.

An example of an implementation of qubits of a quantum computer could start with the use of particles with two spin states: "down" and "up" (typically written $|{\downarrow}\rangle$ and $|{\uparrow}\rangle$, or $|0\rangle$ and $|1\rangle$). But in fact any system possessing an observable quantity A, which is *conserved* under time evolution such that A has at least two discrete and sufficiently spaced consecutive eigenvalues, is a suitable candidate for implementing a qubit. This is true because any such system can be mapped onto an effective spin-1/2 system.

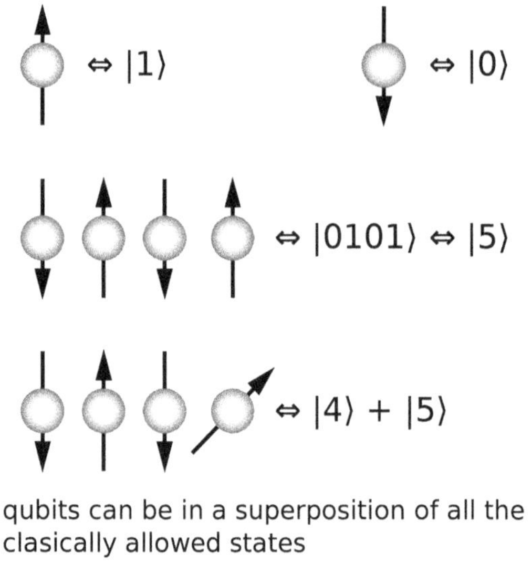

Qubits are made up of controlled particles and the means of control (e.g. devices that trap particles and switch them from one state to another).[11]

1.2 Mechanics

A quantum computer with a given number of qubits is fundamentally different from a classical computer composed of the same number of classical bits. For example, to represent the state of an n-qubit system on a classical computer would require the storage of 2^n complex coefficients. Although this fact may seem to indicate that qubits can hold exponentially more information than their classical counterparts, care must be taken not to overlook the fact that the qubits are only in a probabilistic superposition of all of their states. This means that when the final state of the qubits is measured, they will only be found in one of the possible configurations they were in before measurement. Moreover, it is incorrect to think of the qubits as only being in one particular state before measurement since the fact that they were in a superposition of states before the measurement was made directly affects the possible outcomes of the computation.

For example: Consider first a classical computer that operates on a three-bit register. The state of the computer at any time is a probability distribution over the $2^3 = 8$ different three-bit strings 000, 001, 010, 011, 100, 101, 110, 111. If it is a deterministic computer, then it is in exactly one of these states with probability 1. However, if it is a probabilistic computer, then there is a possibility of it being in any *one* of a number of different states. We can describe this probabilistic state by eight nonnegative numbers *A,B,C,D,E,F,G,H* (where *A* = is the probability that the computer is in state 000, *B* = is the probability that the computer is in state 001, etc.). There is a restriction that these probabilities sum to 1.

The state of a three-qubit quantum computer is similarly described by an eight-dimensional vector (*a,b,c,d,e,f,g,h*), called a ket. Here, however, the coefficients can have complex values, and it is the sum of the *squares* of the coefficients' magnitudes, $|a|^2 + |b|^2 + \cdots + |h|^2$, that must equal 1. These squared magnitudes represent the probability of each of the given states. However, because a complex number encodes not just a magnitude but also a direction in the complex plane, the phase difference between any two coefficients (states) represents a meaningful parameter. This is a fundamental difference between quantum computing and probabilistic classical computing.[12]

If you measure the three qubits, you will observe a three-bit string. The probability of measuring a given string is the squared magnitude of that string's coefficient (i.e., the probability of measuring 000 = $|a|^2$, the probability of measuring 001 = $|b|^2$, etc..). Thus, measuring a quantum state described by complex coefficients (*a,b,...,h*) gives the classical probability distribution $(|a|^2, |b|^2, \ldots, |h|^2)$ and we say that the quantum state "collapses" to a classical state as a result of making the measurement.

Note that an eight-dimensional vector can be specified in many different ways depending on what basis is chosen for the space. The basis of bit strings (e.g., 000, 001, ..., 111) is known as the computational basis. Other possible bases are unit-length, orthogonal vectors and the eigenvectors of the Pauli-x operator. Ket notation is often used to make the choice of basis explicit. For example, the state (*a,b,c,d,e,f,g,h*) in the computational basis can be written as:

$$a\,|000\rangle + b\,|001\rangle + c\,|010\rangle + d\,|011\rangle +$$
$$e\,|100\rangle + f\,|101\rangle + g\,|110\rangle + h\,|111\rangle$$

$$|010\rangle = (0, 0, 1, 0, 0, 0, 0, 0)$$

The computational basis for a single qubit (two dimensions) is $|0\rangle = (1, 0)$ and $|1\rangle = (0, 1)$.

Using the eigenvectors of the Pauli-x operator, a single qubit is $|+\rangle = \frac{1}{\sqrt{2}}(1, 1)$ and $|-\rangle = \frac{1}{\sqrt{2}}(1, -1)$.

1.3 Operation

While a classical three-bit state and a quantum three-qubit state are both eight-dimensional vectors, they are manipulated quite differently for classical or quantum computation. For computing in either case, the system must be initialized, for example into the all-zeros string, $|000\rangle$, corresponding to the vector (1,0,0,0,0,0,0,0). In classical randomized computation, the system evolves according to the application of stochastic matrices, which preserve that the probabilities add up to one (i.e., preserve the L1 norm). In quantum computation, on the other hand, allowed operations are unitary matrices, which are effectively rotations (they preserve that the sum of the squares add up to one, the Euclidean or L2 norm). (Exactly what unitaries can be applied depend on the physics of the quantum device.) Consequently, since rotations can be undone by rotating backward, quantum computations are reversible. (Technically, quantum operations can be probabilistic combinations of unitaries, so quantum computation really does generalize classical computation. See quantum circuit for a more precise formulation.)

Finally, upon termination of the algorithm, the result needs to be read off. In the case of a classical computer, we *sample* from the probability distribution on the three-bit register to obtain one definite three-bit string, say 000. Quantum mechanically, we *measure* the three-qubit state, which is equivalent to collapsing the quantum state down to a classical distribution (with the coefficients in the classical state being the squared magnitudes of the coefficients for the quantum state, as described above), followed by sampling from that distribution. Note that this destroys the original quantum state. Many algorithms will only give the correct answer with a certain probability. However, by repeatedly initializing, running and measuring the quantum computer's results, the probability of getting the correct answer can be increased. In contrast, counterfactual quantum computation allows the correct answer to be inferred when the quantum computer is not actually running in a technical sense, though earlier initialization and frequent measurements are part of the counterfactual computation protocol.

For more details on the sequences of operations used for various quantum algorithms, see universal quantum computer, Shor's algorithm, Grover's algorithm, Deutsch–Jozsa algorithm, amplitude amplification, quantum Fourier transform, quantum gate, quantum adiabatic algorithm and quantum error correction.

1.4 Potential

Integer factorization, which underpins the security of public key cryptographic systems, is believed to be computationally infeasible with an ordinary computer for large integers if they are the product of few prime numbers (e.g., products of two 300-digit primes).[13] By comparison, a quantum computer could efficiently solve this problem using Shor's algorithm to find its factors. This ability would allow a quantum computer to decrypt many of the cryptographic systems in use today, in the sense that there would be a polynomial time (in the number of digits of the integer) algorithm for solving the problem. In particular, most of the popular public key ciphers are based on the difficulty of factoring integers or the discrete logarithm problem, both of which can be solved by Shor's algorithm. In particular the RSA, Diffie-Hellman, and Elliptic curve Diffie-Hellman algorithms could be broken. These are used to protect secure Web pages, encrypted email, and many other types of data. Breaking these would have significant ramifications for electronic privacy and security.

However, other cryptographic algorithms do not appear to be broken by those algorithms.[14][15] Some public-key algorithms are based on problems other than the integer factorization and discrete logarithm problems to which Shor's algorithm applies, like the McEliece cryptosystem based on a problem in coding theory.[14][16] Lattice-based cryptosystems are also not known to be broken by quantum computers, and finding a polynomial time algorithm for solving the dihedral hidden subgroup problem, which would break many lattice based cryptosystems, is a well-studied open problem.[17] It has been proven that applying Grover's algorithm to break a symmetric (secret key) algorithm by brute force requires time equal to roughly $2^{n/2}$ invocations of the underlying cryptographic algorithm, compared with roughly 2^n in the classical case,[18] meaning that symmetric key lengths are effectively halved: AES-256 would have the same security against an attack using Grover's algorithm that AES-128 has against classical brute-force search (see Key size). Quantum cryptography could potentially fulfill some of the functions of public key cryptography.

Besides factorization and discrete logarithms, quantum algorithms offering a more than polynomial speedup over the best known classical algorithm have been found for several problems,[19] including the simulation of quantum physical processes from chemistry and solid state physics, the approximation of Jones polynomials, and solving Pell's equation. No mathematical proof has been found that shows that an equally fast classical algorithm cannot be discovered, although this is considered unlikely . For some problems, quantum computers offer a polynomial speedup. The most well-known example of this is *quantum database search*, which can be solved by Grover's algorithm using quadratically fewer queries to the database than are required by classical algorithms. In this case the advantage is provable. Several other examples of provable quantum speedups for query problems have subsequently been discovered, such as for finding collisions in two-to-one functions and evaluating NAND trees.

Consider a problem that has these four properties:

1. The only way to solve it is to guess answers repeatedly and check them,
2. The number of possible answers to check is the same as the number of inputs,
3. Every possible answer takes the same amount of time to check, and
4. There are no clues about which answers might be better: generating possibilities randomly is just as good as checking them in some special order.

An example of this is a password cracker that attempts to guess the password for an encrypted file (assuming that the password has a maximum possible length).

For problems with all four properties, the time for a quantum computer to solve this will be proportional to the square root of the number of inputs. It can be used to attack symmetric ciphers such as Triple DES and AES by attempting to guess the secret key.[20]

Grover's algorithm can also be used to obtain a quadratic speed-up over a brute-force search for a class of problems known as NP-complete.

Since chemistry and nanotechnology rely on understanding quantum systems, and such systems are impossible to simulate in an efficient manner classically, many believe quantum simulation will be one of the most important applications of quantum computing.[21] Quantum simulation could also be used to simulate the behavior of atoms and particles at unusual conditions such as the reactions inside a collider.[22]

There are a number of technical challenges in building a large-scale quantum computer, and thus far quantum computers have yet to solve a problem faster than a classical computer. David DiVincenzo, of IBM, listed the following requirements for a practical quantum computer:[23]

- scalable physically to increase the number of qubits;
- qubits that can be initialized to arbitrary values;
- quantum gates that are faster than decoherence time;
- universal gate set;
- qubits that can be read easily.

1.4.1 Quantum decoherence

One of the greatest challenges is controlling or removing quantum decoherence. This usually means isolating the system from its environment as interactions with the external world cause the system to decohere. However, other sources of decoherence also exist. Examples include the quantum gates, and the lattice vibrations and background thermonuclear spin of the physical system used to implement the qubits. Decoherence is irreversible, as it is non-unitary, and is usually something that should be highly controlled, if not avoided. Decoherence times for candidate systems, in particular the transverse relaxation time T_2 (for NMR and MRI technology, also called the *dephasing time*), typically range between nanoseconds and seconds at low temperature.[12] Currently, some quantum computers require their qubits to be cooled to 20 millikelvin in order to prevent significant decoherence.[24]

These issues are more difficult for optical approaches as the timescales are orders of magnitude shorter and an often-cited approach to overcoming them is optical pulse shaping. Error rates are typically proportional to the ratio of operating time to decoherence time, hence any operation must be completed much more quickly than the decoherence time.

If the error rate is small enough, it is thought to be possible to use quantum error correction, which corrects errors due to decoherence, thereby allowing the total calculation time to be longer than the decoherence time. An often cited figure for required error rate in each gate is 10^{-4}. This implies that each gate must be able to perform its task in one 10,000th of the coherence time of the system.

Meeting this scalability condition is possible for a wide range of systems. However, the use of error correction brings with it the cost of a greatly increased number of required bits. The number required to factor integers using Shor's algorithm is still polynomial, and thought to be between L and L^2, where L is the number of bits in the number to be factored; error correction algorithms would inflate this figure by an additional factor of L. For a 1000-bit number, this implies a need for about 10^4 bits without error correction.[25] With error correction, the figure would rise to about 10^7 bits. Note that computation time is about L^2 or about 10^7 steps and on 1 MHz, about 10 seconds.

A very different approach to the stability-decoherence problem is to create a topological quantum computer with anyons, quasi-particles used as threads and relying on braid theory to form stable logic gates.[26][27]

1.5 Developments

There are a number of quantum computing models, distinguished by the basic elements in which the computation is decomposed. The four main models of practical importance are:

- *Quantum gate array* (computation decomposed into sequence of few-qubit quantum gates)

- *One-way quantum computer* (computation decomposed into sequence of one-qubit measurements applied to a highly entangled initial state or cluster state)
- *Adiabatic quantum computer*, based on Quantum annealing (computation decomposed into a slow continuous transformation of an initial Hamiltonian into a final Hamiltonian, whose ground states contain the solution)[28]
- Topological quantum computer[29] (computation decomposed into the braiding of anyons in a 2D lattice)

The *Quantum Turing machine* is theoretically important but direct implementation of this model is not pursued. All four models of computation have been shown to be equivalent; each can simulate the other with no more than polynomial overhead.

For physically implementing a quantum computer, many different candidates are being pursued, among them (distinguished by the physical system used to realize the qubits):

- Superconductor-based quantum computers (including SQUID-based quantum computers)[30][31] (qubit implemented by the state of small superconducting circuits (Josephson junctions))
- Trapped ion quantum computer (qubit implemented by the internal state of trapped ions)
- Optical lattices (qubit implemented by internal states of neutral atoms trapped in an optical lattice)
- Quantum dot computer, spin-based (e.g. the Loss-DiVincenzo quantum computer [32]) (qubit given by the spin states of trapped electrons)
- Quantum dot computer, spatial-based (qubit given by electron position in double quantum dot)[33]
- Nuclear magnetic resonance on molecules in solution (liquid-state NMR) (qubit provided by nuclear spins within the dissolved molecule)
- Solid-state NMR Kane quantum computers (qubit realized by the nuclear spin state of phosphorus donors in silicon)
- Electrons-on-helium quantum computers (qubit is the electron spin)
- Cavity quantum electrodynamics (CQED) (qubit provided by the internal state of trapped atoms coupled to high-finesse cavities)
- Molecular magnet[34] (qubit given by spin states)
- Fullerene-based ESR quantum computer (qubit based on the electronic spin of atoms or molecules encased in fullerenes)
- Linear optical quantum computer (qubits realized by processing states of different modes of light through linear elements e.g. mirrors, beam splitters and phase shifters)[35]
- Diamond-based quantum computer[36][37][38] (qubit realized by electronic or nuclear spin of nitrogen-vacancy centers in diamond)
- Bose–Einstein condensate-based quantum computer[39]
- Transistor-based quantum computer – string quantum computers with entrainment of positive holes using an electrostatic trap
- Rare-earth-metal-ion-doped inorganic crystal based quantum computers[40][41] (qubit realized by the internal electronic state of dopants in optical fibers)

The large number of candidates demonstrates that the topic, in spite of rapid progress, is still in its infancy. There is also a vast amount of flexibility.

1.5.1 Timeline

Main article: Timeline of quantum computing

In 2001, researchers demonstrated Shor's algorithm to factor 15 using a 7-qubit NMR computer.[42]

In 2005, researchers at the University of Michigan built a semiconductor chip ion trap. Such devices from standard lithography, may point the way to scalable quantum computing.[43]

In 2009, researchers at Yale University created the first solid-state quantum processor. The two-qubit superconducting chip had artificial atom qubits made of a billion aluminum atoms that acted like a single atom that could occupy two states.[44][45]

A team at the University of Bristol, also created a silicon chip based on quantum optics, able to run Shor's algorithm.[46] Further developments were made in 2010.[47] Springer publishes a journal (*Quantum Information Processing*) devoted to the subject.[48]

In August 2010, Digital Combinational Circuits like adder, subtractor etc. are designed with the help of Symmetric Functions organized from different quantum gates.[49]

April 2011, a team of scientists from Australia and Japan made a breakthrough in quantum teleportation. They successfully transferred a complex set of quantum data with full transmission integrity, without affecting the qubits' superpositions.[50][51]

In 2011, D-Wave Systems announced the first commercial quantum annealer, the D-Wave One, claiming a 128

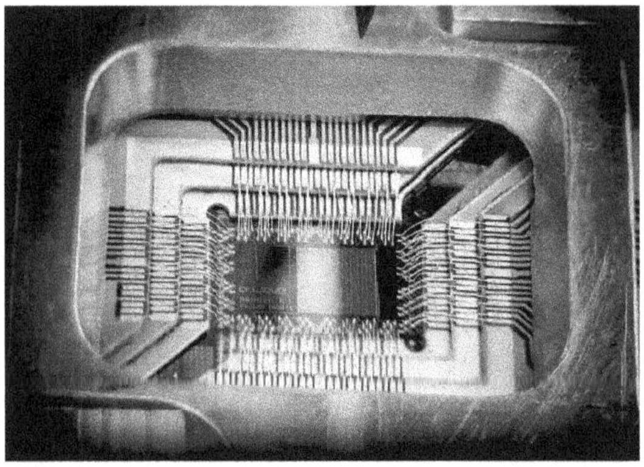

Photograph of a chip constructed by D-Wave Systems Inc., mounted and wire-bonded in a sample holder. The D-Wave processor is designed to use 128 superconducting logic elements that exhibit controllable and tunable coupling to perform operations.

qubit processor.[52] On May 25, 2011 Lockheed Martin agreed to purchase a D-Wave One system.[53] Lockheed and the University of Southern California (USC) will house the D-Wave One at the newly formed USC Lockheed Martin Quantum Computing Center.[54] D-Wave's engineers designed the chips with an empirical approach, focusing on solving particular problems. Investors liked this more than academics, who said D-Wave had not demonstrated they really had a quantum computer. Criticism softened after a D-Wave paper in Nature, that proved the chips have some quantum properties.[55][56] Two published papers have suggested that the D-Wave machine's operation can be explained classically, rather than requiring quantum models.[57][58] Later work showed that classical models are insufficient when all available data is considered.[59] Experts remain divided on the ultimate classification of the D-Wave systems though their quantum behavior was established concretely with a demonstration of entanglement.[60]

During the same year, researchers at the University of Bristol created an all-bulk optics system that ran a version of Shor's algorithm to successfully factor 21.[61]

In September 2011 researchers proved quantum computers can be made with a Von Neumann architecture (separation of RAM).[62]

In November 2011 researchers factorized 143 using 4 qubits.[63]

In February 2012 IBM scientists said that they had made several breakthroughs in quantum computing with superconducting integrated circuits.[64]

In April 2012 a multinational team of researchers from the University of Southern California, Delft University of Technology, the Iowa State University of Science and Technology, and the University of California, Santa Barbara, constructed a two-qubit quantum computer on a doped diamond crystal that can easily be scaled up and is functional at room temperature. Two logical qubit directions of electron spin and nitrogen kernels spin were used, with microwave impulses. This computer ran Grover's algorithm generating the right answer from the first try in 95% of cases.[65]

In September 2012, Australian researchers at the University of New South Wales said the world's first quantum computer was just 5 to 10 years away, after announcing a global breakthrough enabling manufacture of its memory building blocks. A research team led by Australian engineers created the first working qubit based on a single atom in silicon, invoking the same technological platform that forms the building blocks of modern-day computers.[66] [67]

In October 2012, Nobel Prizes were presented to David J. Wineland and Serge Haroche for their basic work on understanding the quantum world, which may help make quantum computing possible.[68][69]

In November 2012, the first quantum teleportation from one macroscopic object to another was reported.[70][71]

In December 2012, the first dedicated quantum computing software company, 1QBit was founded in Vancouver, BC.[72] 1QBit is the first company to focus exclusively on commercializing software applications for commercially available quantum computers, including the D-Wave Two. 1QBit's research demonstrated the ability of superconducting quantum annealing processors to solve real-world problems.[73]

In February 2013, a new technique, boson sampling, was reported by two groups using photons in an optical lattice that is not a universal quantum computer but may be good enough for practical problems. *Science* Feb 15, 2013

In May 2013, Google announced that it was launching the Quantum Artificial Intelligence Lab, hosted by NASA's Ames Research Center, with a 512-qubit D-Wave quantum computer. The USRA (Universities Space Research Association) will invite researchers to share time on it with the goal of studying quantum computing for machine learning.[74]

In early 2014 it was reported, based on documents provided by former NSA contractor Edward Snowden, that the U.S. National Security Agency (NSA) is running a $79.7 million research program (titled "Penetrating Hard Targets") to develop a quantum computer capable of breaking vulnerable encryption.[75]

In 2014, a group of researchers from ETH Zürich, USC, Google and Microsoft reported a definition of quantum speedup, and were not able to measure quantum speedup with the D-Wave Two device, but did not explicitly rule it out.[76][77]

In 2014, researchers at University of New South Wales used silicon as a protectant shell around qubits, making them more accurate, increasing the length of time they will hold information and possibly made quantum computers easier to build.[78]

In April 2015 IBM scientists claimed two critical advances towards the realization of a practical quantum computer. They claimed the ability to detect and measure both kinds of quantum errors simultaneously, as well as a new, square quantum bit circuit design that could scale to larger dimensions.[79]

In October 2015 researchers at University of New South Wales built a quantum logic gate in silicon for the first time.[80]

In December 2015 NASA publicly displayed the world's first fully operational $15-million quantum computer made by the Canadian company D-Wave at the Quantum Artificial Intelligence Laboratory at its Ames Research Center in California's Moffett Field. The device was purchased in 2013 via a partnership with Google and Universities Space Research Association. Despite using quantum effects the algorithm run on the quantum computer does not outperform Selby's algorithm run on a classical computer.[81]

1.6 Relation to computational complexity theory

Main article: Quantum complexity theory

The class of problems that can be efficiently solved by

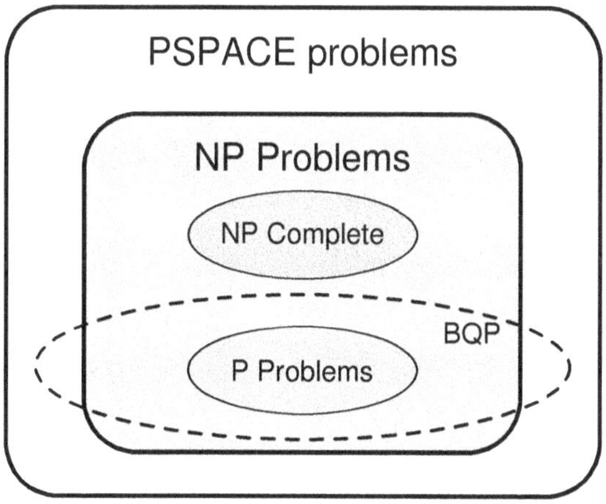

The suspected relationship of BQP to other problem spaces.[82]

quantum computers is called BQP, for "bounded error, quantum, polynomial time". Quantum computers only run probabilistic algorithms, so BQP on quantum computers is the counterpart of BPP ("bounded error, probabilistic, polynomial time") on classical computers. It is defined as the set of problems solvable with a polynomial-time algorithm, whose probability of error is bounded away from one half.[83] A quantum computer is said to "solve" a problem if, for every instance, its answer will be right with high probability. If that solution runs in polynomial time, then that problem is in BQP.

BQP is contained in the complexity class *#P* (or more precisely in the associated class of decision problems $P^{\#P}$),[84] which is a subclass of PSPACE.

BQP is suspected to be disjoint from NP-complete and a strict superset of P, but that is not known. Both integer factorization and discrete log are in BQP. Both of these problems are NP problems suspected to be outside BPP, and hence outside P. Both are suspected to not be NP-complete. There is a common misconception that quantum computers can solve NP-complete problems in polynomial time. That is not known to be true, and is generally suspected to be false.[84]

The capacity of a quantum computer to accelerate classical algorithms has rigid limits—upper bounds of quantum computation's complexity. The overwhelming part of classical calculations cannot be accelerated on a quantum computer.[85] A similar fact takes place for particular computational tasks, like the search problem, for which Grover's algorithm is optimal.[86]

Although quantum computers may be faster than classical computers for some problem types, those described above can't solve any problem that classical computers can't already solve. A Turing machine can simulate these quantum computers, so such a quantum computer could never solve an undecidable problem like the halting problem. The existence of "standard" quantum computers does not disprove the Church–Turing thesis.[87] It has been speculated that theories of quantum gravity, such as M-theory or loop quantum gravity, may allow even faster computers to be built. Currently, *defining* computation in such theories is an open problem due to the *problem of time*, i.e., there currently exists no obvious way to describe what it means for an observer to submit input to a computer and later receive output.[88]

1.7 See also

- Chemical computer
- David Deutsch
- DNA computer
- Electronic quantum holography
- List of emerging technologies
- Richard Feynman
- IARPA
- Kane quantum computer
- Natural computing
- Normal mode
- Photonic computing
- Post-quantum cryptography
- Quantum annealing

- Quantum bus
- Quantum cognition
- Quantum gate
- Quantum threshold theorem
- Soliton
- Theoretical computer science
- Timeline of quantum computing
- Topological quantum computer
- Valleytronics
- D-Wave Two

1.8 References

[1] Gershenfeld, Neil; Chuang, Isaac L. (June 1998). “Quantum Computing with Molecules” (PDF). *Scientific American*.

[2] Benioff, Paul (1980). “The computer as a physical system: A microscopic quantum mechanical Hamiltonian model of computers as represented by Turing machines”. *Journal of statistical physics* **22** (5): 563–591. Bibcode:1980JSP....22..563B. doi:10.1007/BF01011339.

[3] Manin, Yu. I. (1980). *Vychislimoe i nevychislimoe* [*Computable and Noncomputable*] (in Russian). Sov.Radio. pp. 13–15. Retrieved 2013-03-04.

[4] Feynman, R. P. (1982). “Simulating physics with computers”. *International Journal of Theoretical Physics* **21** (6): 467–488. Bibcode:1982IJTP...21..467F. doi:10.1007/BF02650179.

[5] Deutsch, David (1985). “Quantum Theory, the Church-Turing Principle and the Universal Quantum Computer”. *Proceedings of the Royal Society of London A* **400** (1818): 97–117. Bibcode:1985RSPSA.400...97D. doi:10.1098/rspa.1985.0070.

[6] Finkelstein, David (1968). “Space-Time Structure in High Energy Interactions”. In Gudehus, T.; Kaiser, G. *Fundamental Interactions at High Energy*. New York: Gordon & Breach.

[7] Gershon, Eric (2013-01-14). “New qubit control bodes well for future of quantum computing”. Phys.org. Retrieved 2014-10-26.

[8] Quantum Information Science and Technology Roadmap for a sense of where the research is heading.

[9] Simon, D.R. (1994). “On the power of quantum computation”. *Foundations of Computer Science, 1994 Proceedings., 35th Annual Symposium on*: 116–123. doi:10.1109/SFCS.1994.365701. ISBN 0-8186-6580-7.

[10] Nielsen, Michael A.; Chuang, Isaac L. *Quantum Computation and Quantum Information*. p. 202.

[11] Waldner, Jean-Baptiste (2007). *Nanocomputers and Swarm Intelligence*. London: ISTE. p. 157. ISBN 2-7462-1516-0.

[12] DiVincenzo, David P. (1995). “Quantum Computation”. *Science* **270** (5234): 255–261. Bibcode:1995Sci...270..255D. doi:10.1126/science.270.5234.255. (subscription required)

[13] Lenstra, Arjen K. (2000). “Integer Factoring” (PDF). *Designs, Codes and Cryptography* **19** (2/3). 101–128. doi:10.1023/A:1008397921377.

[14] Daniel J. Bernstein, *Introduction to Post-Quantum Cryptography*. Introduction to Daniel J. Bernstein, Johannes Buchmann, Erik Dahmen (editors). Post-quantum cryptography. Springer, Berlin, 2009. ISBN 978-3-540-88701-0

[15] See also pqcrypto.org, a bibliography maintained by Daniel J. Bernstein and Tanja Lange on cryptography not known to be broken by quantum computing.

[16] Robert J. McEliece. "A public-key cryptosystem based on algebraic coding theory." Jet Propulsion Laboratory DSN Progress Report 42–44, 114–116.

[17] Kobayashi, H.; Gall, F.L. (2006). “Dihedral Hidden Subgroup Problem: A Survey”. *Information and Media Technologies* **1** (1): 178–185.

[18] Bennett C.H., Bernstein E., Brassard G., Vazirani U., "The strengths and weaknesses of quantum computation". *SIAM Journal on Computing* 26(5): 1510–1523 (1997).

[19] Quantum Algorithm Zoo – Stephen Jordan’s Homepage

[20] Rich, Steven; Gellman, Barton (2014-02-01). “NSA seeks to build quantum computer that could crack most types of encryption”. *Washington Post*.

[21] Norton, Quinn (2007-02-15). “The Father of Quantum Computing”. Wired.com.

[22] Ambainis, Andris (Spring 2014). “What Can We Do with a Quantum Computer?". Institute for Advanced Study.

[23] DiVincenzo, David P. (2000-04-13). “The Physical Implementation of Quantum Computation”. arXiv:quant-ph/0002077 [quant-ph].

[24] Jones, Nicola (19 June 2013). “Computing: The quantum company”. *Nature* **498** (7454): 286–288. doi:10.1038/498286a.

[25] Dyakonov, M. I. (2006-10-14). “Is Fault-Tolerant Quantum Computation Really Possible?". *In: Future Trends in Microelectronics. Up the Nano Creek, S. Luryi, J. Xu, and A. Zaslavsky (eds), Wiley, pp.*: 4–18. arXiv:quant-ph/0610117.

[26] Freedman, Michael H.; Kitaev, Alexei; Larsen, Michael J.; Wang, Zhenghan (2003). “Topological quantum computation”. *Bulletin of the American Mathematical Society* **40** (1): 31–38. arXiv:quant-ph/0101025. doi:10.1090/S0273-0979-02-00964-3. MR 1943131.

[27] Monroe, Don (2008-10-01). "Anyons: The breakthrough quantum computing needs?". *New Scientist*.

[28] Das, A.; Chakrabarti, B. K. (2008). "Quantum Annealing and Analog Quantum Computation". *Rev. Mod. Phys.* **80** (3): 1061–1081. Bibcode:2008RvMP...80.1061D. doi:10.1103/RevModPhys.80.1061

[29] Nayak, Chetan; Simon, Steven; Stern, Ady; Das Sarma, Sankar (2008). "Nonabelian Anyons and Quantum Computation". *Rev Mod Phys* **80** (3): 1083. arXiv:0707.1889. Bibcode:2008RvMP...80.1083N. doi:10.1103/RevModPhys.80.1083.

[30] Clarke, John; Wilhelm, Frank (June 19, 2008). "Superconducting quantum bits". *Nature* **453** (7198): 1031–1042. Bibcode:2008Natur.453.1031C. doi:10.1038/nature07128. PMID 18563154.

[31] Kaminsky, William M (2004). "Scalable Superconducting Architecture for Adiabatic Quantum Computation". arXiv:quant-ph/0403090 [quant-ph].

[32] Imamoğlu, Atac; Awschalom, D. D.; Burkard, Guido; DiVincenzo, D. P.; Loss, D.; Sherwin, M.; Small, A. (1999). "Quantum information processing using quantum dot spins and cavity-QED". *Physical Review Letters* **83** (20): 4204. Bibcode:1999PhRvL..83.4204I. doi:10.1103/PhysRevLett.83.4204.

[33] Fedichkin, Leonid; Yanchenko, Maxim; Valiev, Kamil (2000). "Novel coherent quantum bit using spatial quantization levels in semiconductor quantum dot". *Quantum Computers and Computing* **1**: 58–76. arXiv:quant-ph/0006097. Bibcode:2000quant.ph..6097F.

[34] "Quantum computing in molecular magnets.". *Nature* **410** (6830): 789–93. Apr 12, 2001. doi:10.1038/35071024. PMID 11298441.

[35] Knill, G. J.; Laflamme, R.; Milburn, G. J. (2001). "A scheme for efficient quantum computation with linear optics". *Nature* **409** (6816): 46–52. Bibcode:2001Natur.409...46K. doi:10.1038/35051009. PMID 11343107.

[36] Nizovtsev, A. P. (August 2005). "A quantum computer based on NV centers in diamond: Optically detected nutations of single electron and nuclear spins". *Optics and Spectroscopy* **99** (2): 248–260. Bibcode:2005OptSp..99..233N. doi:10.1134/1.2034610.

[37] Gruener, Wolfgang (2007-06-01). "Research indicates diamonds could be key to quantum storage". Retrieved 2007-06-04.

[38] Neumann, P.; et al. (June 6, 2008). "Multipartite Entanglement Among Single Spins in Diamond". *Science* **320** (5881): 1326–1329. Bibcode:2008Sci...320.1326N. doi:10.1126/science.1157233. PMID 18535240.

[39] Millman, Rene (2007-08-03). "Trapped atoms could advance quantum computing". ITPro. Archived from the original on 2007-09-27. Retrieved 2007-07-26.

[40] Ohlsson, N.; Mohan, R. K.; Kröll, S. (January 1, 2002). "Quantum computer hardware based on rare-earth-ion-doped inorganic crystals". *Opt. Commun.* **201** (1–3): 71–77. Bibcode:2002OptCo.201...71O. doi:10.1016/S0030-4018(01)01666-2.

[41] Longdell, J. J.; Sellars, M. J.; Manson, N. B. (September 23, 2004). "Demonstration of conditional quantum phase shift between ions in a solid". *Phys. Rev. Lett.* **93** (13): 130503. arXiv:quant-ph/0404083. Bibcode:2004PhRvL..93m0503L. doi:10.1103/PhysRevLett.93.130503. PMID 15524694.

[42] Vandersypen, Lieven M. K.; Steffen, Matthias; Breyta, Gregory; Yannoni, Costantino S.; Sherwood, Mark H.; Chuang, Isaac L. (2001). "Experimental realization of Shor's quantum factoring algorithm using nuclear magnetic resonance". *Nature* **414** (6866): 883–7. doi:10.1038/414883a. PMID 11780055.

[43] "U-M develops scalable and mass-producible quantum computer chip". University of Michigan. 2005-12-12. Retrieved 2006-11-17.

[44] DiCarlo, L.; Chow, J. M.; Gambetta, J. M.; Bishop, Lev S.; Johnson, B. R.; Schuster, D. I.; Majer, J.; Blais, A.; Frunzio, L.; S. M. Girvin; R. J. Schoelkopf (9 July 2009). "Demonstration of two-qubit algorithms with a superconducting quantum processor" (PDF). *Nature* **460** (7252): 240–4. Bibcode:2009Natur.460..240D. doi:10.1038/nature08121. PMID 19561592. Retrieved 2009-07-02.

[45] "Scientists Create First Electronic Quantum Processor". Yale University. 2009-07-02. Retrieved 2009-07-02.

[46] "Code-breaking quantum algorithm runs on a silicon chip". *New Scientist*. 2009-09-04. Retrieved 2009-10-14.

[47] "New Trends in Quantum Computation". *Simons Conference on New Trends in Quantum Computation 2010: Program*. C.N. Yang Institute for Theoretical Physics.

[48] "Quantum Information Processing". Springer.com. Retrieved on 2011-05-19.

[49] Bhattacharjee, Pijush Kanti (2010). "Digital Combinational Circuits Design with the Help of Symmetric Functions Considering Heat Dissipation by Each QCA Gate" (PDF). International Journal of Computer and Electrical Engineering (IJCEE), Singapore, vol. 2, no. 4, pp. 666-672, August 2010.

[50] "Quantum teleporter breakthrough". University of New South Wales. 2011-04-15. Archived from the original on 2011-04-18.

[51] Lai, Richard (2011-04-18). "First light wave quantum teleportation achieved, opens door to ultra fast data transmission". Engadget.

[52] "Learning to program the D-Wave One". *Hack The Multiverse*. D-Wave. Retrieved 2011-05-11.

[53] "D-Wave Systems sells its first Quantum Computing System to Lockheed Martin Corporation". D-Wave. 2011-05-25. Retrieved 2011-05-30.

[54] "Operational Quantum Computing Center Established at USC". University of Southern California. 2011-10-29. Retrieved 2011-12-06.

[55] "Quantum annealing with manufactured spins". *Nature* **473** (7346): 194–198. 12 May 2011. doi:10.1038/nature10012.

[56] Simonite, Tom (October 4, 2012). "The CIA and Jeff Bezos Bet on Quantum Computing". *Technology Review*.

[57] "How "Quantum" is the D-Wave Machine?". Arxiv. 2014-05-02.

[58] "Quantum Annealing With More Than 100 Qbits". Arxiv. 2013-04-16.

[59] "Reexamining classical and quantum models for the D-Wave One processor". Arxiv. 2014-09-12.

[60] "Entanglement in a quantum annealing processor". prx. 2014-05-29.

[61] Lopez, Enrique Martin; Laing, Anthony; Lawson, Thomas; Alvarez, Roberto; Zhou, Xiao-Qi; O'Brien, Jeremy L. (2011). "Implementation of an iterative quantum order finding algorithm". *Nature Photonics* **6** (11): 773–776. arXiv:1111.4147. doi:10.1038/nphoton.2012.259.

[62] "Quantum computer with Von Neumann architecture". Retrieved 2014-10-26.

[63] "Quantum Factorization of 143 on a Dipolar-Coupling NMR system". Retrieved 2014-10-26.

[64] "IBM Says It's 'On the Cusp' of Building a Quantum Computer". *PCMAG*. Retrieved 2014-10-26.

[65] "Quantum computer built inside diamond". *Futurity*. Retrieved 2014-10-26.

[66] "Australian engineers write quantum computer 'qubit' in global breakthrough". *The Australian*. Retrieved 2012-10-03.

[67] "Breakthrough in bid to create first quantum computer". University of New South Wales. Retrieved 2012-10-03.

[68] Frank, Adam (October 14, 2012). "Cracking the Quantum Safe". *New York Times*. Retrieved 2012-10-14.

[69] Overbye, Dennis (October 9, 2012). "A Nobel for Teasing Out the Secret Life of Atoms". *New York Times*. Retrieved 2012-10-14.

[70] "First Teleportation from One Macroscopic Object to Another: The Physics arXiv Blog". *MIT Technology Review*. November 15, 2012. Retrieved 2012-11-17.

[71] Bao, Xiao-Hui; Xu, Xiao-Fan; Li, Che-Ming; Yuan, Zhen-Sheng; Lu, Chao-Yang; Pan, Jian-wei (November 13, 2012). "Quantum teleportation between remote atomic-ensemble quantum memories". *arXiv*. arXiv:1211.2892.

[72] "1QBit Founded". *1QBit.com*. Retrieved 2014-06-22.

[73] "1QBit Research". *1QBit.com*. Retrieved 2014-06-22.

[74] "Launching the Quantum Artificial Intelligence Lab". Research@Google Blog. Retrieved 2013-05-16.

[75] "NSA seeks to build quantum computer that could crack most types of encryption". *Washington Post*. January 2, 2014.

[76] Defining and detecting quantum speedup, Troels F. Rønnow, Zhihui Wang, Joshua Job, Sergio Boixo, Sergei V. Isakov, David Wecker, John M. Martinis, Daniel A. Lidar, Matthias Troyer, 2014-01-13.

[77] "Quantum Chaos: After a Failed Speed Test, the D-Wave Debate Continues". *Scientific American*. 2014-06-19.

[78] Gaudin, Sharon (23 October 2014). "Researchers use silicon to push quantum computing toward reality". *Computer World*.

[79] IBM Scientists Achieve Critical Steps to Building First Practical Quantum Computer

[80] World's First Silicon Quantum Logic Gate Brings Quantum Computing One Step Closer

[81] "3Q: Scott Aaronson on Google's new quantum-computing paper". *MIT News*. Retrieved 2016-01-05.

[82] Nielsen, p. 42

[83] Nielsen, p. 41

[84] Bernstein, Ethan; Vazirani, Umesh (1997). "Quantum Complexity Theory". *SIAM Journal on Computing* **26** (5): 1411. doi:10.1137/S0097539796300921.

[85] Ozhigov, Yuri (1999). "Quantum Computers Speed Up Classical with Probability Zero". *Chaos Solitons Fractals* **10** (10): 1707–1714. arXiv:quant-ph/9803064. Bibcode:1998quant.ph..3064O. doi:10.1016/S0960-0779(98)00226-4.

[86] Ozhigov, Yuri (1999). "Lower Bounds of Quantum Search for Extreme Point". *Proceedings of the London Royal Society* **A455** (1986): 2165–2172. arXiv:quant-ph/9806001. Bibcode:1999RSPSA.455.2165O. doi:10.1098/rspa.1999.0397.

[87] Nielsen, p. 126

[88] Scott Aaronson, *NP-complete Problems and Physical Reality*, ACM SIGACT News, Vol. 36, No. 1. (March 2005), pp. 30–52, section 7 "Quantum Gravity": "[...] to anyone who wants a test or benchmark for a favorite quantum gravity theory,[author's footnote: That is, one without all the bother of making numerical predictions and comparing them to observation] let me humbly propose the following: *can you define Quantum Gravity Polynomial-Time?* [...] until we can say what it means for a 'user' to specify an 'input' and 'later' receive an 'output'—*there is no such thing as computation, not even theoretically.*" (emphasis in original)

1.9 Further reading

- Nielsen, Michael; Chuang, Isaac (2000). *Quantum Computation and Quantum Information*. Cambridge: Cambridge University Press. ISBN 0-521-63503-9. OCLC 174527496.
- Abbot, Derek; Doering, Charles R.; Caves, Carlton M.; Lidar, Daniel M.; Brandt, Howard E.; Hamilton, Alexander R.; Ferry, David K.; Gea-Banacloche, Julio; Bezrukov, Sergey M.; Kish, Laszlo B. (2003). "Dreams versus Reality: Plenary Debate Session on Quantum Computing". *Quantum Information Processing* **2** (6): 449–472. arXiv:quant-ph/0310130. doi:10.1023/B:QINP.0000042203.24782.9a. hdl:2027.42/45526.
- DiVincenzo, David P. (2000). "The Physical Implementation of Quantum Computation". *Experimental Proposals for Quantum Computation*. arXiv:quant-ph/0002077
- DiVincenzo, David P. (1995). "Quantum Computation". *Science* **270** (5234): 255–261. Bibcode:1995Sci...270..255D. doi:10.1126/science.270.5234.255. Table 1 lists switching and dephasing times for various systems.
- Feynman, Richard (1982). "Simulating physics with computers". *International Journal of Theoretical Physics* **21** (6–7): 467. Bibcode:1982IJTP...21..467F. doi:10.1007/BF02650179.
- Jaeger, Gregg (2006). *Quantum Information: An Overview*. Berlin: Springer. ISBN 0-387-35725-4. OCLC 255569451.
- Singer, Stephanie Frank (2005). *Linearity, Symmetry, and Prediction in the Hydrogen Atom*. New York: Springer. ISBN 0-387-24637-1. OCLC 253709076.
- Benenti, Giuliano (2004). *Principles of Quantum Computation and Information Volume 1*. New Jersey: World Scientific. ISBN 981-238-830-3. OCLC 179950736.
- Lomonaco, Sam. Four Lectures on Quantum Computing given at Oxford University in July 2006
- C. Adami, N.J. Cerf. (1998). "Quantum computation with linear optics". arXiv:quant-ph/9806048v1.
- Stolze, Joachim; Suter, Dieter (2004). *Quantum Computing*. Wiley-VCH. ISBN 3-527-40438-4.
- Mitchell, Ian (1998). "Computing Power into the 21st Century: Moore's Law and Beyond".
- Landauer, Rolf (1961). "Irreversibility and heat generation in the computing process" (PDF).
- Moore, Gordon E. (1965). *Cramming more components onto integrated circuits. Electronics Magazine*.
- Keyes, R. W. (1988). *Miniaturization of electronics and its limits. IBM Journal of Research and Development*.
- Nielsen, M. A.; Knill, E.; Laflamme, R. "Complete Quantum Teleportation By Nuclear Magnetic Resonance".
- Vandersypen, Lieven M.K.; Yannoni, Constantino S.; Chuang, Isaac L. (2000). *Liquid state NMR Quantum Computing*.
- Hiroshi, Imai; Masahito, Hayashi (2006). *Quantum Computation and Information*. Berlin: Springer. ISBN 3-540-33132-8.
- Berthiaume, Andre (1997). "Quantum Computation".
- Simon, Daniel R. (1994). "On the Power of Quantum Computation". Institute of Electrical and Electronic Engineers Computer Society Press.
- "Seminar Post Quantum Cryptology". Chair for communication security at the Ruhr-University Bochum.
- Sanders, Laura (2009). "First programmable quantum computer created".
- "New trends in quantum computation".
- Wichert, Andreas (2014). *Principles of Quantum Artificial Intelligence*. World Scientific Publishing Co. ISBN 978-981-4566-74-2.
- Akama, Seiki (2014). *Elements of Quantum Computing: History, Theories and Engineering Applications*. Springer International Publishing. ISBN 978-3-319-08284-4.

1.10 External links

- Stanford Encyclopedia of Philosophy: "Quantum Computing" by Amit Hagar.
- Quantum Annealing and Computation: A Brief Documentary Note, A. Ghosh and S. Mukherjee
- Maryland University Laboratory for Physical Sciences: conducts researches for the quantum computer-based project led by the NSA, named 'Penetrating Hard Target'.
- Visualized history of quantum computing

- Quantum Annealing and Analog Quantum Computation by Arnab Das and BK Chakrabarti

Lectures

- Quantum computing for the determined – 22 video lectures by Michael Nielsen
- Video Lectures by David Deutsch
- Lectures at the Institut Henri Poincaré (slides and videos)
- Online lecture on An Introduction to Quantum Computing, Edward Gerjuoy (2008)
- Quantum Computing research by Mikko Möttönen at Aalto University (video) on YouTube

Chapter 2

Quantum finite automata

In quantum computing, **quantum finite automata** or **QFA** or quantum state machines are a quantum analog of probabilistic automata or a Markov decision process. They are related to quantum computers in a similar fashion as finite automata are related to Turing machines. Several types of automata may be defined, including *measure-once* and *measure-many* automata. Quantum finite automata can also be understood as the quantization of subshifts of finite type, or as a quantization of Markov chains. QFA's are, in turn, special cases of **geometric finite automata** or **topological finite automata**.

The automata work by accepting a finite-length string $\sigma = (\sigma_0, \sigma_1, \cdots, \sigma_k)$ of letters σ_i from a finite alphabet Σ, and assigning to each such string a probability $\Pr(\sigma)$ indicating the probability of the automaton being in an accept state; that is, indicating whether the automaton accepted or rejected the string.

The languages accepted by QFA's are not the regular languages of deterministic finite automata, nor are they the stochastic languages of probabilistic finite automata. Study of these **quantum languages** remains an active area of research.

2.1 Informal description

There is a simple, intuitive way of understanding quantum finite automata. One begins with a graph-theoretic interpretation of deterministic finite automata (DFA). A DFA can be represented as a directed graph, with states as nodes in the graph, and arrows representing state transitions. Each arrow is labelled with a possible input symbol, so that, given a specific state and an input symbol, the arrow points at the next state. One way of representing such a graph is by means of a set of adjacency matrices, with one matrix for each input symbol. In this case, the list of possible DFA states is written as a column vector. For a given input symbol, the adjacency matrix indicates how any given state (row in the state vector) will transition to the next state; a state transition is given by matrix multiplication.

One needs a distinct adjacency matrix for each possible input symbol, since each input symbol can result in a different transition. The entries in the adjacency matrix must be zero's and one's. For any given column in the matrix, only one entry can be non-zero: this is the entry that indicates the next (unique) state transition. Similarly, the state of the system is a column vector, in which only one entry is non-zero: this entry corresponds to the current state of the system. Let $\Sigma = \{\alpha\}$ denote the set of input symbols. For a given input symbol $\alpha \in \Sigma$, write U_α as the adjacency matrix that describes the evolution of the DFA to its next state. The set $\{U_\alpha | \alpha \in \Sigma\}$ then completely describes the state transition function of the DFA. Let Q represent the set of possible states of the DFA. If there are N states in Q, then each matrix U_α is N by N-dimensional. The initial state $q_0 \in Q$ corresponds to a column vector with a one in the q_0'th row. A general state q is then a column vector with a one in the q'th row. By abuse of notation, let q_0 and q also denote these two vectors. Then, after reading input symbols $\alpha\beta\gamma\cdots$ from the input tape, the state of the DFA will be given by $q = \cdots U_\gamma U_\beta U_\alpha q_0$. The state transitions are given by ordinary matrix multiplication (that is, multiply q_0 by U_α, *etc.*); the order of application is 'reversed' only because we follow the standard application order in linear algebra.

The above description of a DFA, in terms of linear operators and vectors, almost begs for generalization, by replacing the state-vector q by some general vector, and the matrices $\{U_\alpha\}$ by some general operators. This is essentially what a QFA does: it replaces q by a probability amplitude, and the $\{U_\alpha\}$ by unitary matrices. Other, similar generalizations also become obvious: the vector q can be some distribution on a manifold; the set of transition matrices become automorphisms of the manifold; this defines a topological finite automaton. Similarly, the matrices could be taken as automorphisms of a homogeneous space; this defines a geometric finite automaton.

Before moving on to the formal description of a QFA, there are two noteworthy generalizations that should be mentioned and understood. The first is the non-deterministic finite automaton (NFA). In this case, the vector q is replaced by a vector which can have more than one entry that is non-zero. Such a vector then represents an element of the power set of Q; its just an indicator function on Q. Likewise, the state transition matrices $\{U_\alpha\}$ are defined in such a way that a given column can have several non-zero entries in it. After each application of $\{U_\alpha\}$, though, the column vector q must be renormalized so that it only contains zeros and ones. Equivalently, the multiply-add operations performed during component-wise matrix multiplication should be replaced by Boolean and-or operations, that is, so that one is working with a ring of characteristic 2.

A well-known theorem states that, for each DFA, there is an equivalent NFA, and vice versa. This implies that the set of languages that can be recognized by DFA's and NFA's are the same; these are the regular languages. In the generalization to QFA's, the set of recognized languages will be different. Describing that set is one of the outstanding research problems in QFA theory.

Another generalization that should be immediately apparent is to use a stochastic matrix for the transition matrices, and a probability vector for the state; this gives a probabilistic finite automaton. The entries in the state vector must be real numbers, positive, and sum to one, in order for the state vector to be interpreted as a probability. The transition matrices must preserve this property: this is why they must be stochastic. Each state vector should be imagined as specifying a point in a simplex; thus, this is a topological automaton, with the simplex being the manifold, and the stochastic matrices being linear automorphisms of the simplex onto itself. Since each transition is (essentially) independent of the previous (if we disregard the distinction between accepted and rejected languages), the PFA essentially becomes a kind of Markov chain.

By contrast, in a QFA, the manifold is complex projective space $\mathbb{C}P^N$, and the transition matrices are unitary matrices. Each point in $\mathbb{C}P^N$ corresponds to a quantum-mechanical probability amplitude or pure state; the unitary matrices can be thought of as governing the time evolution of the system (viz in the Schrödinger picture). The generalization from pure states to mixed states should be straightforward: A mixed state is simply a measure-theoretic probability distribution on $\mathbb{C}P^N$.

A worthy point to contemplate is the distributions that result on the manifold during the input of a language. In order for an automaton to be 'efficient' in recognizing a language, that distribution should be 'as uniform as possible'. This need for uniformity is the underlying principle behind maximum entropy methods: these simply guarantee crisp, compact operation of the automaton. Put in other words, the machine learning methods used to train hidden Markov models generalize to QFA's as well: the Viterbi algorithm and the forward-backward algorithm generalize readily to the QFA.

Although the study of QFA was popularized in the work of Kondacs and Watrous in 1997[1] and later by Moore and Crutchfeld, they were described as early as 1971, by Ion Baianu.[2][3]

2.2 Measure-once automata

Measure-once automata were introduced by Cris Moore and James P. Crutchfield.[4] They may be defined formally as follows.

As with an ordinary finite automaton, the quantum automaton is considered to have N possible internal states, represented in this case by an N -state qubit $|\psi\rangle$. More precisely, the N -state qubit $|\psi\rangle \in \mathbb{C}P^N$ is an element of N -dimensional complex projective space, carrying an inner product $\|\cdot\|$ that is the Fubini–Study metric.

The state transitions, transition matrixes or de Bruijn graphs are represented by a collection of $N \times N$ unitary matrixes U_α , with one unitary matrix for each letter $\alpha \in \Sigma$. That is, given an input letter α , the unitary matrix describes the transition of the automaton from its current state $|\psi\rangle$ to its next state $|\psi'\rangle$:

$$|\psi'\rangle = U_\alpha|\psi\rangle$$

Thus, the triple $(\mathbb{C}P^N, \Sigma, \{U_\alpha|\alpha \in \Sigma\})$ form a quantum semiautomaton.

The accept state of the automaton is given by an $N \times N$ projection matrix P , so that, given a N -dimensional quantum state $|\psi\rangle$, the probability of $|\psi\rangle$ being in the accept state is

$$\langle\psi|P|\psi\rangle = \|P|\psi\rangle\|^2$$

The probability of the state machine accepting a given finite input string $\sigma = (\sigma_0, \sigma_1, \cdots, \sigma_k)$ is given by

$$\Pr(\sigma) = \|PU_{\sigma_k} \cdots U_{\sigma_1} U_{\sigma_0}|\psi\rangle\|^2$$

Here, the vector $|\psi\rangle$ is understood to represent the initial state of the automaton, that is, the state the automaton was in before it started accepting the string input. The empty string $\varnothing$ is understood to be just the unit matrix, so that

$$\Pr(\varnothing) = \|P|\psi\rangle\|^2$$

is just the probability of the initial state being an accepted state.

Because the left-action of U_α on $|\psi\rangle$ reverses the order of the letters in the string σ , it is not uncommon for QFA's to be defined using a right action on the Hermitian transpose states, simply in order to keep the order of the letters the same.

A regular language is accepted with probability p by a quantum finite automaton, if, for all sentences σ in the language, (and a given, fixed initial state $|\psi\rangle$), one has $p < \Pr(\sigma)$.

2.3 Example

Consider the classical deterministic finite automaton given by the state transition table

The quantum state is a vector, in bra–ket notation

$$|\psi\rangle = a_1|S_1\rangle + a_2|S_2\rangle = \begin{bmatrix} a_1 \\ a_2 \end{bmatrix}$$

with the complex numbers a_1, a_2 normalized so that

$$\begin{bmatrix} a_1^* & a_2^* \end{bmatrix} \begin{bmatrix} a_1 \\ a_2 \end{bmatrix} = a_1^* a_1 + a_2^* a_2 = 1$$

The unitary transition matrices are

$$U_0 = \begin{bmatrix} 0 & 1 \\ 1 & 0 \end{bmatrix}$$

and

$$U_1 = \begin{bmatrix} 1 & 0 \\ 0 & 1 \end{bmatrix}$$

Taking S_1 to be the accept state, the projection matrix is

$$P = \begin{bmatrix} 1 & 0 \\ 0 & 0 \end{bmatrix}$$

As should be readily apparent, if the initial state is the pure state $|S_1\rangle$ or $|S_2\rangle$, then the result of running the machine will be exactly identical to the classical deterministic finite state machine. In particular, there is a language accepted by this automaton with probability one, for these initial states, and it is identical to the regular language for the classical DFA, and is given by the regular expression:

$$(1^*(01^*0)^*)^*$$

The non-classical behaviour occurs if both a_1 and a_2 are non-zero. More subtle behaviour occurs when the matrices U_0 and U_1 are not so simple; see, for example, the de Rham curve as an example of a quantum finite state machine acting on the set of all possible finite binary strings.

2.4 Measure-many automata

Measure-many automata were introduced by Kondacs and Watrous in 1997.[1] The general framework resembles that of the measure-once automaton, except that instead of there being one projection, at the end, there is a projection, or quantum measurement, performed after each letter is read. A formal definition follows.

The Hilbert space $\mathcal{H}_Q$ is decomposed into three orthogonal subspaces

$$\mathcal{H}_Q = \mathcal{H}_{\text{accept}} \oplus \mathcal{H}_{\text{reject}} \oplus \mathcal{H}_{\text{non-halting}}$$

In the literature, these orthogonal subspaces are usually formulated in terms of the set Q of orthogonal basis vectors for the Hilbert space $\mathcal{H}_Q$. This set of basis vectors is divided up into subsets $Q_{\text{acc}} \subset Q$ and $Q_{\text{rej}} \subset Q$, such that

$$\mathcal{H}_{\text{accept}} = \text{span}\{|q\rangle : |q\rangle \in Q_{\text{acc}}\}$$

is the linear span of the basis vectors in the accept set. The reject space is defined analogously, and the remaining space is designated the *non-halting* subspace. There are three projection matrices, P_{acc}, P_{rej} and P_{non}, each projecting to the respective subspace:

$$P_{\text{acc}} : \mathcal{H}_Q \to \mathcal{H}_{\text{accept}}$$

and so on. The parsing of the input string proceeds as follows. Consider the automaton to be in a state $|\psi\rangle$. After reading an input letter α, the automaton will be in the state

$$|\psi'\rangle = U_\alpha|\psi\rangle$$

At this point, a measurement is performed on the state $|\psi'\rangle$, using the projection operators P, at which time its wave-function collapses into one of the three subspaces $\mathcal{H}_{\text{accept}}$ or $\mathcal{H}_{\text{reject}}$ or $\mathcal{H}_{\text{non-halting}}$. The probability of collapse is given by

$$\Pr_{\text{acc}}(\sigma) = \|P_{\text{acc}}|\psi'\rangle\|^2$$

for the "accept" subspace, and analogously for the other two spaces.

If the wave function has collapsed to either the "accept" or "reject" subspaces, then further processing halts. Otherwise, processing continues, with the next letter read from the input, and applied to what must be an eigenstate of P_{non}. Processing continues until the whole string is read, or the machine halts. Often, additional symbols κ and \$ are adjoined to the alphabet, to act as the left and right end-markers for the string.

In the literature, the meaure-many automaton is often denoted by the tuple $(Q; \Sigma; \delta; q_0; Q_{\text{acc}}; Q_{\text{rej}})$. Here, Q, Σ, Qacc and Qrej are as defined above. The initial state is denoted by $|\psi\rangle = |q_0\rangle$. The unitary transformations are denoted by the map δ ,

$$\delta : Q \times \Sigma \times Q \to \mathbb{C}$$

so that

$$U_\alpha |q_1\rangle = \sum_{q_2 \in Q} \delta(q_1, \alpha, q_2) |q_2\rangle$$

2.5 Geometric generalizations

The above constructions indicate how the concept of a quantum finite automaton can be generalized to arbitrary topological spaces. For example, one may take some (N-dimensional) Riemann symmetric space to take the place of $\mathbb{C}P^N$. In place of the unitary matrices, one uses the isometries of the Riemannian manifold, or, more generally, some set of open functions appropriate for the given topological space. The initial state may be taken to be a point in the space. The set of accept states can be taken to be some arbitrary subset of the topological space. One then says that a formal language is accepted by this **topological automaton** if the point, after iteration by the homeomorphisms, intersects the accept set. But, of course, this is nothing more than the standard definition of an M-automaton. The behaviour of topological automata is studied in the field of topological dynamics.

The quantum automaton differs from the topological automaton in that, instead of having a binary result (is the iterated point in, or not in, the final set?), one has a probability. The quantum probability is the (square of) the initial state projected onto some final state *P*; that is $\mathbf{Pr} = |\langle P|\psi\rangle|^2$. But this probability amplitude is just a very simple function of the distance between the point $|P\rangle$ and the point $|\psi\rangle$ in $\mathbb{C}P^N$, under the distance metric given by the Fubini–Study metric. To recap, the quantum probability of a language being accepted can be interpreted as a metric, with the probability of accept being unity, if the metric distance between the initial and final states is zero, and otherwise the probability of accept is less than one, if the metric distance is non-zero. Thus, it follows that the quantum finite automaton is just a special case of a **geometric automaton** or a **metric automaton**, where $\mathbb{C}P^N$ is generalized to some metric space, and the probability measure is replaced by a simple function of the metric on that space.

2.6 See also

- Quantum Markov chain

2.7 References

[1] Kondacs, A.; Watrous, J. (1997), "On the power of quantum finite state automata", *Proceedings of the 38th Annual Symposium on Foundations of Computer Science*, pp. 66–75

[2] I. Bainau, "Organismic Supercategories and Qualitative Dynamics of Systems" (1971), Bulletin of Mathematical Biophysics, **33** pp.339-354.

[3] I. Baianu, "Categories, Functors and Quantum Automata Theory" (1971). The 4th Intl.Congress LMPS, August-Sept.1971

[4] C. Moore, J. Crutchfield, "Quantum automata and quantum grammars", *Theoretical Computer Science*, **237** (2000) pp 275-306.

- L. Accardi (2001), "Quantum stochastic processes", in Hazewinkel, Michiel, *Encyclopedia of Mathematics*, Springer, ISBN 978-1-55608-010-4 *(Provides an intro to quantum Markov chains.)*
- Alex Brodsky, Nicholas Pippenger, "Characterization of 1-way Quantum Finite Automata", *SIAM Journal on Computing* **31**(2002) pp 1456–1478.
- Vincent D. Blondel, Emmanual Jeandel, Pascal Koiran and Natacha Portier, "Decidable and Undecidable Problems about Quantum Automata", *SIAM Journal on Computing* **34** (2005) pp 1464–1473.

Chapter 3

Quantum information

In physics and computer science, **quantum information** is information that is held in the state of a quantum system. Quantum information is the basic entity of study in **quantum information theory**, and can be manipulated using engineering techniques known as quantum information processing. Much like classical information can be processed with digital computers, transmitted from place to place, manipulated with algorithms, and analyzed with the mathematics of computer science, so also analogous concepts apply to quantum information.

3.1 Quantum information

Quantum information differs strongly from classical information, epitomized by the bit, in many striking and unfamiliar ways. Among these are the following:

- A unit of quantum information is the qubit. Unlike classical digital states (which are discrete), a qubit is continuous-valued, describable by a direction on the Bloch sphere. Despite being continuously valued in this way, a qubit is the *smallest* possible unit of quantum information. The reason for this indivisibility is due to the Heisenberg uncertainty principle: despite the qubit state being continuously-valued, it is impossible to measure the value precisely.

- A qubit cannot be (wholly) converted into classical bits; that is, it cannot be "read". This is the no-teleportation theorem.

- Despite the awkwardly-named no-teleportation theorem, qubits can be moved from one physical particle to another, by means of quantum teleportation. That is, qubits can be transported, independently of the underlying physical particle.

- An arbitrary qubit can neither be copied, nor destroyed. This is the content of the no cloning theorem and the no-deleting theorem.

- Although a single qubit can be transported from place to place (*e.g.* via quantum teleportation), it cannot be delivered to multiple recipients; this is the no-broadcast theorem, and is essentially implied by the no-cloning theorem.

- Qubits can be changed, by applying linear transformations or quantum gates to them, to alter their state.

- Classical bits may be combined with and extracted from configurations of multiple qubits, through the use of quantum gates. That is, two or more qubits can be arranged in such a way as to convey classical bits. The simplest such configuration is the Bell state, which consists of two qubits and four classical bits (*i.e.* requires two qubits and four classical bits to fully describe).

- Quantum information can be moved about, in a quantum channel, analogous to the concept of a classical communications channel. Quantum messages have a finite size, measured in qubits; quantum channels have a finite channel capacity, measured in qubits per second.

- Multiple qubits can be used to carry classical bits. Although n qubits can carry more than n classical bits of information, the greatest amount of classical information that can be retrieved is n. This is Holevo's theorem.

- Quantum information, and changes in quantum information, can be quantitatively measured by using an analogue of Shannon entropy, called the von Neumann entropy. Given a statistical ensemble of quantum mechanical systems with the density matrix ρ , it is given by $S(\rho) = -\mathrm{Tr}(\rho \ln \rho)$. Many of the same entropy measures in classical information theory can also be generalized to the quantum case, such as Holevo entropy and the conditional quantum entropy.

- Quantum algorithms have a different computational complexity than classical algorithms. The most famous example of this is Shor's factoring algorithm, which is not known to have a polynomial time classical algorithm, but does have a polynomial time quantum algorithm. Other examples include

Grover's search algorithm, where the quantum algorithm gives a quadratic speed-up over the best possible classical algorithm.

- Quantum encryption allows unconditionally secure transmission of classical information, unlike classical encryption, which can always be broken in principle, if not in practice. (Note that certain subtle points are hotly debated).
- Linear logic describes the logic of quantum information, in analogy to how classical logic works with classical bits. Linear logic is much like classical logic, except that Gentzen's rules for cloning are omitted. That is, entailment cannot be used to clone or delete logical premises, since qubits cannot be cloned or deleted.
- The simplest description[1] of generalized quantum information is provided by dagger compact categories, in much the same way that categorical logic and type theory provide the foundations for computer science. This extends the Curry–Howard correspondence between proof theory and computation to quantum domains.
- The general framework for the manipulation of quantum states is given by categorical quantum mechanics.

The study of all of the above topics and differences comprises quantum information theory.

3.2 Quantum information theory

The theory of quantum information is a result of the effort to generalize classical information theory to the quantum world. Quantum information theory aims to investigate the question "How is information stored in a state of a quantum system?". Under the no-teleportation theorem, a quantum state cannot be precisely converted into classical bits. The information content of a message M can nevertheless be measured in terms of the minimum number n of qubits needed to encode the message. Such a message M is encoded with n qubits and n^2 classical bits that describe the relative arrangement of the n qubits. The qubit is the smallest possible unit of quantum information.

Quantum information can be transmitted through quantum channels. These have finite capacity and are analogous to the classical case, described by the noisy-channel coding theorem which defines the maximum channel capacity of a classical communications channel. An important breakthrough for the theory of quantum information occurred when quantum error correction codes and fault-tolerant quantum computation schemes were discovered .

An important step in quantum information theory is the manipulation of quantum information. This requires quantum logic gates, in rough analog to the processing of classical information with digital circuits.

3.3 Journals

Many journals publish research in quantum information science, although only a few are dedicated to this area. Among these are

- *International Journal of Quantum Information*
- *Quantum Information & Computation*
- *Quantum Information Processing*
- *Quantum Information*[2]

3.4 See also

- Information theory
- Interpretations of quantum mechanics
- POVM (positive operator valued measure)
- Quantum clock
- Quantum computing
- Quantum gravity
- Quantum information science
- Quantum statistical mechanics
- Qutrit
- Typical subspace

3.5 References

[1] Bob Coecke, "Quantum Picturalism", (2009) *Contemporary Physics* vol **51**, pp59-83. (ArXiv 0908.1787)

[2] npj Quantum Information

3.6 External links and references

- Quantiki - A wiki portal for quantum information with introductory tutorials.
- Charles H. Bennett and Peter W. Shor, "Quantum Information Theory," *IEEE Transactions on Information Theory,* Vol 44, pp 2724–2742, Oct 1998
- Gregg Jaeger's book on Quantum Information(published by Springer, New York, 2007, ISBN 0-387-35725-4)

- Lectures at the Institut Henri Poincaré (slides and videos)
- International Journal of Quantum Information World Scientific
- Quantum Information Processing Springer
- Mark M. Wilde, "From Classical to Quantum Shannon Theory", arXiv:1106.1445.
- Quantum information can be negative
- Centres and groups doing research on quantum information include:
    - Quantum Information Theory at ETH Zurich
    - Quantum Information Perimeter Institute for Theoretical Physics
    - Institute for Quantum Computing - The Institute for Quantum Computing, based in Waterloo, ON Canada, is a research institute working in conjunction with the University of Waterloo and Perimeter Institute on the subject of Quantum Information.
    - Centre for Quantum Technologies - CQT is a research centre at the National University of Singapore bringing together quantum physicists and computer scientists
    - Center for Quantum Computation - The CQC, part of Cambridge University, is a group of researchers studying quantum information, and is a useful portal for those interested in this field.
    - Quantum Information Group The quantum information research group at the University of Nottingham.
    - Research Group on Mathematics and Quantum Information Madrid
    - Institute for Quantum Information and Matter Caltech
    - Quantum Information Theory Imperial College
    - Quantum Information University College London
    - Quantum Information Technology Toshiba Research
    - USC Center for Quantum Information Science & Technology
    - Center for Quantum Information and Control Theoretical and experimental groups from University of New Mexico and University of Arizona with adjunct faculty associates from the Sandia National Labs and the Los Alamos National Labs. Another site to view their research activities (more on the UNM site) is at http://cquic.unm.edu/.
- Group of Quantum Information Theory Kyungnam University in Korea

Chapter 4

Quantum mutual information

In quantum information theory, **quantum mutual information**, or **von Neumann mutual information**, after John von Neumann, is a measure of correlation between subsystems of quantum state. It is the quantum mechanical analog of Shannon mutual information.

4.1 Motivation

For simplicity, it will be assumed that all objects in the article are finite-dimensional.

The definition of quantum mutual entropy is motivated by the classical case. For a probability distribution of two variables $p(x, y)$, the two marginal distributions are

$$p(x) = \sum_y p(x,y)\ ,\ p(y) = \sum_x p(x,y).$$

The classical mutual information $I(X, Y)$ is defined by

$$I(X,Y) = S(p(x)) + S(p(y)) - S(p(x,y))$$

where $S(q)$ denotes the Shannon entropy of the probability distribution q.

One can calculate directly

$$S(p(x)) + S(p(y))$$

$$= -(\sum_x p_x \log p(x) + \sum_y p_y \log p(y))$$

$$= -(\sum_x (\sum_{y'} p(x,y') \log \sum_{y'} p(x,y')) + \sum_y (\sum_{x'} p(x' \ _{x'} p(x',y)))$$

$$= -(\sum_{x,y} p(x,y)(\log \sum_{y'} p(x,y') + \log \sum_{x'} p(x',y)))$$

$$= -\sum_{x,y} p(x,y) \log p(x)p(y).$$

So the mutual information is

$$I(X,Y) = \sum_{x,y} p(x,y) \log \frac{p(x,y)}{p(x)p(y)}.$$

But this is precisely the relative entropy between $p(x, y)$ and $p(x)p(y)$. In other words, if we assume the two variables x and y to be uncorrelated, mutual information is the *discrepancy in uncertainty* resulting from this (possibly erroneous) assumption.

It follows from the property of relative entropy that $I(X,Y) \geq 0$ and equality holds if and only if $p(x, y) = p(x)p(y)$.

4.2 Definition

The quantum mechanical counterpart of classical probability distributions are density matrices.

Consider a composite quantum system whose state space is the tensor product

$$H = H_A \otimes H_B.$$

Let ϱ^{AB} be a density matrix acting on H. The von Neumann entropy of ϱ, which is the quantum mechanical analogy of the Shannon entropy, is given by

$$S(\rho^{AB}) = -\operatorname{Tr} \rho^{AB} \log \rho^{AB}.$$

For a probability distribution $p(x,y)$, the marginal distributions are obtained by integrating away the variables x or y. The corresponding operation for density matrices is the partial trace. So one can assign to ϱ a state on the subsystem A by

$$\rho^A = \operatorname{Tr}_B\ \rho^{AB}$$

where TrB is partial trace with respect to system B. This is the **reduced state** of ϱ^{AB} on system A. The **reduced von Neumann entropy** of ϱ^{AB} with respect to system A is

$$S(\rho^A).$$

$S(\varrho^B)$ is defined in the same way.

Technical Note: In mathematical language, passing from the classical to quantum setting can be described as follows. The *algebra of observables* of a physical system is a C*-algebra and states are unital linear functionals on the algebra. Classical systems are described by commutative C*-algebras, therefore classical states are probability measures. Quantum mechanical systems have non-commutative observable algebras. In concrete considerations, quantum states are density operators. If the probability measure μ is a state on classical composite system consisting of two subsystem A and B, we project μ onto the system A to obtain the reduced state. As stated above, the quantum analog of this is the partial trace operation, which can be viewed as projection onto a tensor component. *End of note*

It can now be seen that the appropriate definition of quantum mutual information should be

$$I(\rho^{AB}) = S(\rho^A) + S(\rho^B) - S(\rho^{AB}).$$

Quantum mutual information can be interpreted the same way as in the classical case: it can be shown that

$$I(\rho^{AB}) = S(\rho^{AB} \| \rho^A \otimes \rho^B)$$

where $S(\cdot\|\cdot)$ denotes quantum relative entropy.

Chapter 5

Quantum information science

Quantum information science is an area of study based on the idea that information science depends on quantum effects in physics. It includes theoretical issues in computational models as well as more experimental topics in quantum physics including what can and cannot be done with quantum information. The term **quantum information theory** is sometimes used, but it fails to encompass experimental research in the area.

Subfields include:

- Quantum computing, which deals on the one hand with the question how and whether one can build a quantum computer and on the other hand, algorithms that harness its power (see quantum algorithm)
- Quantum complexity theory
- Quantum cryptography and its generalization, quantum communication
- Quantum error correction
- Quantum communication complexity
- Quantum entanglement, as seen from an information-theoretic point of view
- Quantum dense coding
- Quantum teleportation is a well-known quantum information processing operation, which can be used to move any arbitrary quantum state from one particle (at one location) to another.

5.1 See also

- No-communication theorem
- Quantum decision tree complexity
- Quantum capacity
- Quantum communication channel
- Entanglement-assisted classical capacity

5.2 References

- Nielsen, M.A. and Chuang, I.L. *Quantum computation and quantum information*. Cambridge University Press, 2000.

5.3 External links

- Quantiki – quantum information science portal and wiki.
- ERA-Pilot QIST WP1 European roadmap on Quantum Information Processing and Communication
- QIIC – Quantum Information, Imperial College London.
- QIP – Quantum Information Group, University of Leeds. The quantum information group at the University of Leeds is engaged in researching a wide spectrum of aspects of quantum information. This ranges from algorithms, quantum computation, to physical implementations of information processing and fundamental issues in quantum mechanics. Also contains some basic tutorials for the lay audience.
- mathQI Research Group on Mathematics and Quantum Information.
- CQIST Center for Quantum Information Science & Technology at the University of Southern California
- CQuIC Center for Quantum Information and Control, including theoretical and experimental groups from University of New Mexico, University of Arizona.
- CQT Centre for Quantum Technologies at the National University of Singapore

Chapter 6

Quantum mechanics

For a more accessible and less technical introduction to this topic, see Introduction to quantum mechanics.

Quantum mechanics (**QM**; also known as **quantum physics** or **quantum theory**), including quantum field theory, is a fundamental branch of physics concerned with processes involving, for example, atoms and photons. In such processes, said to be quantized, the action has been observed to be only in integer multiples of the Planck constant. This is utterly inexplicable in classical physics.

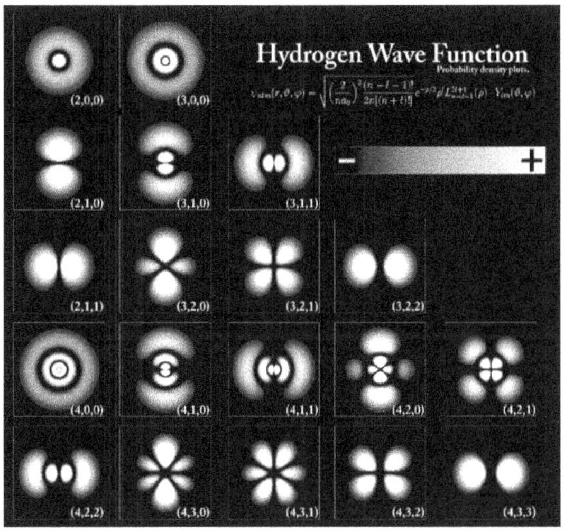

Solution to Schrödinger's equation for the hydrogen atom at different energy levels. The brighter areas represent a higher probability of finding an electron

Quantum mechanics gradually arose from Max Planck's solution in 1900 to the black-body radiation problem (reported 1859) and Albert Einstein's 1905 paper which offered a quantum-based theory to explain the photoelectric effect (reported 1887). Early quantum theory was profoundly reconceived in the mid-1920s.

The reconceived theory is formulated in various specially developed mathematical formalisms. In one of them, a mathematical function, the wave function, provides information about the probability amplitude of position, momentum, and other physical properties of a particle.

Important applications of quantum mechanical theory include superconducting magnets, light-emitting diodes and the laser, the transistor and semiconductors such as the microprocessor, medical and research imaging such as magnetic resonance imaging and electron microscopy, and explanations for many biological and physical phenomena.

6.1 History

Main article: History of quantum mechanics

Scientific inquiry into the wave nature of light began in the 17th and 18th centuries, when scientists such as Robert Hooke, Christiaan Huygens and Leonhard Euler proposed a wave theory of light based on experimental observations.[1] In 1803, Thomas Young, an English polymath, performed the famous double-slit experiment that he later described in a paper entitled *On the nature of light and colours*. This experiment played a major role in the general acceptance of the wave theory of light.

In 1838, Michael Faraday discovered cathode rays. These studies were followed by the 1859 statement of the black-body radiation problem by Gustav Kirchhoff, the 1877 suggestion by Ludwig Boltzmann that the energy states of a physical system can be discrete, and the 1900 quantum hypothesis of Max Planck.[2] Planck's hypothesis that energy is radiated and absorbed in discrete "quanta" (or energy elements) precisely matched the observed patterns of black-body radiation.

In 1896, Wilhelm Wien empirically determined a distribution law of black-body radiation,[3] known as Wien's law in his honor. Ludwig Boltzmann independently arrived at this result by considerations of Maxwell's equations. However, it was valid only at high frequencies and underestimated the radiance at low frequencies. Later, Planck corrected this model using Boltzmann's statistical interpretation of thermodynamics and proposed what is now called Planck's law, which led to the development of quantum mechanics.

Following Max Planck's solution in 1900 to the black-body radiation problem (reported 1859), Albert Einstein offered a quantum-based theory to explain the photoelectric effect (1905, reported 1887). Around 1900-1910, the atomic theory and the corpuscular theory of light[4] first came to be widely accepted as scientific fact; these latter theories can be viewed as quantum theories of matter and electromagnetic radiation, respectively.

Among the first to study quantum phenomena in nature were Arthur Compton, C. V. Raman, and Pieter Zeeman, each of whom has a quantum effect named after him. Robert Andrews Millikan studied the photoelectric effect experimentally, and Albert Einstein developed a theory for it. At the same time, Niels Bohr developed his theory of the atomic structure, which was later confirmed by the experiments of Henry Moseley. In 1913, Peter Debye extended Niels Bohr's theory of atomic structure, introducing elliptical orbits, a concept also introduced by Arnold Sommerfeld.[5] This phase is known as old quantum theory.

According to Planck, each energy element (E) is proportional to its frequency (ν):

$$E = h\nu$$

where h is Planck's constant.

Max Planck is considered the father of the quantum theory.

Planck cautiously insisted that this was simply an aspect of the *processes* of absorption and emission of radiation and had nothing to do with the *physical reality* of the radiation itself.[6] In fact, he considered his quantum hypothesis a mathematical trick to get the right answer rather than a sizable discovery.[7] However, in 1905 Albert Einstein interpreted Planck's quantum hypothesis realistically and used it to explain the photoelectric effect, in which shining light on certain materials can eject electrons from the material. He won the 1921 Nobel Prize in Physics for this work.

Einstein further developed this idea to show that an electromagnetic wave such as light could also be described as a particle (later called the photon), with a discrete quantum of energy that was dependent on its frequency.[8]

The 1927 Solvay Conference in Brussels.

The foundations of quantum mechanics were established during the first half of the 20th century by Max Planck, Niels Bohr, Werner Heisenberg, Louis de Broglie, Arthur Compton, Albert Einstein, Erwin Schrödinger, Max Born, John von Neumann, Paul Dirac, Enrico Fermi, Wolfgang Pauli, Max von Laue, Freeman Dyson, David Hilbert, Wilhelm Wien, Satyendra Nath Bose, Arnold Sommerfeld, and others. The Copenhagen interpretation of Niels Bohr became widely accepted.

In the mid-1920s, developments in quantum mechanics led to its becoming the standard formulation for atomic physics. In the summer of 1925, Bohr and Heisenberg published results that closed the old quantum theory. Out of deference to their particle-like behavior in certain processes and measurements, light quanta came to be called photons (1926). From Einstein's simple postulation was born a flurry of debating, theorizing, and testing. Thus, the entire field of quantum physics emerged, leading to its wider acceptance at the Fifth Solvay Conference in 1927.

It was found that subatomic particles and electromagnetic waves are neither simply particle nor wave but have certain properties of each. This originated the concept of wave–particle duality.

By 1930, quantum mechanics had been further unified and formalized by the work of David Hilbert, Paul Dirac and John von Neumann[9] with greater emphasis on measurement, the statistical nature of our knowledge of reality, and philosophical speculation about the 'observer'. It has since permeated many disciplines including quantum chemistry, quantum electronics, quantum optics, and quantum information science. Its speculative modern developments include string theory and quantum gravity theories. It also provides a useful framework for many features of the modern periodic table of elements, and describes the behaviors of atoms during chemical bonding and the flow of electrons in computer semiconductors, and therefore plays a crucial role in many modern technologies.

While quantum mechanics was constructed to describe the world of the very small, it is also needed to explain some macroscopic phenomena such as superconductors,[10] and superfluids.[11]

The word *quantum* derives from the Latin, meaning "how great" or "how much".[12] In quantum mechanics, it refers to a discrete unit assigned to certain physical quantities such as the energy of an atom at rest (see Figure 1). The discovery that particles are discrete packets of energy with wave-like properties led to the branch of physics dealing with atomic and subatomic systems which is today called quantum mechanics. It underlies the mathematical framework of many fields of physics and chemistry, including condensed matter physics, solid-state physics, atomic physics, molecular physics, computational physics, computational chemistry, quantum chemistry, particle physics, nuclear chemistry, and nuclear physics.[13] Some fundamental aspects of the theory are still actively studied.[14]

Quantum mechanics is essential to understanding the behavior of systems at atomic length scales and smaller. If the physical nature of an atom was solely described by classical mechanics, electrons would not *orbit* the nucleus, since orbiting electrons emit radiation (due to circular motion) and would eventually collide with the nucleus due to this loss of energy. This framework was unable to explain the stability of atoms. Instead, electrons remain in an uncertain, non-deterministic, *smeared*, probabilistic wave–particle orbital about the nucleus, defying the traditional assumptions of classical mechanics and electromagnetism.[15]

Quantum mechanics was initially developed to provide a better explanation and description of the atom, especially the differences in the spectra of light emitted by different isotopes of the same chemical element, as well as subatomic particles. In short, the quantum-mechanical atomic model has succeeded spectacularly in the realm where classical mechanics and electromagnetism falter.

Broadly speaking, quantum mechanics incorporates four classes of phenomena for which classical physics cannot account:

- quantization of certain physical properties
- quantum entanglement
- principle of uncertainty
- wave–particle duality

6.2 Mathematical formulations

Main article: Mathematical formulation of quantum mechanics
See also: Quantum logic

In the mathematically rigorous formulation of quantum mechanics developed by Paul Dirac,[16] David Hilbert,[17] John von Neumann,[18] and Hermann Weyl,[19] the possible states of a quantum mechanical system are symbolized[20] as unit vectors (called *state vectors*). Formally, these reside in a complex separable Hilbert space—variously called the *state space* or the *associated Hilbert space* of the system—that is well defined up to a complex number of norm 1 (the phase factor). In other words, the possible states are points in the projective space of a Hilbert space, usually called the complex projective space. The exact nature of this Hilbert space is dependent on the system—for example, the state space for position and momentum states is the space of square-integrable functions, while the state space for the spin of a single proton is just the product of two complex planes. Each observable is represented by a maximally Hermitian (precisely: by a self-adjoint) linear operator acting on the state space. Each eigenstate of an observable corresponds to an eigenvector of the operator, and the associated eigenvalue corresponds to the value of the observable in that eigenstate. If the operator's spectrum is discrete, the observable can attain only those discrete eigenvalues.

In the formalism of quantum mechanics, the state of a system at a given time is described by a complex wave function, also referred to as state vector in a complex vector space.[21] This abstract mathematical object allows for the calculation of probabilities of outcomes of concrete experiments. For example, it allows one to compute the probability of finding an electron in a particular region around the nucleus at a particular time. Contrary to classical mechanics, one can never make simultaneous predictions of conjugate variables, such as position and momentum, with accuracy. For instance, electrons may be considered (to a certain probability) to be located somewhere within a given region of space, but with their exact positions unknown. Contours of constant probability, often referred to as "clouds", may be drawn around the nucleus of an atom to conceptualize where the electron might be located with the most probability. Heisenberg's uncertainty principle quantifies the inability to precisely locate the particle given its conjugate momentum.[22]

According to one interpretation, as the result of a measurement the wave function containing the probability information for a system collapses from a given initial state to a particular eigenstate. The possible results of a measurement are the eigenvalues of the operator representing the observable—which explains the choice of *Hermitian* operators, for which all the eigenvalues are real. The probability distribution of an observable in a given state can be found by computing the spectral decomposition of the corresponding operator. Heisenberg's uncertainty principle is represented by the statement that the operators corresponding to certain observables do not commute.

The probabilistic nature of quantum mechanics thus stems from the act of measurement. This is one of the most difficult aspects of quantum systems to understand. It was the central topic in the famous Bohr–Einstein debates, in which the two scientists attempted to clarify these fundamental principles by way of thought experiments. In the decades after the formulation of quantum mechanics, the question of what constitutes a "measurement" has been extensively studied. Newer interpretations of quantum mechanics have been formulated that do away with the concept of "wave function collapse" (see, for example, the relative state interpretation). The basic idea is that when a quantum system interacts with a measuring apparatus, their respective wave functions become entangled, so that the original quantum system ceases to exist as an independent entity. For details, see the article on measurement in quantum mechanics.[23]

Generally, quantum mechanics does not assign definite values. Instead, it makes a prediction using a probability distribution; that is, it describes the probability of obtaining the possible outcomes from measuring an observable. Often these results are skewed by many causes, such as dense probability clouds. Probability clouds are approximate (but better than the Bohr model) whereby electron location is given by a probability function, the wave function eigenvalue, such that the probability is the squared modulus of the complex amplitude, or quantum state nuclear attraction.[24][25] Naturally, these probabilities will depend on the quantum state at the "instant" of the measurement. Hence, uncertainty is involved in the value. There are, however, certain states that are associated with a definite value of a particular observable. These are known as eigenstates of the observable ("eigen" can be translated from German as meaning "inherent" or "characteristic").[26]

In the everyday world, it is natural and intuitive to think of everything (every observable) as being in an eigenstate. Everything appears to have a definite position, a definite momentum, a definite energy, and a definite time of occurrence. However, quantum mechanics does not pinpoint the exact values of a particle's position and momentum (since they are conjugate pairs) or its energy and time (since they too are conjugate pairs); rather, it provides only a range of probabilities in which that particle might be given its momentum and momentum probability. Therefore, it is helpful to use different words to describe states having *uncertain* values and states having *definite* values (eigenstates). Usually, a system will not be in an eigenstate of the observable (particle) we are interested in. However, if one measures the observable, the wave function will instantaneously be an eigenstate (or "generalized" eigenstate) of that observable. This process is known as wave function collapse, a controversial and much-debated process[27] that involves expanding the system under study to include the measurement device. If one knows the corresponding wave function at the instant before the measurement, one will be able to compute the probability of the wave function collapsing into each of the possible eigenstates. For example, the free particle in the previous example will usually have a wave function that is a wave packet centered around some mean position x_0 (neither an eigenstate of position nor of momentum). When one measures the position of the particle, it is impossible to predict with certainty the result.[23] It is probable, but not certain, that it will be near x_0, where the amplitude of the wave function is large. After the measurement is performed, having obtained some result x, the wave function collapses into a position eigenstate centered at x.[28]

The time evolution of a quantum state is described by the Schrödinger equation, in which the Hamiltonian (the operator corresponding to the total energy of the system) generates the time evolution. The time evolution of wave functions is deterministic in the sense that - given a wave function at an *initial* time - it makes a definite prediction of what the wave function will be at any *later* time.[29]

During a measurement, on the other hand, the change of the initial wave function into another, later wave function is not deterministic, it is unpredictable (i.e., random). A time-evolution simulation can be seen here.[30][31]

Wave functions change as time progresses. The Schrödinger equation describes how wave functions change in time, playing a role similar to Newton's second law in classical mechanics. The Schrödinger equation, applied to the aforementioned example of the free particle, predicts that the center of a wave packet will move through space at a constant velocity (like a classical particle with no forces acting on it). However, the wave packet will also spread out as time progresses, which means that the position becomes more uncertain with time. This also has the effect of turning a position eigenstate (which can be thought of as an infinitely sharp wave packet) into a broadened wave packet that no longer represents a (definite, certain) position eigenstate.[32]

Some wave functions produce probability distributions that are constant, or independent of time—such as when in a stationary state of constant energy, time vanishes in the absolute square of the wave function. Many systems that are treated dynamically in classical mechanics are described by such "static" wave functions. For example, a single electron in an unexcited atom is pictured classically as a particle moving in a circular trajectory around the atomic nucleus, whereas in quantum mechanics it is described by a static, spherically symmetric wave function surrounding the nucleus (Fig. 1) (note, however, that only the lowest angular momentum states, labeled *s*, are spherically symmetric).[33]

The Schrödinger equation acts on the *entire* probability amplitude, not merely its absolute value. Whereas the

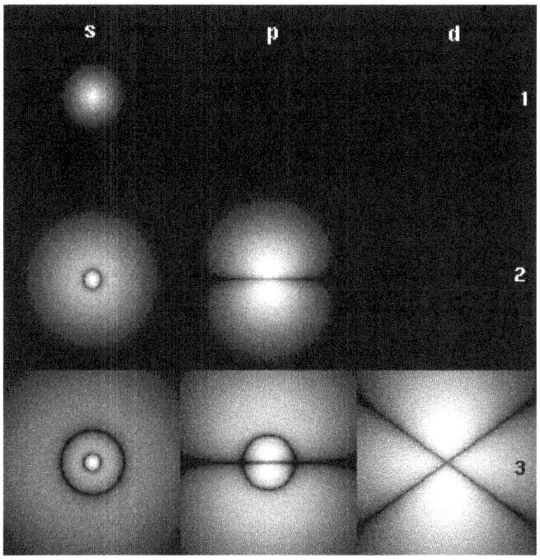

Fig. 1: Probability densities corresponding to the wave functions of an electron in a hydrogen atom possessing definite energy levels (increasing from the top of the image to the bottom: n = *1, 2, 3, ...) and angular momenta (increasing across from left to right:* s, p, d, *...). Brighter areas correspond to higher probability density in a position measurement. Such wave functions are directly comparable to Chladni's figures of acoustic modes of vibration in classical physics, and are modes of oscillation as well, possessing a sharp energy and, thus, a definite frequency. The angular momentum and energy are quantized, and take* ***only*** *discrete values like those shown (as is the case for resonant frequencies in acoustics)*

absolute value of the probability amplitude encodes information about probabilities, its phase encodes information about the interference between quantum states. This gives rise to the "wave-like" behavior of quantum states. As it turns out, analytic solutions of the Schrödinger equation are available for only a very small number of relatively simple model Hamiltonians, of which the quantum harmonic oscillator, the particle in a box, the dihydrogen cation, and the hydrogen atom are the most important representatives. Even the helium atom—which contains just one more electron than does the hydrogen atom—has defied all attempts at a fully analytic treatment.

There exist several techniques for generating approximate solutions, however. In the important method known as perturbation theory, one uses the analytic result for a simple quantum mechanical model to generate a result for a more complicated model that is related to the simpler model by (for one example) the addition of a weak potential energy. Another method is the "semi-classical equation of motion" approach, which applies to systems for which quantum mechanics produces only weak (small) deviations from classical behavior. These deviations can then be computed based on the classical motion. This approach is particularly important in the field of quantum chaos.

6.3 Mathematically equivalent formulations of quantum mechanics

There are numerous mathematically equivalent formulations of quantum mechanics. One of the oldest and most commonly used formulations is the "transformation theory" proposed by Paul Dirac, which unifies and generalizes the two earliest formulations of quantum mechanics - matrix mechanics (invented by Werner Heisenberg) and wave mechanics (invented by Erwin Schrödinger).[34]

Especially since Werner Heisenberg was awarded the Nobel Prize in Physics in 1932 for the creation of quantum mechanics, the role of Max Born in the development of QM was overlooked until the 1954 Nobel award. The role is noted in a 2005 biography of Born, which recounts his role in the matrix formulation of quantum mechanics, and the use of probability amplitudes. Heisenberg himself acknowledges having learned matrices from Born, as published in a 1940 *festschrift* honoring Max Planck.[35] In the matrix formulation, the instantaneous state of a quantum system encodes the probabilities of its measurable properties, or "observables". Examples of observables include energy, position, momentum, and angular momentum. Observables can be either continuous (e.g., the position of a particle) or discrete (e.g., the energy of an electron bound to a hydrogen atom).[36] An alternative formulation of quantum mechanics is Feynman's path integral formulation, in which a quantum-mechanical amplitude is considered as a sum over all possible classical and non-classical paths between the initial and final states. This is the quantum-mechanical counterpart of the action principle in classical mechanics.

6.4 Interactions with other scientific theories

The rules of quantum mechanics are fundamental. They assert that the state space of a system is a Hilbert space and that observables of that system are Hermitian operators acting on that space—although they do not tell us which Hilbert space or which operators. These can be chosen appropriately in order to obtain a quantitative description of a quantum system. An important guide for making these choices is the correspondence principle, which states that the predictions of quantum mechanics reduce to those of classical mechanics when a system moves to higher energies or, equivalently, larger quantum numbers, i.e. whereas a single particle exhibits a degree of randomness, in systems incorporating millions of particles averaging takes over and, at the high energy limit, the statistical probability of random behaviour approaches zero. In other words, classical mechanics is simply a quantum mechanics of large systems. This "high energy" limit is known as the *classical* or *correspondence limit*. One can even start from an established classical model of a particular system, then attempt to guess the underlying quantum model that would give rise to the classical model in the correspondence limit.

When quantum mechanics was originally formulated, it was applied to models whose correspondence limit was non-relativistic classical mechanics. For instance, the well-known model of the quantum harmonic oscillator uses an explicitly non-relativistic expression for the kinetic energy of the oscillator, and is thus a quantum version of the classical harmonic oscillator.

Early attempts to merge quantum mechanics with special relativity involved the replacement of the Schrödinger equation with a covariant equation such as the Klein–Gordon equation or the Dirac equation. While these theories were successful in explaining many experimental results, they had certain unsatisfactory qualities stemming from their neglect of the relativistic creation and annihilation of particles. A fully relativistic quantum theory required the development of quantum field theory, which applies quantization to a field (rather than a fixed set of particles). The first complete quantum field theory, quantum electrodynamics, provides a fully quantum description of the electromagnetic interaction. The full apparatus of quantum field theory is often unnecessary for describing electrodynamic systems. A simpler approach, one that has been employed since the inception of quantum mechanics, is to treat charged particles as quantum mechanical objects being acted on by a classical electromagnetic field. For example, the elementary quantum model of the hydrogen atom describes the electric field of the hydrogen atom using a classical $-e^2/(4\pi\ \epsilon_0\ r)$ Coulomb potential. This "semi-classical" approach fails if quantum fluctuations in the electromagnetic field play an important role, such as in the emission of photons by charged particles.

Quantum field theories for the strong nuclear force and the weak nuclear force have also been developed. The quantum field theory of the strong nuclear force is called quantum chromodynamics, and describes the interactions of subnuclear particles such as quarks and gluons. The weak nuclear force and the electromagnetic force were unified, in their quantized forms, into a single quantum field theory (known as electroweak theory), by the physicists Abdus Salam, Sheldon Glashow and Steven Weinberg. These three men shared the Nobel Prize in Physics in 1979 for this work.[37]

It has proven difficult to construct quantum models of gravity, the remaining fundamental force. Semi-classical approximations are workable, and have led to predictions such as Hawking radiation. However, the formulation of a complete theory of quantum gravity is hindered by apparent incompatibilities between general relativity (the most accurate theory of gravity currently known) and some of the fundamental assumptions of quantum theory. The resolution of these incompatibilities is an area of active research, and theories such as string theory are among the possible candidates for a future theory of quantum gravity.

Classical mechanics has also been extended into the complex domain, with complex classical mechanics exhibiting behaviors similar to quantum mechanics.[38]

6.4.1 Quantum mechanics and classical physics

Predictions of quantum mechanics have been verified experimentally to an extremely high degree of accuracy.[39] According to the correspondence principle between classical and quantum mechanics, all objects obey the laws of quantum mechanics, and classical mechanics is just an approximation for large systems of objects (or a statistical quantum mechanics of a large collection of particles).[40] The laws of classical mechanics thus follow from the laws of quantum mechanics as a statistical average at the limit of large systems or large quantum numbers.[41] However, chaotic systems do not have good quantum numbers, and quantum chaos studies the relationship between classical and quantum descriptions in these systems.

Quantum coherence is an essential difference between classical and quantum theories as illustrated by the Einstein–Podolsky–Rosen (EPR) paradox — an attack on a certain philosophical interpretation of quantum mechanics by an appeal to local realism.[42] Quantum interference involves adding together *probability amplitudes*, whereas classical "waves" infer that there is an adding together of *intensities*. For microscopic bodies, the extension of the system is much smaller than the coherence length, which gives rise to long-range entanglement and other nonlocal phenomena characteristic of quantum systems.[43] Quantum coherence is not typically evident at macroscopic scales, though an exception to this rule may occur at extremely low temperatures (i.e. approaching absolute zero) at which quantum behavior may manifest itself macroscopically.[44] This is in accordance with the following observations:

- Many macroscopic properties of a classical system are a direct consequence of the quantum behavior of its parts. For example, the stability of bulk matter (consisting of atoms and molecules which would quickly collapse under electric forces alone), the rigidity of solids, and the mechanical, thermal, chemical, optical and magnetic properties of matter are all results of the interaction of electric charges under the rules of quantum mechanics.[45]
- While the seemingly "exotic" behavior of matter posited by quantum mechanics and relativity theory become more apparent when dealing with particles of extremely small size or velocities approaching the speed of light, the laws of classical, often considered

"Newtonian", physics remain accurate in predicting the behavior of the vast majority of "large" objects (on the order of the size of large molecules or bigger) at velocities much smaller than the velocity of light.[46]

6.4.2 Copenhagen interpretation of quantum versus classical kinematics

A big difference between classical and quantum mechanics is that they use very different kinematic descriptions.[47]

In Niels Bohr's mature view, quantum mechanical phenomena are required to be experiments, with complete descriptions of all the devices for the system, preparative, intermediary, and finally measuring. The descriptions are in macroscopic terms, expressed in ordinary language, supplemented with the concepts of classical mechanics.[48][49][50][51] The initial condition and the final condition of the system are respectively described by values in a configuration space, for example a position space, or some equivalent space such as a momentum space. Quantum mechanics does not admit a completely precise description, in terms of both position and momentum, of an initial condition or "state" (in the classical sense of the word) that would support a precisely deterministic and causal prediction of a final condition.[52][53] In this sense, advocated by Bohr in his mature writings, a quantum phenomenon is a process, a passage from initial to final condition, not an instantaneous "state" in the classical sense of that word.[54][55] Thus there are two kinds of processes in quantum mechanics: stationary and transitional. For a stationary process, the initial and final condition are the same. For a transition, they are different. Obviously by definition, if only the initial condition is given, the process is not determined.[52] Given its initial condition, prediction of its final condition is possible, causally but only probabilistically, because the Schrödinger equation is deterministic for wave function evolution, but the wave function describes the system only probabilistically.[56][57]

For many experiments, it is possible to think of the initial and final conditions of the system as being a particle. In some cases it appears that there are potentially several spatially distinct pathways or trajectories by which a particle might pass from initial to final condition. It is an important feature of the quantum kinematic description that it does not permit a unique definite statement of which of those pathways is actually followed. Only the initial and final conditions are definite, and, as stated in the foregoing paragraph, they are defined only as precisely as allowed by the configuration space description or its equivalent. In every case for which a quantum kinematic description is needed, there is always a compelling reason for this restriction of kinematic precision. An example of such a reason is that for a particle to be experimentally found in a definite position, it must be held motionless; for it to be experimentally found to have a definite momentum, it must have free motion; these two are logically incompatible.[58][59]

Classical kinematics does not primarily demand experimental description of its phenomena. It allows completely precise description of an instantaneous state by a value in phase space, the Cartesian product of configuration and momentum spaces. This description simply assumes or imagines a state as a physically existing entity without concern about its experimental measurability. Such a description of an initial condition, together with Newton's laws of motion, allows a precise deterministic and causal prediction of a final condition, with a definite trajectory of passage. Hamiltonian dynamics can be used for this. Classical kinematics also allows the description of a process analogous to the initial and final condition description used by quantum mechanics. Lagrangian mechanics applies to this.[60] For processes that need account to be taken of actions of a small number of Planck constants, classical kinematics is not adequate; quantum mechanics is needed.

6.4.3 General relativity and quantum mechanics

Even with the defining postulates of both Einstein's theory of general relativity and quantum theory being indisputably supported by rigorous and repeated empirical evidence, and while they do not directly contradict each other theoretically (at least with regard to their primary claims), they have proven extremely difficult to incorporate into one consistent, cohesive model.[61]

Gravity is negligible in many areas of particle physics, so that unification between general relativity and quantum mechanics is not an urgent issue in those particular applications. However, the lack of a correct theory of quantum gravity is an important issue in cosmology and the search by physicists for an elegant "Theory of Everything" (TOE). Consequently, resolving the inconsistencies between both theories has been a major goal of 20th and 21st century physics. Many prominent physicists, including Stephen Hawking, have labored for many years in the attempt to discover a theory underlying *everything*. This TOE would combine not only the different models of subatomic physics, but also derive the four fundamental forces of nature - the strong force, electromagnetism, the weak force, and gravity - from a single force or phenomenon. While Stephen Hawking was initially a believer in the Theory of Everything, after considering Gödel's Incompleteness Theorem, he has concluded that one is not obtainable, and has stated so publicly in his lecture "Gödel and the End of Physics" (2002).[62]

6.4.4 Attempts at a unified field theory

Main article: Grand unified theory

The quest to unify the fundamental forces through quantum mechanics is still ongoing. Quantum electrodynamics (or "quantum electromagnetism"), which is currently (in the perturbative regime at least) the most accurately tested physical theory in competition with general relativity,[63][64] has been successfully merged with the weak nuclear force into the electroweak force and work is currently being done to merge the electroweak and strong force into the electrostrong force. Current predictions state that at around 10^{14} GeV the three aforementioned forces are fused into a single unified field.[65] Beyond this "grand unification", it is speculated that it may be possible to merge gravity with the other three gauge symmetries, expected to occur at roughly 10^{19} GeV. However — and while special relativity is parsimoniously incorporated into quantum electrodynamics — the expanded general relativity, currently the best theory describing the gravitation force, has not been fully incorporated into quantum theory. One of those searching for a coherent TOE is Edward Witten, a theoretical physicist who formulated the M-theory, which is an attempt at describing the supersymmetrical based string theory. M-theory posits that our apparent 4-dimensional spacetime is, in reality, actually an 11-dimensional spacetime containing 10 spatial dimensions and 1 time dimension, although 7 of the spatial dimensions are - at lower energies - completely "compactified" (or infinitely curved) and not readily amenable to measurement or probing.

Another popular theory is Loop quantum gravity (LQG), a theory first proposed by Carlo Rovelli that describes the quantum properties of gravity. It is also a theory of quantum space and quantum time, because in general relativity the geometry of spacetime is a manifestation of gravity. LQG is an attempt to merge and adapt standard quantum mechanics and standard general relativity. The main output of the theory is a physical picture of space where space is granular. The granularity is a direct consequence of the quantization. It has the same nature of the granularity of the photons in the quantum theory of electromagnetism or the discrete levels of the energy of the atoms. But here it is space itself which is discrete. More precisely, space can be viewed as an extremely fine fabric or network "woven" of finite loops. These networks of loops are called spin networks. The evolution of a spin network over time is called a spin foam. The predicted size of this structure is the Planck length, which is approximately 1.616×10^{-35} m. According to theory, there is no meaning to length shorter than this (cf. Planck scale energy). Therefore, LQG predicts that not just matter, but also space itself, has an atomic structure.

6.5 Philosophical implications

Main article: Interpretations of quantum mechanics

Since its inception, the many counter-intuitive aspects and results of quantum mechanics have provoked strong philosophical debates and many interpretations. Even fundamental issues, such as Max Born's basic rules concerning probability amplitudes and probability distributions, took decades to be appreciated by society and many leading scientists. Richard Feynman once said, "I think I can safely say that nobody understands quantum mechanics."[66] According to Steven Weinberg, "There is now in my opinion no entirely satisfactory interpretation of quantum mechanics."[67]

The Copenhagen interpretation — due largely to Niels Bohr and Werner Heisenberg — remains most widely accepted amongst physicists, some 75 years after its enunciation. According to this interpretation, the probabilistic nature of quantum mechanics is not a *temporary* feature which will eventually be replaced by a deterministic theory, but instead must be considered a *final* renunciation of the classical idea of "causality." It is also believed therein that any well-defined application of the quantum mechanical formalism must always make reference to the experimental arrangement, due to the conjugate nature of evidence obtained under different experimental situations.

Albert Einstein, himself one of the founders of quantum theory, did not accept some of the more philosophical or metaphysical interpretations of quantum mechanics, such as rejection of determinism and of causality. He is famously quoted as saying, in response to this aspect, "My God does not play with dice". He rejected the concept that the state of a physical system depends on the experimental arrangement for its measurement. He held that a state of nature occurs in its own right, regardless of whether or how it might be observed. In that view, he is supported by the currently accepted definition of a quantum state, which remains invariant under arbitrary choice of configuration space for its representation, that is to say, manner of observation. He also held that underlying quantum mechanics there should be a theory that thoroughly and directly expresses the rule against action at a distance; in other words, he insisted on the principle of locality. He considered, but rejected on theoretical grounds, a particular proposal for hidden variables to obviate the indeterminism or acausality of quantum mechanical measurement. He considered that quantum mechanics was a currently valid but not a permanently definitive theory for quantum phenomena. He thought its future replacement would require profound conceptual advances, and would not come quickly or easily. The *Bohr-Einstein debates* provide a vibrant critique of the Copenhagen Interpretation from an epistemological point of view. In arguing for his views, he produced a series of objections, the most famous of which has become known as the Einstein–Podolsky–Rosen paradox.

John Bell showed that this "EPR" paradox led to experimentally testable differences between quantum mechanics and theories that rely on added hidden variables. Experiments have been performed confirming the accuracy of quantum mechanics, thereby demonstrating that quantum mechanics cannot be improved upon by addition of hidden variables.[68] Alain Aspect's initial experiments in 1982, and many subsequent experiments since, have definitively verified quantum entanglement.

Entanglement, as demonstrated in Bell-type experiments, does not, however, violate causality, since no transfer of information happens. Quantum entanglement forms the basis of quantum cryptography, which is proposed for use in high-security commercial applications in banking and government.

The Everett many-worlds interpretation, formulated in 1956, holds that *all* the possibilities described by quantum theory *simultaneously* occur in a multiverse composed of mostly independent parallel universes.[69] This is not accomplished by introducing some "new axiom" to quantum mechanics, but on the contrary, by *removing* the axiom of the collapse of the wave packet. *All* of the possible consistent states of the measured system and the measuring apparatus (including the observer) are present in a *real* physical - not just formally mathematical, as in other interpretations - quantum superposition. Such a superposition of consistent state combinations of different systems is called an entangled state. While the multiverse is deterministic, we perceive non-deterministic behavior governed by probabilities, because we can only observe the universe (i.e., the consistent state contribution to the aforementioned superposition) that we, as observers, inhabit. Everett's interpretation is perfectly consistent with John Bell's experiments and makes them intuitively understandable. However, according to the theory of quantum decoherence, these "parallel universes" will never be accessible to us. The inaccessibility can be understood as follows: once a measurement is done, the measured system becomes entangled with *both* the physicist who measured it *and* a huge number of other particles, some of which are photons flying away at the speed of light towards the other end of the universe. In order to prove that the wave function did not collapse, one would have to bring *all* these particles back and measure them again, together with the system that was originally measured. Not only is this completely impractical, but even if one *could* theoretically do this, it would have to destroy any evidence that the original measurement took place (including the physicist's memory). In light of these Bell tests, Cramer (1986) formulated his transactional interpretation.[70] Relational quantum mechanics appeared in the late 1990s as the modern derivative of the Copenhagen Interpretation.

6.6 Applications

Quantum mechanics has had enormous[71] success in explaining many of the features of our universe. Quantum mechanics is often the only tool available that can reveal the individual behaviors of the subatomic particles that make up all forms of matter (electrons, protons, neutrons, photons, and others). Quantum mechanics has strongly influenced string theories, candidates for a Theory of Everything (see reductionism).

Quantum mechanics is also critically important for understanding how individual atoms combine covalently to form molecules. The application of quantum mechanics to chemistry is known as quantum chemistry. Relativistic quantum mechanics can, in principle, mathematically describe most of chemistry. Quantum mechanics can also provide quantitative insight into ionic and covalent bonding processes by explicitly showing which molecules are energetically favorable to which others and the magnitudes of the energies involved.[72] Furthermore, most of the calculations performed in modern computational chemistry rely on quantum mechanics.

In many aspects modern technology operates at a scale where quantum effects are significant.

6.6.1 Electronics

Many modern electronic devices are designed using quantum mechanics. Examples include the laser, the transistor (and thus the microchip), the electron microscope, and magnetic resonance imaging (MRI). The study of semiconductors led to the invention of the diode and the transistor, which are indispensable parts of modern electronics systems, computer and telecommunication devices. Another application is the light emitting diode which is a high-efficiency source of light.

Many electronic devices operate under effect of Quantum tunneling. It even exists in the simple light switch. The switch would not work if electrons could not quantum tunnel through the layer of oxidation on the metal contact surfaces. Flash memory chips found in USB drives use quantum tunneling to erase their memory cells. Some negative differential resistance devices also utilizes quantum tunneling effect, such as resonant tunneling diode .Unlike classical diodes, its current is carried by resonant tunneling through two potential barriers (see right figure). Its negative resistance behavior can only be understood with quantum mechanics: As the confined state moves close to Fermi level, tunnel current increases. As it moves away, current decreases. Quantum mechanics is vital to understanding and designing such electronic devices.

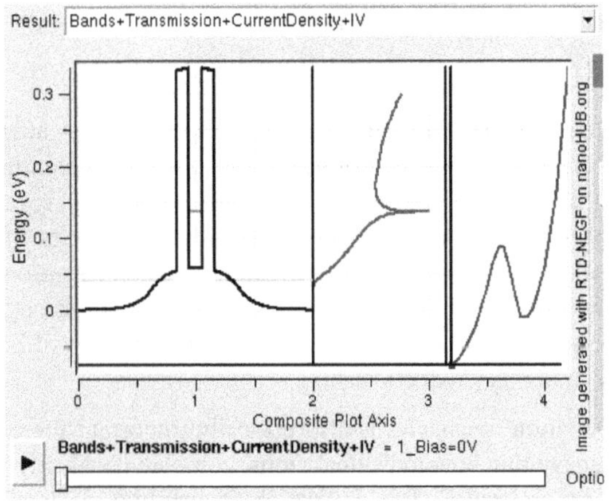

A working mechanism of a resonant tunneling diode device, based on the phenomenon of quantum tunneling through potential barriers.(Left: band diagram; Center: transmission coefficient; Right: current-voltage characteristics) As shown in the band diagram(left), although there are two barriers, electrons still tunnel through via the confined states between two barriers(center), conducting current.

6.6.2 Cryptography

Researchers are currently seeking robust methods of directly manipulating quantum states. Efforts are being made to more fully develop quantum cryptography, which will theoretically allow guaranteed secure transmission of information.

6.6.3 Quantum computing

A more distant goal is the development of quantum computers, which are expected to perform certain computational tasks exponentially faster than classical computers. Instead of using classical bits, quantum computers use qubits, which can be in superpositions of states. Another active research topic is quantum teleportation, which deals with techniques to transmit quantum information over arbitrary distances.

6.6.4 Macroscale quantum effects

While quantum mechanics primarily applies to the smaller atomic regimes of matter and energy, some systems exhibit quantum mechanical effects on a large scale. Superfluidity, the frictionless flow of a liquid at temperatures near absolute zero, is one well-known example. So is the closely related phenomenon of superconductivity, the frictionless flow of an electron gas in a conducting material (an electric current) at sufficiently low temperatures.

6.6.5 Quantum theory

Quantum theory also provides accurate descriptions for many previously unexplained phenomena, such as black-body radiation and the stability of the orbitals of electrons in atoms. It has also given insight into the workings of many different biological systems, including smell receptors and protein structures.[73] Recent work on photosynthesis has provided evidence that quantum correlations play an essential role in this fundamental process of plants and many other organisms.[74] Even so, classical physics can often provide good approximations to results otherwise obtained by quantum physics, typically in circumstances with large numbers of particles or large quantum numbers. Since classical formulas are much simpler and easier to compute than quantum formulas, classical approximations are used and preferred when the system is large enough to render the effects of quantum mechanics insignificant.

6.7 Examples

6.7.1 Free particle

For example, consider a free particle. In quantum mechanics, there is wave–particle duality, so the properties of the particle can be described as the properties of a wave. Therefore, its quantum state can be represented as a wave of arbitrary shape and extending over space as a wave function. The position and momentum of the particle are observables. The Uncertainty Principle states that both the position and the momentum cannot simultaneously be measured with complete precision. However, one *can* measure the position (alone) of a moving free particle, creating an eigenstate of position with a wave function that is very large (a Dirac delta) at a particular position x, and zero everywhere else. If one performs a position measurement on such a wave function, the resultant x will be obtained with 100% probability (i.e., with full certainty, or complete precision). This is called an eigenstate of position—or, stated in mathematical terms, a *generalized position eigenstate (eigendistribution)*. If the particle is in an eigenstate of position, then its momentum is completely unknown. On the other hand, if the particle is in an eigenstate of momentum, then its position is completely unknown.[75] In an eigenstate of momentum having a plane wave form, it can be shown that the wavelength is equal to h/p, where h is Planck's constant and p is the momentum of the eigenstate.[76]

6.7.2 Step potential

Main article: Solution of Schrödinger equation for a step potential

The potential in this case is given by:

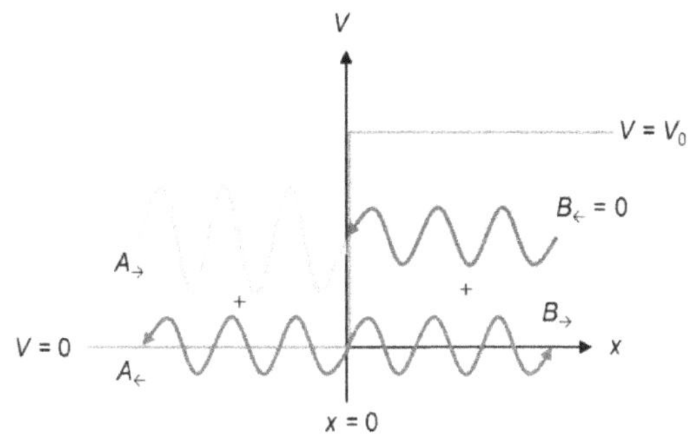

Scattering at a finite potential step of height V_0*, shown in green. The amplitudes and direction of left- and right-moving waves are indicated. Yellow is the incident wave, blue are reflected and transmitted waves, red does not occur.* $E > V_0$ *for this figure.*

$$V(x) = \begin{cases} 0, & x < 0, \\ V_0, & x \geq 0. \end{cases}$$

The solutions are superpositions of left- and right-moving waves:

$$\psi_1(x) = \frac{1}{\sqrt{k_1}}\left(A_{\rightarrow}e^{ik_1x} + A_{\leftarrow}e^{-ik_1x}\right) \quad x < 0$$

$$\psi_2(x) = \frac{1}{\sqrt{k_2}}\left(B_{\rightarrow}e^{ik_2x} + B_{\leftarrow}e^{-ik_2x}\right) \quad x > 0$$

where the wave vectors are related to the energy via

$$k_1 = \sqrt{2mE/\hbar^2}$$

$$k_2 = \sqrt{2m(E - V_0)/\hbar^2}$$

with coefficients A and B determined from the boundary conditions and by imposing a continuous derivative on the solution.

Each term of the solution can be interpreted as an incident, reflected, or transmitted component of the wave, allowing the calculation of transmission and reflection coefficients. Notably, in contrast to classical mechanics, incident particles with energies greater than the potential step are partially reflected.

6.7.3 Rectangular potential barrier

Main article: Rectangular potential barrier

This is a model for the quantum tunneling effect which plays an important role in the performance of modern technologies such as flash memory and scanning tunneling microscopy. Quantum tunneling is central to physical phenomena involved in superlattices.

6.7.4 Particle in a box

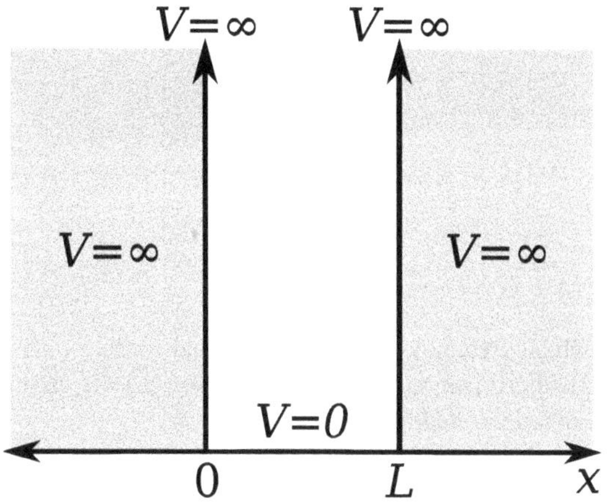

1-dimensional potential energy box (or infinite potential well)

Main article: Particle in a box

The particle in a one-dimensional potential energy box is the most mathematically simple example where restraints lead to the quantization of energy levels. The box is defined as having zero potential energy everywhere *inside* a certain region, and infinite potential energy everywhere *outside* that region. For the one-dimensional case in the x direction, the time-independent Schrödinger equation may be written[77]

$$-\frac{\hbar^2}{2m}\frac{d^2\psi}{dx^2} = E\psi.$$

With the differential operator defined by

$$\hat{p}_x = -i\hbar\frac{d}{dx}$$

the previous equation is evocative of the classic kinetic energy analogue,

$$\frac{1}{2m}\hat{p}_x^2 = E,$$

with state ψ in this case having energy E coincident with the kinetic energy of the particle.

The general solutions of the Schrödinger equation for the particle in a box are

$$\psi(x) = Ae^{ikx} + Be^{-ikx} \qquad E = \frac{\hbar^2k^2}{2m}$$

or, from Euler's formula,

$$\psi(x) = C\sin kx + D\cos kx.$$

The infinite potential walls of the box determine the values of C, D, and k at $x = 0$ and $x = L$ where ψ must be zero. Thus, at $x = 0$,

$$\psi(0) = 0 = C\sin 0 + D\cos 0 = D$$

and $D = 0$. At $x = L$,

$$\psi(L) = 0 = C\sin kL.$$

in which C cannot be zero as this would conflict with the Born interpretation. Therefore, since $\sin(kL) = 0$, kL must be an integer multiple of π,

$$k = \frac{n\pi}{L} \qquad n = 1, 2, 3, \ldots.$$

The quantization of energy levels follows from this constraint on k, since

$$E = \frac{\hbar^2\pi^2n^2}{2mL^2} = \frac{n^2h^2}{8mL^2}.$$

6.7.5 Finite potential well

Main article: Finite potential well

A finite potential well is the generalization of the infinite potential well problem to potential wells having finite depth.

The finite potential well problem is mathematically more complicated than the infinite particle-in-a-box problem as the wave function is not pinned to zero at the walls of the well. Instead, the wave function must satisfy more complicated mathematical boundary conditions as it is nonzero in regions outside the well.

6.7.6 Harmonic oscillator

Main article: Quantum harmonic oscillator

As in the classical case, the potential for the quantum harmonic oscillator is given by

$$V(x) = \frac{1}{2}m\omega^2x^2$$

This problem can either be treated by directly solving the Schrödinger equation, which is not trivial, or by using the more elegant "ladder method" first proposed by Paul Dirac. The eigenstates are given by

$$\psi_n(x) = \sqrt{\frac{1}{2^n\,n!}}\cdot\left(\frac{m\omega}{\pi\hbar}\right)^{1/4}\cdot e^{-\frac{m\omega x^2}{2\hbar}}\cdot H_n\left(\sqrt{\frac{m\omega}{\hbar}}x\right), \qquad n = 0, 1, 2, \ldots.$$

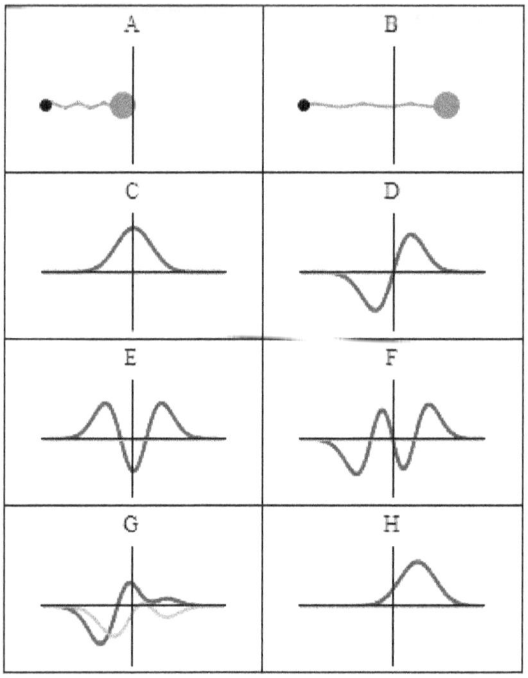

Some trajectories of a harmonic oscillator (i.e. a ball attached to a spring) in classical mechanics (A-B) and quantum mechanics (C-H). In quantum mechanics, the position of the ball is represented by a wave (called the wave function), with the real part shown in blue and the imaginary part shown in red. Some of the trajectories (such as C,D,E,and F) are standing waves (or "stationary states"). Each standing-wave frequency is proportional to a possible energy level of the oscillator. This "energy quantization" does not occur in classical physics, where the oscillator can have any *energy.*

where H_n are the Hermite polynomials,

$$H_n(x) = (-1)^n e^{x^2}\frac{d^n}{dx^n}\left(e^{-x^2}\right)$$

and the corresponding energy levels are

$$E_n = \hbar\omega\left(n + \frac{1}{2}\right)$$

This is another example illustrating the quantization of energy for bound states.

6.8 See also

- Angular momentum diagrams (quantum mechanics)
- EPR paradox
- Fractional quantum mechanics
- List of quantum-mechanical systems with analytical solutions

- Macroscopic quantum phenomena
- Phase space formulation
- Regularization (physics)
- Spherical basis

6.9 Notes

[1] Max Born & Emil Wolf, Principles of Optics, 1999, Cambridge University Press

[2] Mehra, J.; Rechenberg, H. (1982). *The historical development of quantum theory*. New York: Springer-Verlag. ISBN 0387906428.

[3] Kragh, Helge (2002). *Quantum Generations: A History of Physics in the Twentieth Century*. Princeton University Press. p. 58. ISBN 0-691-09552-3. Extract of page 58

[4] Ben-Menahem, Ari (2009). *Historical Encyclopedia of Natural and Mathematical Sciences, Volume 1*. Springer. p. 3678. ISBN 3540688315. Extract of page 3678

[5] E Arunan (2010). "Peter Debye" (PDF). *Resonance (journal)* (Indian Academy of Sciences) **15** (12).

[6] Kuhn, T. S. (1978). *Black-body theory and the quantum discontinuity 1894-1912*. Oxford: Clarendon Press. ISBN 0195023838.

[7] Kragh, Helge (1 December 2000), *Max Planck: the reluctant revolutionary*, PhysicsWorld.com

[8] Einstein, A. (1905). "Über einen die Erzeugung und Verwandlung des Lichtes betreffenden heuristischen Gesichtspunkt" [On a heuristic point of view concerning the production and transformation of light]. *Annalen der Physik* **17** (6): 132–148. Bibcode:1905AnP...322..132E. doi:10.1002/andp.19053220607. Reprinted in *The collected papers of Albert Einstein*, John Stachel, editor, Princeton University Press, 1989, Vol. 2, pp. 149-166, in German; see also *Einstein's early work on the quantum hypothesis*, ibid. pp. 134-148.

[9] van Hove, Leon (1958). "Von Neumann's contributions to quantum mechanics" (PDF). *Bulletin of the American Mathematical Society* **64**: Part2:95–99. doi:10.1090/s0002-9904-1958-10206-2.

[10] *The Feynman Lectures on Physics* **III** 21-4 "...it was long believed that the wave function of the Schrödinger equation would never have a macroscopic representation analogous to the macroscopic representation of the amplitude for photons. On the other hand, it is now realized that the phenomena of superconductivity presents us with just this situation. accessdate=2015-11-24

[11] Richard Packard (2006) "Berkeley Experiments on Superfluid Macroscopic Quantum Effects" accessdate=2015-11-24

[12] "Quantum - Definition and More from the Free Merriam-Webster Dictionary". Merriam-webster.com. Retrieved 2012-08-18.

[13] http://web.archive.org/web/20091007133943/http://mooni.fccj.org/%7Eethall/quantum/quant.htm. Archived from the original on October 7, 2009. Retrieved May 23, 2009. Missing or empty |title= (help)

[14] "ysfine.com". *ysfine.com*. Retrieved 11 September 2015.

[15] Oocities.com at the Wayback Machine (archived October 26, 2009)

[16] P.A.M. Dirac, *The Principles of Quantum Mechanics*, Clarendon Press, Oxford, 1930.

[17] D. Hilbert *Lectures on Quantum Theory*, 1915–1927

[18] J. von Neumann, *Mathematische Grundlagen der Quantenmechanik*, Springer, Berlin, 1932 (English translation: *Mathematical Foundations of Quantum Mechanics*, Princeton University Press, 1955).

[19] H.Weyl "The Theory of Groups and Quantum Mechanics", 1931 (original title: "Gruppentheorie und Quantenmechanik").

[20] Dirac, P.A.M. (1958). *The Principles of Quantum Mechanics*, 4th edition, Oxford University Press, Oxford UK, p. ix: "For this reason I have chosen the symbolic method, introducing the representatives later merely as an aid to practical calculation."

[21] Greiner, Walter; Müller, Berndt (1994). *Quantum Mechanics Symmetries, Second edition*. Springer-Verlag. p. 52. ISBN 3-540-58080-8., Chapter 1, p. 52

[22] "Heisenberg - Quantum Mechanics, 1925–1927: The Uncertainty Relations". Aip.org. Retrieved 2012-08-18.

[23] Greenstein, George; Zajonc, Arthur (2006). *The Quantum Challenge: Modern Research on the Foundations of Quantum Mechanics, Second edition*. Jones and Bartlett Publishers, Inc. p. 215. ISBN 0-7637-2470-X., Chapter 8, p. 215

[24] "[Abstract] Visualization of Uncertain Particle Movement". Actapress.com. Retrieved 2012-08-18.

[25] Hirshleifer, Jack (2001). *The Dark Side of the Force: Economic Foundations of Conflict Theory*. Campbridge University Press. p. 265. ISBN 0-521-80412-4., Chapter , p.

[26] "dict.cc dictionary :: eigen :: German-English translation". *dict.cc*. Retrieved 11 September 2015.

[27] "Topics: Wave-Function Collapse". Phy.olemiss.edu. 2012-07-27. Retrieved 2012-08-18.

[28] "Collapse of the wave-function". Farside.ph.utexas.edu. Retrieved 2012-08-18.

[29] "Determinism and Naive Realism : philosophy". Reddit.com. 2009-06-01. Retrieved 2012-08-18.

[30] Michael Trott. "Time-Evolution of a Wavepacket in a Square Well — Wolfram Demonstrations Project". Demonstrations.wolfram.com. Retrieved 2010-10-15.

[31] Michael Trott. "Time Evolution of a Wavepacket In a Square Well". Demonstrations.wolfram.com. Retrieved 2010-10-15.

[32] Mathews, Piravonu Mathews; Venkatesan, K. (1976). *A Textbook of Quantum Mechanics*. Tata McGraw-Hill. p. 36. ISBN 0-07-096510-2., Chapter 2, p. 36

[33] "Wave Functions and the Schrödinger Equation" (PDF). Retrieved 2010-10-15.

[34] (PDF) http://th-www.if.uj.edu.pl/acta/vol19/pdf/v19p0683.pdf. Retrieved June 4, 2009. Missing or empty |title= (help)

[35] Nancy Thorndike Greenspan, "The End of the Certain World: The Life and Science of Max Born" (Basic Books, 2005), pp. 124-8 and 285-6.

[36] http://ocw.usu.edu/physics/classical-mechanics/pdf_lectures/06.pdf

[37] "The Nobel Prize in Physics 1979". Nobel Foundation. Retrieved 2010-02-16.

[38] Carl M. Bender, Daniel W. Hook, Karta Kooner (2009-12-31). "Complex Elliptic Pendulum". arXiv:1001.0131 [hep-th].

[39] See, for example, Precision tests of QED. The relativistic refinement of quantum mechanics known as quantum electrodynamics (QED) has been shown to agree with experiment to within 1 part in 10^8 for some atomic properties.

[40] Tipler, Paul; Llewellyn, Ralph (2008). *Modern Physics* (5 ed.). W. H. Freeman and Company. pp. 160–161. ISBN 978-0-7167-7550-8.

[41] "Quantum mechanics course iwhatisquantummechanics". Scribd.com. 2008-09-14. Retrieved 2012-08-18.

[42] A. Einstein, B. Podolsky, and N. Rosen, *Can quantum-mechanical description of physical reality be considered complete?* Phys. Rev. **47** 777 (1935).

[43] "Between classical and quantum�" (PDF). Retrieved 2012-08-19. replacement character in |title= at position 30 (help)

[44] (see macroscopic quantum phenomena, Bose–Einstein condensate, and Quantum machine)

[45] "Atomic Properties". Academic.brooklyn.cuny.edu. Retrieved 2012-08-18.

[46] http://assets.cambridge.org/97805218/29526/excerpt/9780521829526_excerpt.pdf

[47] Born, M., Heisenberg, W., Jordan, P. (1926). *Z. Phys.* **35**: 557–615. Translated as 'On quantum mechanics II', pp. 321–385 in Van der Waerden, B.L. (1967), *Sources of Quantum Mechanics*, North-Holland, Amsterdam, "The basic difference between the theory proposed here and that used hitherto ... lies in the characteristic kinematics ...", p. 385.

[48] Dirac, P.A.M. (1930/1958). *The Principles of Quantum Mechanics*, fourth edition, Oxford University Press, Oxford UK, p. 5: "A question about what will happen to a particular photon under certain conditions is not really very precise. To make it precise one must imagine some experiment performed having a bearing on the question, and enquire what will be the result of the experiment. Only questions about the results of experiments have a real significance and it is only such questions that theoretical physics has to consider."

[49] Bohr, N. (1939). The Causality Problem in Atomic Physics, in *New Theories in Physics, Conference organized in collaboration with the International Union of Physics and the Polish Intellectual Co-operation Committee, Warsaw, May 30th – June 3rd 1938*, International Institute of Intellectual Co-operation, Paris, 1939, pp. 11–30, reprinted in *Niels Bohr, Collected Works*, volume 7 (1933 – 1958) edited by J. Kalckar, Elsevier, Amsterdam, ISBN 0-444-89892-1, pp. 303–322. "The essential lesson of the analysis of measurements in quantum theory is thus the emphasis on the necessity, in the account of the phenomena, of taking the whole experimental arrangement into consideration, in complete conformity with the fact that all unambiguous interpretation of the quantum mechanical formalism involves the fixation of the external conditions, defining the initial state of the atomic system and the character of the possible predictions as regards subsequent observable properties of that system. Any measurement in quantum theory can in fact only refer either to a fixation of the initial state or to the test of such predictions, and it is first the combination of both kinds which constitutes a well-defined phenomenon."

[50] Bohr, N. (1948). On the notions of complementarity and causality, *Dialectica* **2**: 312–319. "As a more appropriate way of expression, one may advocate limitation of the use of the word *phenomenon* to refer to observations obtained under specified circumstances, including an account of the whole experiment."

[51] Ludwig, G. (1987). *An Axiomatic Basis for Quantum Mechanics*, volume 2, *Quantum Mechanics and Macrosystems*, translated by K. Just, Springer, Berlin, ISBN 978-3-642-71899-1, Chapter XIII, Special Structures in Preparation and Registration Devices, §1, Measurement chains, p. 132.

[52] Heisenberg, W. (1927). Über den anschaulichen Inhalt der quantentheoretischen Kinematik und Mechanik, *Z. Phys.* **43**: 172–198. Translation as 'The actual content of quantum theoretical kinematics and mechanics' here , "But in the rigorous formulation of the law of causality, — "If we know the present precisely, we can calculate the future" — it is not the conclusion that is faulty, but the premise."

[53] Green, H.S. (1965). *Matrix Mechanics*, with a foreword by Max Born, P. Noordhoff Ltd, Groningen. "It is not possible, therefore, to provide 'initial conditions' for the prediction of the behaviour of atomic systems, in the way contemplated by classical physics. This is accepted by quantum theory, not merely as an experimental difficulty, but as a fundamental law of nature", p. 32.

[54] Rosenfeld, L. (1957). Misunderstandings about the foundations of quantum theory, pp. 41–45 in *Observation and Interpretation*, edited by S. Körner, Butterworths, London. "A phenomenon is therefore a process (endowed with the characteristic quantal wholeness) involving a definite type of interaction between the system and the apparatus."

[55] Dirac, P.A.M. (1973). Development of the physicist's conception of nature, pp. 1–55 in *The Physicist's Conception of Nature*, edited by J. Mehra, D. Reidel, Dordrecht, ISBN 90-277-0345-0, p. 5: "That led Heisenberg to his really masterful step forward, resulting in the new quantum mechanics. His idea was to build up a theory entirely in terms of quantities referring to two states."

[56] Born, M. (1927). Physical aspects of quantum mechanics, *Nature* **119**: 354–357, "These probabilities are thus dynamically determined. But what the system actually does is not determined ..."

[57] Messiah, A. (1961). *Quantum Mechanics*, volume 1, translated by G.M. Temmer from the French *Mécanique Quantique*, North-Holland, Amsterdam, p. 157.

[58] Bohr, N. (1928). The Quantum postulate and the recent development of atomic theory, *Nature* **121**: 580–590.

[59] Heisenberg, W. (1930). *The Physical Principles of the Quantum Theory*, translated by C. Eckart and F.C. Hoyt, University of Chicago Press.

[60] Goldstein, H. (1950). *Classical Mechanics*, Addison-Wesley, ISBN 0-201-02510-8.

[61] "There is as yet no logically consistent and complete relativistic quantum field theory.", p. 4. — V. B. Berestetskii, E. M. Lifshitz, L P Pitaevskii (1971). J. B. Sykes, J. S. Bell (translators). *Relativistic Quantum Theory* **4, part I**. *Course of Theoretical Physics (Landau and Lifshitz)* ISBN 0-08-016025-5

[62] "Stephen Hawking; Gödel and the end of physics". *cam.ac.uk*. Retrieved 11 September 2015.

[63] "The Nature of Space and Time". *google.com*. Retrieved 11 September 2015.

[64] Tatsumi Aoyama, Masashi Hayakawa, Toichiro Kinoshita, Makiko Nio (2012). "Tenth-Order QED Contribution to the Electron g-2 and an Improved Value of the Fine Structure Constant". *Physical Review Letters* **109** (11): 111807. arXiv:1205.5368v2. Bibcode:2012PhRvL.109k1807A. doi:10.1103/PhysRevLett.109.111807.

[65] Parker, B. (1993). *Overcoming some of the problems*. pp. 259–279.

[66] The Character of Physical Law (1965) Ch. 6; also quoted in The New Quantum Universe (2003), by Tony Hey and Patrick Walters

[67] Weinberg, S. "Collapse of the State Vector", Phys. Rev. A 85, 062116 (2012).

[68] "Action at a Distance in Quantum Mechanics (Stanford Encyclopedia of Philosophy)". Plato.stanford.edu. 2007-01-26. Retrieved 2012-08-18.

[69] "Everett's Relative-State Formulation of Quantum Mechanics (Stanford Encyclopedia of Philosophy)". Plato.stanford.edu. Retrieved 2012-08-18.

[70] The Transactional Interpretation of Quantum Mechanics by John Cramer. *Reviews of Modern Physics* 58, 647-688, July (1986)

[71] See, for example, the Feynman Lectures on Physics for some of the technological applications which use quantum mechanics, e.g., transistors (vol **III**, pp. 14–11 ff), integrated circuits, which are follow-on technology in solid-state physics (vol **II**, pp. 8–6), and lasers (vol **III**, pp. 9–13).

[72] *Introduction to Quantum Mechanics with Applications to Chemistry - Linus Pauling, E. Bright Wilson*. 1985-03-01. ISBN 9780486648712. Retrieved 2012-08-18.

[73] Anderson, Mark (2009-01-13). "Is Quantum Mechanics Controlling Your Thoughts? | Subatomic Particles". DISCOVER Magazine. Retrieved 2012-08-18.

[74] "Quantum mechanics boosts photosynthesis". physicsworld.com. Retrieved 2010-10-23.

[75] Davies, P. C. W.; Betts, David S. (1984). *Quantum Mechanics, Second edition*. Chapman and Hall. p. 79. ISBN 0-7487-4446-0., Chapter 6, p. 79

[76] Baofu, Peter (2007-12-31). *The Future of Complexity: Conceiving a Better Way to Understand Order and Chaos*. ISBN 9789812708991. Retrieved 2012-08-18.

[77] Derivation of particle in a box, chemistry.tidalswan.com

6.10 References

The following titles, all by working physicists, attempt to communicate quantum theory to lay people, using a minimum of technical apparatus.

- Chester, Marvin (1987) *Primer of Quantum Mechanics*. John Wiley. ISBN 0-486-42878-8
- Cox, Brian; Forshaw, Jeff (2011). *The Quantum Universe: Everything That Can Happen Does Happen:*. Allen Lane. ISBN 1-84614-432-9.
- Richard Feynman, 1985. *QED: The Strange Theory of Light and Matter*, Princeton University Press. ISBN 0-691-08388-6. Four elementary lectures on quantum electrodynamics and quantum field theory, yet containing many insights for the expert.
- Ghirardi, GianCarlo, 2004. *Sneaking a Look at God's Cards*, Gerald Malsbary, trans. Princeton Univ. Press. The most technical of the works cited here. Passages using algebra, trigonometry, and bra–ket notation can be passed over on a first reading.
- N. David Mermin, 1990, "Spooky actions at a distance: mysteries of the QT" in his *Boojums all the way through*. Cambridge University Press: 110-76.
- Victor Stenger, 2000. *Timeless Reality: Symmetry, Simplicity, and Multiple Universes*. Buffalo NY: Prometheus Books. Chpts. 5-8. Includes cosmological and philosophical considerations.

More technical:

- Bryce DeWitt, R. Neill Graham, eds., 1973. *The Many-Worlds Interpretation of Quantum Mechanics*, Princeton Series in Physics, Princeton University Press. ISBN 0-691-08131-X
- Dirac, P. A. M. (1930). *The Principles of Quantum Mechanics*. ISBN 0-19-852011-5. The beginning chapters make up a very clear and comprehensible introduction.
- Hugh Everett, 1957, "Relative State Formulation of Quantum Mechanics", *Reviews of Modern Physics* 29: 454-62.
- Feynman, Richard P.; Leighton, Robert B.; Sands, Matthew (1965). *The Feynman Lectures on Physics* **1–3**. Addison-Wesley. ISBN 0-7382-0008-5.
- Griffiths, David J. (2004). *Introduction to Quantum Mechanics (2nd ed.)*. Prentice Hall. ISBN 0-13-111892-7. OCLC 40251748. A standard undergraduate text.
- Max Jammer, 1966. *The Conceptual Development of Quantum Mechanics*. McGraw Hill.
- Hagen Kleinert, 2004. *Path Integrals in Quantum Mechanics, Statistics, Polymer Physics, and Financial Markets*, 3rd ed. Singapore: World Scientific. Draft of 4th edition.
- Gunther Ludwig, 1968. *Wave Mechanics*. London: Pergamon Press. ISBN 0-08-203204-1
- George Mackey (2004). *The mathematical foundations of quantum mechanics*. Dover Publications. ISBN 0-486-43517-2.
- Albert Messiah, 1966. *Quantum Mechanics* (Vol. I), English translation from French by G. M. Temmer. North Holland, John Wiley & Sons. Cf. chpt. IV, section III.
- Omnès, Roland (1999). *Understanding Quantum Mechanics*. Princeton University Press. ISBN 0-691-00435-8. OCLC 39849482.
- Scerri, Eric R., 2006. *The Periodic Table: Its Story and Its Significance*. Oxford University Press. Considers the extent to which chemistry and the periodic system have been reduced to quantum mechanics. ISBN 0-19-530573-6
- Transnational College of Lex (1996). *What is Quantum Mechanics? A Physics Adventure*. Language Research Foundation, Boston. ISBN 0-9643504-1-6. OCLC 34661512.
- von Neumann, John (1955). *Mathematical Foundations of Quantum Mechanics*. Princeton University Press. ISBN 0-691-02893-1.
- Hermann Weyl, 1950. *The Theory of Groups and Quantum Mechanics*, Dover Publications.
- D. Greenberger, K. Hentschel, F. Weinert, eds., 2009. *Compendium of quantum physics, Concepts, experiments, history and philosophy*, Springer-Verlag, Berlin, Heidelberg.

6.11 Further reading

- Bernstein, Jeremy (2009). *Quantum Leaps*. Cambridge, Massachusetts: Belknap Press of Harvard University Press. ISBN 978-0-674-03541-6.
- Bohm, David (1989). *Quantum Theory*. Dover Publications. ISBN 0-486-65969-0.
- Eisberg, Robert; Resnick, Robert (1985). *Quantum Physics of Atoms, Molecules, Solids, Nuclei, and Particles (2nd ed.)*. Wiley. ISBN 0-471-87373-X.
- Liboff, Richard L. (2002). *Introductory Quantum Mechanics*. Addison-Wesley. ISBN 0-8053-8714-5.
- Merzbacher, Eugen (1998). *Quantum Mechanics*. Wiley, John & Sons, Inc. ISBN 0-471-88702-1.
- Sakurai, J. J. (1994). *Modern Quantum Mechanics*. Addison Wesley. ISBN 0-201-53929-2.
- Shankar, R. (1994). *Principles of Quantum Mechanics*. Springer. ISBN 0-306-44790-8.
- Stone, A. Douglas (2013). *Einstein and the Quantum*. Princeton University Press. ISBN 978-0-691-13968-5.
- Martinus J. G. Veltman, 2003 *Facts and Mysteries in Elementary Particle Physics*.
- Shushi, Tomer (2014). *The Influence of Particle Interactions on the Existence of Quantum Particles Properties* (PDF). Haifa, Israel: Journal of Physical Science and Application.

6.12 External links

- 3D animations, applications and research for basic quantum effects (animations also available in commons.wikimedia.org (Université paris Sud))
- Quantum Cook Book by R. Shankar, Open Yale PHYS 201 material (4pp)
- The Modern Revolution in Physics - an online textbook.
- J. O'Connor and E. F. Robertson: A history of quantum mechanics.

- Introduction to Quantum Theory at Quantiki.
- Quantum Physics Made Relatively Simple: three video lectures by Hans Bethe
- H is for h-bar.
- Quantum Mechanics Books Collection: Collection of free books

Course material

- Quantum Physics Database - Fundamentals and Historical Background of Quantum Theory.
- Doron Cohen: Lecture notes in Quantum Mechanics (comprehensive, with advanced topics).
- MIT OpenCourseWare: Chemistry.
- MIT OpenCourseWare: Physics. See 8.04
- Stanford Continuing Education PHY 25: Quantum Mechanics by Leonard Susskind, see course description Fall 2007
- 5½ Examples in Quantum Mechanics
- Imperial College Quantum Mechanics Course.
- Spark Notes - Quantum Physics.
- Quantum Physics Online : interactive introduction to quantum mechanics (RS applets).
- Experiments to the foundations of quantum physics with single photons.
- AQME : Advancing Quantum Mechanics for Engineers — by T.Barzso, D.Vasileska and G.Klimeck online learning resource with simulation tools on nanohub
- Quantum Mechanics by Martin Plenio
- Quantum Mechanics by Richard Fitzpatrick
- Online course on *Quantum Transport*

FAQs

- Many-worlds or relative-state interpretation.
- Measurement in Quantum mechanics.

Media

- PHYS 201: Fundamentals of Physics II by Ramamurti Shankar, Open Yale Course
- Lectures on Quantum Mechanics by Leonard Susskind
- Everything you wanted to know about the quantum world — archive of articles from *New Scientist*.
- Quantum Physics Research from *Science Daily*
- Overbye, Dennis (December 27, 2005). "Quantum Trickery: Testing Einstein's Strangest Theory". *The New York Times*. Retrieved April 12, 2010.
- Audio: Astronomy Cast Quantum Mechanics — June 2009. Fraser Cain interviews Pamela L. Gay.

Philosophy

- Jenann Ismael. ""Quantum Mechanics"". *Stanford Encyclopedia of Philosophy*.
- Henry Krips. ""Measurement in Quantum Theory"". *Stanford Encyclopedia of Philosophy*.

Chapter 7

Quantum superposition

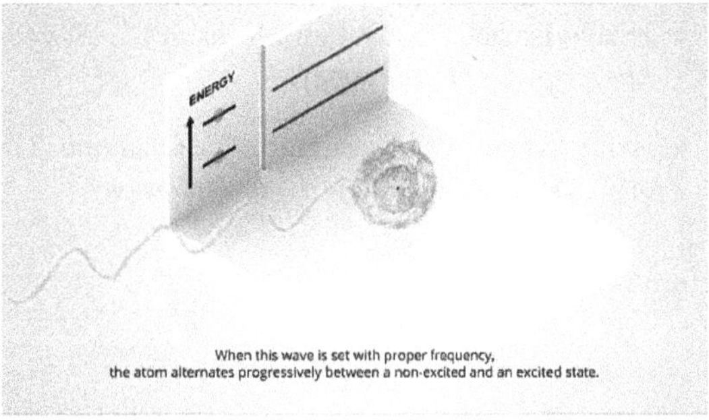
ENERGY
When this wave is set with proper frequency,
the atom alternates progressively between a non-excited and an excited state.

Quantum superposition of states and decoherence

Quantum superposition is a fundamental principle of quantum mechanics. It states that, much like waves in classical physics, any two (or more) quantum states can be added together ("superposed") and the result will be another valid quantum state; and conversely, that every quantum state can be represented as a sum of two or more other distinct states. Mathematically, it refers to a property of solutions to the Schrödinger equation; since the Schrödinger equation is linear, any linear combination of solutions will also be a solution.

An example of a physically observable manifestation of superposition is interference peaks from an electron wave in a double-slit experiment.

Another example is a quantum logical qubit state, as used in quantum information processing, which is a linear superposition of the "basis states" $|0\rangle$ and $|1\rangle$. Here $|0\rangle$ is the Dirac notation for the quantum state that will always give the result 0 when converted to classical logic by a measurement. Likewise $|1\rangle$ is the state that will always convert to 1.

7.1 Theory

7.1.1 Examples

For an equation describing a physical phenomenon, the superposition principle states that a combination of solutions to a linear equation is also a solution of it. When this is true the equation is said to obey the superposition principle. Thus if state vectors f_1, f_2 and f_3 each solve the linear equation on ψ, then $\psi = c_1 f_1 + c_2 f_2 + c_3 f_3$ would also be a solution, in which each c is a coefficient. The Schrödinger equation is linear, so quantum mechanics follows this.

For example, consider an electron with two possible configurations, up and down. This describes the physical system of a qubit.

$$c_1 \, |\uparrow\rangle + c_2 \, |\downarrow\rangle$$

is the most general state. But these coefficients dictate probabilities for the system to be in either configuration. The probability for a specified configuration is given by the square of the absolute value of the coefficient. So the probabilities should add up to 1. The electron is in one of those two states for sure.

$$p_{\text{up}} = | \, c_1 \, |^2$$

$$p_{\text{down}} = | \, c_2 \, |^2$$

$$p_{\text{down or up}} = p_{\text{up}} + p_{\text{down}} = 1$$

Continuing with this example: If a particle can be in state up and can be in state down, it can also be in a state where it is an amount $3i/5$ in up and an amount 4/5 in down.

$$|\psi\rangle = \frac{3}{5} i | \uparrow\rangle + \frac{4}{5} | \downarrow\rangle.$$

In this, the probability for up is $\left| \frac{3i}{5} \right|^2 = \frac{9}{25}$. The probability for down is $\left| \frac{4}{5} \right|^2 = \frac{16}{25}$. Note that $\frac{9}{25} + \frac{16}{25} = 1$.

In the description, only the relative size of the different components matter, and their angle to each other on the complex plane. This is usually stated by declaring that two states which are a multiple of one another are the same as far as the description of the situation is concerned. Either of these describe the same state for any nonzero α

$$|\psi\rangle \approx \alpha |\psi\rangle$$

The fundamental law of quantum mechanics is that the evolution is linear, meaning that if state A turns into A′ and B turns into B′ after 10 seconds, then after 10 seconds the superposition ψ turns into a superposition of A′ and B′ with the same coefficients as A and B.

For example, if we have the following

$$|\uparrow\rangle \rightarrow |\downarrow\rangle$$

$$|\downarrow\rangle \rightarrow \frac{3i}{5}\,|\uparrow\rangle + \frac{4}{5}\,|\downarrow\rangle$$

Then after those 10 seconds our state will change to

$$c_1\,|\uparrow\rangle + c_2\,|\downarrow\rangle \rightarrow c_1\,(|\downarrow\rangle) + c_2\left(\frac{3i}{5}\,|\uparrow\rangle + \frac{4}{5}\,|\downarrow\rangle\right)$$

So far there have just been 2 configurations, but there can be infinitely many.

In illustration, a particle can have any position, so that there are different configurations which have any value of the position x. These are written:

$$|x\rangle$$

The principle of superposition guarantees that there are states which are arbitrary superpositions of all the positions with complex coefficients:

$$\sum_x \psi(x)|x\rangle$$

This sum is defined only if the index x is discrete. If the index is over $\mathbb{R}$, then the sum replaced by an integral. The quantity $\psi(x)$ is called the wavefunction of the particle.

If we consider a qubit with both position and spin, the state is a superposition of all possibilities for both:

$$\sum_x \psi_+(x)|x,\uparrow\rangle + \psi_-(x)|x,\downarrow\rangle$$

The configuration space of a quantum mechanical system cannot be worked out without some physical knowledge. The input is usually the allowed different classical configurations, but without the duplication of including both position and momentum.

A pair of particles can be in any combination of pairs of positions. A state where one particle is at position x and the other is at position y is written $|x,y\rangle$. The most general state is a superposition of the possibilities:

$$\sum_{xy} A(x,y)|x,y\rangle$$

The description of the two particles is much larger than the description of one particle—it is a function in twice the number of dimensions. This is also true in probability, when the statistics of two random variables are correlated. If two particles are uncorrelated, the probability distribution for their joint position P(*x*, *y*) is a product of the probability of finding one at one position and the other at the other position:

$$P(x,y) = P_x(x)P_y(y)$$

In quantum mechanics, two particles can be in special states where the amplitudes of their position are uncorrelated. For quantum amplitudes, the word entanglement replaces the word correlation, but the analogy is exact. A disentangled wave function has the form:

$$A(x,y) = \psi_x(x)\psi_y(y)$$

while an entangled wavefunction does not have this form.

7.1.2 Hamiltonian evolution

The numbers that describe the amplitudes for different possibilities define the kinematics, the space of different states. The dynamics describes how these numbers change with time. For a particle that can be in any one of infinitely many discrete positions, a particle on a lattice, the superposition principle tells you how to make a state:

$$\sum_n \psi_n|n\rangle$$

So that the infinite list of amplitudes $(...\psi_{-2},\psi_{-1},\psi_0,\psi_1,\psi_2...)$ completely describes the quantum state of the particle. This list is called the **state vector**, and formally it is an element of a Hilbert space, an infinite dimensional complex vector space. It is usual to represent the state so that the sum of the absolute squares of the amplitudes add up to one:

$$\sum \psi_n^*\psi_n = 1$$

For a particle described by probability theory random walking on a line, the analogous thing is the list of probabilities $(...P_{-2}, P_{-1}, P_0, P_1, P_2, ...)$, which give the probability of any position. The quantities that describe how they change in time are the transition probabilities $K_{x\rightarrow y}(t)$, which gives the probability that, starting at x, the particle ends up at y after time t. The total probability of ending up at y is given by the sum over all the possibilities

$$P_y(t_0+t) = \sum_x P_x(t_0)K_{x\rightarrow y}(t)$$

The condition of conservation of probability states that starting at any x, the total probability to end up *somewhere* must add up to 1:

$$\sum_y K_{x\to y} = 1$$

So that the total probability will be preserved, K is what is called a stochastic matrix.

When no time passes, nothing changes: for zero elapsed time $K_{x\to y}(0)=\delta_{xy}$, the K matrix is zero except from a state to itself. So in the case that the time is short, it is better to talk about the rate of change of the probability instead of the absolute change in the probability.

$$P_y(t+dt) = P_y(t) + dt\sum_x P_x R_{x\to y}$$

where $R_{x\to y}$ is the time derivative of the K matrix:

$$R_{x\to y} = \frac{K_{x\to y}(dt) - \delta_{xy}}{dt}$$

The equation for the probabilities is a differential equation which is sometimes called the **master equation**:

$$\frac{dP_y}{dt} = \sum_x P_x R_{x\to y}$$

The R matrix is the probability per unit time for the particle to make a transition from x to y. The condition that the K matrix elements add up to one becomes the condition that the R matrix elements add up to zero:

$$\sum_y R_{x\to y} = 0$$

One simple case to study is when the R matrix has an equal probability to go one unit to the left or to the right, describing a particle which has a constant rate of random walking. In this case $R_{x\to y}$ is zero unless y is either x+1,x, or x−1, when y is x+1 or x−1, the R matrix has value c, and in order for the sum of the R matrix coefficients to equal zero, the value of $R_{x\to x}$ must be −2c. So the probabilities obey the **discretized diffusion equation**:

$$\frac{dP_x}{dt} = c(P_{x+1} - 2P_x + P_{x-1})$$

which, when c is scaled appropriately and the P distribution is smooth enough to think of the system in a continuum limit becomes:

$$\frac{\partial P(x,t)}{\partial t} = c\frac{\partial^2 P}{\partial x^2}$$

Which is the **diffusion equation**.

Quantum amplitudes give the rate at which amplitudes change in time, and they are mathematically exactly the same except that they are complex numbers. The analog of the finite time K matrix is called the U matrix:

$$\psi_n(t) = \sum_m U_{nm}(t)\psi_m$$

Since the sum of the absolute squares of the amplitudes must be constant, U must be unitary:

$$\sum_n U^*_{nm}U_{np} = \delta_{mp}$$

or, in matrix notation,

$$U^\dagger U = I$$

The rate of change of U is called the Hamiltonian H, up to a traditional factor of i:

$$H_{mn} = i\frac{d}{dt}U_{mn}$$

The Hamiltonian gives the rate at which the particle has an amplitude to go from m to n. The reason it is multiplied by i is that the condition that U is unitary translates to the condition:

$$(I + iH^\dagger dt)(I - iHdt) = I$$

$$H^\dagger - H = 0$$

which says that H is Hermitian. The eigenvalues of the Hermitian matrix H are real quantities which have a physical interpretation as energy levels. If the factor i were absent, the H matrix would be antihermitian and would have purely imaginary eigenvalues, which is not the traditional way quantum mechanics represents observable quantities like the energy.

For a particle which has equal amplitude to move left and right, the Hermitian matrix H is zero except for nearest neighbors, where it has the value c. If the coefficient is everywhere constant, the condition that H is Hermitian demands that the amplitude to move to the left is the complex conjugate of the amplitude to move to the right. The equation of motion for ψ is the time differential equation:

$$i\frac{d\psi_n}{dt} = c^*\psi_{n+1} + c\psi_{n-1}$$

In the case that left and right are symmetric, c is real. By redefining the phase of the wavefunction in time, $\psi \to$

ψe^{i2ct} , the amplitudes for being at different locations are only rescaled, so that the physical situation is unchanged. But this phase rotation introduces a linear term.

$$i\frac{d\psi_n}{dt} = c\psi_{n+1} - 2c\psi_n + c\psi_{n-1}$$

which is the right choice of phase to take the continuum limit. When c is very large and psi is slowly varying so that the lattice can be thought of as a line, this becomes the free Schrödinger equation:

$$i\frac{\partial\psi}{\partial t} = -\frac{\partial^2\psi}{\partial x^2}$$

If there is an additional term in the H matrix which is an extra phase rotation which varies from point to point, the continuum limit is the Schrödinger equation with a potential energy:

$$i\frac{\partial\psi}{\partial t} = -\frac{\partial^2\psi}{\partial x^2} + V(x)\psi$$

These equations describe the motion of a single particle in non-relativistic quantum mechanics.

7.1.3 Quantum mechanics in imaginary time

The analogy between quantum mechanics and probability is very strong, so that there are many mathematical links between them. In a statistical system in discrete time, t=1,2,3, described by a transition matrix for one time step $K_{m\to n}$, the probability to go between two points after a finite number of time steps can be represented as a sum over all paths of the probability of taking each path:

$$K_{x\to y}(T) = \sum_{x(t)} \prod_t K_{x(t)x(t+1)}$$

where the sum extends over all paths $x(t)$ with the property that $x(0) = 0$ and $x(T) = y$. The analogous expression in quantum mechanics is the path integral.

A generic transition matrix in probability has a stationary distribution, which is the eventual probability to be found at any point no matter what the starting point. If there is a nonzero probability for any two paths to reach the same point at the same time, this stationary distribution does not depend on the initial conditions. In probability theory, the probability m for the stochastic matrix obeys detailed balance when the stationary distribution ρ_n has the property:

$$\rho_n K_{n\to m} = \rho_m K_{m\to n}$$

Detailed balance says that the total probability of going from m to n in the stationary distribution, which is the probability of starting at m ρ_m times the probability of hopping from m to n, is equal to the probability of going from n to m, so that the total back-and-forth flow of probability in equilibrium is zero along any hop. The condition is automatically satisfied when n=m, so it has the same form when written as a condition for the transition-probability R matrix.

$$\rho_n R_{n\to m} = \rho_m R_{m\to n}$$

When the R matrix obeys detailed balance, the scale of the probabilities can be redefined using the stationary distribution so that they no longer sum to 1:

$$p'_n = \sqrt{\rho_n}\, p_n$$

In the new coordinates, the R matrix is rescaled as follows:

$$\sqrt{\rho_n} R_{n\to m} \frac{1}{\sqrt{\rho_m}} = H_{nm}$$

and H is symmetric

$$H_{nm} = H_{mn}$$

This matrix H defines a quantum mechanical system:

$$i\frac{d}{dt}\psi_n = \sum H_{nm}\psi_m$$

whose Hamiltonian has the same eigenvalues as those of the R matrix of the statistical system. The eigenvectors are the same too, except expressed in the rescaled basis. The stationary distribution of the statistical system is the *ground state* of the Hamiltonian and it has energy exactly zero, while all the other energies are positive. If H is exponentiated to find the U matrix:

$$U(t) = e^{-iHt}$$

and t is allowed to take on complex values, the K' matrix is found by taking time imaginary.

$$K'(t) = e^{-Ht}$$

For quantum systems which are invariant under time reversal the Hamiltonian can be made real and symmetric, so that the action of time-reversal on the wave-function is just complex conjugation. If such a Hamiltonian has a unique lowest energy state with a positive real wave-function, as it often does for physical reasons, it is connected to a stochastic system in imaginary time. This relationship between stochastic systems and quantum systems sheds much light on supersymmetry.

7.2 Experiments and applications

Successful experiments involving superpositions of relatively large (by the standards of quantum physics) objects have been performed.[1]

- A "cat state" has been achieved with photons.[2]
- A beryllium ion has been trapped in a superposed state.[3]
- A double slit experiment has been performed with molecules as large as buckyballs.[4][5]
- A 2013 experiment superposed molecules containing 15,000 each of protons, neutrons and electrons. The molecules were of compounds selected for their good thermal stability, and were evaporated into a beam at a temperature of 600 K. The beam was prepared from highly purified chemical substances, but still contained a mixture of different molecular species. Each species of molecule interfered only with itself, as verified by mass spectrometry.[6]
- An experiment involving a superconducting quantum interference device ("SQUID") has been linked to theme of the "cat state" thought experiment.[7]

  By use of very low temperatures, very fine experimental arrangements were made to protect in near isolation and preserve the coherence of intermediate states, for a duration of time, between preparation and detection, of SQUID currents. Such a SQUID current is a coherent physical assembly of perhaps billions of electrons. Because of its coherence, such an assembly may be regarded as exhibiting "collective states" of a macroscopic quantal entity. For the principle of superposition, after it is prepared but before it is detected, it may be regarded as exhibiting an intermediate state. It is not a single-particle state such as is often considered in discussions of interference, for example by Dirac in his famous dictum stated above.[8] Morever, though the 'intermediate' state may be loosely regarded as such, it has not been produced as an output of a secondary quantum analyser that was fed a pure state from a primary analyser, and so this is not an example of superposition as strictly and narrowly defined.

  Nevertheless, after preparation, but before measurement, such a SQUID state may be regarded in a manner of speaking as a "pure" state that is a superposition of a clockwise and an anti-clockwise current state. In a SQUID, collective electron states can be physically prepared in near isolation, at very low temperatures, so as to result in protected coherent intermediate states. Remarkable here is that there are found two well-separated respectively self-coherent collective states that exhibit such metastability. The crowd of electrons tunnels back and forth between the clockwise and the anti-clockwise states, as opposed to forming a single intermediate state in which there is no definite collective sense of current flow.[9][10]

  In contrast, for actual real cats, such well-separated metastable collective states states do not exist and consequently cannot be physically prepared. Schrödinger's point was that classical thinking does not in general anticipate such physically distinct and separate metastable quantum states. In classical thinking, distinct quantum states even of single atoms can indeed be regarded as metastable, and are remarkable and unexpected. In the days when Schrödinger raised his argumentative example, no one had imagined the invention of SQUIDs that exhibit such states on a macroscopic scale. The present-day physicist here pays close attention to the requirement mentioned above, that the intermediate states must be carefully physically shielded to protect them from any factor that affects some of the independent quantal entities (in this case collective not single particle) differently from others. Contrary to this requirement, the living cat breathes. This destroys intermediate state coherence, and so the conditions required for exhibition of the principle of superposition are not fulfilled.

- An experiment involving a flu virus has been proposed.[11]
- A piezoelectric "tuning fork" has been constructed, which can be placed into a superposition of vibrating and non vibrating states. The resonator comprises about 10 trillion atoms.[12]
- Recent research indicates that chlorophyll within plants appears to exploit the feature of quantum superposition to achieve greater efficiency in transporting energy, allowing pigment proteins to be spaced further apart than would otherwise be possible.[13][14]
- An experiment has been proposed, with a bacterial cell cooled to 10 mK, using an electromechanical oscillator.[15] At that temperature, all metabolism would be stopped, and the cell might behave virtually as a definite chemical species. For detection of interference, it would be necessary that the cells be supplied in large numbers as pure samples of identical and detectably recognizable virtual chemical species. It is not known whether this requirement

can be met by bacterial cells. They would be in a state of suspended animation during the experiment.

In quantum computing the phrase "cat state" often refers to the special entanglement of qubits wherein the qubits are in an equal superposition of all being 0 and all being 1; i.e.,

$$|\psi\rangle = \frac{1}{\sqrt{2}}\Big(|00...0\rangle + |11...1\rangle\Big)$$

7.3 Formal interpretation

Applying the superposition principle to a quantum mechanical particle, the configurations of the particle are all positions, so the superpositions make a complex wave in space. The coefficients of the linear superposition are a wave which describes the particle as best as is possible, and whose amplitude interferes according to the Huygens principle.

For any physical property in quantum mechanics, there is a list of all the states where that property has some value. These states are necessarily perpendicular to each other using the Euclidean notion of perpendicularity which comes from sums-of-squares length, except that they also must not be i multiples of each other. This list of perpendicular states has an associated value which is the value of the physical property. The superposition principle guarantees that any state can be written as a combination of states of this form with complex coefficients.

Write each state with the value q of the physical quantity as a vector in some basis ψ_n^q , a list of numbers at each value of n for the vector which has value q for the physical quantity. Now form the outer product of the vectors by multiplying all the vector components and add them with coefficients to make the matrix

$$A_{nm} = \sum_q q\psi_n^{*q}\psi_m^q$$

where the sum extends over all possible values of q. This matrix is necessarily symmetric because it is formed from the orthogonal states, and has eigenvalues q. The matrix A is called the observable associated to the physical quantity. It has the property that the eigenvalues and eigenvectors determine the physical quantity and the states which have definite values for this quantity.

Every physical quantity has a Hermitian linear operator associated to it, and the states where the value of this physical quantity is definite are the eigenstates of this linear operator. The linear combination of two or more eigenstates results in quantum superposition of two or more values of the quantity. If the quantity is measured, the value of the physical quantity will be random, with a probability equal to the square of the coefficient of the superposition in the linear combination. Immediately after the measurement, the state will be given by the eigenvector corresponding to the measured eigenvalue.

7.4 Physical interpretation

It is natural to ask why ordinary everyday "real" (macroscopic, Newtonian) objects and events do not seem empirically to display quantum mechanical features such as superposition. Indeed, this is sometimes regarded even as "mysterious", for example by Richard Feynman.[16] In 1935, Erwin Schrödinger devised a well-known thought experiment, now known as Schrödinger's cat, which highlighted the dissonance between quantum mechanics and Newtonian physics, where only one configuration occurs, although a configuration for a particle in Newtonian physics specifies both position and momentum.

Physically, according to Dirac, this is explained as follows. It is a logical truism that a single detection of a quantum system, observed alone, empirically considered, is not an example of a relation of several states. For the several states are not empirically defined when the quantum system is observed alone. It would therefore be nonsense to try to say that it, a single state, observed alone, empirically shows superposition. It is convenient to describe superposition for an original primary beam that consists of quantum systems in a pure state. Superposition is a relation of several states that are empirically defined when the original superposed beam is split by some diffractive object into several intermediate sub-beams, empirically observable by distinct particle detectors respectively in each. The detectors should be removed when it is desired to verify superposition by re-composition of the sub-beams back into the original pure state. The sub-beams can be considered in two ways. Either they can be considered as joint constituents of the primary beam, an expression of the original pure state. Or they can be considered as separate sub-beams, each respectively pure with respect to the diffractive object.[17][18] To produce sub-beams, the diffractive object must be characterized by an operator that does not commute with at least one of the operators that define the production of the pure state of the original primary beam. It is classically inexplicable how a quantum analyser or diffractive object can have several pure states as outputs. That is Feynman's "mystery".

Here may be found reason for differences of opinion, as between the Copenhagen or other interpretations. Neil Bohr famously insisted that the wave function refers to a single individual quantum system. What did he mean by this? He was expressing the idea that Dirac expressed when he famously wrote: "Each photon then interferes only with itself. Interference between different photons never occurs.".[19] Dirac clarified this by writing: "This, of course, is true only provided the two states that are superposed refer to the same beam of light, *i.e.* all that is known about the position and momentum of a photon in either of these states must be the same for each."[20] Bohr wanted to emphasize that a superposition is different from a mixture. He seemed to think that those who spoke of a "statistical interpretation" were not taking that into account. To create, by a superposition experiment, a new and different pure state, from an original pure beam, one can put absorbers and phase-shifters into some of the sub-beams, so as to alter the composition of the re-constituted superposition. But one cannot do so by mixing a fragment of the original unsplit beam with component split sub-beams. That is because one photon cannot both go into the unsplit fragment and go into the split component sub-beams. Bohr felt that talk in statistical terms might hide this fact.

Quantum superposition is exhibited in fact in many directly observable phenomena, such as interference peaks from an electron wave in a double-slit experiment. Superposition persists at all scales, provided that coherence is shielded from disruption by intermittent external factors.

The Heisenberg uncertainty principle states that for any given instant of time, the position and velocity of an electron or other subatomic particle cannot both be exactly determined.

If the operators corresponding to two observables do not commute, a state where one of them has a definite value corresponds to a superposition of many states for the other.

7.5 See also

- Eigenstates
- Mach-Zehnder interferometer
- Penrose Interpretation
- Pure qubit state
- Quantum computation
- Schrödinger's cat
- Wave packet

7.6 References

[1] What is the World's Biggest Schrodinger Cat?

[2] Schrödinger's Cat Now Made of Light

[3] C. Monroe, et. al. *A "Schrodinger Cat" Superposition State of an Atom*

[4] Wave Particle Duality of C60

[5] Diffraction of the Fullerenes C60 and C70 by a standing light wave

[6] Eibenberger, S., Gerlich, S., Arndt, M., Mayor, M., Tüxen, J. (2013). Matter-wave interference with particles selected from a molecular library with masses exceeding 10 000 amu, *Phys. Chem. Chem. Phys.*, **15**: 14696-14700.

[7] Leggett, A.J. (1986). The superposition principle in macroscopic systems, pp. 28–40 in *Quantum Concepts of Space and Time*, edited by R. Penrose and C.J. Isham, ISBN 0-19-851972-9.

[8] Dirac, P.A.M. (1930/1958), p. 9.

[9] Physics World: *Schrodinger's cat comes into view*

[10] Friedman, J.R., Patel, V., Chen, W., Tolpygo, S.K., Lukens, J.E. (2000).Quantum superposition of distinct macroscopic states, *Nature* **406**: 43–46.

[11] How to Create Quantum Superpositions of Living Things>

[12] Scientific American : *Macro-Weirdness: "Quantum Microphone" Puts Naked-Eye Object in 2 Places at Once: A new device tests the limits of Schrödinger's cat*

[13] Scholes, Gregory; Elisabetta Collini; Cathy Y. Wong; Krystyna E. Wilk; Paul M. G. Curmi; Paul Brumer; Gregory D. Scholes (4 February 2010). "Coherently wired light-harvesting in photosynthetic marine algae at ambient temperature". *Nature* **463** (7281): 644–647. Bibcode:2010Natur.463..644C. doi:10.1038/nature08811. PMID 20130647.

[14] Moyer, Michael (September 2009). "Quantum Entanglement, Photosynthesis and Better Solar Cells". *Scientific American.* Retrieved 12 May 2010.

[15] Could 'Schrödinger's bacterium' be placed in a quantum superposition?>

[16] Feynman, R.P., Leighton, R.B., Sands, M. (1965), § 1-1.

[17] Dirac, P.A.M. (1958). *The Principles of Quantum Mechanics*, 4th edition, Oxford University Press, Oxford UK, p. 8: "For a photon to be in a definite translational state it need not be associated with one single beam of light, but may be associated with two or more beams of light which are the components into which one original beam has been split."

[18] Feynman, R.P., Leighton, R.B., Sands, M. (1963). *The Feynman Lectures on Physics*, Volume 3, Addison-Wesley, Reading MA, also here, Chapter 5, 'Spin One': "a filtered beam in a *pure state* with respect to *S*.

[19] Dirac, P.A.M., *The Principles of Quantum Mechanics*, (1930), 1st edition, p. 15; (1935), 2nd edition, p. 9; (1947), 3rd edition, p. 9; (1958), 4th edition, p. 9.

[20] Dirac, P.A.M., *The Principles of Quantum Mechanics*, (1930), 1st edition, p. 8.

7.6.1 Bibliography of cited references

- Bohr, N. (1927/1928). The quantum postulate and the recent development of atomic theory, *Nature* Supplement 14 April 1928, **121**: 580–590.
- Cohen-Tannoudji, C., Diu, B., Laloë, F. (1973/1977). *Quantum Mechanics*, translated from the French by S.R. Hemley, N. Ostrowsky, D. Ostrowsky, second edition, volume 1, Wiley, New York, ISBN 0471164321.
- Dirac, P.A.M. (1930/1958). *The Principles of Quantum Mechanics*, 4th edition, Oxford University Press.
- Einstein, A. (1949). Remarks concerning the essays brought together in this co-operative volume, translated from the original German by the editor, pp. 665–688 in Schilpp, P.A. editor (1949), *Albert Einstein: Philosopher-Scientist*, volume II, Open Court, La Salle IL.
- Feynman, R.P., Leighton, R.B., Sands, M. (1965). *The Feynman Lectures on Physics*, volume 3, Addison-Wesley, Reading, MA.
- Merzbacher, E. (1961/1970). *Quantum Mechanics*, second edition, Wiley, New York.
- Messiah, A. (1961). *Quantum Mechanics*, volume 1, translated by G.M. Temmer from the French *Mécanique Quantique*, North-Holland, Amsterdam.
- Wheeler, J.A.; Zurek, W.H. (1983). *Quantum Theory and Measurement.* Princeton NJ: Princeton University Press.

Chapter 8

Bit

This article is about the unit of information. For other uses, see Bit (disambiguation).

The **bit** is a basic unit of information in computing and digital communications.[1] A bit can have only one of two values, and may therefore be physically implemented with a two-state device. These values are most commonly represented as either a 0or1. The term *bit* is a portmanteau of **binary digit**. In information theory, the bit is equivalent to the unit **shannon**,[2] named after Claude Shannon.

The two values can also be interpreted as logical values (true/false, yes/no), algebraic signs (+/−), activation states (on/off), or any other two-valued attribute. The correspondence between these values and the physical states of the underlying storage or device is a matter of convention, and different assignments may be used even within the same device or program. The length of a binary number may be referred to as its bit-length.

In information theory, one bit is typically defined as the uncertainty of a binary random variable that is 0 or 1 with equal probability,[3] or the information that is gained when the value of such a variable becomes known.[4]

In quantum computing, a *quantum bit* or qubit is a quantum system that can exist in superposition of two classical (i.e., non-quantum) bit values.

The symbol for bit, as a unit of information, is either simply *bit* (recommended by the IEC 80000-13:2008 standard) or lowercase *b* (recommended by the IEEE 1541-2002 standard). A group of eight bits is commonly called one byte, but historically the size of the byte is not strictly defined.

8.1 History

The encoding of data by discrete bits was used in the punched cards invented by Basile Bouchon and Jean-Baptiste Falcon (1732), developed by Joseph Marie Jacquard (1804), and later adopted by Semen Korsakov, Charles Babbage, Hermann Hollerith, and early computer manufacturers like IBM. Another variant of that idea was the perforated paper tape. In all those systems, the medium (card or tape) conceptually carried an array of hole positions; each position could be either punched through or not, thus carrying one bit of information. The encoding of text by bits was also used in Morse code (1844) and early digital communications machines such as teletypes and stock ticker machines (1870).

Ralph Hartley suggested the use of a logarithmic measure of information in 1928.[5] Claude E. Shannon first used the word ***bit*** in his seminal 1948 paper *A Mathematical Theory of Communication*. [6] He attributed its origin to John W. Tukey, who had written a Bell Labs memo on 9 January 1947 in which he contracted "binary digit" to simply "bit". Interestingly, Vannevar Bush had written in 1936 of "bits of information" that could be stored on the punched cards used in the mechanical computers of that time.[7] The first programmable computer built by Konrad Zuse used binary notation for numbers.

8.2 Physical representation

A bit can be stored by a digital device or other physical system that exists in either of two possible distinct states. These may be the two stable states of a flip-flop, two positions of an electrical switch, two distinct voltage or current levels allowed by a circuit, two distinct levels of light intensity, two directions of magnetization or polarization, the orientation of reversible double stranded DNA, etc.

Bits can be implemented in several forms. In most modern computing devices, a bit is usually represented by an electrical voltage or current pulse, or by the electrical state of a flip-flop circuit.

For devices using positive logic, a digit value of 1 (or a logical value of true) is represented by a more positive voltage relative to the representation of 0. The specific voltages are different for different logic families and variations are permitted to allow for component aging and noise immunity. For example, in transistor–transistor logic (TTL) and compatible circuits, digit values 0 and 1 at the output of a device are represented by no higher than 0.4 volts and no lower than 2.6 volts, respectively; while TTL inputs are specified to recognize 0.8 volts or below as 0 and 2.2 volts or above as 1.

8.2.1 Transmission and processing

Bits are transmitted one at a time in serial transmission, and by a multiple number of bits in parallel transmission. A bitwise operation optionally process bits one at a time. Data transfer rates are usually measured in decimal SI multiples of the unit bit per second (bit/s), such as kbit/s.

8.2.2 Storage

In the earliest non-electronic information processing devices, such as Jacquard's loom or Babbage's Analytical Engine, a bit was often stored as the position of a mechanical lever or gear, or the presence or absence of a hole at a specific point of a paper card or tape. The first electrical devices for discrete logic (such as elevator and traffic light control circuits, telephone switches, and Konrad Zuse's computer) represented bits as the states of electrical relays which could be either "open" or "closed". When relays were replaced by vacuum tubes, starting in the 1940s, computer builders experimented with a variety of storage methods, such as pressure pulses traveling down a mercury delay line, charges stored on the inside surface of a cathode-ray tube, or opaque spots printed on glass discs by photolithographic techniques.

In the 1950s and 1960s, these methods were largely supplanted by magnetic storage devices such as magnetic core memory, magnetic tapes, drums, and disks, where a bit was represented by the polarity of magnetization of a certain area of a ferromagnetic film, or by a change in polarity from one direction to the other. The same principle was later used in the magnetic bubble memory developed in the 1980s, and is still found in various magnetic strip items such as metro tickets and some credit cards.

In modern semiconductor memory, such as dynamic random-access memory, the two values of a bit may be represented by two levels of electric charge stored in a capacitor. In certain types of programmable logic arrays and read-only memory, a bit may be represented by the presence or absence of a conducting path at a certain point of a circuit. In optical discs, a bit is encoded as the presence or absence of a microscopic pit on a reflective surface. In one-dimensional bar codes, bits are encoded as the thickness of alternating black and white lines.

8.3 Unit and symbol

The bit is not defined in the International System of Units (SI). However, the International Electrotechnical Commission issued standard IEC 60027, which specifies that the symbol for binary digit should be *bit*, and this should be used in all multiples, such as *kbit*, for kilobit.[8] However, the lower-case letter b is widely used as well and was recommended by the IEEE 1541 Standard (2002). In contrast, the upper case letter B is the standard and customary symbol for byte.

8.3.1 Multiple bits

Multiple bits may be expressed and represented in several ways. For convenience of representing commonly reoccurring groups of bits in information technology, several units of information have traditionally been used. The most common is the unit byte, coined by Werner Buchholz in July 1956, which historically was used to represent the number of bits used to encode a single character of text (until UTF-8 multibyte encoding took over) in a computer[9][10] and for this reason it was used as the basic addressable element in many computer architectures. The trend in hardware design converged on the most common implementation of using eight bits per byte, as it is widely used today. However, because of the ambiguity of relying on the underlying hardware design, the unit octet was defined to explicitly denote a sequence of eight bits.

Computers usually manipulate bits in groups of a fixed size, conventionally named "words". Like the byte, the number of bits in a word also varies with the hardware design, and is typically between 8 and 80 bits, or even more in some specialized computers. In the 21st century, retail personal or server computers have a word size of 32 or 64 bits.

The International System of Units defines a series of decimal prefixes for multiples of standardized units which are commonly also used with the bit and the byte. The prefixes kilo (10^3) through yotta (10^{24}) increment by multiples of 1000, and the corresponding units are the kilobit (kbit) through the yottabit (Ybit).

8.4 Information capacity and information compression

When the information *capacity* of a storage system or a communication channel is presented in bits or bits per second, this often refers to binary digits, which is a computer hardware capacity to store binary code (0 or 1, up or down, current or not, etc.). Information *capacity* of a storage system is only an upper bound to the actual *quantity of information* stored therein. If the two possible values of one bit of storage are not equally likely, that bit of storage will contain less than one bit of information. Indeed, if the value is completely predictable, then the reading of that value will provide no information at all (zero entropic bits, because no resolution of uncertainty and therefore no information). If a computer file that uses n bits of storage contains only $m < n$ bits of information, then that information can in principle be encoded in about m bits, at least on the average. This principle is the basis of data compression technology. Using an analogy, the hardware binary digits refer to the amount of storage space available (like the number of buckets available to store things), and the information content the filling, which comes in different levels of granularity (fine or coarse, that is, compressed or uncompressed information). When the granularity is finer (when information is more compressed), the same bucket can hold more.

For example, it is estimated that the combined technological capacity of the world to store information provides 1,300 exabytes of hardware digits in 2007. However, when this storage space is filled and the corresponding content is optimally compressed, this only represents 295 exabytes of information.[11] When optimally compressed, the resulting carrying capacity approaches Shannon information or information entropy.

8.5 Bit-based computing

Certain bitwise computer processor instructions (such as *bit set*) operate at the level of manipulating bits rather than manipulating data interpreted as an aggregate of bits.

In the 1980s, when bitmapped computer displays became popular, some computers provided specialized bit block transfer ("bitblt" or "blit") instructions to set or copy the bits that corresponded to a given rectangular area on the screen.

In most computers and programming languages, when a bit within a group of bits, such as a byte or word, is referred to, it is usually specified by a number from 0 upwards corresponding to its position within the byte or word. However, 0 can refer to either the most or least significant bit depending on the context.

8.6 Other information units

Main article: Units of information

Other units of information, sometimes used in information theory, include the *natural digit* also called a *nat* or *nit* and defined as $\log_2 e$ ($\approx$ 1.443) bits, where *e* is the base of the natural logarithms; and the *dit*, *ban*, or *hartley*, defined as $\log_2 10$ ($\approx$ 3.322) bits.[5] This value, slightly less than 10/3, may be understood because $10^3 = 1000 \approx 1024 = 2^{10}$: three decimal digits are slightly less information than ten binary digits, so one decimal digit is slightly less than 10/3 binary digits. Conversely, one bit of information corresponds to about $\ln 2$ ($\approx$ 0.693) nats, or $\log_{10} 2$ ($\approx$ 0.301) hartleys. As with the inverse ratio, this value, approximately 3/10, but slightly more, corresponds to the fact that $2^{10} = 1024 \sim 1000 = 10^3$: ten binary digits are slightly more information than three decimal digits, so one binary digit is slightly more than 3/10 decimal digits.

Some authors also define a **binit** as an arbitrary information unit equivalent to some fixed but unspecified number of bits.[12]

8.7 See also

- Integer (computer science)
- Primitive data type
- Trit (Trinary digit)
- Bitstream
- Entropy (information theory)
- Baud (bits per second)
- Binary numeral system
- Ternary numeral system
- Shannon (unit)

8.8 Notes

8.9 References

[1] http://www.merriam-webster.com/dictionary/bit

[2] https://www.unc.edu/~{}rowlett/units/dictB.html#bit

[3] John B. Anderson, Rolf Johnnesson (2006) *Understanding Information Transmission.*

[4] Simon Haykin (2006), *Digital Communications*

[5] Norman Abramson (1963), *Information theory and coding*. McGraw-Hill.

[6] Shannon, Claude. "A Mathematical Theory of Communication" (PDF). *Bell Labs Technical Journal.*

[7] Bush, Vannevar (1936). "Instrumental analysis". *Bulletin of the American Mathematical Society* **42** (10): 649–669. doi:10.1090/S0002-9904-1936-06390-1.

[8] National Institute of Standards and Technology (2008), *Guide for the Use of the International System of Units.* Online version.

[9] Bemer, RW; Buchholz, Werner (1962), "4, Natural Data Units", in Buchholz, Werner, *Planning a Computer System – Project Stretch* (PDF), pp. 39–40

[10] Bemer, RW (1959), "A proposal for a generalized card code of 256 characters", *Communications of the ACM* **2** (9): 19–23, doi:10.1145/368424.368435

[11] "The World's Technological Capacity to Store, Communicate, and Compute Information", especially Supporting online material, Martin Hilbert and Priscila López (2011), Science (journal), 332(6025), 60-65; free access to the article through here: martinhilbert.net/WorldInfoCapacity.html

[12] Amitabha Bhattacharya, *Digital Communication*

8.10 External links

- Bit Calculator - Convert between bit, byte, kilobit, kilobyte, megabit, megabyte, gigabit, gigabyte
- BitXByteConverter - Best tool for file size, storage capacity, digital information and data conversion

Chapter 9

Qubit

This article is about the quantum computing unit. For other uses, see Qubit (disambiguation).

In quantum computing, a **qubit** (/ˈkjuːbɪt/) or **quantum bit** (sometimes **qbit**) is a unit of quantum information—the quantum analogue of the classical bit. A qubit is a two-state quantum-mechanical system, such as the polarization of a single photon: here the two states are vertical polarization and horizontal polarization. In a classical system, a bit would have to be in one state or the other. However quantum mechanics allows the qubit to be in a superposition of both states at the same time, a property which is fundamental to quantum computing.

9.1 Origin of the concept and name

The concept of the qubit was unknowingly introduced by Stephen Wiesner in 1983, in his proposal for quantum money, which he had tried to publish for over a decade.[1][2]

The coining of the term "qubit" is attributed to Benjamin Schumacher.[3] In the acknowledgments of his paper, Schumacher states that the term *qubit* was invented in jest due to its phonological resemblance with an ancient unit of length called cubit, during a conversation with William Wootters. The paper describes a way of compressing states emitted by a quantum source of information so that they require fewer physical resources to store. This procedure is now known as Schumacher compression.

9.2 Bit versus qubit

The bit is the basic unit of information. It is used to represent information by computers. Regardless of its physical realization, a bit has two possible states typically thought of as 0 and 1, but more generally—and according to applications—interpretable as true and false, or any other dichotomous choice. An analogy to this is a light switch—its off position can be thought of as 0 and its on position as 1.

A qubit has a few similarities to a classical bit, but is overall very different. There are two possible outcomes for the measurement of a qubit—usually 0 and 1, like a bit. The difference is that whereas the state of a bit is either 0 or 1, the state of a qubit can also be a superposition of both.[4] It is possible to fully encode one bit in one qubit. However, a qubit can hold even more information, e.g. up to two bits using superdense coding. A complete description of the state of a classical system requires only n bits, in quantum physics, a complete description of the state of a system requires 2^n-1 complex numbers.[5]

9.3 Representation

The two states in which a qubit may be measured are known as basis states (or basis vectors). As is the tradition with any sort of quantum states, they are represented by Dirac—or "bra–ket"—notation. This means that the two computational basis states are conventionally written as $|0\rangle$ and $|1\rangle$ (pronounced "ket 0" and "ket 1").

9.4 Qubit states

A pure qubit state is a linear superposition of the basis states. This means that the qubit can be represented as a linear combination of $|0\rangle$ and $|1\rangle$:

$$|\psi\rangle = \alpha|0\rangle + \beta|1\rangle,$$

where α and β are probability amplitudes and can in general both be complex numbers.

When we measure this qubit in the standard basis, the probability of outcome $|0\rangle$ is $|\alpha|^2$ and the probability of outcome $|1\rangle$ is $|\beta|^2$. Because the absolute squares of the amplitudes equate to probabilities, it follows that α and β must be constrained by the equation

$$|\alpha|^2 + |\beta|^2 = 1$$

simply because this ensures you must measure either one state or the other (the total probability of all possible outcomes must be 1).

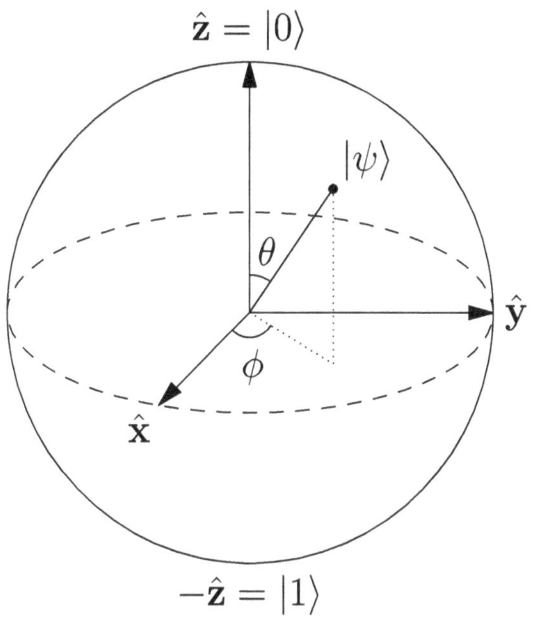

Bloch sphere representation of a qubit. The probability amplitudes in the text are given by $\alpha = \cos\left(\frac{\theta}{2}\right)$ *and* $\beta = e^{i\phi}\sin\left(\frac{\theta}{2}\right)$
.

9.4.1 Bloch sphere

The possible states for a single qubit can be visualised using a Bloch sphere (see diagram). Represented on such a sphere, a classical bit could only be at the "North Pole" or the "South Pole", in the locations where $|0\rangle$ and $|1\rangle$ are respectively. The rest of the surface of the sphere is inaccessible to a classical bit, but a pure qubit state can be represented by any point on the surface. For example, the pure qubit state $\frac{|0\rangle+i|1\rangle}{\sqrt{2}}$ would lie on the equator of the sphere, on the positive y axis.

The surface of the sphere is two-dimensional space, which represents the state space of the pure qubit states. This state space has two local degrees of freedom. It might at first sight seem that there should be four degrees of freedom, as α and β are complex numbers with two degrees of freedom each. However, one degree of freedom is removed by the constraint $|\alpha|^2 + |\beta|^2 = 1$. Another, the overall phase of the state, has no physically observable consequences, so we can arbitrarily choose α to be real, leaving just two degrees of freedom.

It is possible to put the qubit in a mixed state, a statistical combination of different pure states. Mixed states can be represented by points inside the Bloch sphere. A mixed qubit state has three degrees of freedom: the angles ϕ and θ , as well as the length r of the vector that represents the mixed state.

9.4.2 Operations on pure qubit states

There are various kinds of physical operations that can be performed on pure qubit states.

- A quantum logic gate can operate on a qubit: mathematically speaking, the qubit undergoes a unitary transformation. Unitary transformations correspond to rotations of the qubit vector in the Bloch sphere.

- Standard basis measurement is an operation in which information is gained about the state of the qubit. The result of the measurement will be either $|0\rangle$, with probability $|\alpha|^2$, or $|1\rangle$, with probability $|\beta|^2$. Measurement of the state of the qubit alters the values of α and β. For instance, if the result of the measurement is $|0\rangle$, α is changed to 1 (up to phase) and β is changed to 0. Note that a measurement of a qubit state entangled with another quantum system transforms a pure state into a mixed state.

9.5 Entanglement

An important distinguishing feature between a qubit and a classical bit is that multiple qubits can exhibit quantum entanglement. Entanglement is a nonlocal property that allows a set of qubits to express higher correlation than is possible in classical systems. Take, for example, two entangled qubits in the Bell state

$$\frac{1}{\sqrt{2}}(|00\rangle + |11\rangle).$$

In this state, called an *equal superposition*, there are equal probabilities of measuring either $|00\rangle$ or $|11\rangle$, as $|1/\sqrt{2}|^2 = 1/2$.

Imagine that these two entangled qubits are separated, with one each given to Alice and Bob. Alice makes a measurement of her qubit, obtaining—with equal probabilities—either $|0\rangle$ or $|1\rangle$. Because of the qubits' entanglement, Bob must now get exactly the same measurement as Alice; i.e., if she measures a $|0\rangle$, Bob must measure the same, as $|00\rangle$ is the only state where Alice's qubit is a $|0\rangle$. Entanglement also allows multiple states (such as the Bell state mentioned above) to be acted on simultaneously, unlike classical bits that can only have one value at a time. Entanglement is a necessary ingredient of any quantum computation that cannot be done efficiently on a classical computer. Many of the successes of quantum computation and communication, such as quantum teleportation and superdense coding, make use of entanglement, suggesting that entanglement is a resource that is unique to quantum computation.

9.6 Quantum register

A number of qubits taken together is a qubit register. Quantum computers perform calculations by manipulating qubits within a register. A **qubyte** (quantum byte) is a collection of eight qubits.[6]

9.6.1 Variations of the qubit

Similar to the qubit, a qutrit is a unit of quantum information in a 3-level quantum system. This is analogous to the unit of classical information trit. The term "**qudit**" is used to denote a unit of quantum information in a *d*-level quantum system.

9.7 Physical representation

Any two-level system can be used as a qubit. Multi-level systems can be used as well, if they possess two states that can be effectively decoupled from the rest (e.g., ground state and first excited state of a nonlinear oscillator). There are various proposals. Several physical implementations which approximate two-level systems to various degrees were successfully realized. Similarly to a classical bit where the state of a transistor in a processor, the magnetization of a surface in a hard disk and the presence of current in a cable can all be used to represent bits in the same computer, an eventual quantum computer is likely to use various combinations of qubits in its design.

The following is an incomplete list of physical implementations of qubits, and the choices of basis are by convention only.

9.8 Qubit storage

In a paper entitled: "Solid-state quantum memory using the ^{31}P nuclear spin", published in the October 23, 2008 issue of the journal *Nature*,[7] a team of scientists from the U.K. and U.S. reported the first relatively long (1.75 seconds) and coherent transfer of a superposition state in an electron spin "processing" qubit to a nuclear spin "memory" qubit. This event can be considered the first relatively consistent quantum data storage, a vital step towards the development of quantum computing. Recently, a modification of similar systems (using charged rather than neutral donors) has dramatically extended this time, to 3 hours at very low temperatures and 39 minutes at room temperature.[8]

9.9 See also

- Ancilla bit
- D-Wave
- Photonic computer
- W state

9.10 References

[1] S. Weisner (1983). "Conjugate coding". *Association for Computing Machinery, Special Interest Group in Algorithms and Computation Theory* **15**: 78–88.

[2] A. Zelinger, *Dance of the Photons: From Einstein to Quantum Teleportation*, Farrar, Straus & Giroux, New York, 2010, pp. 189, 192, ISBN 0374239665

[3] B. Schumacher (1995). "Quantum coding". *Physical Review A* **51** (4): 2738–2747. Bibcode:1995PhRvA..51.2738S. doi:10.1103/PhysRevA.51.2738.

[4] Nielsen, Michael A.; Chuang, Isaac L. (2010). *Quantum Computation and Quantum Information*. Cambridge University Press. p. 13. ISBN 978-1-107-00217-3.

[5] Shor, Peter (1996). "Polynomial-Time Algorithms for Prime Factorization and Discrete Logarithms on a Quantum Computer*". *arXiv*. Retrieved 4/15/2016. Check date values in: |access-date= (help)

[6] R. Tanburn; E. Okada; N. S. Dattani (2015). "Reducing multi-qubit interactions in adiabatic quantum computation without adding auxiliary qubits. Part 1: The "deduc-reduc" method and its application to quantum factorization of numbers".

[7] J. J. L. Morton; et al. (2008). "Solid-state quantum memory using the ^{31}P nuclear spin". *Nature* **455** (7216): 1085–1088. arXiv:0803.2021. Bibcode:2008Natur.455.1085M. doi:10.1038/nature07295.

[8] Kamyar Saeedi; et al. (2013). "Room-Temperature Quantum Bit Storage Exceeding 39 Minutes Using Ionized Donors in Silicon-28". *Science* **342** (6160): 830–833. Bibcode:2013Sci...342..830S. doi:10.1126/science.1239584.

9.11 External links

- Qubit.org—cofounded by one of the pioneers in quantum computation, David Deutsch

Chapter 10

Qutrit

A **qutrit** is a unit of quantum information that exists as a superposition of three orthogonal quantum states.

The qutrit is analogous to the classical trit, just as the qubit, a quantum particle of two possible states, is analogous to the classical bit.

10.1 Representation

A qutrit has three orthogonal basis states, or vectors, often denoted $|0\rangle$, $|1\rangle$, and $|2\rangle$ in Dirac or bra–ket notation. These are used to describe the qutrit as a superposition in the form of a linear combination of the three states:

$$|\psi\rangle = \alpha|0\rangle + \beta|1\rangle + \gamma|2\rangle$$

where the coefficients are probability amplitudes, such that the sum of their squares is unity:

$$|\alpha|^2 + |\beta|^2 + |\gamma|^2 = 1$$

The qutrit's basis states are orthogonal. Qubits achieve this by utilizing Hilbert space H_2 , corresponding to spin-up and spin-down. Qutrits require a Hilbert space of higher dimension, namely H_3 .

A string of n qutrits represents 3^n different states simultaneously.

Qutrits have several peculiar features when used for storing quantum information. For example, they are more robust to decoherence under certain environmental interactions.[1] In reality, manipulating qutrits directly might be tricky, and one way to do that is by using an entanglement with a qubit.[2]

10.2 See also

- Mutually unbiased bases
- Quantum computing
- Ternary computing

10.3 References

[1] A. Melikidze, V. V. Dobrovitski, H. A. De Raedt, M. I. Katsnelson, and B. N. Harmon, *Parity effects in spin decoherence*, Phys. Rev. B **70**, 014435 (2004) (link)

[2] B. P. Lanyon,1 T. J. Weinhold, N. K. Langford, J. L. O'Brien, K. J. Resch, A. Gilchrist, and A. G. White, *Manipulating Biphotonic Qutrits*, Phys. Rev. Lett. **100**, 060504 (2008) (link)

10.4 External links

- Physicists Demonstrate Qubit-Qutrit Entanglement by Lisa Zyga at Physorg.com, February 26, 2008 . Accessed March 2008
- qudit—Wiktionary.

Chapter 11

1QBit

1QB Information Technologies, Inc. (**1QBit**) is a quantum computing software company, based in Vancouver, British Columbia. 1QBit was founded on December 1, 2012[1] and a longstanding partnership with D-Wave Systems was formally announced on June 9, 2014.[2] While 1QBit develops general purpose algorithms for quantum computing hardware, the organization is primarily focused on computational finance, the energy industry, and the life sciences.[3]

11.1 Technology description

1QBit's software reformulates optimization problems into the quadratic unconstrained binary optimization (QUBO) format necessary to compute with D-Wave's quantum annealing processors.[4]

11.2 History

1QBit was founded as the first dedicated quantum computing software company in 2012.[5] In 2013, 1QBit raised seed funding from US and Canadian angel investors, before closing a Series A financing round led by the Chicago Mercantile Exchange in 2014.[6] On August 5th, 2015 the World Economic Forum announced 1QBit as a recipient of the 2015 Technology Pioneer Award[7] recognizing 1QBit as a leader among the world's most promising technology companies.[8]

11.3 Locations

1QBit is headquartered in Vancouver, British Columbia, Canada.[9] In early 2014, 1QBit was invited to join the OneEleven data community located in Toronto, Ontario, Canada.[10] This second location serves as the data science and software production arm of the organization.

11.4 See also

- D-Wave Systems
- Timeline of quantum computing
- Adiabatic quantum computation

11.5 References

[1] "Founding 1QBit". December 1, 2012.

[2] "D-Wave Systems Building Quantum Application Ecosystem, Announces Partnerships with DNA-SEQ Alliance and 1QBit". June 9, 2014.

[3] "Recommended Reading and Discussion". *1QBit.com*. Retrieved 16 June 2014.

[4] Dion, Marco (November 4, 2013). "Europe Equity Research" (PDF). *J.P. Morgan Equity Quant Conference 2013* **6**: 12. Retrieved 16 June 2014.

[5] "CNBC Exponential Finance". *CNBC Online*. CNBC. Retrieved 14 April 2016.

[6] Marek, Lynne (May 5, 2014). "CME makes a new bet on the future". Crain's Chicago Business. Retrieved 16 June 2014.

[7] "2015 Technology Pioneers". *The World Economic Forum*. Retrieved 16 August 2015.

[8] SHAW, GILLIAN (August 5, 2015). "Vancouver company named among world's most promising tech pioneers". Vancouver Sun. Retrieved August 16, 2015.

[9] "1QBit Locations". *1QBit Website*. Retrieved 17 June 2014.

[10] "1QBit @ OneEleven". *OneEleven.com*. Retrieved 17 June 2014.

11.6 External links

- Official website

Chapter 12

Quantum state

In quantum physics, **quantum state** refers to the state of an isolated quantum system. The quantum state assigns a probability distribution to each observable. Knowledge of the quantum state and the (deterministic) rules for its evolution in time exhausts all that can be predicted about the behavior of the system. A quantum state can be either pure or mixed.

A **pure quantum state** is characterized by a set of observables and their values, which are all obtained with certainty upon measurement on a system in this and only this state.[1] Measurement of these observables will not disturb the system (i.e. change its state),[1] while measurement of anything, that cannot be inferred from these values, will. Different pure states differ in the sets of observables and/or their values.

Mathematically, a **pure quantum state** corresponds[2][4] to a non-zero **state vector** in the Hilbert space of solutions of the relevant Schrödinger equation over the complex numbers. Two vectors differing by just respective non-net-zero complex factors correspond to the same physical state and they are said to be equivalent. Thus, a physical pure quantum state corresponds to a unique unit ray in the Hilbert space.[5] Nevertheless, the factors are important when pure states are added together to form a superposition.

Hilbert space is a generalization of the ordinary Euclidean space[6]:93–96 and it contains all possible pure quantum states of the given system. If this Hilbert space, by choice of representation (essentially a choice of basis corresponding to a complete set of observables), is exhibited as a function space, a Hilbert space in its own right, then the representatives are called wave functions.

For example, when dealing with the energy spectrum of the electron in a hydrogen atom, the relevant state vectors are identified by the principal quantum number n, the angular momentum quantum number l, the magnetic quantum number m, and the spin z-component sz. A more complicated case is given (in bra–ket notation) by the spin part of a state vector

$$|\psi\rangle = \frac{1}{\sqrt{2}}\Big(|\uparrow\downarrow\rangle - |\downarrow\uparrow\rangle\Big),$$

which involves superposition of joint spin states for two particles with spin $^1\!/_2$.

A **mixed quantum state** corresponds to a probabilistic mixture of pure states; however, different distributions of pure states can generate equivalent (i.e., physically indistinguishable) mixed states. Mixed states are described by so-called density matrices. A pure state can also be recast as a density matrix; in this way, pure states can be represented as a subset of the more general mixed states.

For example, if the spin of an electron is measured in any direction, e.g. with a Stern–Gerlach experiment, there are two possible results: up or down. The Hilbert space for the electron's spin is therefore two-dimensional. A pure state here is represented by a two-dimensional complex vector (α, β) , with a length of one; that is, with

$$|\alpha|^2 + |\beta|^2 = 1,$$

where $|\alpha|$ and $|\beta|$ are the absolute values of α and β . A mixed state, in this case, is a 2×2 matrix that is Hermitian, positive-definite, and has trace 1.

Before a particular measurement is performed on a quantum system, the theory usually gives only a probability distribution for the outcome, and the form that this distribution takes is completely determined by the quantum state and the observable describing the measurement. These probability distributions arise for both mixed states and pure states: it is impossible in quantum mechanics (unlike classical mechanics) to prepare a state in which all properties of the system are fixed and certain. This is exemplified by the uncertainty principle, and reflects a core difference between classical and quantum physics. Even in quantum theory, however, for every observable there are some states that have an exact and determined value for that observable.[6]:4–5[7]

12.1 Conceptual description

12.1.1 Pure states

In the mathematical formulation of quantum mechanics, pure quantum states correspond to vectors in a Hilbert

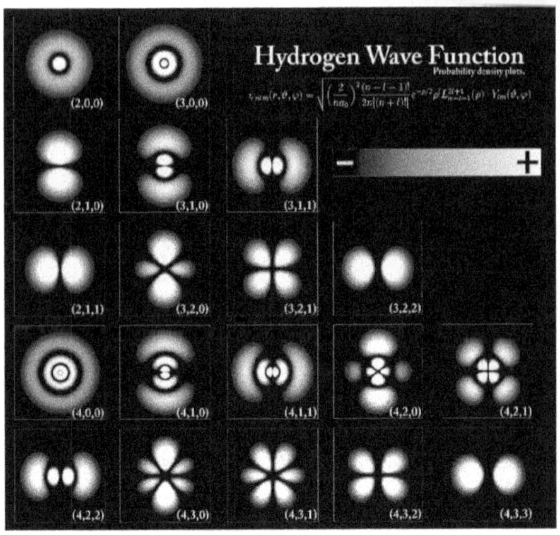

Probability densities for the electron of a hydrogen atom in different quantum states.

space, while each observable quantity (such as the energy or momentum of a particle) is associated with a mathematical operator. The operator serves as a linear function which acts on the states of the system. The eigenvalues of the operator correspond to the possible values of the observable, i.e. it is possible to observe a particle with a momentum of 1 kg⋅m/s if and only if one of the eigenvalues of the momentum operator is 1 kg⋅m/s. The corresponding eigenvector (which physicists call an **eigenstate**) with eigenvalue 1 kg⋅m/s would be a quantum state with a definite, well-defined value of momentum of 1 kg⋅m/s, with no quantum uncertainty. If its momentum were measured, the result is guaranteed to be 1 kg⋅m/s.

On the other hand, a system in a linear combination of multiple different eigenstates *does* in general have quantum uncertainty for the given observable. We can represent this linear combination of eigenstates as:

$$|\Psi(t)\rangle = \sum_n C_n(t)|\Phi_n\rangle$$

The coefficient which corresponds to a particular state in the linear combination is complex thus allowing interference effects between states. The coefficients are time dependent. How a quantum system changes in time is governed by the time evolution operator. The symbols $|$ and $\rangle$ [lower-alpha 1] surrounding the Ψ are part of bra–ket notation.

Statistical mixtures of states are different from a linear combination. A statistical mixture of states is a statistical ensemble of independent systems. Statistical mixtures represent the degree of knowledge whilst the uncertainty within quantum mechanics is fundamental. Mathematically, a statistical mixture is not a combination using complex coefficients, but rather a combination using real-valued, positive probabilities of different states Φ_n . A number P_n represents the probability of a randomly selected system being in the state Φ_n . Unlike the linear combination case each system is in a definite eigenstate.[8][9]

The expectation value $\langle A \rangle_\sigma$ of an observable A is a statistical mean of measured values of the observable. It is this mean, and the distribution of probabilities, that is predicted by physical theories.

There is no state which is simultaneously an eigenstate for *all* observables. For example, we cannot prepare a state such that both the position measurement $Q(t)$ and the momentum measurement $P(t)$ (at the same time t) are known exactly; at least one of them will have a range of possible values.[lower-alpha 2] This is the content of the Heisenberg uncertainty relation.

Moreover, in contrast to classical mechanics, it is unavoidable that *performing a measurement on the system generally changes its state*.[10][11][12] More precisely: After measuring an observable A, the system will be in an eigenstate of A; thus the state has changed, unless the system was already in that eigenstate. This expresses a kind of logical consistency: If we measure A twice in the same run of the experiment, the measurements being directly consecutive in time,[lower-alpha 3] then they will produce the same results. This has some strange consequences, however, as follows.

Consider two incompatible observables, A and B, where A corresponds to a measurement earlier in time than B.[lower-alpha 4] Suppose that the system is in an eigenstate of B at the experiment's begin. If we measure only B, all runs of the experiment will yield the same result. If we measure first A and then B in the same run of the experiment, the system will transfer to an eigenstate of A after the first measurement, and we will generally notice that the results of B are statistical. Thus: *Quantum mechanical measurements influence one another*, and it is important in which order they are performed.

Another feature of quantum states becomes relevant if we consider a physical system that consists of multiple subsystems; for example, an experiment with two particles rather than one. Quantum physics allows for certain states, called *entangled states*, that show certain statistical correlations between measurements on the two particles which cannot be explained by classical theory. For details, see entanglement. These entangled states lead to experimentally testable properties (Bell's theorem) that allow us to distinguish between quantum theory and alternative classical (non-quantum) models.

12.1.2 Schrödinger picture vs. Heisenberg picture

One can take the observables to be dependent on time, while the state σ was fixed once at the beginning of the experiment. This approach is called the Heisenberg picture. (This approach was taken in the later part of the discussion above, with time-varying observables *P*(*t*), *Q*(*t*).) One can, equivalently, treat the observables as fixed, while the state of the system depends on time; that is known as the Schrödinger picture. (This approach was taken in the earlier part of the discussion above, with a time-varying state $|\Psi(t)\rangle = \sum_n C_n(t)|\Phi_n\rangle$.) Conceptually (and mathematically), the two approaches are equivalent; choosing one of them is a matter of convention.

Both viewpoints are used in quantum theory. While non-relativistic quantum mechanics is usually formulated in terms of the Schrödinger picture, the Heisenberg picture is often preferred in a relativistic context, that is, for quantum field theory. Compare with Dirac picture.[13]:65

12.2 Formalism in quantum physics

See also: Mathematical formulation of quantum mechanics

12.2.1 Pure states as rays in a Hilbert space

Quantum physics is most commonly formulated in terms of linear algebra, as follows. Any given system is identified with some finite- or infinite-dimensional Hilbert space. The pure states correspond to vectors of norm 1. Thus the set of all pure states corresponds to the unit sphere in the Hilbert space.

Multiplying a pure state by a scalar is physically inconsequential (as long as the state is considered by itself). If one vector is obtained from the other by multiplying by a scalar of unit magnitude, the two vectors are said to correspond to the same "ray" in Hilbert space[14] and also to the same point in the projective Hilbert space.

12.2.2 Bra–ket notation

Main article: Bra–ket notation

Calculations in quantum mechanics make frequent use of linear operators, scalar products, dual spaces and Hermitian conjugation. In order to make such calculations flow smoothly, and to make it unnecessary (in some contexts) to fully understand the underlying linear algebra, Paul Dirac invented a notation to describe quantum states, known as *bra–ket notation*. Although the details of this are beyond the scope of this article, some consequences of this are:

- The expression used to denote a state vector (which corresponds to a pure quantum state) takes the form $|\psi\rangle$ (where the " ψ " can be replaced by any other symbols, letters, numbers, or even words). This can be contrasted with the usual *mathematical* notation, where vectors are usually bold, lower-case letters, or letters with arrows on top.
- Dirac defined two kinds of vector, *bra* and *ket*, dual to each other.[15]
- Each ket $|\psi\rangle$ is uniquely associated with a so-called *bra*, denoted $\langle\psi|$, which corresponds to the same physical quantum state. Technically, the bra is the adjoint of the ket. It is an element of the dual space, and related to the ket by the Riesz representation theorem. In a finite-dimensional space with a chosen basis, writing $|\psi\rangle$ as a column vector, $\langle\psi|$ is a row vector; to obtain it just take the transpose and entry-wise complex conjugate of $|\psi\rangle$.
- Scalar products[16][17] (also called *brackets*) are written so as to look like a bra and ket next to each other: $\langle\psi_1|\psi_2\rangle$. (The phrase "bra-ket" is supposed to resemble "bracket".)

12.2.3 Spin

Main article: Mathematical formulation of quantum mechanics § Spin

The angular momentum has the same dimension as the Planck constant and, at quantum scale, behaves as a *discrete* degree of freedom. Most particles possess a kind of intrinsic angular momentum that does not appear at all in classical mechanics and arises from Dirac's relativistic generalization of the theory. Mathematically it is described with spinors. In non-relativistic quantum mechanics the group representations of the Lie group SU(2) are used to describe this additional freedom. For a given particle, the choice of representation (and hence the range of possible values of the spin observable) is specified by a non-negative number *S* that, in units of Planck's reduced constant $\hbar$, is either an integer (0, 1, 2 ...) or a half-integer (1/2, 3/2, 5/2 ...). For a massive particle with spin *S*, its spin quantum number *m* always assumes one of the 2*S* + 1 possible values in the set

$$\{-S, -S+1, \ldots + S-1, +S\}$$

As a consequence, the quantum state of a particle with spin is described by a vector-valued wave function with values in $\mathbf{C}^{2S+1}$. Equivalently, it is represented by a complex-valued function of four variables: one discrete quantum number variable (for the spin) is added to the usual three continuous variables (for the position in space).

12.2.4 Many-body states and particle statistics

Further information: Particle statistics

The quantum state of a system of *N* particles, each potentially with spin, is described by a complex-valued function with four variables per particle, e.g.

$$|\psi(\mathbf{r}_1, m_1; \ldots; \mathbf{r}_N, m_N)\rangle.$$

Here, the spin variables *mν* assume values from the set

$$\{-S_\nu, -S_\nu + 1, \ldots + S_\nu - 1, +S_\nu\}$$

where S_ν is the spin of *ν*th particle. $S_\nu = 0$ for a particle that does not exhibit spin.

The treatment of identical particles is very different for bosons (particles with integer spin) versus fermions (particles with half-integer spin). The above N-particle function must either be symmetrized (in the bosonic case) or anti-symmetrized (in the fermionic case) with respect to the particle numbers. If not all *N* particles are identical, but some of them are, then the function must be (anti)symmetrized separately over the variables corresponding to each group of identical variables, according to its statistics (bosonic or fermionic).

Electrons are fermions with *S* = 1/2, photons (quanta of light) are bosons with *S* = 1 (although in the vacuum they are massless and can't be described with Schrödingerian mechanics).

When symmetrization or anti-symmetrization is unnecessary, *N*-particle spaces of states can be obtained simply by tensor products of one-particle spaces, to which we will return later.

12.2.5 Basis states of one-particle systems

As with any Hilbert space, if a basis is chosen for the Hilbert space of a system, then any ket can be expanded as a linear combination of those basis elements. Symbolically, given basis kets $|k_i\rangle$, any ket $|\psi\rangle$ can be written

$$|\psi\rangle = \sum_i c_i |k_i\rangle$$

where *ci* are complex numbers. In physical terms, this is described by saying that $|\psi\rangle$ has been expressed as a *quantum superposition* of the states $|k_i\rangle$. If the basis kets are chosen to be orthonormal (as is often the case), then $c_i = \langle k_i|\psi\rangle$.

One property worth noting is that the *normalized* states $|\psi\rangle$ are characterized by

$$\langle\psi|\psi\rangle = 1,$$

and for orthonormal basis this translates to

$$\sum_i |c_i|^2 = 1.$$

Expansions of this sort play an important role in measurement in quantum mechanics. In particular, if the $|k_i\rangle$ are eigenstates (with eigenvalues *ki*) of an observable, and that observable is measured on the normalized state $|\psi\rangle$, then the probability that the result of the measurement is *ki* is |*ci*|^2. (The normalization condition above mandates that the total sum of probabilities is equal to one.)

A particularly important example is the *position basis*, which is the basis consisting of eigenstates $|\mathbf{r}\rangle$ with eigenvalues **r** of the observable which corresponds to measuring position.[lower-alpha 5] If these eigenstates are nondegenerate (for example, if the system is a single, spinless particle), then any ket $|\psi\rangle$ is associated with a complex-valued function of three-dimensional space

> $\psi(\mathbf{r}) \equiv \langle\mathbf{r}|\psi\rangle$. [lower-alpha 6] i.e. $\langle\mathbf{r}|\mathbf{r}'\rangle = \delta(\mathbf{r}' - \mathbf{r})$ Dirac delta function), which means that $\langle\mathbf{r}|\mathbf{r}\rangle = \infty$.

This function is called the **wave function** corresponding to $|\psi\rangle$. Similarly to the discrete case above, the probability *density* of the particle being found at position **r** is $|\psi(\mathbf{r})|^2$ and the normalized states have

$$\int d^3\mathbf{r} |\psi(\mathbf{r})|^2 = 1$$

In terms of the continuous set of position basis $|\mathbf{r}\rangle$, the state $|\psi\rangle$ is:

$$|\psi\rangle = \int d^3\mathbf{r}\, \psi(\mathbf{r})|\mathbf{r}\rangle$$

12.2.6 Superposition of pure states

Main article: Quantum superposition

One aspect of quantum states, mentioned above, is that superpositions of them can be formed. If $|\alpha\rangle$ and $|\beta\rangle$ are two kets corresponding to quantum states, the ket

$$c_\alpha|\alpha\rangle + c_\beta|\beta\rangle$$

is a different quantum state (possibly not normalized). Note that *which* quantum state it is depends on both the amplitudes and phases (arguments) of c_α and c_β . In other words, for example, even though $|\psi\rangle$ and $e^{i\theta}|\psi\rangle$ (for real θ) correspond to the same physical quantum state, they are *not interchangeable*, since for example $|\phi\rangle + |\psi\rangle$ and $|\phi\rangle + e^{i\theta}|\psi\rangle$ do *not* (in general) correspond to the same physical state. However, $|\phi\rangle + |\psi\rangle$ and $e^{i\theta}(|\phi\rangle + |\psi\rangle)$ *do* correspond to the same physical state. This is sometimes described by saying that "global" phase factors are unphysical, but "relative" phase factors are physical and important.

One example of a quantum interference phenomenon that arises from superposition is the double-slit experiment. The photon state is a superposition of two different states, one of which corresponds to the photon having passed through the left slit, and the other corresponding to passage through the right slit. The relative phase of those two states has a value which depends on the distance from each of the two slits. Depending on what that phase is, the interference is constructive at some locations and destructive in others, creating the interference pattern. By the analogy with coherence in other wave phenomena, a superposed state can be referred to as a *coherent superposition*.

Another example of the importance of relative phase in quantum superposition is Rabi oscillations, where the relative phase of two states varies in time due to the Schrödinger equation. The resulting superposition ends up oscillating back and forth between two different states.

12.2.7 Mixed states

See also: Density matrix

A *pure quantum state* is a state which can be described by a single ket vector, as described above. A *mixed quantum state* is a statistical ensemble of pure states (see quantum statistical mechanics). Mixed states inevitably arise from pure states when, for a composite quantum system $H_1 \otimes H_2$ with an entangled state on it, the part H_2 is inaccessible to the observer. The state of the part H_1 is expressed then as the partial trace over H_2 .

A mixed state *cannot* be described as a ket vector. Instead, it is described by its associated *density matrix* (or *density operator*), usually denoted ϱ. Note that density matrices can describe both mixed *and* pure states, treating them on the same footing. Moreover, a mixed quantum state on a given quantum system described by a Hilbert space H can be always represented as the partial trace of a pure quantum state (called a purification) on a larger bipartite system $H \otimes K$ for a sufficiently large Hilbert space K .

The density matrix describing a mixed state is defined to be an operator of the form

$$\rho = \sum_s p_s |\psi_s\rangle\langle\psi_s|$$

where p_s is the fraction of the ensemble in each pure state $|\psi_s\rangle$. The density matrix can be thought of as a way of using the one-particle formalism to describe the behavior of many similar particles by giving a probability distribution (or ensemble) of states that these particles can be found in.

A simple criterion for checking whether a density matrix is describing a pure or mixed state is that the trace of ϱ^2 is equal to 1 if the state is pure, and less than 1 if the state is mixed.[lower-alpha 7][19] Another, equivalent, criterion is that the von Neumann entropy is 0 for a pure state, and strictly positive for a mixed state.

The rules for measurement in quantum mechanics are particularly simple to state in terms of density matrices. For example, the ensemble average (expectation value) of a measurement corresponding to an observable *A* is given by

$$\langle A\rangle = \sum_s p_s \langle\psi_s|A|\psi_s\rangle = \sum_s \sum_i p_s a_i |\langle\alpha_i|\psi_s\rangle|^2 = \mathrm{tr}(\rho A)$$

where $|\alpha_i\rangle$, a_i are eigenkets and eigenvalues, respectively, for the operator *A*, and "tr" denotes trace. It is important to note that two types of averaging are occurring, one being a weighted quantum superposition over the basis kets $|\psi_s\rangle$ of the pure states, and the other being a statistical (said *incoherent*) average with the probabilities *ps* of those states.

According to Wigner,[20] the concept of mixture was put forward by Landau.[21][22]:38–41

12.3 Interpretation

Main article: Interpretations of quantum mechanics

Although theoretically, for a given quantum system, a state vector provides the full information about its evolution, it is not easy to understand what information about the "real world" it carries. Due to the uncertainty principle, a state, even if it has the value of one observable exactly defined (i.e. the observable has this state as an eigenstate), cannot exactly define values of *all* observables.

For state vectors (pure states), probability amplitudes offer a probabilistic interpretation. It can be generalized for all states (including mixed), for instance, as expectation values mentioned above.

12.4 Mathematical generalizations

States can be formulated in terms of observables, rather than as vectors in a vector space. These are positive normalized linear functionals on a C*-algebra, or sometimes other classes of algebras of observables. See State on a C*-algebra and Gelfand–Naimark–Segal construction for more details.

12.5 See also

- Atomic electron transition
- Bloch sphere
- Ground state
- Introduction to quantum mechanics
- No-cloning theorem
- Orthonormal basis
- PBR theorem
- Quantum harmonic oscillator
- Qubit
- State vector reduction, for historical reasons called a *wave function collapse*
- Stationary state
- W state

12.6 Notes

[1] Sometimes written ">"; see angle brackets.

[2] To avoid misunderstandings: Here we mean that *Q*(*t*) and *P*(*t*) are measured in the same state, but *not* in the same run of the experiment.

[3] i.e. separated by a zero delay. One can think of it as stopping the time, then making the two measurements one after the other, then resuming the time. Thus, the measurements occurred at the same time, but it is still possible to tell which was first.

[4] For concreteness' sake, suppose that $A = Q(t_1)$ and $B = P(t_2)$ in the above example, with $t_2 > t_1 > 0$.

[5] Note that a state $|\psi\rangle$ is a superposition of different basis states $|\mathbf{r}\rangle$, so $|\psi\rangle$ and $|\mathbf{r}\rangle$ are elements of the same Hilbert space. A particle in state $|\mathbf{r}\rangle$ is located precisely at position $\mathbf{r} = (x, y, z)$, while a particle in state $|\psi\rangle$ can be found at different positions with corresponding probabilities.

[6] In the continuous case, the basis kets $|\mathbf{r}\rangle$ are not unit kets (unlike the state $|\psi\rangle$): They are normalized according to $\int d^3\mathbf{r}'\langle\mathbf{r}|\mathbf{r}'\rangle = 1$, [18] p. 17: "∫ Ψf′Ψf* dq = δ(f′ − f)" (the left side corresponds to ⟨f|f′⟩), "∫ δ(f′ − f) df′ = 1".

[7] Note that this criterion works when the density matrix is normalized so that the trace of ρ is 1, as it is for the standard definition given in this section. Occasionally a density matrix will be normalized differently, in which case the criterion is $\mathrm{Tr}(\rho^2) = (\mathrm{Tr}\,\rho)^2$

12.7 References

[1] U. Fano (1957), 'Description of states in quantum mechanics by density matrix and operator techniques', *Rev. Mod. Phys.*, **29**(1): 74–93, pp. 75–76

[2] Dirac (1958),[3] p. 16: "each state of a dynamical system at a particular time corresponds to a ket vector."

[3] Dirac, P.A.M. (1958). *The Principles of Quantum Mechanics*, 4th edition, Oxford University Press, Oxford UK.

[4] Feynman, R.P., Leighton, R.B., Sands, M. (1963). *The Feynman Lectures on Physics*, Addison-Wesley, Reading MA, available at http://www.feynmanlectures.info/, Volume III, p. 8–2: "The states χ and φ correspond to the two vectors ***B*** and ***A***."

[5] Weinberg, S. (2002), *The Quantum Theory of Fields* **I**, Cambridge University Press, ISBN 0-521-55001-7

[6] Griffiths, David J. (2004), *Introduction to Quantum Mechanics (2nd ed.)*, Prentice Hall, ISBN 0-13-111892-7

[7] Ballentine, L. E. (1970), "The Statistical Interpretation of Quantum Mechanics", *Reviews of Modern Physics* **42**: 358–381, Bibcode:1970RvMP...42..358B, doi:10.1103/RevModPhys.42.358

[8] Statistical Mixture of States

[9] http://electron6.phys.utk.edu/qm1/modules/m6/statistical.htm

[10] Heisenberg, W. (1927). Über den anschaulichen Inhalt der quantentheoretischen Kinematik und Mechanik, *Z. Phys.* **43**: 172–198. Translation as 'The actual content of quantum theoretical kinematics and mechanics'. Also translated as 'The physical content of quantum kinematics and mechanics' at pp. 62–84 by editors John Wheeler and Wojciech Zurek, in *Quantum Theory and Measurement* (1983), Princeton University Press, Princeton NJ.

[11] Bohr, N. (1927/1928). The quantum postulate and the recent development of atomic theory, *Nature* Supplement April 14 1928, **121**: 580–590.

[12] Dirac (1958),[3] p. 4: "If a system is small, we cannot observe it without producing a serious disturbance."

[13] Gottfried, Kurt; Yan, Tung-Mow (2003). *Quantum Mechanics: Fundamentals* (2nd, illustrated ed.). Springer. ISBN 9780387955766.

[14] Weinberg, Steven. "The Quantum Theory of Fields", Vol. 1. Cambridge University Press, 1995 p. 50.

[15] Dirac (1958),[3] p. 20: "The bra vectors, as they have been here introduced, are quite a different kind of vector from the kets, and so far there is no connexion between them except for the existence of a scalar product of a bra and a ket."

[16] Dirac (1958),[3] p. 19: "A scalar product $\langle B|A\rangle$ now appears as a complete bracket expression."

[17] Gottfried (2013),[13] p. 31: "to define the scalar products as being between bras and kets."

[18] Landau (1965),<ref name='Landau (1965)' group=">

[19] Blum, *Density matrix theory and applications*, page 39.

[20] Eugene Wigner (1962). "Remarks on the mind-body question" (PDF). In I.J. Good. *The Scientist Speculates*. London: Heinemann. pp. 284–302. Footnote 13 on p.180

[21] Lev Landau (1927). "Das Dämpfungsproblem in der Wellenmechanik (The Damping Problem in Wave Mechanics)". *Zeitschrift für Physik* **45** (5–6): 430–441. Bibcode:1927ZPhy...45..430L. doi:10.1007/bf01343064. English translation reprinted in: D. Ter Haar, ed. (1965). *Collected papers of L.D. Landau*. Oxford: Pergamon Press. p.8–18

[22] Lev Landau; Evgeny Lifshitz (1965). *Quantum Mechanics — Non-Relativistic Theory* (PDF). Course of Theoretical Physics **3** (2nd ed.). London: Pergamon Press.

12.8 Further reading

The concept of quantum states, in particular the content of the section Formalism in quantum physics above, is covered in most standard textbooks on quantum mechanics.

For a discussion of conceptual aspects and a comparison with classical states, see:

- Isham, Chris J (1995). *Lectures on Quantum Theory: Mathematical and Structural Foundations*. Imperial College Press. ISBN 978-1-86094-001-9.

For a more detailed coverage of mathematical aspects, see:

- Bratteli, Ola; Robinson, Derek W (1987). *Operator Algebras and Quantum Statistical Mechanics 1*. Springer. ISBN 978-3-540-17093-8. 2nd edition. In particular, see Sec. 2.3.

For a discussion of purifications of mixed quantum states, see Chapter 2 of John Preskill's lecture notes for Physics 219 at Caltech.

Chapter 13

Quantum algorithm

In quantum computing, a **quantum algorithm** is an algorithm which runs on a realistic model of quantum computation, the most commonly used model being the quantum circuit model of computation.[1][2] A classical (or non-quantum) algorithm is a finite sequence of instructions, or a step-by-step procedure for solving a problem, where each step or instruction can be performed on a classical computer. Similarly, a quantum algorithm is a step-by-step procedure, where each of the steps can be performed on a quantum computer. Although all classical algorithms can also be performed on a quantum computer,[3] the term quantum algorithm is usually used for those algorithms which seem inherently quantum, or use some essential feature of quantum computation such as quantum superposition or quantum entanglement.

Problems which are undecidable using classical computers remain undecidable using quantum computers. What makes quantum algorithms interesting is that they might be able to solve some problems faster than classical algorithms.

The most well known algorithms are Shor's algorithm for factoring, and Grover's algorithm for searching an unstructured database or an unordered list. Shor's algorithms runs exponentially faster than the best known classical algorithm for factoring, the general number field sieve. Grover's algorithm runs quadratically faster than the best possible classical algorithm for the same task.

13.1 Overview

Quantum algorithms are usually described, in the commonly used circuit model of quantum computation, by a quantum circuit which acts on some input qubits and terminates with a measurement. A quantum circuit consists of simple quantum gates which act on at most a fixed number of qubits, usually two or three. Quantum algorithms may also be stated in other models of quantum computation, such as the Hamiltonian oracle model.[4]

Quantum algorithms can be categorized by the main techniques used by the algorithm. Some commonly used techniques/ideas in quantum algorithms include phase kickback, phase estimation, the quantum Fourier transform, quantum walks, amplitude amplification and topological quantum field theory. Quantum algorithms may also be grouped by the type of problem solved, for instance see the survey on quantum algorithms for algebraic problems.[5]

13.2 Algorithms based on the quantum Fourier transform

The quantum Fourier transform is the quantum analogue of the discrete Fourier transform, and is used in several quantum algorithms. The Hadamard transform is also an example of a quantum Fourier transform over an n-dimensional vector space over the field $\mathbf{F}_2$. The quantum Fourier transform can be efficiently implemented on a quantum computer using only a polynomial number of quantum gates.

13.2.1 Deutsch–Jozsa algorithm

Main article: Deutsch–Jozsa algorithm

The Deutsch–Jozsa algorithm solves a black-box problem which probably requires exponentially many queries to the black box for any deterministic classical computer, but can be done with exactly one query by a quantum computer. If we allow both bounded-error quantum and classical algorithms, then there is no speedup since a classical probabilistic algorithm can solve the problem with a constant number of queries with small probability of error. The algorithm determines whether a function f is either constant (0 on all inputs or 1 on all inputs) or balanced (returns 1 for half of the input domain and 0 for the other half).

13.2.2 Simon's algorithm

Main article: Simon's algorithm

Simon's algorithm solves a black-box problem exponentially faster than any classical algorithm, including bounded-error probabilistic algorithms. This algorithm, which achieves an exponential speedup over all classical algorithms that we consider efficient, was the motivation for Shor's factoring algorithm.

13.2.3 Quantum phase estimation algorithm

Main article: Quantum phase estimation algorithm

The quantum phase estimation algorithm is used to determine the eigenphase of an eigenvector of a unitary gate given a quantum state proportional to the eigenvector and access to the gate. The algorithm is frequently used as a subroutine in other algorithms.

13.2.4 Shor's algorithm

Main article: Shor's algorithm

Shor's algorithm solves the discrete logarithm problem and the integer factorization problem in polynomial time,[6] whereas the best known classical algorithms take super-polynomial time. These problems are not known to be in P or NP-complete. It is also one of the few quantum algorithms that solves a non–black-box problem in polynomial time where the best known classical algorithms run in super-polynomial time.

13.2.5 Hidden subgroup problem

The abelian hidden subgroup problem is a generalization of many problems that can be solved by a quantum computer, such as Simon's problem, solving Pell's equation, testing the principal ideal of a ring R and factoring. There are efficient quantum algorithms known for the Abelian hidden subgroup problem.[7] The more general hidden subgroup problem, where the group isn't necessarily abelian, is a generalization of the previously mentioned problems and graph isomorphism and certain lattice problems. Efficient quantum algorithms are known for certain non-abelian groups. However, no efficient algorithms are known for the symmetric group, which would give an efficient algorithm for graph isomorphism[8] and the dihedral group, which would solve certain lattice problems.[9]

13.2.6 Boson sampling problem

Main article: Boson sampling

The Boson Sampling Problem in an experimental configuration assumes[10] an input of bosons (ex. photons of light) of moderate number getting randomly scattered into a large number of output modes constrained by a defined unitarity. The problem is then to produce a fair sample of the probability distribution of the output which is dependent on the input arrangement of bosons and the Unitarity.[11] Solving this problem with a classical computer algorithm requires computing the permanent of the unitary transform matrix, which may be either impossible or take a prohibitively long time. In 2014, it was proposed[12] that existing technology and standard probabilistic methods of generating single photon states could be used as input into a suitable quantum computable linear optical network and that sampling of the output probability distribution would be demonstrably superior using quantum algorithms. In 2015, investigation predicted[13] the sampling problem had similar complexity for inputs other than Fock state photons and identified a transition in computational complexity from classically simulatable to just as hard as the Boson Sampling Problem, dependent on the size of coherent amplitude inputs.

13.2.7 Estimating Gauss sums

A Gauss sum is a type of exponential sum. The best known classical algorithm for estimating these sums takes exponential time. Since the discrete logarithm problem reduces to Gauss sum estimation, an efficient classical algorithm for estimating Gauss sums would imply an efficient classical algorithm for computing discrete logarithms, which is considered unlikely. However, quantum computers can estimate Gauss sums to polynomial precision in polynomial time.[14]

13.2.8 Fourier fishing and Fourier checking

We have an oracle consisting of n random Boolean functions mapping n-bit strings to a Boolean value. We are required to find n n-bit strings $z_1,..., z_n$ such that for the Hadamard-Fourier transform, at least 3/4 of the strings satisfy

$$\left|\tilde{f}(z_i)\right| \geqslant 1$$

and at least 1/4 satisfies

$$\left|\tilde{f}(z_i)\right| \geqslant 2$$

This can be done in BQP.[15]

13.3 Algorithms based on amplitude amplification

Amplitude amplification is a technique that allows the amplification of a chosen subspace of a quantum state.

Applications of amplitude amplification usually lead to quadratic speedups over the corresponding classical algorithms. It can be considered to be a generalization of Grover's algorithm.

13.3.1 Grover's algorithm

Main article: Grover's algorithm

Grover's algorithm searches an unstructured database (or an unordered list) with N entries, for a marked entry, using only $O(\sqrt{N})$ queries instead of the Ω(*N*) queries required classically.[16] Classically, Ω(*N*) queries are required, even if we allow bounded-error probabilistic algorithms.

13.3.2 Quantum counting

Quantum counting solves a generalization of the search problem. It solves the problem of counting the number of marked entries in an unordered list, instead of just detecting if one exists. Specifically, it counts the number of marked entries in an N -element list, with error ϵ making only $\Theta\left(\frac{1}{\epsilon}\sqrt{\frac{N}{k}}\right)$ queries, where k is the number of marked elements in the list.[17][18] More precisely, the algorithm outputs an estimate k' for k , the number of marked entries, with the following accuracy: $|k - k'| \leq \epsilon k$.

13.4 Algorithms based on quantum walks

Main article: Quantum walk

A quantum walk is the quantum analogue of a classical random walk, which can be described by a probability distribution over some states. A quantum walk can be described by a quantum superposition over states. Quantum walks are known to give exponential speedups for some black-box problems.[19][20] They also provide polynomial speedups for many problems. A framework for the creation quantum walk algorithms exists and is quite a versatile tool.[21]

13.4.1 Element distinctness problem

Main article: Element distinctness problem

The element distinctness problem is the problem of determining whether all the elements of a list are distinct. Classically, Ω(*N*) queries are required for a list of size *N*, since this problem is harder than the search problem which requires Ω(*N*) queries. However, it can be solved in $\Theta(N^{2/3})$ queries on a quantum computer. The optimal algorithm is by Andris Ambainis.[22] Yaoyun Shi first proved a tight lower bound when the size of the range is sufficiently large.[23] Ambainis[24] and Kutin[25] independently (and via different proofs) extended his work to obtain the lower bound for all functions.

13.4.2 Triangle-finding problem

Main article: Triangle finding problem

The triangle-finding problem is the problem of determining whether a given graph contains a triangle (a clique of size 3). The best-known lower bound for quantum algorithms is Ω(*N*), but the best algorithm known requires O($N^{1.297}$) queries,[26] an improvement over the previous best O($N^{1.3}$) queries.[21][27]

13.4.3 Formula evaluation

A formula is a tree with a gate at each internal node and an input bit at each leaf node. The problem is to evaluate the formula, which is the output of the root node, given oracle access to the input.

A well studied formula is the balanced binary tree with only NAND gates.[28] This type of formula requires Θ(N^c) queries using randomness,[29] where $c = \log_2(1+\sqrt{33})/4 \approx 0.754$. With a quantum algorithm however, it can be solved in Θ($N^{0.5}$) queries. No better quantum algorithm for this case was known until one was found for the unconventional Hamiltonian oracle model.[4] The same result for the standard setting soon followed.[30]

Fast quantum algorithms for more complicated formulas are also known.[31]

13.4.4 Group commutativity

The problem is to determine if a black box group, given by *k* generators, is commutative. A black box group is a group with an oracle function, which must be used to perform the group operations (multiplication, inversion, and comparison with identity). We are interested in the query complexity, which is the number of oracle calls needed to solve the problem. The deterministic and randomized query complexities are $\Theta(k^2)$ and $\Theta(k)$ respectively.[32] A quantum algorithm requires $\Omega(k^{2/3})$ queries but the best known algorithm uses $O(k^{2/3} \log k)$ queries.[33]

13.5 BQP-complete problems

13.5.1 Computing knot invariants

Witten had shown that the Chern-Simons topological quantum field theory (TQFT) can be solved in terms of Jones polynomials. A quantum computer can simulate a TQFT, and thereby approximate the Jones polynomial,[34] which as far as we know, is hard to compute classically in the worst-case scenario.

13.5.2 Quantum simulation

The idea that quantum computers might be more powerful than classical computers originated in Richard Feynman's observation that classical computers seem to require exponential time to simulate many-particle quantum systems.[35] Since then, the idea that quantum computers can simulate quantum physical processes exponentially faster than classical computers has been greatly fleshed out and elaborated. Efficient (that is, polynomial-time) quantum algorithms have been developed for simulating both Bosonic and Fermionic systems[36] and in particular, the simulation of chemical reactions beyond the capabilities of current classical supercomputers requires only a few hundred qubits.[37] Quantum computers can also efficiently simulate topological quantum field theories.[38] In addition to its intrinsic interest, this result has led to efficient quantum algorithms for estimating quantum topological invariants such as Jones[39] and HOMFLY[40] polynomials, and the Turaev-Viro invariant of three-dimensional manifolds.[41]

13.6 See also

- Quantum sort
- Primality test

13.7 References

[1] Nielsen, M.; Chuang, I. (2000). *Quantum Computation and Quantum Information*. Cambridge University Press. ISBN 0-521-63503-9.

[2] Mosca, M. (2008). "Quantum Algorithms". arXiv:0808.0369 [quant-ph].

[3] Lanzagorta, Marco; Uhlmann, Jeffrey K. (2009-01-01). *Quantum Computer Science*. Morgan & Claypool Publishers. ISBN 9781598297324.

[4] Farhi, E.; Goldstone, J.; Gutmann, S. (2007). "A Quantum Algorithm for the Hamiltonian NAND Tree". arXiv:quant-ph/0702144 [quant-ph].

[5] Childs, A. M.; van Dam, W. (2008). "Quantum algorithms for algebraic problems". *Reviews of Modern Physics* **82**: 1–52. arXiv:0812.0380. Bibcode:2010RvMP...82....1C. doi:10.1103/RevModPhys.82.1.

[6] Shor, P. W. (1997). "Polynomial-Time Algorithms for Prime Factorization and Discrete Logarithms on a Quantum Computer". *SIAM Journal on Scientific and Statistical Computing* **26**: 1484. arXiv:quant-ph/9508027. Bibcode:1995quant.ph..8027S.

[7] Boneh, D.; Lipton, R. J. (1995). "Quantum cryptoanalysis of hidden linear functions". In Coppersmith, D. *Proceedings of the 15th Annual International Cryptology Conference on Advances in Cryptology*. Springer-Verlag. pp. 424–437. ISBN 3-540-60221-6.

[8] Moore, C.; Russell, A.; Schulman, L. J. (2005). "The Symmetric Group Defies Strong Fourier Sampling: Part I". arXiv:quant-ph/0501056 [quant-ph].

[9] Regev, O. (2003). "Quantum Computation and Lattice Problems". arXiv:cs/0304005 [cs.DS].

[10] Ralph, T.C. "Figure 1: The boson-sampling problem". *Nature Photonics*. Nature. Retrieved 12 September 2014.

[11] Lund, A.P.; Laing, A.; Rahimi-Keshari, S.; Rudolph, T.; O'Brien, J.L.; Ralph, T.C. (September 5, 2014). "Boson Sampling from Gaussian States". *Phys. Rev. Lett.* 113, 100502. arXiv:1305.4346. Bibcode:2014PhRvL.113j0502L. doi:10.1103/PhysRevLett.113.100502. Retrieved 12 September 2014.

[12] "The quantum revolution is a step closer". *Phys.org*. Omicron Technology Limited. Retrieved 12 September 2014.

[13] Seshadreesan, Kaushik P.; Olson, Jonathan P.; Motes, Keith R.; Rohde, Peter P.; Dowling, Jonathan P. "Boson sampling with displaced single-photon Fock states versus single-photon-added coherent states: The quantum-classical divide and computational-complexity transitions in linear optics". *Physical Review A* **91** (2): 022334. arXiv:1402.0531. Bibcode:2015PhRvA..91b2334S. doi:10.1103/PhysRevA.91.022334. Retrieved 31 May 2015.

[14] van Dam, W.; Seroussi, G. (2002). "Efficient Quantum Algorithms for Estimating Gauss Sums". arXiv:quant-ph/0207131 [quant-ph].

[15] Aaronson, S. (2009). "BQP and the Polynomial Hierarchy". arXiv:0910.4698 [quant-ph].

[16] Grover, L. K. (1996). "A fast quantum mechanical algorithm for database search". arXiv:quant-ph/9605043 [quant-ph].

[17] Brassard, G.; Hoyer, P.; Tapp, A. (1998). "Quantum Counting". arXiv:quant-ph/9805082 [quant-ph].

[18] Brassard, G.; Hoyer, P.; Mosca, M.; Tapp, A. (2000). "Quantum Amplitude Amplification and Estimation". arXiv:quant-ph/0005055 [quant-ph].

[19] Childs, A. M.; Cleve, R.; Deotto, E.; Farhi, E.; Gutmann, S.; Spielman, D. A. (2003). "Exponential algorithmic

speedup by quantum walk". *Proceedings of the 35th Symposium on Theory of Computing*. Association for Computing Machinery. pp. 59–68. arXiv:quant-ph/0209131. doi:10.1145/780542.780552. ISBN 1-58113-674-9.

[20] Childs, A. M.; Schulman, L. J.; Vazirani, U. V. (2007). "Quantum Algorithms for Hidden Nonlinear Structures". *Proceedings of the 48th Annual IEEE Symposium on Foundations of Computer Science*. IEEE. pp. 395–404. arXiv:0705.2784. doi:10.1109/FOCS.2007.18. ISBN 0-7695-3010-9.

[21] Magniez, F.; Nayak, A.; Roland, J.; Santha, M. (2007). "Search via quantum walk". *Proceedings of the 39th Annual ACM Symposium on Theory of Computing*. Association for Computing Machinery. pp. 575–584. doi:10.1145/1250790.1250874. ISBN 978-1-59593-631-8.

[22] Ambainis, A. (2007). "Quantum Walk Algorithm for Element Distinctness". *SIAM Journal on Computing* **37** (1): 210–239. doi:10.1137/S0097539705447311.

[23] Shi, Y. (2002). *Quantum lower bounds for the collision and the element distinctness problems*. Proceedings of the 43rd Symposium on Foundations of Computer Science. pp. 513–519. arXiv:quant-ph/0112086. doi:10.1109/SFCS.2002.1181975.

[24] Ambainis, A. (2005). "Polynomial Degree and Lower Bounds in Quantum Complexity: Collision and Element Distinctness with Small Range". *Theory of Computing* **1** (1): 37–46. doi:10.4086/toc.2005.v001a003.

[25] Kutin, S. (2005). "Quantum Lower Bound for the Collision Problem with Small Range". *Theory of Computing* **1** (1): 29–36. doi:10.4086/toc.2005.v001a002.

[26] Aleksandrs Belovs (2011). "Span Programs for Functions with Constant-Sized 1-certificates". arXiv:1105.4024 [quant-ph].

[27] Magniez, F.; Santha, M.; Szegedy, M. (2007). "Quantum Algorithms for the Triangle Problem". *SIAM Journal on Computing* **37** (2): 413–424. doi:10.1137/050643684.

[28] Aaronson, S. (3 February 2007). "NAND now for something completely different". *Shtetl-Optimized*. Retrieved 2009-12-17.

[29] Saks, M.E.; Wigderson, A. (1986). "Probabilistic Boolean Decision Trees and the Complexity of Evaluating Game Trees" (PDF). *Proceedings of the 27th Annual Symposium on Foundations of Computer Science*. IEEE. pp. 29–38. doi:10.1109/SFCS.1986.44. ISBN 0-8186-0740-8.

[30] Ambainis, A. (2007). "A nearly optimal discrete query quantum algorithm for evaluating NAND formulas". arXiv:0704.3628 [quant-ph].

[31] Reichardt, B. W.; Spalek, R. (2008). "Span-program-based quantum algorithm for evaluating formulas". *Proceedings of the 40th Annual ACM symposium on Theory of Computing*. Association for Computing Machinery. pp. 103–112. doi:10.1145/1374376.1374394. ISBN 978-1-60558-047-0.

[32] Pak, Igor (2012). "Testing commutativity of a group and the power of randomization". *LMS Journal of Computation and Mathematics* **15**: 38–43. doi:10.1112/S1461157012000046.

[33] Magniez, F.; Nayak, A. (2007). "Quantum Complexity of Testing Group Commutativity". *Algorithmica* **48** (3): 221–232. doi:10.1007/s00453-007-0057-8.

[34] Aharonov, D.; Jones, V.; Landau, Z. (2006). "A polynomial quantum algorithm for approximating the Jones polynomial". *Proceedings of the 38th Annual ACM symposium on Theory of Computing*. Association for Computing Machinery. pp. 427–436. doi:10.1145/1132516.1132579.

[35] Feynman, R. P. (1982). "Simulating physics with computers". *International Journal of Theoretical Physics* **21** (6–7): 467. Bibcode:1982IJTP...21..467F. doi:10.1007/BF02650179.

[36] Abrams, D. S.; Lloyd, S. (1997). "Simulation of many-body Fermi systems on a universal quantum computer". *Physical Review Letters* **79** (13): 2586–2589. arXiv:quant-ph/9703054. Bibcode:1997PhRvL..79.2586A. doi:10.1103/PhysRevLett.79.2586.

[37] Kassal, I.; Jordan, S. P.; Love, P. J.; Mohseni, M.; Aspuru-Guzik, A. (2008). "Polynomial-time quantum algorithm for the simulation of chemical dynamics". *Proceedings of the National Academy of Sciences of the United States of America* **105** (48): 18681–86. arXiv:0801.2986. Bibcode:2008PNAS..10518681K. doi:10.1073/pnas.0808245105. PMC 2596249. PMID 19033207.

[38] Freedman, M.; Kitaev, A.; Wang, Z. (2002). "Simulation of Topological Field Theories by Quantum Computers". *Communications in Mathematical Physics* **227** (3): 587–603. arXiv:quant-ph/0001071. Bibcode:2002CMaPh.227..587F. doi:10.1007/s002200200635.

[39] Aharonov, D.; Jones, V.; Landau, Z. (2009). "A polynomial quantum algorithm for approximating the Jones polynomial". *Algorithmica* **55** (3): 395–421. arXiv:quant-ph/0511096. doi:10.1007/s00453-008-9168-0.

[40] Wocjan, P.; Yard, J. (2008). "The Jones polynomial: quantum algorithms and applications in quantum complexity theory". *Quantum Information and Computation* **8** (1): 147–180. arXiv:quant-ph/0603069. Bibcode:2006quant.ph..3069W.

[41] Alagic, G.; Jordan, S.P.; König, R.; Reichardt, B. W. (2010). "Approximating Turaev-Viro 3-manifold invariants is universal for quantum computation". *Physical Review A* **82** (4): 040302. arXiv:1003.0923. Bibcode:2010PhRvA..82d0302A. doi:10.1103/PhysRevA.82.040302.

13.8 External links

- The Quantum Algorithm Zoo: A comprehensive list of quantum algorithms that provide a speedup over the fastest known classical algorithms.

13.8.1 Surveys

- Smith, J.; Mosca, M. (2012). "Algorithms for Quantum Computers". *Handbook of Natural Computing*. p. 1451. doi:10.1007/978-3-540-92910-9_43. ISBN 978-3-540-92909-3.
- Childs, A. M.; Van Dam, W. (2010). "Quantum algorithms for algebraic problems". *Reviews of Modern Physics* **82**: 1. doi:10.1103/RevModPhys.82.1.

Chapter 14

Quantum algorithm for linear systems of equations

The **quantum algorithm for linear systems of equations**, designed by Aram Harrow, Avinatan Hassidim, and Seth Lloyd, is a quantum algorithm for solving linear systems formulated in 2009. The algorithm estimates the result of a scalar measurement on the solution vector to a given linear system of equations.[1]

The algorithm is one of the main fundamental algorithms expected to provide an exponential speedup over their classical counterparts, along with Shor's factoring algorithm, Grover's search algorithm and quantum simulation. Provided the linear system is a sparse and has a low condition number κ , and that the user is interested in the result of a scalar measurement on the solution vector, instead of the values of the solution vector itself, then the algorithm has a runtime of $O(\log(N)\kappa^2)$, where N is the number of variables in the linear system.. This offers an exponential speedup over the fastest classical algorithm, which runs in $O(N\kappa)$ (or $O(N\sqrt{\kappa})$ for positive semidefinite matrices).

An implementation of the quantum algorithm for linear systems of equations was first demonstrated in 2013 by Cai et al., Barz et al.and Pan et al. in parallel. The demonstrations consisted of simple linear equations on specially designed quantum devices.[2][3] [4]

Due to the prevalence of linear systems in virtually all areas of science and engineering, the quantum algorithm for linear systems of equations has the potential for widespread applicability.[5]

14.1 Procedure

The problem we are trying to solve is: given a Hermitian $N \times N$ matrix A and a unit vector $\overrightarrow{b}$, find the solution vector $\overrightarrow{x}$ satisfying $A\overrightarrow{x} = \overrightarrow{b}$. This algorithm assumes that the user is not interested in the values of $\overrightarrow{x}$ itself, but rather the result of applying some operator M onto x, $\langle x|M|x\rangle$.

First, the algorithm represents the vector $\overrightarrow{b}$ as a quantum state of the form:

$$|b\rangle = \sum_{i=1}^{N} b_i|i\rangle.$$

Next, Hamiltonian simulation techniques are used to apply the unitary operator e^{iAt} to $|b\rangle$ for a superposition of different times t . The ability to decompose $|b\rangle$ into the eigenbasis of A and to find the corresponding eigenvalues λ_j is facilitated by the use of quantum phase estimation.

The state of the system after this decomposition is approximately:

$$\sum_{j=1}^{N} \beta_j|u_j\rangle|\lambda_j\rangle,$$

where u_j is the eigenvector basis of A , and $|b\rangle = \sum_{j=1}^{N} \beta_j|u_j\rangle$.

We would then like to perform the linear map taking $|\lambda_j\rangle$ to $C\lambda_j^{-1}|\lambda_j\rangle$, where C is a normalizing constant. The linear mapping operation is not unitary and thus will require a number of repetitions as it has some probability of failing. After it succeeds, we uncompute the $|\lambda_j\rangle$ register and are left with a state proportional to:

$$\sum_{i=1}^{N} \beta_i\lambda_j^{-1}|u_j\rangle = A^{-1}|b\rangle = |x\rangle,$$

Where $|x\rangle$ is a quantum-mechanical representation of the desired solution vector *x*. To read out all components of *x* would require the procedure be repeated at least *N* times. However, it is often the case that one is not interested in x itself, but rather some expectation value of a linear operator *M* acting on *x*. By mapping *M* to a quantum-mechanical operator and performing the quantum measurement corresponding to *M*, we obtain an estimate of the expectation value $\langle x|M|x\rangle$. This allows for a wide variety of features of the vector *x* to be extracted including normalization, weights in different parts of the state space, and moments without actually computing all the values of the solution vector *x*.

14.2 Explanation of the algorithm

14.2.1 Initialization

Firstly, the algorithm requires that the matrix A be Hermitian so that it can be converted into a unitary operator. In the case were A is not Hermitian, define

$$\mathbf{C} = \begin{bmatrix} 0 & A \\ A^t & 0 \end{bmatrix}.$$

As C is Hermitian, the algorithm can now be used to solve $Cy = \begin{bmatrix} b \\ 0 \end{bmatrix}$. to obtain $y = \begin{bmatrix} 0 \\ x \end{bmatrix}$.

Secondly, The algorithm requires an efficient procedure to prepare $|b\rangle$, the quantum representation of b. It is assumed that there exists some linear operator B that can take some arbitrary quantum state $|\text{initial}\rangle$ to $|b\rangle$ efficiently or that this algorithm is a subroutine in a larger algorithm and is given $|b\rangle$ as input. Any error in the preparation of state $|b\rangle$ is ignored.

Finally, the algorithm assumes that the state $|\psi_0\rangle$ can be prepared efficiently. Where

$$|\psi_0\rangle := \sqrt{2/T} \sum_{\tau=0}^{T-1} \sin \pi \left(\frac{\tau + \frac{1}{2}}{T} \right) |\tau\rangle$$

for some large T . The coefficients of $|\psi_0\rangle$ are chosen to minimize a certain quadratic loss function which induces error in the U_{invert} subroutine described below.

14.2.2 Phase estimation

Phase estimation is used to transform the Hermitian matrix A into a unitary operator, which can then be applied at will. This is possible if A is s-sparse and efficiently row computable, meaning it has at most s nonzero entries per row and given a row index these entries can be computed in time O(s). Under these assumptions, quantum phase estimation allows $e^i At$ to be simulated in time $O(\log(N)s^2 t)$.

14.2.3 Uinvert subroutine

The key subroutine to the algorithm, denoted U_{invert} , is defined as follows:

1. Prepare $|\psi_0\rangle^C$ on register C

2. Apply the conditional Hamiltonian evolution (sum)

3. Apply the Fourier transform to the register C. Denote the resulting basis states with $|k\rangle$ for k = 0, ..., T − 1. Define $\lambda_k := 2\pi k / t_0$.

4. Adjoin a three-dimensional register S in the state

$$|h(\lambda_k)\rangle^S := \sqrt{1 - f(\lambda_k)^2 - g(\lambda_k)^2} |\text{nothing}\rangle^S$$

$$+ f(\lambda_k)|\text{well}\rangle^S + g(\lambda_k)|\text{ill}\rangle^S,$$

5. Reverse steps 1–3, uncomputing any garbage produced along the way.

where functions f, g, are filter functions. The states 'nothing', 'well' and 'ill' are used to instruct the loop body on how to proceed; 'nothing' indicates that the desired matrix inversion has not yet taken place, 'well' indicates that the inversion has taken place and the loop should halt, and 'ill' indicates that part of $|b\rangle$ is in the ill-conditioned subspace of A and the algorithm will not be able to produce the desired inversion.

14.2.4 Main loop

The body of the algorithm follows the amplitude amplification procedure: starting with $U_{\text{invert}} B |\text{initial}\rangle$, the following operation is repeatedly applied:

$$U_{\text{invert}} B R_{\text{init}} B^\dagger U_{\text{invert}}^\dagger R_{\text{succ}}$$

where

$$R_{\text{succ}} = I^2 - 2|\text{well}\rangle\langle\text{well}|^2,$$

and

$$R_{\text{init}} = I^2 - 2|\text{initial}\rangle\langle\text{initial}|.$$

After each repetition, S is measured and will produce a value of 'nothing', 'well', or 'ill' as described above. This loop is repeated until S is measured, which occurs with a probability p . Rather than repeating $\frac{1}{p}$ times to minimize error, amplitude amplification is used to achieve the same error resilience using only $O\left(\frac{1}{\sqrt{p}}\right)$ repetitions.

14.2.5 Scalar measurement

After successfully measuring 'well' on S the system will be in a state proportional to:

$$\sum_{i=1}^{N} \beta_i \lambda_j^{-1} |u_j\rangle = A^{-1}|b\rangle = |x\rangle.$$

Finally, we perform the quantum-mechanical operator corresponding to M and obtain an estimate of the value of $\langle x|M|x\rangle$.

14.3 Run time analysis

14.3.1 Classical efficiency

The best classical algorithm which produces the actual solution vector $\overrightarrow{x}$ is Gaussian elimination, which runs in $O(N^3)$ time.

If A is s-sparse and positive semi-definite, then the Conjugate Gradient method can be used to find the solution vector $\overrightarrow{x}$ can be found in $O(Ns\kappa)$ time by minimizing the quadratic function $|A\overrightarrow{x} - \overrightarrow{b}|^2$.

When only a summary statistic of the solution vector $\overrightarrow{x}$ is needed, as is the case for the quantum algorithm for linear systems of equations, a classical computer can find an estimate of $\overrightarrow{x}^\dagger M \overrightarrow{x}$ in $O(N\sqrt{\kappa})$.

14.3.2 Quantum efficiency

The quantum algorithm for solving linear systems of equations originally proposed by Harrow et al. was shown to be $O(\kappa^2 \log N)$. The runtime of this algorithm was subsequently improved to $O(\kappa \log^3 \kappa \log N)$ by Andris Ambainis.[6]

14.3.3 Optimality

An important factor in the performance of the matrix inversion algorithm is the condition number of A κ , which represents the ratio of A 's largest and smallest eigenvalues. As the condition number increases, the ease with which the solution vector can be found using gradient descent methods such as the conjugate gradient method decreases, as A becomes closer to a matrix which cannot be inverted and the solution vector becomes less stable. This algorithm assumes that all elements of the matrix A lie between $\frac{1}{\kappa}$ and 1, in which case the claimed run-time proportional to κ^2 will be achieved. Therefore, the speedup over classical algorithms is increased further when κ is a poly(log(N)) .[1]

If the run-time of the algorithm were made poly-logarithmic in κ then problems solvable on n qubits could be solved in poly(n) time, causing the complexity class BQP to be equal to PSPACE.[1]

14.4 Error analysis

Performing the phase estimation, which is the dominant source of error, is done by simulating e^{iAt} . Assuming that A is s-sparse, this can be done with an error bounded by a constant ε , which will translate to the additive error achieved in the output state $|x\rangle$.

The phase estimation step errs by $O\left(\frac{1}{t_0}\right)$ in estimating λ , which translates into a relative error of $O\left(\frac{1}{\lambda t_0}\right)$ in λ^{-1} . If $\lambda \geq 1/\kappa$, taking $t_0 = O(\kappa\varepsilon)$ induces a final error of ε . This requires that the overall run-time efficiency be increased proportional to $O\left(\frac{1}{\varepsilon}\right)$ to minimize error.

14.5 Experimental realization

While there does not yet exist a quantum computer that can truly offer a speedup over a classical computer, implementation of a "proof of concept" remains an important milestone in the development of a new quantum algorithm. Demonstrating the quantum algorithm for linear systems of equations remained a challenge for years after its proposal until 2013 when it was demonstrated by Cai et al., Barz et al. and Pan et al. in parallel.

14.5.1 Cai et al.

Published in Physical Review Letters 110, 230501 (2013), Cai et al. reported an experimental demonstration of the simplest meaningful instance of this algorithm, that is, solving 2*2 linear equations for various input vectors. The quantum circuit is optimized and compiled into a linear optical network with four photonic quantum bits (qubits) and four controlled logic gates, which is used to coherently implement every subroutine for this algorithm. For various input vectors, the quantum computer gives solutions for the linear equations with reasonably high precision, ranging from fidelities of 0.825 to 0.993.

14.5.2 Barz et al.

On February 5, 2013, Barz et al. demonstrated the quantum algorithm for linear systems of equations on a photonic quantum computing architecture. This implementation used two consecutive entangling gates on the same pair of polarization-encoded qubits. Two separately controlled NOT gates were realized where the successful operation of the first was heralded by a measurement of two ancillary photons. Barz et al. found that the fidelity in the obtained output state ranged from 64.7% to 98.1% due to the influence of higher-order emissions from spontaneous parametric down-conversion.[3]

14.5.3 Pan et al.

On February 8, 2013 Pan et al. reported a proof-of-concept experimental demonstration of the quantum algorithm using a 4-qubit nuclear magnetic resonance quantum information processor. The implementation was tested using simple linear systems of only 2 variables. Across three experiments they obtain the solution vector with over 96% fidelity.[4]

14.6 Applications

Quantum computers are devices that harness quantum mechanics to perform computations in ways that classical computers cannot. For certain problems, quantum algorithms supply exponential speedups over their classical counterparts, the most famous example being Shor's factoring algorithm. Few such exponential speedups are known, and those that are (such as the use of quantum computers to simulate other quantum systems) have so far found limited use outside the domain of quantum mechanics. This algorithm provides an exponentially faster method of estimating features of the solution of a set of linear equations, which is a problem ubiquitous in science an engineering, both on its own and as a subroutine in more complex problems.

14.6.1 Linear differential equation solving

Dominic Berry proposed a new algorithm for solving linear time dependent differential equations as an extension of the quantum algorithm for solving linear systems of equations. Berry provides an efficient algorithm for solving the full-time evolution under sparse linear differential equations on a quantum computer.[7]

14.6.2 Least-squares fitting

Wiebe et al. provide a new quantum algorithm to determine the quality of a least-squares fit in which a continuous function is used to approximate a set of discrete points by extending the quantum algorithm for linear systems of equations. As the amount of discrete points increases, the time required to produce a least-squares fit using even a quantum computer running a quantum state tomography algorithm becomes very large. Wiebe et al. find that in many cases, their algorithm can efficiently find a concise approximation of the data points, eliminating the need for the higher-complexity tomography algorithm.[8]

14.6.3 Machine learning and big data analysis

Main article: Quantum machine learning

Machine learning is the study of systems that can identify trends in data. Tasks in machine learning frequently involve manipulating and classifying a large volume of data in high-dimensional vector spaces. The runtime of classical machine learning algorithms is limited by a polynomial dependence on both the volume of data and the dimensions of the space. Quantum computers are capable of manipulating high-dimensional vectors using tensor product spaces are thus the perfect platform for machine learning algorithms.[9]

The quantum algorithm for linear systems of equations has been applied to a support vector machine, which is an optimized linear or non-linear binary classifier. A support vector machine can be used for supervised machine learning, in which training set of already classified data is available, or unsupervised machine learning, in which all data given to the system is unclassified. Rebentrost et al. show that a quantum support vector machine can be used for big data classification and achieve an exponential speedup over classical computers.[10]

14.7 References

[1] Quantum algorithm for solving linear systems of equations, by Harrow et al..

[2] Experimental quantum computing to solve systems of linear equations by Cai et al..

[3] Barz, Stefanie; Kassal, Ivan; Ringbauer, Martin; Lipp, Yannick Ole; Dakić, Borivoje; Aspuru-Guzik, Alán; Walther, Philip (2014). "A two-qubit photonic quantum processor and its application to solving systems of linear equations". *Scientific Reports* **4**: 6115. doi:10.1038/srep06115. ISSN 2045-2322.

[4] Experimental realization of quantum algorithm for solving linear systems of equations, by Pan et al..

[5] Quantum Computer Runs The Most Practically Useful Quantum Algorithm, by Lu and Pan.

[6] [http://arxiv.org/abs/1010.4458 Variable time amplitude amplification and a faster quantum algorithm for solving systems of linear equations by Adris Ambainis].

[7] [http://arxiv.org/abs/1010.2745 High-order quantum algorithm for solving linear differential equations by Dominic Berry].

[8] Quantum Data Fitting by Wiebe et al..

[9] Quantum algorithms for supervised and unsupervised machine learning, by Lloyd et al..

[10] Quantum support vector machine for big feature and big data classification, by Rebentrost et al..

Chapter 15

Quantum programming

Quantum programming is a set of computer programming languages that allow the expression of quantum algorithms using high-level constructs.[1] The point of quantum languages is not so much to provide a tool for programmers, but to provide tools for researchers to understand better how quantum computation works and how to reason formally about quantum algorithms.

One can single out two main groups of quantum programming languages: imperative quantum programming languages and functional quantum programming languages.

The most prominent representatives of the first group are QCL[2] and LanQ.[3]

Efforts are underway to develop functional programming languages for quantum computing. Examples include Selinger's QPL,[4] and the Haskell-like language QML by Altenkirch and Grattage.[5][6] Higher-order quantum programming languages, based on lambda calculus, have been proposed by van Tonder,[7] Selinger and Valiron [8] and by Arrighi and Dowek.[9]

Simon Gay's Quantum Programming Languages Survey provides information on the state of research and a comprehensive bibliography of resources about quantum programming as of 2007.

15.1 Imperative quantum programming languages

15.1.1 Quantum pseudocode

Quantum pseudocode proposed by E. Knill is the first formalized language for description of quantum algorithms. It was introduced and, moreover, was tightly connected with a model of quantum machine called Quantum Random Access Machine (QRAM).

15.1.2 Quantum computing language

QCL (Quantum Computation Language) is one of the first implemented quantum programming languages. Its syntax resembles the syntax of the C programming language and its classical data types are similar to primitive data types in C. One can combine classical code and quantum code in the same program.

The basic built-in quantum data type in QCL is the qureg (quantum register). It can be interpreted as an array of qubits (quantum bits).

qureg x1[2]; // 2-qubit quantum register x1 qureg x2[2]; // 2-qubit quantum register x2 H(x1); // Hadamard operation on x1 H(x2[1]); // Hadamard operation on the first qubit of the register x2

Since the qcl interpreter uses qlib simulation library, it is possible to observe the internal state of the quantum machine during execution of the quantum program.

qcl> dump : STATE: 4 / 32 qubits allocated, 28 / 32 qubits free 0.35355 |0> + 0.35355 |1> + 0.35355 |2> + 0.35355 |3> + 0.35355 |8> + 0.35355 |9> + 0.35355 |10> + 0.35355 |11>

Note that the dump operation is different from measurement, since it does not influence the state of the quantum machine and can be realized only using a simulator.

The QCL standard library provides standard quantum operators used in quantum algorithms such as:

- controlled-not with many target qubits,
- Hadamard operation on many qubits,
- parse and controlled phase.

The most important feature of QCL is the support for user-defined operators and functions. Like in modern programming languages, it is possible to define new operations which can be used to manipulate quantum data. For example:

operator diffuse (qureg q) { H(q); // Hadamard Transform Not(q); // Invert q CPhase(pi, q); // Rotate if q=1111.. !Not(q); // undo inversion !H(q); // undo Hadamard Transform }

defines inverse about the mean operator used in Grover's algorithm. This allows one to define algorithms on a higher level of abstraction and extend the library of functions available for programmers.

Syntax

- Data types
  - Quantum - qureg, quvoid, quconst, quscratch, qucond
  - Classical - int, real, complex, boolean, string, vector, matrix, tensor
- Function types
  - qufunct - Pseudo-classic operators. Can only change the permutation of basic states.
  - operator - General unitary operators. Can change the amplitude.
  - procedure - Can call measure, print, and dump inside this function. This function is non-invertible.
- Built-in functions
  - Quantum
    - qufunct - Fanout, Swap, Perm2, Perm4, Perm8, Not, CNot
    - operator - Matrix2x2, Matrix4x4, Matrix8x8, Rot, Mix, H, CPhase, SqrtNot, X, Y, Z, S, T
    - procedure - measure, dump, reset
  - Classical
    - Arithmetic - sin, cos, tan, log, sqrt, ...
    - Complex - Re, Im, conj

15.1.3 Q language

Q Language is the second implemented imperative quantum programming language.

Q Language was implemented as an extension of C++ programming language. It provides classes for basic quantum operations like QHadamard, QFourier, QNot, and QSwap, which are derived from the base class Qop. New operators can be defined using C++ class mechanism.

Quantum memory is represented by class Qreg.

Qreg x1; // 1-qubit quantum register with initial value 0 Qreg x2(2,0); // 2-qubit quantum register with initial value 0

The computation process is executed using a provided simulator. Noisy environment can be simulated using parameters of the simulator.

15.1.4 qGCL

Quantum Guarded Command Language (qGCL) was defined by P. Zuliani in his PhD thesis. It is based on Guarded Command Language created by Edsger Dijkstra.

It can be described as a language of quantum programs specification.

15.2 Functional quantum programming languages

During the last few years many quantum programming languages based on the functional programming paradigm were proposed. Functional programming languages are well-suited for reasoning about programs.

15.2.1 QFC and QPL

QFC and QPL are two closely related quantum programming languages defined by Peter Selinger. They differ only in their syntax: QFC uses a flow chart syntax, whereas QPL uses a textual syntax. These languages have classical control flow but can operate on quantum or classical data. Selinger gives a denotational semantics for these languages in a category of superoperators.

15.2.2 QML

QML is a Haskell-like quantum programming language by Altenkirch and Grattage.[5] Unlike Selinger's QPL, this language takes duplication, rather than discarding, of quantum information as a primitive operation. Duplication in this context is understood to be the operation that maps $|\phi\rangle$ to $|\phi\rangle \otimes |\phi\rangle$, and is not to be confused with the impossible operation of cloning; the authors claim it is akin to how sharing is modeled in classical languages. QML also introduces both classical and quantum control operators, whereas most other languages rely on classical control.

An operational semantics for QML is given in terms of quantum circuits, while a denotational semantics is presented in terms of superoperators, and these are shown to agree. Both the operational and denotational semantics have been implemented (classically) in Haskell.[10]

15.2.3 Quantum lambda calculi

Quantum lambda calculi are extensions of the classical lambda calculus introduced by Alonzo Church and Stephen Cole Kleene in the 1930s. The purpose of quantum lambda calculi is to extend quantum programming languages with a theory of higher-order functions.

The first attempt to define a quantum lambda calculus was made by Philip Maymin in 1996.[11] His lambda-q calculus is powerful enough to express any quantum computation. However, this language can efficiently solve NP-complete problems, and therefore appears to be strictly stronger than the standard quantum computational models (such as the quantum Turing machine or the quantum circuit model). Therefore, Maymin's lambda-q calculus is probably not implementable on a physical device.

In 2003, André van Tonder defined an extension of the lambda calculus suitable for proving correctness of quantum programs. He also provided an implementation in the Scheme programming language.[12]

In 2004, Selinger and Valiron defined a strongly typed lambda calculus for quantum computation with a type system based on linear logic.

15.2.4 Quipper

Quipper was published in 2013.[13] It is implemented as an embedded language, using Haskell as the host language.[14] For this reason, quantum programs written in Quipper are written in Haskell using provided libraries. For example, the following code implements preparation of a superposition

import Quipper spos :: Bool -> Circ Qubit spos b = do q <- qinit b r <- hadamard q return r

15.3 References

[1] Jarosław Adam Miszczak. "High-level Structures in Quantum Computing". Retrieved 12 December 2015.

[2] Bernhard Omer. "The QCL Programming Language".

[3] Hynek Mlnařík. "LanQ – a quantum imperative programming language".

[4] Peter Selinger, "Towards a quantum programming language", Mathematical Structures in Computer Science 14(4):527-586, 2004.

[5] Jonathan Grattage: QML Research (website)

[6] T. Altenkirch, V. Belavkin, J. Grattage, A. Green, A. Sabry, J. K. Vizzotto, QML: A Functional Quantum Programming Language (website)

[7] Andre van Tonder, "A Lambda Calculus for Quantum Computation", SIAM J. Comput., 33(5), 1109–1135. (27 pages), 2004. Also available from arXiv:quant-ph/0307150

[8] Peter Selinger and Benoît Valiron, "A lambda calculus for quantum computation with classical control", Mathematical Structures in Computer Science 16(3):527-552, 2006.

[9] Pablo Arrighi, Gilles Dowek, "Linear-algebraic lambda-calculus: higher-order, encodings and confluence", 2006

[10] Jonathan Grattage, QML: A Functional Quantum Programming Language (compiler), 2005–2008

[11] Philip Maymin, "Extending the Lambda Calculus to Express Randomized and Quantumized Algorithms", 1996

[12] André van Tonder. "A lambda calculus for quantum computation (website)".

[13] Alexander S. Green, Peter LeFanu Lumsdaine, Neil J. Ross, Peter Selinger, Benoît Valiron. "The Quipper Language (website)".

[14] Alexander S. Green, Peter LeFanu Lumsdaine, Neil J. Ross, Peter Selinger, Benoît Valiron (2013). "An Introduction to Quantum Programming in Quipper".

15.4 External links

- 5th International Workshop on Quantum Physics and Logic
- 4th International Workshop on Quantum Programming Languages
- 3rd International Workshop on Quantum Programming Languages
- 2nd International Workshop on Quantum Programming Languages
- Bibliography on Quantum Programming Languages (updated in May 2007)
- Quantum programming language in Quantiki

Chapter 16

Quantum error correction

Quantum error correction is used in quantum computing to protect quantum information from errors due to decoherence and other quantum noise. Quantum error correction is essential if one is to achieve fault-tolerant quantum computation that can deal not only with noise on stored quantum information, but also with faulty quantum gates, faulty quantum preparation, and faulty measurements.

Classical error correction employs redundancy. The simplest way is to store the information multiple times, and—if these copies are later found to disagree—just take a majority vote; e.g. Suppose we copy a bit three times. Suppose further that a noisy error corrupts the three-bit state so that one bit is equal to zero but the other two are equal to one. If we assume that noisy errors are independent and occur with some probability p. It is most likely that the error is a single-bit error and the transmitted message is three ones. It is possible that a double-bit error occurs and the transmitted message is equal to three zeros, but this outcome is less likely than the above outcome.

Copying quantum information is not possible due to the no-cloning theorem. This theorem seems to present an obstacle to formulating a theory of quantum error correction. But it is possible to *spread* the information of one qubit onto a highly entangled state of several (*physical*) qubits. Peter Shor first discovered this method of formulating a *quantum error correcting code* by storing the information of one qubit onto a highly entangled state of nine qubits. A quantum error correcting code protects quantum information against errors of a limited form.

Classical error correcting codes use a *syndrome measurement* to diagnose which error corrupts an encoded state. We then reverse an error by applying a corrective operation based on the syndrome. Quantum error correction also employs syndrome measurements. We perform a multi-qubit measurement that does not disturb the quantum information in the encoded state but retrieves information about the error. A syndrome measurement can determine whether a qubit has been corrupted, and if so, which one. What is more, the outcome of this operation (the *syndrome*) tells us not only which physical qubit was affected, but also, in which of several possible ways it was affected. The latter is counter-intuitive at first sight: Since noise is arbitrary, how can the effect of noise be one of only few distinct possibilities? In most codes, the effect is either a bit flip, or a sign (of the phase) flip, or both (corresponding to the Pauli matrices X, Z, and Y). The reason is that the measurement of the syndrome has the projective effect of a quantum measurement. So even if the error due to the noise was arbitrary, it can be expressed as a superposition of basis operations—the *error basis* (which is here given by the Pauli matrices and the identity). The syndrome measurement "forces" the qubit to "decide" for a certain specific "Pauli error" to "have happened", and the syndrome tells us which, so that we can let the same Pauli operator act again on the corrupted qubit to revert the effect of the error.

The syndrome measurement tells us as much as possible about the error that has happened, but *nothing* at all about the *value* that is stored in the logical qubit—as otherwise the measurement would destroy any quantum superposition of this logical qubit with other qubits in the quantum computer.

16.1 The bit flip code

The repetition code works in a classical channel, because classical bits are easy to measure and to repeat. However, in a quantum channel, it is no longer possible, due to the no-cloning theorem, which forbids the creation of identical copies of an arbitrary unknown quantum state. So a single qubit can not be repeated three times as in the previous example, as any measurement of the qubit will change its wave function. Nevertheless, in quantum computing there is another method, namely the three qubit bit flip code. It uses entanglement and syndrome measurements and is comparable in performance with the repetition code.

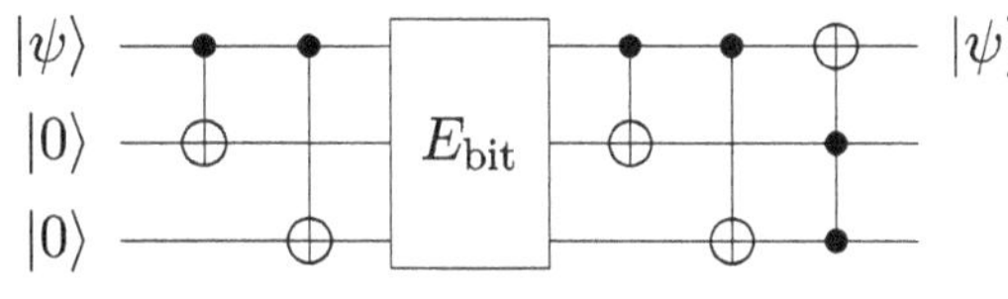

Quantum circuit of the bit flip code

Let $|\psi\rangle = \alpha_0|0\rangle + \alpha_1|1\rangle$ be an arbitrary qubit. The first step of the three qubit bit flip code is to entangle the qubit with two other qubits using two CNOT gates with input $|0\rangle$.[1] The result will be $|\psi'\rangle = \alpha_0|000\rangle + \alpha_1|111\rangle$. This is just a tensor product of three qubits, and different from cloning a state.

Now these qubits will be sent through a channel E_{bit} where we assume that at most one bit flip may occur. For example, in the case where the first qubit is flipped, the result would be $|\psi_r'\rangle = \alpha_0|100\rangle + \alpha_1|011\rangle$. To diagnose bit flips in any of the three possible qubits, syndrome diagnosis is needed, which includes four projection operators:

$P_0 = |000\rangle\langle 000| + |111\rangle\langle 111|$

$P_1 = |100\rangle\langle 100| + |011\rangle\langle 011|$

$P_2 = |010\rangle\langle 010| + |101\rangle\langle 101|$

$P_3 = |001\rangle\langle 001| + |110\rangle\langle 110|$

It can be obtained:

$\langle\psi_r'|P_0|\psi_r'\rangle = 0$

$\langle\psi_r'|P_1|\psi_r'\rangle = 1$

$\langle\psi_r'|P_2|\psi_r'\rangle = 0$

$\langle\psi_r'|P_3|\psi_r'\rangle = 0$

So it will be known that the error syndrome corresponds to P_1 . This three qubits bit flip code can correct one error if at most one bit-flip-error occurred in the channel. It is similar to the three bits repetition code in a classical computer.

16.2 The sign flip code

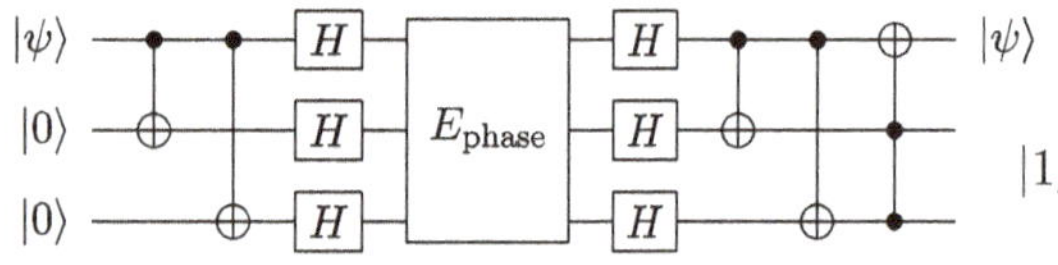

Quantum circuit of the phase flip code

Flipped bits are the only kind of error in classical computer, but there is another possibility of an error with quantum computers, the sign flip. Through the transmission in a channel the relative sign between $|0\rangle$ and $|1\rangle$ can become inverted. For instance, a qubit in the state $|-\rangle = (|0\rangle - |1\rangle)/\sqrt{2}$ may have its sign flip to $|+\rangle = (|0\rangle + |1\rangle)/\sqrt{2}$.

The original state of the qubit

$|\psi\rangle = \alpha_0|+\rangle + \alpha_1|-\rangle$

will be changed into the state

$|\psi'\rangle = \alpha_0|{+}{+}{+}\rangle + \alpha_1|{-}{-}{-}\rangle$.

In the Hadamard basis, bit flips become sign flips and sign flips become bit flips. Let E_{phase} be a quantum channel that can cause at most one phase flip. Then the bit flip code from above can recover $|\psi\rangle$ by transforming into the Hadamard basis before and after transmission through E_{phase} .

16.3 The Shor code

The error channel may induce either a bit flip, a sign flip, or both. It is possible to correct for both types of errors using one code, and the Shor code does just that. In fact, the Shor code corrects arbitrary single-qubit errors.

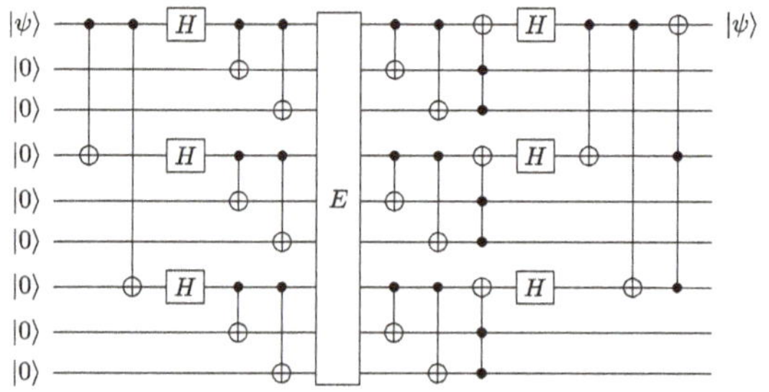

Quantum circuit of the Shor code

Let E be a quantum channel that can arbitrarily corrupt a single qubit. The 1st, 4th and 7th qubits are for the sign flip code, while the three group of qubits (1,2,3), (4,5,6), and (7,8,9) are designed for the bit flip code. With the Shor code, a qubit state $|\psi\rangle = \alpha_0|0\rangle + \alpha_1|1\rangle$ will be transformed into the product of 9 qubits $|\psi'\rangle = \alpha_0|0_S\rangle + \alpha_1|1_S\rangle$, where

$$|0_S\rangle = \frac{1}{2\sqrt{2}}(|000\rangle+|111\rangle)\otimes(|000\rangle+|111\rangle)\otimes(|000\rangle+|111\rangle)$$

$$|1_S\rangle = \frac{1}{2\sqrt{2}}(|000\rangle-|111\rangle)\otimes(|000\rangle-|111\rangle)\otimes(|000\rangle-|111\rangle)$$

If a bit flip error happens to a qubit, the syndrome analysis will be performed on each set of states (1,2,3), (4,5,6), and (7,8,9), then correct the error.

If the three bit flip group (1,2,3), (4,5,6), and (7,8,9) are considered as three inputs, then the Shor code circuit can be reduced as a sign flip code. This means that the Shor code can also repair sign flip error for a single qubit.[2]

The Shor code also can correct for any arbitrary errors (both bit flip and sign flip) to a single qubit. If an error is modeled by a unitary transform U, which will act on a qubit $|\psi\rangle$, then U can be described in the form

$$U = c_0 I + c_1\sigma_x + c_2\sigma_y + c_3\sigma_z$$

where c_0 , c_1 , c_2 , and c_3 are complex constants, I is the identity, and the Pauli matrices are given by

$$\sigma_x = \begin{pmatrix} 0 & 1 \\ 1 & 0 \end{pmatrix};$$

$$\sigma_y = \begin{pmatrix} 0 & -i \\ i & 0 \end{pmatrix};$$

$$\sigma_z = \begin{pmatrix} 1 & 0 \\ 0 & -1 \end{pmatrix}$$

If U is equal to I, then no error occurs. If $U = \sigma_x$, a bit flip error occurs. If $U = \sigma_z$, a sign flip error occurs. If $U = i\sigma_y$ then both a bit flip error and a sign flip error occur. Due to linearity, it follows that the Shor code can correct arbitrary 1-qubit errors.

16.4 General codes

In general, a *quantum code* for a quantum channel $\mathcal{E}$ is a subspace $\mathcal{C} \subseteq \mathcal{H}$, where $\mathcal{H}$ is the state Hilbert space, such that there exists another quantum channel $\mathcal{R}$ with

$$(\mathcal{R} \circ \mathcal{E})(\rho) = \rho \quad \forall \rho = P_{\mathcal{C}} \rho P_{\mathcal{C}},$$

where $P_{\mathcal{C}}$ is the orthogonal projection onto $\mathcal{C}$. Here $\mathcal{R}$ is known as the *correction operation*.

16.5 Models

Over time, researchers have come up with several codes:

- Peter Shor's 9-qubit-code, a.k.a. the Shor code, encodes 1 logical qubit in 9 physical qubits and can correct for arbitrary errors in a single qubit.
- Andrew Steane found a code which does the same with 7 instead of 9 qubits, see Steane code.
- Raymond Laflamme and collaborators found a class of 5-qubit codes which do the same, which also have the property of being fault-tolerant. A 5-qubit code is the smallest possible code which protects a single logical qubit against single-qubit errors.
- A generalisation of this concept are the CSS codes, named for their inventors: A. R. Calderbank, Peter Shor and Andrew Steane. According to the quantum Hamming bound, encoding a single logical qubit and providing for arbitrary error correction in a single qubit requires a minimum of 5 physical qubits.
- A more general class of codes (encompassing the former) are the stabilizer codes discovered by Daniel Gottesman (), and by A. R. Calderbank, Eric Rains, Peter Shor, and N. J. A. Sloane (,); these are also called additive codes.
- A newer idea is Alexei Kitaev's topological quantum codes and the more general idea of a topological quantum computer.
- Todd Brun, Igor Devetak, and Min-Hsiu Hsieh also constructed the entanglement-assisted stabilizer formalism as an extension of the standard stabilizer formalism that incorporates quantum entanglement shared between a sender and a receiver.

That these codes allow indeed for quantum computations of arbitrary length is the content of the *threshold theorem*, found by Michael Ben-Or and Dorit Aharonov, which asserts that you can correct for all errors if you concatenate quantum codes such as the CSS codes—i.e. re-encode each logical qubit by the same code again, and so on, on logarithmically many levels—*provided* the error rate of individual quantum gates is below a certain threshold; as otherwise, the attempts to measure the syndrome and correct the errors would introduce more new errors than they correct for.

As of late 2004, estimates for this threshold indicate that it could be as high as 1-3% , provided that there are sufficiently many qubits available.

16.6 Experimental realization

There have been several experimental realizations of CSS-based codes. The first demonstration was with NMR qubits.[3] Subsequently demonstrations have been made with linear optics,[4] trapped ions,[5][6] and superconducting (transmon) qubits.[7]

Other error correcting codes have also been implemented, such as one aimed at correcting for photon loss, the dominant error source in photonic qubit schemes.[8]

16.7 See also

- Error detection and correction
- Soft error

16.8 Notes

[1] Michael A. Nielsen and Isaac L. Chuang (2000). "Quantum Computation and Quantum Information". *Cambridge University Press.*

[2] W.Shor, Peter (1995). "Scheme for reducing decoherence in quantum computer memory". *AT&T Bell Laboratories.*

[3] D. G. Cory, M. D. Price, W. Maas, E. Knill, R. Laflamme, W. H. Zurek, T. F. Havel and S. S. Somaroo, "Experimental Quantum Error Correction," *Phys. Rev. Lett.* **81**, 2152–2155 (1998), doi:10.1103/PhysRevLett.81.2152

[4] T. B. Pittman, B. C. Jacobs and J. D. Franson, "Demonstration of quantum error correction using linear optics," *Phys. Rev. A* **71**, 052332 (2005), doi:10.1103/PhysRevA.71.052332

[5] J. Chiaverini, D. Leibfried, T. Schaetz, M. D. Barrett, R. B. Blakestad, J. Britton, W. M. Itano, J. D. Jost, E. Knill, C. Langer, R. Ozeri and D. J. Wineland, "Realization of quantum error correction," *Nature* **432**, 602-605 (2004), doi:10.1038/nature03074

[6] P. Schindler, J. T. Barreiro, T. Monz, V. Nebendahl, D. Nigg, M. Chwalla, M. Hennrich and R. Blatt, "Experimental Repetitive Quantum Error Correction," *Science* **332**, 1059-1061 (2011), doi:10.1126/science.1203329

[7] M. D. Reed, L. DiCarlo, S. E. Nigg, L. Sun, L. Frunzio, S. M. Girvin and R. J. Schoelkopf, "Realization of Three-Qubit Quantum Error Correction with Superconducting Circuits," *Nature* **482**, 382-385 (2012), doi:10.1038/nature10786, arXiv:1109.4948

[8] M. Lassen, M. Sabuncu, A. Huck, J. Niset, G. Leuchs, N. J. Cerf and U. L. Andersen, "Quantum optical coherence can survive photon losses using a continuous-variable quantum erasure-correcting code," *Nature Photonics* 4, 700 (2010), doi:10.1038/nphoton.2010.168

16.9 Bibliography

- Daniel Lidar and Todd Brun, ed. (2013). "Quantum Error Correction". *Cambridge University Press.*
- Frank Gaitan (2008). "Quantum Error Correction and Fault Tolerant Quantum Computing". *Taylor & Francis.*
- Freedman, Michael H.; Meyer, David A.; Luo, Feng: Z_2-Systolic freedom and quantum codes. *Mathematics of quantum computation*, 287–320, Comput. Math. Ser., Chapman & Hall/CRC, Boca Raton, FL, 2002.
- Freedman, Michael H.; Meyer, David A.: Projective plane and planar quantum codes. *Found. Comput. Math.* 1 (2001), no. 3, 325–332.
- Mikael Lassen, Metin Sabuncu, Alexander Huck, Julien Niset, Gerd Leuchs, Nicolas J. Cerf, Ulrik L. Andersen, *Quantum optical coherence can survive photon losses using a continuous-variable quantum erasure-correcting code* , Nature Photonics **4** 10 (2010)(this document online)

16.10 External links

- Prospects
- Error-check breakthrough in quantum computing
- Quantum error correction on arxiv.org

Chapter 17

Quantum circuit

In quantum information theory, a **quantum circuit** is a model for quantum computation in which a computation is a sequence of quantum gates, which are reversible transformations on a quantum mechanical analog of an n-bit register. This analogous structure is referred to as an n-qubit register.

17.1 Reversible classical logic gates

The elementary logic gates of a classical computer, other than the NOT gate, are not reversible. Thus, for instance, for an AND gate one cannot recover the two input bits from the output bit; for example, if the output bit is 0, we cannot tell from this whether the input bits are 0,1 or 1,0 or 0,0.

However, reversible gates in classical computers are easily constructed for bit strings of any length; moreover, these are actually of practical interest, since they do not increase entropy. A reversible gate is a reversible function on n-bit data that returns n-bit data, where an n-bit data is a string of bits $x_1, x_2, ..., xn$ of length n. The set of n-bit data is the space $\{0,1\}^n$, which consists of 2^n strings of 0's and 1's.

More precisely: an n-bit reversible gate is a bijective mapping f from the set $\{0,1\}^n$ of n-bit data onto itself. An example of such a reversible gate f is a mapping that applies a fixed permutation to its inputs. For reasons of practical engineering, one typically studies gates only for small values of n, e.g. n=1, n=2 or n=3. These gates can be easily described by tables.

17.2 Quantum logic gates

To define quantum gates, we first need to specify the quantum replacement of an n-bit datum. The *quantized version* of classical n-bit space $\{0,1\}^n$ is the Hilbert space

$$H_{\mathrm{QB}(n)} = \ell^2(\{0,1\}^n).$$

This is by definition the space of complex-valued functions on $\{0,1\}^n$ and is naturally an inner product space. This space can also be regarded as consisting of linear superpositions of classical bit strings. Note that $H\mathrm{QB}(n)$ is a vector space over the complex numbers of dimension 2^n. The elements of this space are called n-qubits.

Using Dirac ket notation, if $x_1, x_2, ..., xn$ is a classical bit string, then

$$|x_1, x_2, \cdots, x_n\rangle$$

is a special n-qubit corresponding to the function which maps this classical bit string to 1 and maps all other bit strings to 0; these 2^n special n-qubits are called *computational basis states*. All n-qubits are complex linear combinations of these computational basis states.

Quantum logic gates, in contrast to classical logic gates, are always reversible. One requires a special kind of reversible function, namely a unitary mapping, that is, a linear transformation of a complex inner product space that preserves the Hermitian inner product. An n-qubit (reversible) quantum gate is a unitary mapping U from the space $H\mathrm{QB}(n)$ of n-qubits onto itself.

Typically, we are only interested in gates for small values of n.

A reversible n-bit classical logic gate gives rise to a reversible n-bit quantum gate as follows: to each reversible n-bit logic gate f corresponds a quantum gate Wf defined as follows:

$$W_f(|x_1, x_2, \cdots, x_n\rangle) = |f(x_1, x_2, \cdots, x_n)\rangle.$$

Note that Wf permutes the computational basis states.

Of particular importance is the controlled NOT gate (also called CNOT gate) WCNOT defined on a quantized 2 qubit. Other examples of quantum logic gates derived from classical ones are the Toffoli gate and the Fredkin gate.

However, the Hilbert-space structure of the qubits permits many quantum gates that are not induced by classical ones. For example, a relative phase shift is a 1 qubit gate given by multiplication by the unitary matrix:

$$U_\theta = \begin{bmatrix} e^{i\theta} & 0 \\ 0 & 1 \end{bmatrix},$$

so

$$U_\theta|0\rangle = e^{i\theta}|0\rangle \quad U_\theta|1\rangle = |1\rangle.$$

17.3 Reversible logic circuits

Main article: reversible computing

Again, we consider first *reversible* classical computation. Conceptually, there is no difference between a reversible n-bit circuit and a reversible n-bit logic gate: either one is just an invertible function on the space of n bit data. However, as mentioned in the previous section, for engineering reasons we would like to have a small number of simple reversible gates, that can be put together to assemble any reversible circuit.

To explain this assembly process, suppose we have a reversible n-bit gate f and a reversible m-bit gate g. Putting them together means producing a new circuit by connecting some set of k outputs of f to some set of k inputs of g as in the figure below. In that figure n=5, k=3 and m = 7. The resulting circuit is also reversible and operates on $n+m-k$ bits.

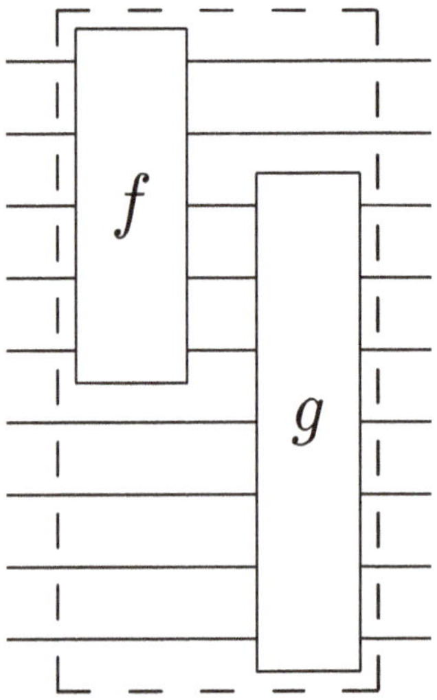

We will refer to this scheme as a *classical assemblage* (This concept corresponds to a technical definition in Kitaev's pioneering paper cited below). In composing these reversible machines, it is important to ensure that the intermediate machines are also reversible. This condition assures that *intermediate* "garbage" is not created (the net physical effect would be to increase entropy, which is one of the motivations for going through this exercise).

Now it is possible to show that the Toffoli gate is a universal gate. This means that given any reversible classical n-bit circuit h, we can construct a classical assemblage of Toffoli gates in the above manner to produce an $(n+m)$-bit circuit f such that

$$f(x_1,\ldots,x_n,\underbrace{0,\ldots,0}) = (y_1,\ldots,y_n,\underbrace{0,\ldots,0})$$

where there are m underbraced zeroed inputs and

$$(y_1,\ldots,y_n) = h(x_1,\ldots,x_n)$$

Notice that the end result always has a string of m zeros as the ancilla bits! No "rubbish" is ever produced, and so this computation is indeed one that, in a physical sense, generates no entropy. This issue is carefully discussed in Kitaev's article.

More generally, any function f (bijective or not) can be simulated by a circuit of Toffoli gates. Obviously, if the mapping fails to be injective, at some point in the simulation (for example as the last step) some "garbage" has to be produced.

For quantum circuits a similar composition of qubit gates can be defined. That is, associated to any *classical assemblage* as above, we can produce a reversible quantum circuit when in place of f we have an n-qubit gate U and in place of g we have an m-qubit gate W. See illustration below:

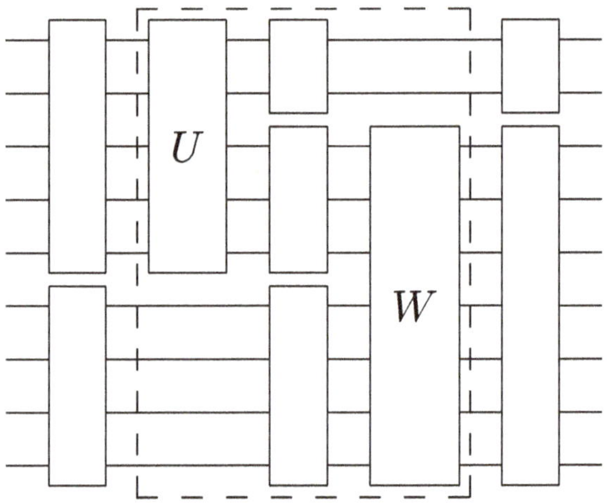

The fact that connecting gates this way gives rise to a unitary mapping on $n+m-k$ qubit space is easy to check. It should also be noted that in a real quantum computer the physical connection between the gates is a major engineering challenge, since it is one of the places where decoherence may occur.

There are also universality theorems for certain sets of well-known gates; such a universality theorem exists, for instance, for the pair consisting of the single qubit phase gate $U\theta$ mentioned above (for a suitable value of θ), together with the 2-qubit CNOT gate *WCNOT*. However, the universality theorem for the quantum case is somewhat weaker than the one for the classical case; it asserts only that any reversible n-qubit circuit can be *approximated* arbitrarily well by circuits assembled from these two elementary gates. Note that there are uncountably many possible single qubit phase gates, one for every possible angle θ, so they cannot all be represented by a finite circuit constructed from $\{U\theta,\ WCNOT)\}$.

17.4 Quantum computations

So far we have not shown how quantum circuits are used to perform computations. Since many important numerical problems reduce to computing a unitary transformation U on a finite-dimensional space (the celebrated discrete Fourier transform being a prime example), one might expect that some quantum circuit could be designed to carry out the transformation U. In principle, one needs only to prepare an n qubit state ψ as an appropriate superposition of computational basis states for the input and measure the output $U\psi$. Unfortunately, there are two problems with this:

- One cannot measure the phase of ψ at any computational basis state so there is no way of reading out the complete answer. This is in the nature of measurement in quantum mechanics.
- There is no way to efficiently prepare the input state ψ.

This does not prevent quantum circuits for the discrete Fourier transform from being used as intermediate steps in other quantum circuits, but the use is more subtle. In fact quantum computations are *probabilistic.*

We now provide a mathematical model for how quantum circuits can simulate *probabilistic* but classical computations. Consider an r-qubit circuit U with register space $H\mathrm{QB}(r)$. U is thus a unitary map

$$H_{\mathrm{QB}(r)} \to H_{\mathrm{QB}(r)}.$$

In order to associate this circuit to a classical mapping on bitstrings, we specify

- An *input register* $X = \{0,1\}^m$ of m (classical) bits.
- An *output register* $Y = \{0,1\}^n$ of n (classical) bits.

The contents $x = x_1, \ldots, xm$ of the classical input register are used to initialize the qubit register in some way. Ideally, this would be done with the computational basis state

$$|\vec{x},0\rangle = |x_1, x_2, \cdots, x_m, \underbrace{0,\ldots,0}\rangle,$$

where there are r-m underbraced zeroed inputs. Nevertheless, this perfect initialization is completely unrealistic. Let us assume therefore that the initialization is a mixed state given by some density operator S which is near the idealized input in some appropriate metric, e.g.

$$\mathrm{Tr}\left(\big||\vec{x},0\rangle\langle\vec{x},0| - S\big|\right) \leq \delta.$$

Similarly, the output register space is related to the qubit register, by a Y valued observable A. Note that observables in quantum mechanics are usually defined in terms of *projection valued measures* on **R**; if the variable happens to be discrete, the projection valued measure reduces to a family $\{E\lambda\}$ indexed on some parameter λ ranging over a countable set. Similarly, a Y valued observable, can be associated with a family of pairwise orthogonal projections $\{Ey\}$ indexed by elements of Y. such that

$$I = \sum_{y\in Y} \mathrm{E}_y\,.$$

Given a mixed state S, there corresponds a probability measure on Y given by

$$\Pr\{y\} = \mathrm{Tr}(S\,\mathrm{E}_y).$$

The function $F{:}X \to Y$ is computed by a circuit $U{:}H\mathrm{QB}(r) \to H\mathrm{QB}(r)$ to within ε if and only if for all bitstrings x of length m

$$\big\langle\vec{x},0\big|U^*\,\mathrm{E}_{F(x)}\,U\big|\vec{x},0\big\rangle = \big\langle\mathrm{E}_{F(x)}\; U(|\vec{x},0\rangle)\big|U(|\vec{x},0\rangle)\big\rangle \geq 1-\epsilon.$$

Now

$$\big|\mathrm{Tr}(SU^*\,\mathrm{E}_{F(x)}\,U) - \big\langle\vec{x},0\big|U^*\,\mathrm{E}_{F(x)}\,U\big|\vec{x},0\big\rangle\big| \leq \mathrm{Tr}(\big||\vec{x},0\rangle\langle\vec{x},0| - S\big|)\|U^*\,\mathrm{E}_{F(x)}$$

so that

$$\mathrm{Tr}(SU^*\,\mathrm{E}_{F(x)}\,U) \geq 1-\epsilon-\delta.$$

Theorem. If $\varepsilon + \delta < 1/2$, then the probability distribution

$$\Pr\{y\} = \mathrm{Tr}(SU^*\,\mathrm{E}_y\,U)$$

on Y can be used to determine $F(x)$ with an arbitrarily small probability of error by majority sampling, for a sufficiently large sample size. Specifically, take k independent samples from the probability distribution Pr on Y

and choose a value on which more than half of the samples agree. The probability that the value $F(x)$ is sampled more than $k/2$ times is at least

$$1 - e^{-2\gamma^2 k},$$

where $\gamma = 1/2 - \varepsilon - \delta$.

This follows by applying the Chernoff bound.

17.5 References

- Biham, Eli; Brassard, Gilles; Kenigsberg, Dan; Mor, Tal (2004), "Quantum computing without entanglement", *Theoretical Computer Science* **320** (1): 15–33, arXiv:quant-ph/0306182, doi:10.1016/j.tcs.2004.03.041, MR 2060181.
- Freedman, Michael H.; Kitaev, Alexei; Larsen, Michael J.; Wang, Zhenghan (2003), "Topological quantum computation", *Bulletin of the American Mathematical Society* **40** (1): 31–38, arXiv:quant-ph/0101025, doi:10.1090/S0273-0979-02-00964-3, MR 1943131.
- Hirvensalo, Mika (2001), *Quantum Computing*, Natural Computing Series, Berlin: Springer-Verlag, ISBN 3-540-66783-0, MR 1931238.
- Kitaev, A. Yu. (1997), "Quantum computations: algorithms and error correction", *Uspekhi Mat. Nauk* (in Russian) **52** (6(318)): 53–112, Bibcode:1997RuMaS..52.1191K, doi:10.1070/RM1997v052n06ABEH002155, MR 1611329.
- Nielsen, Michael A.; Chuang, Isaac L. (2000), *Quantum Computation and Quantum Information*, Cambridge: Cambridge University Press, ISBN 0-521-63235-8, MR 1796805.

17.6 External links

- Q-circuit is a macro package for drawing quantum circuit diagrams in LaTeX.
- Quantum Circuit Simulator a browser-based quantum circuit diagram editor and simulator.

Chapter 18

Quantum clock

A **quantum clock** is a type of atomic clock with laser cooled single ions confined together in an electromagnetic ion trap. Developed by National Institute of Standards and Technology physicists, the clock is 37 times more precise than the than existing international standard.[1] The quantum logic clock is based on an aluminium spectroscopy ion with a logic atom.

Both the aluminium-based quantum clock and the mercury-based optical atomic clock track time by the ion vibration at an optical frequency using a UV laser, that is 100,000 times higher than the microwave frequencies used in NIST-F1 and other similar time standards around the world. Quantum clocks like this are able to be far more precise than microwave standards.

18.1 Accuracy

The NIST team are not able to measure clock ticks per second because the definition of a second is based on the NIST-F1 which cannot measure a more precise machine. However the aluminium ion clock's measured frequency to the current standard is 1121015393207857.4(7)Hz.[2] NIST have attributed the clock's accuracy to the fact that it is insensitive to background magnetic and electric fields, and unaffected by temperature.[3]

In March 2008, physicists at NIST described an experimental quantum logic clock based on individual ions of beryllium and aluminium. This clock was compared to NIST's mercury ion clock. These were the most accurate clocks that had been constructed, with neither clock gaining nor losing time at a rate that would exceed a second in over a billion years.[4]

In February 2010, NIST physicists described a second, enhanced version of the quantum logic clock based on individual ions of magnesium and aluminium. Considered the world's most precise clock in 2010 with a fractional frequency inaccuracy of 8.6×10^{-18}, it offers more than twice the precision of the original.[5] [6] In terms of standard deviation, the quantum logic clock deviates one second every 3.68 billion (3.68×10^{9}) years, while the then current international standard NIST-F1 caesium fountain atomic clock uncertainty was about 3.1×10^{-16} expected to neither gain nor lose a second in more than 100 million (100×10^{6}) years.[7] [8]

18.2 Gravitational time dilation in everyday lab scale

In 2010 an experiment placed two aluminium-ion quantum clocks close to each other, but with the second elevated 12 in (30.5 cm) compared to the first, making the gravitational time dilation effect visible in everyday lab scales.[9]

18.3 More accurate experimental clocks

The accuracy of quantum clocks has since been superseded by optical lattice clocks based on strontium-87 and ytterbium-171. An experimental optical lattice clock was described in a 2014 Nature paper.[10] In 2015 JILA evaluated the absolute frequency uncertainty of their latest strontium-87 optical lattice clock at 2.1×10^{-18}, which corresponds to a measurable gravitational time dilation for an elevation change of 2 cm (0.79 in) on planet Earth that according to JILA/NIST Fellow Jun Ye is "getting really close to being useful for relativistic geodesy".[11][12][13] At this frequency uncertainty, this JILA optical lattice optical clock is expected to neither gain nor lose a second in more than 15 billion (15×10^{9}) years.[14]

18.4 See also

- Atomic clock

18.5 References

[1] Ghose, Tia (5 February 2010). "Ultra-Precise Quantum-Logic Clock Puts Old Atomic Clock to Shame". *Wired*. Retrieved 2010-02-07.

[2] "Frequency Ratio of Al+ and Hg+ Single-ion Optical Clocks; Metrology at the 17th Decimal Place" (pdf). sciencemag.org. 28 March 2008. Retrieved 2013-07-31.

[3] "Quantum Clock Proves to be as Accurate as World's Most Accurate Clock". azonano.com. 7 March 2008. Retrieved 2012-11-06.

[4] "NIST 'Quantum Logic Clock' Rivals Mercury Ion as World's Most Accurate Clock" (PDF). *PhysOrg.com*. 6 March 2008. Retrieved 24 October 2009.

[5] NIST's Second 'Quantum Logic Clock' Based on Aluminum Ion is Now World's Most Precise Clock, NIST, 4 February 2010

[6] C.W Chou, D. Hume, J.C.J. Koelemeij, D.J. Wineland, and T. Rosenband (17 February 2010). "Frequency Comparison of Two High-Accuracy Al+ Optical Clocks" (PDF). *NIST*. Retrieved 9 February 2011.

[7] "NIST's Second 'Quantum Logic Clock' Based on Aluminum Ion is Now World's Most Precise Clock" (Press release). National Institute of Standards and Technology. 4 February 2010. Retrieved 2012-11-04.

[8] "NIST-F1 Cesium Fountain Atomic Clock: The Primary Time and Frequency Standard for the United States". NIST. August 26, 2009. Retrieved 2 May 2011.

[9] "Einstein's time dilation apparent when obeying the speed limit" (Press release). Ars Technica. 24 September 2010. Retrieved 2015-04-10.

[10] Bloom, B. J.; Nicholson, T. L.; Williams, J. R.; Campbell, S. L.; Bishof, M.; Zhang, X.; Zhang, W.; Bromley, S. L.; Ye, J. (22 January 2014). "An optical lattice clock with accuracy and stability at the 10–18 level". *Nature* **506** (7486): 71–5. arXiv:1309.1137. Bibcode:2014Natur.506...71B. doi:10.1038/nature12941. PMID 24463513.

[11] T.L. Nicholson, S.L. Campbell, R.B. Hutson, G.E. Marti, B.J. Bloom, R.L. McNally, W. Zhang, M.D. Barrett, M.S. Safronova, G.F. Strouse, W.L. Tew, J. Ye (21 April 2015). "Systematic evaluation of an atomic clock at 2×10^{-18} total uncertainty". *Nature Communications 6, Article number:6896, 21 April 2015*. doi:10.1038/ncomms7896. Retrieved 24 June 2015.

[12] JILA Scientific Communications (21 April 2015). "About Time". *http://jila.colorado.edu*. Retrieved 27 June 2015. External link in |work= (help)

[13] Laura Ost (21 April 2015). "Getting Better All the Time: JILA Strontium Atomic Clock Sets New Record". *National Institute of Standards and Technology*. Retrieved 17 October 2015.

[14] James Vincent (22 April 2015). "The most accurate clock ever built only loses one second every 15 billion years". *The Verge*. Retrieved 26 June 2015.

Chapter 19

Quantum gate

In quantum computing and specifically the quantum circuit model of computation, a **quantum gate** (or **quantum logic gate**) is a basic quantum circuit operating on a small number of qubits. They are the building blocks of quantum circuits, like classical logic gates are for conventional digital circuits.

Unlike many classical logic gates, quantum logic gates are reversible. However, it is possible to perform classical computing using only reversible gates. For example, the reversible Toffoli gate can implement all Boolean functions. This gate has a direct quantum equivalent, showing that quantum circuits can perform all operations performed by classical circuits.

Quantum logic gates are represented by unitary matrices. The most common quantum gates operate on spaces of one or two qubits, just like the common classical logic gates operate on one or two bits. This means that as matrices, quantum gates can be described by *2 × 2* or *4 × 4* unitary matrices.

19.1 Commonly used gates

Quantum gates are usually represented as matrices. A gate which acts on k qubits is represented by a 2^k x 2^k unitary matrix. The number of qubits in the input and output of the gate have to be equal. The action of the quantum gate is found by multiplying the matrix representing the gate with the vector which represents the quantum state. In the following, the vector representation of a single qubit is:

$$v_0|0\rangle + v_1|1\rangle \rightarrow \begin{bmatrix} v_0 \\ v_1 \end{bmatrix}$$

and the vector representation of two qubits is:

$$v_{00}|00\rangle + v_{01}|01\rangle + v_{10}|10\rangle + v_{11}|11\rangle \rightarrow \begin{bmatrix} v_{00} \\ v_{01} \\ v_{10} \\ v_{11} \end{bmatrix}$$

where $|ab\rangle$ is the state where the first qubit has value a and the second qubit b.

19.1.1 Hadamard gate

Further information: Hadamard_transform § Quantum_computing_applications

The Hadamard gate acts on a single qubit. It maps the basis state $|0\rangle$ to $\frac{|0\rangle+|1\rangle}{\sqrt{2}}$ and $|1\rangle$ to $\frac{|0\rangle-|1\rangle}{\sqrt{2}}$ and represents a rotation of π about the axis $(\hat{x}+\hat{z})/\sqrt{2}$. Equivalently, it is the combination of two rotations, $\pi/2$ about the Y-axis followed by π about the X-axis. It is represented by the Hadamard matrix:

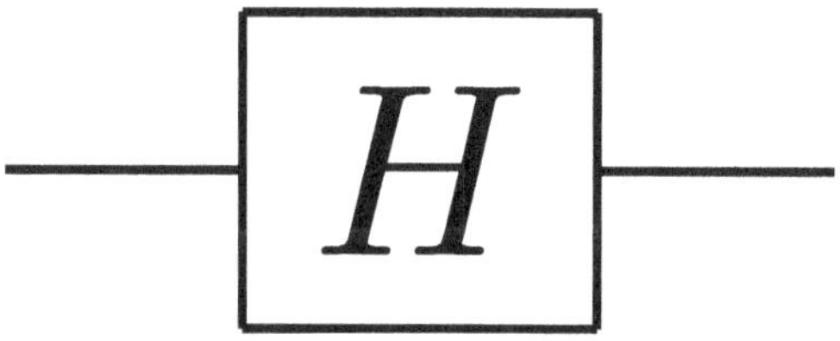

Circuit representation of Hadamard gate

$$H = \frac{1}{\sqrt{2}} \begin{bmatrix} 1 & 1 \\ 1 & -1 \end{bmatrix}$$

Since $HH^* = I$ where *I* is the identity matrix, *H* is indeed a unitary matrix.

19.1.2 Pauli-X gate

The Pauli-X gate acts on a single qubit. It is the quantum equivalent of a NOT gate (with respect to the standard basis $|0\rangle$, $|1\rangle$, which privileges the Z-direction) . It equates to a rotation of the Bloch Sphere around the X-axis by π radians. It maps $|0\rangle$ to $|1\rangle$ and $|1\rangle$ to $|0\rangle$. Due to this nature, it is sometimes called bit-flip. It is represented by the Pauli matrix:

$$X = \begin{bmatrix} 0 & 1 \\ 1 & 0 \end{bmatrix}$$

19.1.3 Pauli-Y gate

The Pauli-Y gate acts on a single qubit. It equates to a rotation around the Y-axis of the Bloch Sphere by π radians. It maps $|0\rangle$ to $i|1\rangle$ and $|1\rangle$ to $-i|0\rangle$. It is represented by the Pauli Y matrix:

$$Y = \begin{bmatrix} 0 & -i \\ i & 0 \end{bmatrix}$$

19.1.4 Pauli-Z gate

The Pauli-Z gate acts on a single qubit. It equates to a rotation around the Z-axis of the Bloch Sphere by π radians. Thus, it is a special case of a phase shift gate (next) with θ=π. It leaves the basis state $|0\rangle$ unchanged and maps $|1\rangle$ to $-|1\rangle$. Due to this nature, it is sometimes called phase-flip. It is represented by the Pauli Z matrix:

$$Z = \begin{bmatrix} 1 & 0 \\ 0 & -1 \end{bmatrix}$$

19.1.5 Phase shift gates

This is a family of single-qubit gates that leave the basis state $|0\rangle$ unchanged and map $|1\rangle$ to $e^{i\phi}|1\rangle$. The probability of measuring a $|0\rangle$ or $|1\rangle$ is unchanged after applying this gate, however it modifies the phase of the quantum state. This is equivalent to tracing a horizontal circle (a line of latitude) on the Bloch Sphere by ϕ radians.

$$R_\phi = \begin{bmatrix} 1 & 0 \\ 0 & e^{i\phi} \end{bmatrix}$$

where ϕ is the *phase shift*. Some common examples are the $\frac{\pi}{8}$ gate where $\phi = \frac{\pi}{4}$, the phase gate where $\phi = \frac{\pi}{2}$ and the Pauli-Z gate where $\phi = \pi$.

19.1.6 Swap gate

The swap gate swaps two qubits. With respect to the basis $|00\rangle$, $|01\rangle$, $|10\rangle$, $|11\rangle$, it is represented by the matrix:

$$\text{SWAP} = \begin{bmatrix} 1 & 0 & 0 & 0 \\ 0 & 0 & 1 & 0 \\ 0 & 1 & 0 & 0 \\ 0 & 0 & 0 & 1 \end{bmatrix}$$

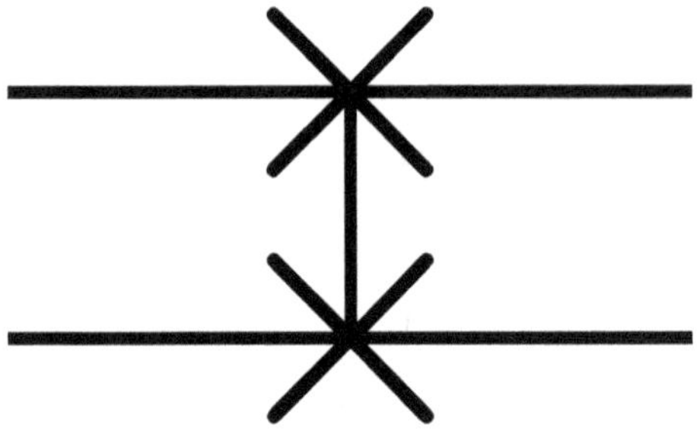

Circuit representation of SWAP gate

19.1.7 Square root of Swap gate

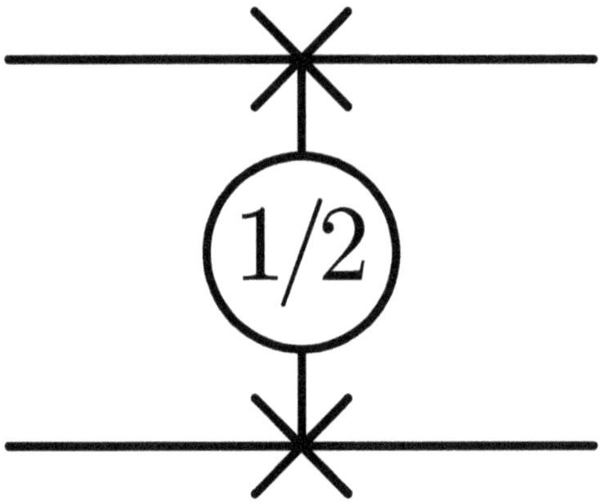

Circuit representation of $\sqrt{SWAP}$ gate

The sqrt(swap) gate performs half-way of a two-qubit swap. It is universal such that any quantum many qubit gate can be constructed from only sqrt(swap) and single qubit gates.

$$\sqrt{\text{SWAP}} = \begin{bmatrix} 1 & 0 & 0 & 0 \\ 0 & \frac{1}{2}(1+i) & \frac{1}{2}(1-i) & 0 \\ 0 & \frac{1}{2}(1-i) & \frac{1}{2}(1+i) & 0 \\ 0 & 0 & 0 & 1 \end{bmatrix}$$

19.1.8 Controlled gates

Controlled gates act on 2 or more qubits, where one or more qubits act as a control for some operation. For example, the controlled NOT gate (or CNOT) acts on 2 qubits, and performs the NOT operation on the second qubit only when the first qubit is $|1\rangle$, and otherwise leaves it unchanged. It is represented by the matrix

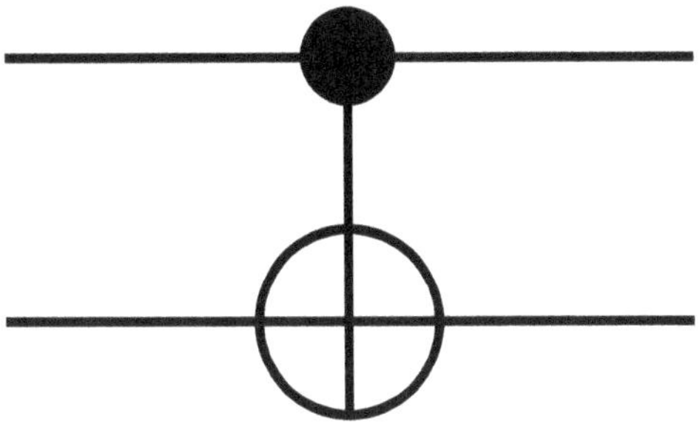

Circuit representation of controlled NOT gate

$$\text{CNOT} = \begin{bmatrix} 1 & 0 & 0 & 0 \\ 0 & 1 & 0 & 0 \\ 0 & 0 & 0 & 1 \\ 0 & 0 & 1 & 0 \end{bmatrix}$$

More generally if U is a gate that operates on single qubits with matrix representation

$$U = \begin{bmatrix} x_{00} & x_{01} \\ x_{10} & x_{11} \end{bmatrix}$$

then the *controlled-U gate* is a gate that operates on two qubits in such a way that the first qubit serves as a control. It maps the basis states as follows.

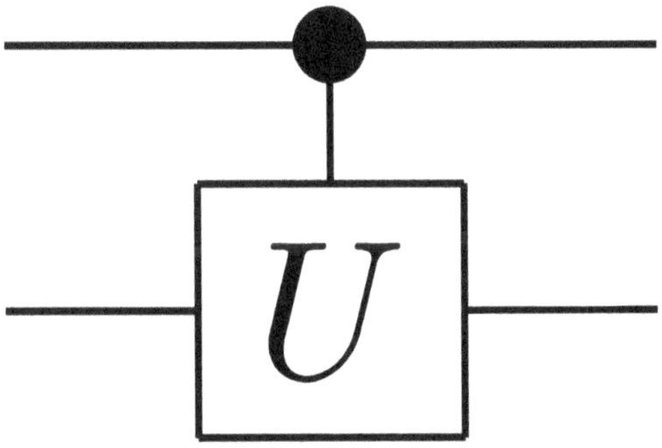

*Circuit representation of controlled-*U *gate*

$$|00\rangle \mapsto |00\rangle$$

$$|01\rangle \mapsto |01\rangle$$

$$|10\rangle \mapsto |1\rangle U|0\rangle = |1\rangle \left(x_{00}|0\rangle + x_{10}|1\rangle\right)$$

$$|11\rangle \mapsto |1\rangle U|1\rangle = |1\rangle \left(x_{01}|0\rangle + x_{11}|1\rangle\right)$$

The matrix representing the controlled U is

$$\text{C}(U) = \begin{bmatrix} 1 & 0 & 0 & 0 \\ 0 & 1 & 0 & 0 \\ 0 & 0 & x_{00} & x_{01} \\ 0 & 0 & x_{10} & x_{11} \end{bmatrix}$$

controlled X-, Y- and Z- gates

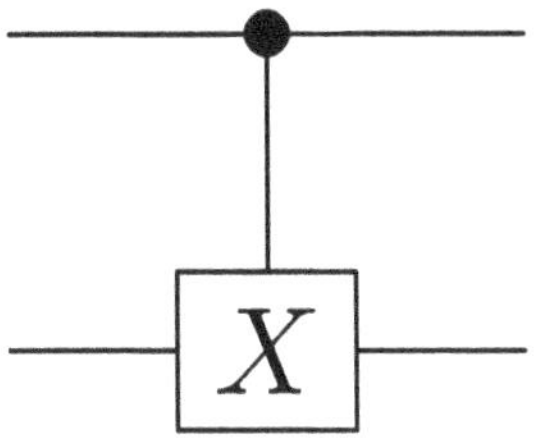

controlled-X gate

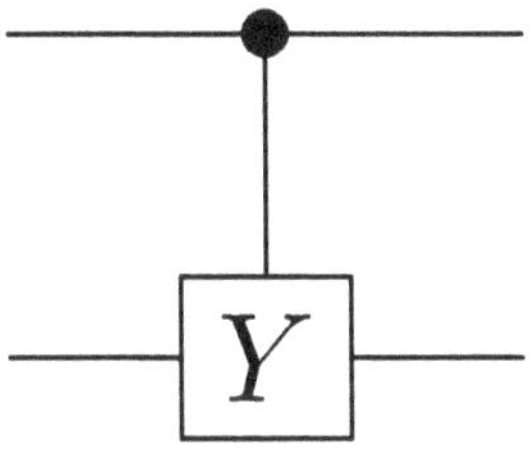

controlled-Y gate

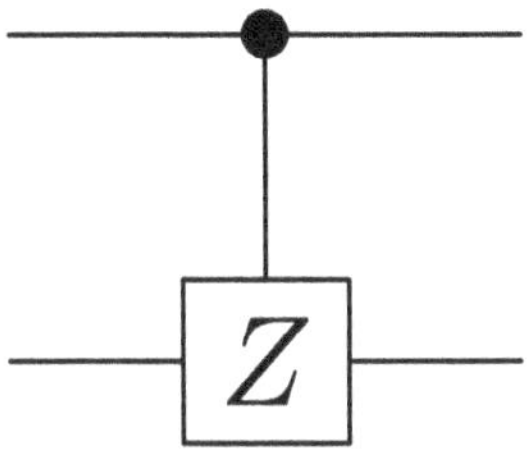

controlled-Z gate

When U is one of the Pauli matrices, σ_x, σ_y, or σ_z, the respective terms "controlled-*X*", "controlled-*Y*", or "controlled-*Z*" are sometimes used.[1]

19.1.9 Toffoli gate

Main article: Toffoli gate

The Toffoli gate, also CCNOT gate, is a 3-bit gate, which

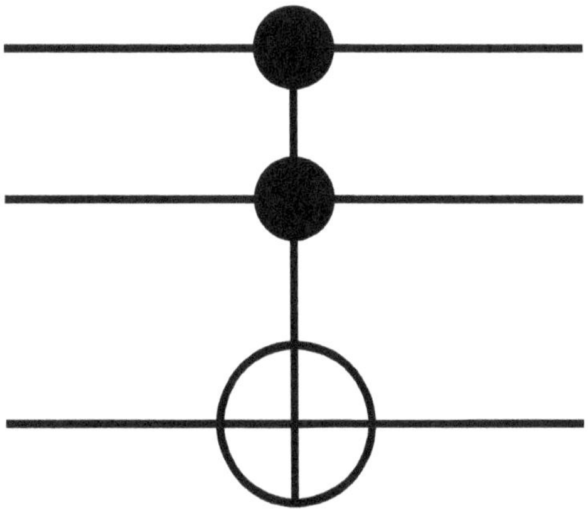

Circuit representation of Toffoli gate

is universal for classical computation. The quantum Toffoli gate is the same gate, defined for 3 qubits. If the first two bits are in the state $|1\rangle$, it applies a Pauli-X on the third bit, else it does nothing. It is an example of a controlled gate. Since it is the quantum analog of a classical gate, it is completely specified by its truth table.

It can be also described as the gate which maps $|a, b, c\rangle$ to $|a, b, c \oplus ab\rangle$.

19.1.10 Fredkin gate

Main article: Fredkin gate
The Fredkin gate (also CSWAP gate) is a 3-bit gate that

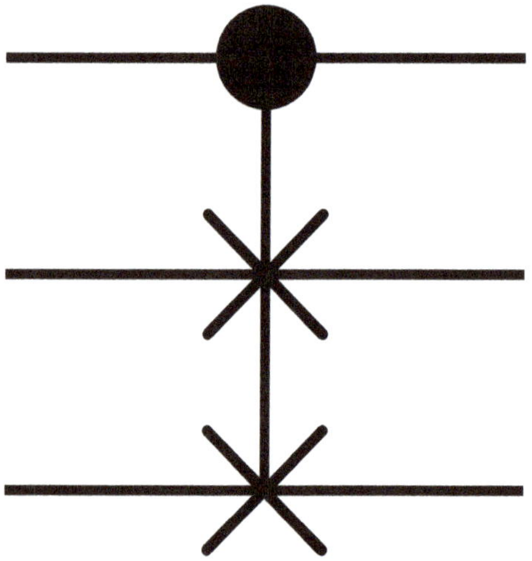

Circuit representation of Fredkin gate

performs a controlled swap. It is universal for classical computation. As with the Toffoli gate it has the useful property that the numbers of 0s and 1s are conserved throughout, which in the billiard ball model means the same number of balls are output as input.

19.2 Universal quantum gates

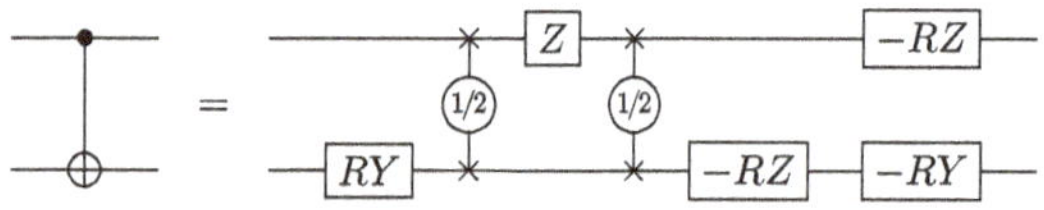

Both CNOT and $\sqrt{SWAP}$ are universal two-qubit gates and can be transformed into each other.

Informally, a set of **universal quantum gates** is any set of gates to which any operation possible on a quantum computer can be reduced, that is, any other unitary operation can be expressed as a finite sequence of gates from the set. Technically, this is impossible since the number of possible quantum gates is uncountable, whereas the number of finite sequences from a finite set is countable. To solve this problem, we only require that any quantum operation can be approximated by a sequence of gates from this finite set. Moreover, for the specific case of single qubit unitaries the Solovay–Kitaev theorem guarantees that this can be done efficiently.

One simple set of two-qubit universal quantum gates is the Hadamard gate (H), the $\pi/8$ gate $R(\pi/4)$, and the controlled NOT gate.

A single-gate set of universal quantum gates can also be formulated using the three-qubit Deutsch gate $D(\theta)$, which performs the transformation[2]

$$|a, b, c\rangle \mapsto \begin{cases} i\cos(\theta)|a, b, c\rangle + \sin(\theta)|a, b, 1-c\rangle & \text{for } a = b = 1 \\ |a, b, c\rangle & \text{otherwise.} \end{cases}$$

The universal classical logic gate, the Toffoli gate, is reducible to the Deutsch gate, $D(\frac{\pi}{2})$, thus showing that all classical logic operations can be performed on a universal quantum computer.

19.3 History

The current notation for quantum gates was developed by Barenco *et al.*,[3] building on notation introduced by Feynman.[4]

19.4 See also

- Pauli matrices

19.5 Notes

[1] M. Nielsen and I. Chuang, *Quantum Computation and Quantum Information*, Cambridge University Press, 2000

[2] Deutsch, David (September 8, 1989), "Quantum computational networks" (PDF), *Proc. R. Soc. Lond. A* **425** (1968): 73–90, Bibcode:1989RSPSA.425...73D, doi:10.1098/rspa.1989.0099

[3] Phys. Rev. A **52** 3457–3467 (1995), DOI:10.1103/PhysRevA.52.3457; e-print arXiv: quant-ph/9503016

[4] R. P. Feynman, "Quantum mechanical computers", Optics News, February 1985, **11**, p. 11; reprinted in Foundations of Physics **16**(6) 507–531

19.6 References

- M. Nielsen and I. Chuang, *Quantum Computation and Quantum Information*, Cambridge University Press, 2000

Chapter 20

Quantum entanglement

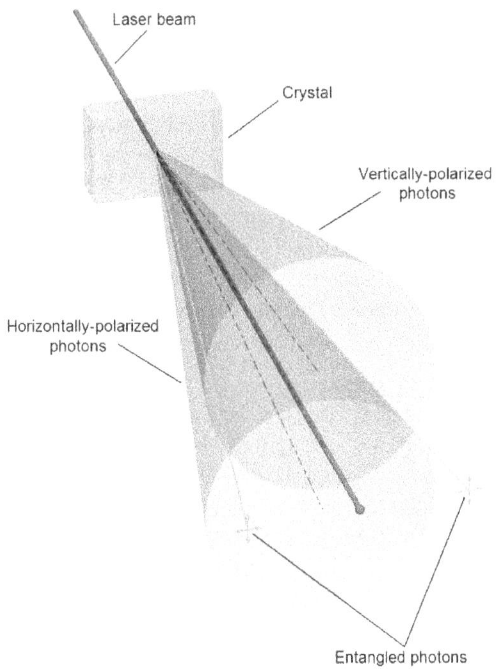

Spontaneous parametric down-conversion process can split photons into type II photon pairs with mutually perpendicular polarization.

Quantum entanglement is a physical phenomenon that occurs when pairs or groups of particles are generated or interact in ways such that the quantum state of each particle cannot be described independently — instead, a quantum state must be described for the system as a whole.

Measurements of physical properties such as position, momentum, spin, polarization, etc., performed on entangled particles are found to be appropriately correlated. For example, if a pair of particles are generated in such a way that their total spin is known to be zero, and one particle is found to have clockwise spin on a certain axis, then the spin of the other particle, measured on the same axis, will be found to be counterclockwise, as to be expected due to their entanglement. However, this behavior gives rise to paradoxical effects: any measurement of a property of a particle can be seen as acting on that particle (e.g., by collapsing a number of superposed states) and will change the original quantum property by some unknown amount; and in the case of entangled particles, such a measurement will be on the entangled system as a whole. It thus appears that one particle of an entangled pair "knows" what measurement has been performed on the other, and with what outcome, even though there is no known means for such information to be communicated between the particles, which at the time of measurement may be separated by arbitrarily large distances.

Such phenomena were the subject of a 1935 paper by Albert Einstein, Boris Podolsky, and Nathan Rosen,[1] and several papers by Erwin Schrödinger shortly thereafter,[2][3] describing what came to be known as the EPR paradox. Einstein and others considered such behavior to be impossible, as it violated the local realist view of causality (Einstein referring to it as "spooky action at a distance")[4] and argued that the accepted formulation of quantum mechanics must therefore be incomplete. Later, however, the counterintuitive predictions of quantum mechanics were verified experimentally.[5] Experiments have been performed involving measuring the polarization or spin of entangled particles in different directions, which — by producing violations of Bell's inequality — demonstrate statistically that the local realist view cannot be correct. This has been shown to occur even when the measurements are performed more quickly than light could travel between the sites of measurement: there is no lightspeed or slower influence that can pass between the entangled particles.[6] Recent experiments have measured entangled particles within less than one one-hundredth of a percent of the travel time of light between them.[7] According to the formalism of quantum theory, the effect of measurement happens instantly.[8][9] It is not possible, however, to use this effect to transmit classical information at faster-than-light speeds[10] (see Faster-than-light § Quantum mechanics).

Quantum entanglement is an area of extremely active research by the physics community, and its effects have been demonstrated experimentally with photons,[11][12][13][14] electrons, molecules the size of buckyballs,[15][16] and even small diamonds.[17][18][19][20] Research is also focused on the utilization of entanglement effects in communication and computation.

20.1 History

EINSTEIN ATTACKS QUANTUM THEORY

Scientist and Two Colleagues Find It Is Not 'Complete' Even Though 'Correct.'

SEE FULLER ONE POSSIBLE

Believe a Whole Description of 'the Physical Reality' Can Be Provided Eventually.

May 4, 1935 New York Times *article headline regarding the imminent EPR paper*

The counterintuitive predictions of quantum mechanics about strongly correlated systems were first discussed by Albert Einstein in 1935, in a joint paper with Boris Podolsky and Nathan Rosen.[1] In this study, they formulated the EPR paradox (Einstein, Podolsky, Rosen paradox), a thought experiment that attempted to show that quantum mechanical theory was incomplete. They wrote: "We are thus forced to conclude that the quantum-mechanical description of physical reality given by wave functions is not complete."[1]

However, they did not coin the word *entanglement*, nor did they generalize the special properties of the state they considered. Following the EPR paper, Erwin Schrödinger wrote a letter (in German) to Einstein in which he used the word *Verschränkung* (translated by himself as *entanglement*) "to describe the correlations between two particles that interact and then separate, as in the EPR experiment."[21] He shortly thereafter published a seminal paper defining and discussing the notion, and terming it "entanglement." In the paper he recognized the importance of the concept, and stated:[2] "I would not call [entanglement] *one* but rather *the* characteristic trait of quantum mechanics, the one that enforces its entire departure from classical lines of thought."

Like Einstein, Schrödinger was dissatisfied with the concept of entanglement, because it seemed to violate the speed limit on the transmission of information implicit in the theory of relativity.[22] Einstein later famously derided entanglement as "*spukhafte Fernwirkung*"[23] or "spooky action at a distance."

The EPR paper generated significant interest among physicists and inspired much discussion about the foundations of quantum mechanics (perhaps most famously Bohm's interpretation of quantum mechanics), but produced relatively little other published work. So, despite the interest, the weak point in EPR's argument was not discovered until 1964, when John Stewart Bell proved that one of their key assumptions, the principle of locality, which underlies the kind of hidden variables interpretation hoped for by EPR, was mathematically inconsistent with the predictions of quantum theory. Specifically, he demonstrated an upper limit, seen in Bell's inequality, regarding the strength of correlations that can be produced in any theory obeying local realism, and he showed that quantum theory predicts violations of this limit for certain entangled systems.[24] His inequality is experimentally testable, and there have been numerous relevant experiments, starting with the pioneering work of Stuart Freedman and John Clauser in 1972[25] and Alain Aspect's experiments in 1982.[26] They have all shown agreement with quantum mechanics rather than the principle of local realism. However, the issue is not finally settled, as each of these experimental tests has left open at least one loophole by which it is possible to question the validity of the results.

The work of Bell raised the possibility of using these super-strong correlations as a resource for communication. It led to the discovery of quantum key distribution protocols, most famously BB84 by Charles H. Bennett and Gilles Brassard[27] and E91 by Artur Ekert.[28] Although BB84 does not use entanglement, Ekert's protocol uses the violation of a Bell's inequality as a proof of security.

20.2 Concept

20.2.1 Meaning of entanglement

An entangled system is defined to be one whose quantum state cannot be factored as a product of states of its local constituents, that is to say, they are not individual particles but are an inseparable whole. If entangled, one constituent cannot be fully described without considering the other(s). Note that the state of a composite system is always expressible as a *sum*, or superposition, of products of states of local constituents; it is entangled if this sum necessarily has more than one term.

Quantum systems can become entangled through various types of interactions. For some ways in which entanglement may be achieved for experimental purposes, see the section below on methods. Entanglement is broken when the entangled particles decohere through interaction with the environment; for example, when a measurement is made.[29]

As an example of entanglement: a subatomic particle

decays into an entangled pair of other particles. The decay events obey the various conservation laws, and as a result, the measurement outcomes of one daughter particle must be highly correlated with the measurement outcomes of the other daughter particle (so that the total momenta, angular momenta, energy, and so forth remains roughly the same before and after this process). For instance, a spin-zero particle could decay into a pair of spin-½ particles. Since the total spin before and after this decay must be zero (conservation of angular momentum), whenever the first particle is measured to be spin up on some axis, the other, when measured on the same axis, is always found to be spin down. (This is called the *spin anti-correlated* case; and if the prior probabilities for measuring each spin are equal, the pair is said to be in the singlet state.)

The special property of entanglement can be better observed if we separate the said two particles. Let's put one of them in the White House in Washington and the other in UC Berkeley (think about this as a thought experiment, not an actual one). Now, if we measure a particular characteristic of one of these particles (say, for example, spin), get a result, and then measure the other particle using the same criterion (spin along the same axis), we find that the result of the measurement of the second particle will match (in a complementary sense) the result of the measurement of the first particle, in that they will be opposite in their values.

The above result may or may not be perceived as surprising. A classical system would display the same property, and a hidden variable theory (see below) would certainly be *required* to do so, based on conservation of angular momentum in classical and quantum mechanics alike. The difference is that a classical system has definite values for all the observables all along while the quantum system does not. In a sense to be discussed below, the quantum system considered here seems to *acquire* a probability distribution for the outcome of a measurement of the spin along *any* axis of the *other* particle upon measurement of the *first* particle. This probability distribution is in general *different* from what it would be *without* measurement of the first particle. This may certainly be perceived as surprising in the case of spatially separated entangled particles.

20.2.2 Paradox

The paradox is that a measurement made on either of the particles apparently collapses the state of the entire entangled system — and does so instantaneously, before any information about the measurement result could have been communicated to the other particle (assuming that information cannot travel faster than light) and hence assured the "proper" outcome of the measurement of the other part of the entangled pair. In the quantum formalism, the result of a spin measurement on one of the particles is a collapse into a state in which each particle has a definite spin (either up or down) along the axis of measurement. The outcome is taken to be random, with each possibility having a probability of 50%. However, if both spins are measured along the same axis, they are found to be anti-correlated. This means that the random outcome of the measurement made on one particle seems to have been transmitted to the other, so that it can make the "right choice" when it too is measured.

The distance and timing of the measurements can be chosen so as to make the interval between the two measurements spacelike, hence, a message connecting the events would have to travel faster than light. According to the principles of special relativity, it is not possible for any information to travel between two such measuring events. It is not even possible to unambiguously say which of the measurements came first. For two spacelike separated events x_1 and x_2 there are inertial systems in which x_1 is first and others in which x_2 is first. Therefore, the correlation between the two measurements cannot appropriately be explained as one measurement determining the other. Different observers would disagree about the role of cause and effect.

In conclusion, the result shows that it is quite impossible for the measurement of one particle's properties to determine the other's properties, even though it seems that way at first, as the speed of light is the universal speed limit, and nothing can travel faster than that speed.

20.2.3 Hidden variables theory

A possible resolution to the paradox might be to assume that the state of the particles contains some hidden variables, whose values effectively determine, right from the moment of separation, what the outcomes of the spin measurements are going to be. This would mean that each particle carries all the required information with it, and nothing needs to be transmitted from one particle to the other at the time of measurement. It was originally believed by Einstein and others (see the previous section) that this was the only way out of the paradox, and therefore that the accepted quantum mechanical description (with a random measurement outcome) must be incomplete. (In fact similar paradoxes can arise even without entanglement: the position of a single particle is spread out over space, and two widely separated detectors attempting to detect the particle in two different places must instantaneously attain appropriate correlation, so that they do not *both* detect the particle.)

20.2.4 Violations of Bell's inequality

The hidden variables theory fails, however, when we consider measurements of the spin of entangled particles along different axes (for example, along any of three axes which make angles of 120 degrees). If a large number of pairs of such measurements are made (on a large number of pairs of entangled particles), then statistically, if the local realist or hidden variables view were correct, the results would always satisfy Bell's inequality. A number of experiments have shown in practice that Bell's inequality is not satisfied. However, all experiments have loophole problems.[30][31] When measurements of the entangled particles are made in moving relativistic reference frames, in which each measurement (in its own relativistic time frame) occurs before the other, the measurement results remain correlated.[32][33]

The fundamental issue about measuring spin along different axes is that these measurements cannot have definite values at the same time—they are incompatible in the sense that these measurements' maximum simultaneous precision is constrained by the uncertainty principle. This is contrary to what is found in classical physics, where any number of properties can be measured simultaneously with arbitrary accuracy. It has been proven mathematically that compatible measurements cannot show Bell-inequality-violating correlations,[34] and thus entanglement is a fundamentally non-classical phenomenon.

20.2.5 Other types of experiments

In a 2012 experiment, "delayed-choice entanglement swapping" was used to decide whether two particles were entangled or not after they had been measured.[35]

In a 2013 experiment, entanglement swapping has been used to create entanglement of photons that never coexisted in time, thus demonstrating that "the nonlocality of quantum mechanics, as manifested by entanglement, does not apply only to particles with spacelike separation, but also to particles with timelike [i.e., temporal] separation".[36] What this means is that two particles can be entangled even if they are distanced from each other in time. Two entangled particles will thus show the property of entanglement even if they are measured in two different times.

In three independent experiments it was shown that classically-communicated separable quantum states can be used to carry entangled states.[37]

In August 2014, researcher Gabriela Barreto Lemos and team were able to "take pictures" of objects using photons that have not interacted with the subjects, but were entangled with photons that did interact with such objects. Lemos, from the University of Vienna, is confident that this new quantum imaging technique could find application where low light imaging is imperative, in fields like biological or medical imaging.[38]

20.2.6 Mystery of time

There are physicists who say that time is an emergent phenomenon that is a side effect of quantum entanglement.[39][40] In other words, time is an entanglement phenomenon, which places all equal clock readings (of correctly prepared clocks - or of any objects usable as clocks) into the same history. This was first understood by physicist Don Page and William Wootters in 1983.[41] The Wheeler–DeWitt equation that combines general relativity and quantum mechanics — by leaving out time altogether — was introduced in the 1960s and it was taken up again in 1983, when the theorists Don Page and William Wootters made a solution based on the quantum phenomenon of entanglement. Page and Wootters argued that entanglement can be used to measure time.[42]

In 2013, at the Istituto Nazionale di Ricerca Metrologica (INRIM) in Turin, Italy, researchers performed the first experimental test of Page and Wootters' ideas. Their result has been interpreted to confirm that time is an emergent phenomenon for internal observers but absent for external observers of the universe just as the Wheeler-DeWitt equation predicts.[42]

20.2.7 Source for the arrow of time

Physicist Seth Lloyd says that quantum uncertainty gives rise to *entanglement*, the putative source of the arrow of time. According to Lloyd; "The arrow of time is an arrow of increasing correlations."[43] The approach to entanglement would be from the perspective of the causal arrow of time, with the assumption that the cause of the measurement of one particle determines the effect of the result of the other particle's measurement.

20.3 Non-locality and hidden variables

There is much confusion about the meaning of entanglement, non-locality and hidden variables and how they relate to each other. As described above, entanglement is an experimentally verified and accepted property of nature, which has critical implications for the interpretations of quantum mechanics. Entanglement is also mathematically well-defined (see below). The question becomes, "How can one account for something that was at one point indefinite with regard to its spin (or whatever is in this case the subject of investigation) suddenly becoming definite in that regard even though no physical interaction with the second object occurred, and, if the two objects are sufficiently far separated, could not even have had the time needed for such an interaction to proceed from the first to the second object?"[44] The latter question involves the issue of locality, i.e. does the agent of change have to be in physical contact (at least via some intermediary such as a field force), for a change to occur in some other thing? The study of entanglement brings into sharp focus the dilemma between locality and the completeness or lack of completeness of quantum mechanics.

Bell's theorem and related results rule out a local realistic explanation for quantum mechanics (one which obeys the principle of locality while also ascribing definite values to quantum observables). However, in other interpretations, the experiments that demonstrate the apparent non-locality can also be described in local terms: If each distant observer regards the other as a quantum system, communication between the two must then be treated as a measurement process, and this communication is strictly local.[45] In particular, in the Many-worlds interpretation, the underlying description is fully local.[46] More generally, the question of locality in quantum physics is extraordinarily subtle and sometimes hinges on precisely how it is defined.

In the media and popular science, quantum non-locality is often portrayed as being equivalent to entanglement. While it is true that a bipartite quantum state must be entangled in order for it to produce non-local correlations, there exist entangled states that do not produce such correlations. A well-known example of this is the Werner state that is entangled for certain values of p_{sym} , but can always be described using local hidden variables.[47] In short, entanglement of a two-party state is necessary but not sufficient for that state to be non-local. Moreover, it was shown that, for arbitrary number of party, there exist states that are genuinely entangled but admits a fully local strategy. It is important to recognize that entanglement is more commonly viewed as an algebraic concept, noted for being a precedent to non-locality as well as to quantum teleportation and to superdense coding, whereas non-locality is defined according to experimental statistics and is much more involved with the foundations and interpretations of quantum mechanics.

20.4 Quantum mechanical framework

The following subsections are for those with a good working knowledge of the formal, mathematical description of quantum mechanics, including familiarity with the formalism and theoretical framework developed in the articles: bra–ket notation and mathematical formulation of quantum mechanics.

20.4.1 Pure states

Consider two noninteracting systems A and B, with respective Hilbert spaces HA and HB. The Hilbert space of the composite system is the tensor product

$$H_A \otimes H_B.$$

If the first system is in state $|\psi\rangle_A$ and the second in state $|\phi\rangle_B$, the state of the composite system is

$$|\psi\rangle_A \otimes |\phi\rangle_B.$$

States of the composite system which can be represented in this form are called *separable states*, or (in the simplest case) *product states*.

Not all states are separable states (and thus product states). Fix a basis $\{|i\rangle_A\}$ for HA and a basis $\{|j\rangle_B\}$ for HB. The most general state in *HA* ⊗ *HB* is of the form

$$|\psi\rangle_{AB} = \sum_{i,j} c_{ij}|i\rangle_A \otimes |j\rangle_B$$

This state is separable if there exist vectors $[c_i^A],[c_j^B]$ so that $c_{ij}=c_i^A c_j^B$, yielding $|\psi\rangle_A=\sum_i c_i^A|i\rangle_A$ and $|\phi\rangle_B=\sum_j c_j^B|j\rangle_B$. It is inseparable if for any vectors $[c_i^A],[c_j^B]$ at least for one pair of coordinates c_i^A,c_j^B we have $c_{ij}\neq c_i^A c_j^B$. If a state is inseparable, it is called an *entangled state*.

For example, given two basis vectors $\{|0\rangle_A,|1\rangle_A\}$ of HA and two basis vectors $\{|0\rangle_B,|1\rangle_B\}$ of HB, the following is an entangled state:

$$\tfrac{1}{\sqrt{2}}\left(|0\rangle_A \otimes |1\rangle_B - |1\rangle_A \otimes |0\rangle_B\right).$$

If the composite system is in this state, it is impossible to attribute to either system A or system B a definite pure state. Another way to say this is that while the von Neumann entropy of the whole state is zero (as it is for any pure state), the entropy of the subsystems is greater than zero. In this sense, the systems are “entangled”. This has specific empirical ramifications for interferometry.[48] It is worthwhile to note that the above example is one of four Bell states, which are (maximally) entangled pure states (pure states of the *HA* ⊗ *HB* space, but which cannot be separated into pure states of each HA and HB).

Now suppose Alice is an observer for system A, and Bob is an observer for system B. If in the entangled state given above Alice makes a measurement in the $\{|0\rangle,|1\rangle\}$ eigenbasis of A, there are two possible outcomes, occurring with equal probability:[49]

1. Alice measures 0, and the state of the system collapses to $|0\rangle_A|1\rangle_B$.
2. Alice measures 1, and the state of the system collapses to $|1\rangle_A|0\rangle_B$.

If the former occurs, then any subsequent measurement performed by Bob, in the same basis, will always return 1. If the latter occurs, (Alice measures 1) then Bob's measurement will return 0 with certainty. Thus, system B has been altered by Alice performing a local measurement on system A. This remains true even if the systems A and B are spatially separated. This is the foundation of the EPR paradox.

The outcome of Alice's measurement is random. Alice cannot decide which state to collapse the composite system into, and therefore cannot transmit information to Bob by acting on her system. Causality is thus preserved, in this particular scheme. For the general argument, see no-communication theorem.

20.4.2 Ensembles

As mentioned above, a state of a quantum system is given by a unit vector in a Hilbert space. More generally, if one has a large number of copies of the same system, then the state of this *ensemble* is described by a density matrix, which is a positive-semidefinite matrix, or a trace class when the state space is infinite-dimensional, and has trace 1. Again, by the spectral theorem, such a matrix takes the general form:

$$\rho = \sum_i w_i |\alpha_i\rangle\langle\alpha_i|,$$

where the w_i are positive-valued probabilities (they sum up to 1), the vectors α_i are unit vectors, and in the infinite-dimensional case, we would take the closure of such states in the trace norm. We can interpret ρ as representing an ensemble where w_i is the proportion of the ensemble whose states are $|\alpha_i\rangle$. When a mixed state has rank 1, it therefore describes a *pure ensemble*. When there is less than total information about the state of a quantum system we need density matrices to represent the state.

Experimentally, a mixed ensemble might be realized as follows. Consider a "black box" apparatus that spits electrons towards an observer. The electrons' Hilbert spaces are identical. The apparatus might produce electrons that are all in the same state; in this case, the electrons received by the observer are then a pure ensemble. However, the apparatus could produce electrons in different states. For example, it could produce two populations of electrons: one with state $|\mathbf{z}+\rangle$ with spins aligned in the positive **z** direction, and the other with state $|\mathbf{y}-\rangle$ with spins aligned in the negative **y** direction. Generally, this is a mixed ensemble, as there can be any number of populations, each corresponding to a different state.

Following the definition above, for a bipartite composite system, mixed states are just density matrices on *HA* ⊗ *HB*. That is, it has the general form

$$\rho = \sum_i w_i \left[\sum_j \bar{c}_{ij}(|\alpha_{ij}\rangle \otimes |\beta_{ij}\rangle)\right] \otimes \left[\sum_k c_{ik}(\langle\alpha_{ik}| \otimes \langle\beta_{ik}|)\right]$$

where the w_i are positively valued probabilities, $\sum_j |c_{ij}|^2 = 1$, and the vectors are unit vectors. This is self-adjoint and positive and has trace 1.

Extending the definition of separability from the pure case, we say that a mixed state is separable if it can be written as[50]:131–132

$$\rho = \sum_i w_i \rho_i^A \otimes \rho_i^B,$$

where the w_i are positively valued probabilities and the ρ_i^A 's and ρ_i^B 's are themselves mixed states (density operators) on the subsystems A and B respectively. In other words, a state is separable if it is a probability distribution over uncorrelated states, or product states. By writing the density matrices as sums of pure ensembles and expanding, we may assume without loss of generality that ρ_i^A and ρ_i^B are themselves pure ensembles. A state is then said to be *entangled* if it is not separable.

In general, finding out whether or not a mixed state is entangled is considered difficult. The general bipartite case has been shown to be NP-hard.[51] For the 2 × 2 and 2 × 3 cases, a necessary and sufficient criterion for separability is given by the famous Positive Partial Transpose (PPT) condition.[52]

20.4.3 Reduced density matrices

The idea of a reduced density matrix was introduced by Paul Dirac in 1930.[53] Consider as above systems A and B each with a Hilbert space HA, HB. Let the state of the composite system be

$$|\Psi\rangle \in H_A \otimes H_B.$$

As indicated above, in general there is no way to associate a pure state to the component system A. However, it still is possible to associate a density matrix. Let

$$\rho_T = |\Psi\rangle \ \langle\Psi|$$

which is the projection operator onto this state. The state of A is the partial trace of ρT over the basis of system B:

$$\rho_A \stackrel{\text{def}}{=} \sum_j \langle j|_B \left(|\Psi\rangle\langle\Psi|\right) |j\rangle_B = \text{Tr}_B \ \rho_T.$$

ρA is sometimes called the reduced density matrix of ρ on subsystem A. Colloquially, we "trace out" system B to obtain the reduced density matrix on A.

For example, the reduced density matrix of A for the entangled state

$$\tfrac{1}{\sqrt{2}} \left(|0\rangle_A \otimes |1\rangle_B - |1\rangle_A \otimes |0\rangle_B\right),$$

discussed above is

$$\rho_A = \tfrac{1}{2}\left(|0\rangle_A\langle 0|_A + |1\rangle_A\langle 1|_A\right)$$

This demonstrates that, as expected, the reduced density matrix for an entangled pure ensemble is a mixed ensemble. Also not surprisingly, the density matrix of A for the pure product state $|\psi\rangle_A \otimes |\phi\rangle_B$ discussed above is

$$\rho_A = |\psi\rangle_A\langle\psi|_A.$$

In general, a bipartite pure state ρ is entangled if and only if its reduced states are mixed rather than pure.

20.4.4 Two applications that use them

Reduced density matrices were explicitly calculated in different spin chains with unique ground state. An example is the one-dimensional AKLT spin chain:[54] the ground state can be divided into a block and an environment. The reduced density matrix of the block is proportional to a projector to a degenerate ground state of another Hamiltonian.

The reduced density matrix also was evaluated for XY spin chains, where it has full rank. It was proved that in the thermodynamic limit, the spectrum of the reduced density matrix of a large block of spins is an exact geometric sequence[55] in this case.

20.4.5 Entropy

In this section, the entropy of a mixed state is discussed as well as how it can be viewed as a measure of quantum entanglement.

Definition

In classical information theory, the Shannon entropy, H is associated to a probability distribution, $p_1, \cdots, p_n$, in the following way:[56]

$$H(p_1, \cdots, p_n) = -\sum_i p_i \log_2 p_i.$$

Since a mixed state ρ is a probability distribution over an ensemble, this leads naturally to the definition of the von Neumann entropy:

$$S(\rho) = -\mathrm{Tr}\left(\rho \log_2 \rho\right).$$

In general, one uses the Borel functional calculus to calculate a non-polynomial function such as $\log_2(\varrho)$. If the nonnegative operator ρ acts on a

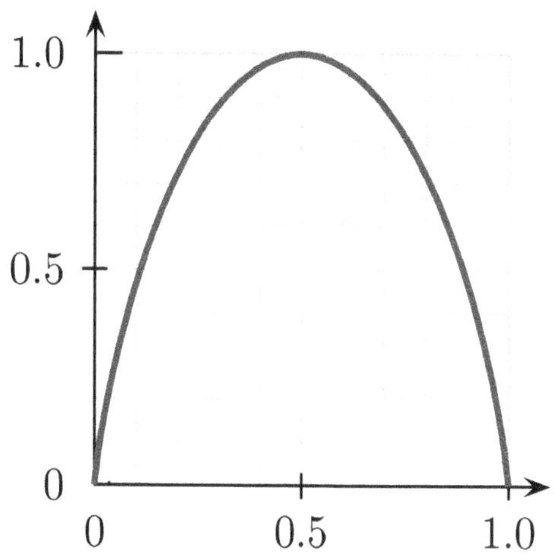

The plot of von Neumann entropy Vs Eigenvalue for a bipartite 2-level pure state. When the eigenvalue has value .5, von Neumann entropy is at a maximum, corresponding to maximum entanglement.

finite-dimensional Hilbert space and has eigenvalues $\lambda_1, \cdots, \lambda_n$, $\log_2(\varrho)$ turns out to be nothing more than the operator with the same eigenvectors, but the eigenvalues $\log_2(\lambda_1), \cdots, \log_2(\lambda_n)$. The Shannon entropy is then:

$$S(\rho) = -\mathrm{Tr}\left(\rho \log_2 \rho\right) = -\sum_i \lambda_i \log_2 \lambda_i$$

Since an event of probability 0 should not contribute to the entropy, and given that

$$\lim_{p \to 0} p \log p = 0,$$

the convention 0 log(0) = 0 is adopted. This extends to the infinite-dimensional case as well: if ρ has spectral resolution

$$\rho = \int \lambda dP_\lambda,$$

assume the same convention when calculating

$$\rho \log_2 \rho = \int \lambda \log_2 \lambda dP_\lambda.$$

As in statistical mechanics, the more uncertainty (number of microstates) the system should possess, the larger the entropy. For example, the entropy of any pure state is zero, which is unsurprising since there is no uncertainty about a system in a pure state. The entropy of any of the two subsystems of the entangled state discussed above is log(2) (which can be shown to be the maximum entropy for 2 × 2 mixed states).

As a measure of entanglement

Entropy provides one tool which can be used to quantify entanglement, although other entanglement measures exist.[57] If the overall system is pure, the entropy of one subsystem can be used to measure its degree of entanglement with the other subsystems.

For bipartite pure states, the von Neumann entropy of reduced states is the unique measure of entanglement in the sense that it is the only function on the family of states that satisfies certain axioms required of an entanglement measure.

It is a classical result that the Shannon entropy achieves its maximum at, and only at, the uniform probability distribution $\{1/n,...,1/n\}$. Therefore, a bipartite pure state $\varrho \in HA \otimes HB$ is said to be a **maximally entangled state** if the reduced state of ρ is the diagonal matrix

$$\begin{bmatrix} \frac{1}{n} & & \\ & \ddots & \\ & & \frac{1}{n} \end{bmatrix}.$$

For mixed states, the reduced von Neumann entropy is not the only reasonable entanglement measure.

As an aside, the information-theoretic definition is closely related to entropy in the sense of statistical mechanics (comparing the two definitions, we note that, in the present context, it is customary to set the Boltzmann constant $k = 1$). For example, by properties of the Borel functional calculus, we see that for any unitary operator U,

$$S(\rho) = S\left(U\rho U^*\right).$$

Indeed, without this property, the von Neumann entropy would not be well-defined.

In particular, U could be the time evolution operator of the system, i.e.,

$$U(t) = \exp\left(\frac{-iHt}{\hbar}\right),$$

where H is the Hamiltonian of the system. Here the entropy is unchanged.

The reversibility of a process is associated with the resulting entropy change, i.e., a process is reversible if, and only if, it leaves the entropy of the system invariant. Therefore, the march of the arrow of time towards thermodynamic equilibrium is simply the growing spread of quantum entanglement.[58] This provides a connection between quantum information theory and thermodynamics.

Rényi entropy also can be used as a measure of entanglement.

20.4.6 Entanglement measures

Entanglement measures quantify the amount of entanglement in a (often viewed as a bipartite) quantum state. As aforementioned, entanglement entropy is the standard measure of entanglement for pure states (but no longer a measure of entanglement for mixed states). For mixed states, there are some entanglement measures in the literature [57] and no single one is standard.

- Entanglement cost
- Distillable entanglement
- Entanglement of formation
- Relative entropy of entanglement
- Squashed entanglement
- Logarithmic negativity

Most (but not all) of these entanglement measures reduce for pure states to entanglement entropy, and are difficult (NP-hard) to compute.[59]

20.4.7 Quantum field theory

The Reeh-Schlieder theorem of quantum field theory is sometimes seen as an analogue of quantum entanglement.

20.5 Applications

Entanglement has many applications in quantum information theory. With the aid of entanglement, otherwise impossible tasks may be achieved.

Among the best-known applications of entanglement are superdense coding and quantum teleportation.[60]

Most researchers believe that entanglement is necessary to realize quantum computing (although this is disputed by some[61]).

Entanglement is used in some protocols of quantum cryptography.[62][63] This is because the “shared noise” of entanglement makes for an excellent one-time pad. Moreover, since measurement of either member of an entangled pair destroys the entanglement they share, entanglement-based quantum cryptography allows the sender and receiver to more easily detect the presence of an interceptor.

In interferometry, entanglement is necessary for surpassing the standard quantum limit and achieving the Heisenberg limit.[64]

20.5.1 Entangled states

There are several canonical entangled states that appear often in theory and experiments.

For two qubits, the Bell states are

$$|\Phi^\pm\rangle = \frac{1}{\sqrt{2}}(|0\rangle_A \otimes |0\rangle_B \pm |1\rangle_A \otimes |1\rangle_B)$$

$$|\Psi^\pm\rangle = \frac{1}{\sqrt{2}}(|0\rangle_A \otimes |1\rangle_B \pm |1\rangle_A \otimes |0\rangle_B)$$

These four pure states are all maximally entangled (according to the entropy of entanglement) and form an orthonormal basis (linear algebra) of the Hilbert space of the two qubits. They play a fundamental role in Bell's theorem.

For M>2 qubits, the GHZ state is

$$|\mathrm{GHZ}\rangle = \frac{|0\rangle^{\otimes M} + |1\rangle^{\otimes M}}{\sqrt{2}},$$

which reduces to the Bell state $|\Phi^+\rangle$ for $M = 2$. The traditional GHZ state was defined for $M = 3$. GHZ states are occasionally extended to *qudits*, i.e., systems of *d* rather than 2 dimensions.

Also for M>2 qubits, there are spin squeezed states.[65] Spin squeezed states are a class of squeezed coherent states satisfying certain restrictions on the uncertainty of spin measurements, and are necessarily entangled.[66] Spin squeezed states are good candidates for enhancing precision measurements using quantum entanglement.[67]

For two bosonic modes, a NOON state is

$$|\psi_{\text{NOON}}\rangle = \frac{|N\rangle_a|0\rangle_b + |0\rangle_a|N\rangle_b}{\sqrt{2}},$$

This is like a Bell state $|\Phi^+\rangle$ except the basis kets 0 and 1 have been replaced with "the *N* photons are in one mode" and "the *N* photons are in the other mode".

Finally, there also exist twin Fock states for bosonic modes, which can be created by feeding a Fock state into two arms leading to a beam splitter. They are the sum of multiple of NOON states, and can used to achieve the Heisenberg limit.[68]

For the appropriately chosen measure of entanglement, Bell, GHZ, and NOON states are maximally entangled while spin squeezed and twin Fock states are only partially entangled. The partially entangled states are generally easier to prepare experimentally.

20.5.2 Methods of creating entanglement

Entanglement is usually created by direct interactions between subatomic particles. These interactions can take numerous forms. One of the most commonly used methods is spontaneous parametric down-conversion to generate a pair of photons entangled in polarisation.[69] Other methods include the use of a fiber coupler to confine and mix photons, the use of quantum dots to trap electrons until decay occurs, the use of the Hong-Ou-Mandel effect, etc., In the earliest tests of Bell's theorem, the entangled particles were generated using atomic cascades.

It is also possible to create entanglement between quantum systems that never directly interacted, through the use of entanglement swapping.

20.5.3 Testing a system for entanglement

Systems which contain no entanglement are said to be separable. For 2-Qubit and Qubit-Qutrit systems (2 × 2 and 2 × 3 respectively) the simple Peres–Horodecki criterion provides both a necessary and a sufficient criterion for separability, and thus for detecting entanglement. However, for the general case, the criterion is merely a sufficient one for separability, as the problem becomes NP-hard.[70][71] A numerical approach to the problem is suggested by Jon Magne Leinaas, Jan Myrheim and Eirik Ovrum in their paper "Geometrical aspects of entanglement".[72] Leinaas et al. offer a numerical approach, iteratively refining an estimated separable state towards the target state to be tested, and checking if the target state can indeed be reached. An implementation of the algorithm (including a built in Peres-Horodecki criterion testing) is brought in the "StateSeparator" web-app.

20.6 Naturally entangled systems

The electron shell of multi-electron atoms always consists of entangled electrons. The correct ionization energy can be calculated only by consideration of electron entanglement.[73]

It has been shown by femtosecond transition spectroscopy, that in the photosystem of plants, entangled photons exist. An efficient conversion of the photon energy into chemical energy is possible only due to this entanglement.[74][75]

20.7 See also

- Concurrence (quantum computing)
- Entanglement distillation
- Entanglement witness
- Faster-than-light communication
- Ghirardi–Rimini–Weber theory
- Multipartite entanglement

- Normally distributed and uncorrelated does not imply independent
- Observer effect (physics)
- Photon entanglement
- Quantum coherence
- Quantum discord
- Quantum phase transition
- Quantum pseudo-telepathy
- Retrocausality
- Separable state
- Squashed entanglement
- Ward's probability amplitude
- Wheeler–Feynman absorber theory

20.8 References

[1] Einstein A, Podolsky B, Rosen N; Podolsky; Rosen (1935). "Can Quantum-Mechanical Description of Physical Reality Be Considered Complete?". *Phys. Rev.* **47** (10): 777–780. Bibcode:1935PhRv...47..777E. doi:10.1103/PhysRev.47.777.

[2] Schrödinger E (1935). "Discussion of probability relations between separated systems". *Mathematical Proceedings of the Cambridge Philosophical Society* **31** (4): 555–563. Bibcode:1935PCPS...31..555S. doi:10.1017/S0305004100013554.

[3] Schrödinger E (1936). "Probability relations between separated systems". *Mathematical Proceedings of the Cambridge Philosophical Society* **32** (3): 446–452. Bibcode:1936PCPS...32..446S. doi:10.1017/S0305004100019137.

[4] Physicist John Bell depicts the Einstein camp in this debate in his article entitled "Bertlmann's socks and the nature of reality", p. 143 of *Speakable and unspeakable in quantum mechanics*: "For EPR that would be an unthinkable 'spooky action at a distance'. To avoid such action at a distance they have to attribute, to the space-time regions in question, real properties in advance of observation, correlated properties, which predetermine the outcomes of these particular observations. Since these real properties, fixed in advance of observation, are not contained in quantum formalism, that formalism for EPR is incomplete. It may be correct, as far as it goes, but the usual quantum formalism cannot be the whole story." And again on p. 144 Bell says: "Einstein had no difficulty accepting that affairs in different places could be correlated. What he could not accept was that an intervention at one place could influence, immediately, affairs at the other." Downloaded 5 July 2011 from Bell, J. S. (1987). *Speakable and Unspeakable in Quantum Mechanics* (PDF). CERN. ISBN 0521334950. Retrieved June 2014.

[5] "75 years of entanglement - Science News". Retrieved 13 October 2014.

[6] Francis, Matthew. Quantum entanglement shows that reality can't be local, *Ars Technica*, 30 October 2012

[7] Juan Yin; et al. (2013). "Bounding the speed of 'spooky action at a distance". *Phys. Rev. Lett. 110, 260407* **1303**: 614. arXiv:1303.0614. Bibcode:2013arXiv1303.0614Y.

[8] Matson, John (13 August 2012). "Quantum teleportation achieved over record distances". Nature.

[9] Griffiths, David J. (2004), *Introduction to Quantum Mechanics (2nd ed.)*, Prentice Hall, ISBN 0-13-111892-7

[10] Roger Penrose, *The Road to Reality: A Complete Guide to the Laws of the Universe*, London, 2004, p. 603.

[11] "New High-Intensity Source of Polarization-Entangled Photon Pairs". *Physical Review Letters* **75**: 4337–4341. Bibcode:1995PhRvL..75.4337K. doi:10.1103/PhysRevLett.75.4337.

[12] "Experimental demonstration of five-photon entanglement and open-destination teleportation". *Nature* **430**: 54–58. Jul 2004. doi:10.1038/nature02643. PMID 15229594.

[13] "Experimental entanglement of six photons in graph states". *Nature Physics* **3**: 91–95. doi:10.1038/nphys507.

[14] "Observation of eight-photon entanglement". *Nature Photonics* **6**: 225–228. doi:10.1038/nphoton.2011.354.

[15] "Wave–particle duality of C_{60} molecules". *Nature* **401**: 680–682. 14 October 1999. doi:10.1038/44348. PMID 18494170. (subscription required)

[16] Olaf Nairz, Markus Arndt, and Anton Zeilinger, "Quantum interference experiments with large molecules", American Journal of Physics, 71 (April 2003) 319-325.

[17] Hensen, B.; et al. (21 October 2015). "Loophole-free Bell inequality violation using electron spins separated by 1.3 kilometres". *Nature* **526**: 682–686. doi:10.1038/nature15759. Retrieved 21 October 2015.

[18] Markoff, Jack (21 October 2015). "Sorry, Einstein. Quantum Study Suggests 'Spooky Action' Is Real.". *New York Times*. Retrieved 21 October 2015.

[19] Lee, K. C.; Sprague, M. R.; Sussman, B. J.; Nunn, J.; Langford, N. K.; Jin, X.- M.; Champion, T.; Michelberger, P.; Reim, K. F.; England, D.; Jaksch, D.; Walmsley, I. A. (2 December 2011). "Entangling macroscopic diamonds at room temperature". *Science* **334** (6060): 1253–1256. Bibcode:2011Sci...334.1253L. doi:10.1126/science.1211914. PMID 22144620. Lay summary.

[20] sciencemag.org, supplementary materials

[21] Kumar, M., *Quantum*, Icon Books, 2009, p. 313.

[22] Alisa Bokulich, Gregg Jaeger, *Philosophy of Quantum Information and Entanglement*, Cambridge University Press, 2010, xv.

[23] Letter from Einstein to Max Born, 3 March 1947; *The Born-Einstein Letters; Correspondence between Albert Einstein and Max and Hedwig Born from 1916 to 1955*, Walker, New York, 1971. (cited in M. P. Hobson; et al., *Quantum Entanglement and Communication Complexity (1998)*, pp. 1/13, CiteSeerX: 10.1.1.20.8324)

[24] J. S. Bell (1964). "On the Einstein-Poldolsky-Rosen paradox". *Physics*.

[25] Freedman, Stuart J.; Clauser, John F. (1972). "Experimental Test of Local Hidden-Variable Theories". *Physical Review Letters* **28** (14): 938–941. Bibcode:1972PhRvL..28..938F. doi:10.1103/PhysRevLett.28.938.

[26] A. Aspect, P. Grangier, and G. Roger (1982). "Experimental Realization of Einstein-Podolsky-Rosen-Bohm Gedankenexperiment: A New Violation of Bell's Inequalities". *Physical Review Letters* **49** (2): 91–94. Bibcode:1982PhRvL..49...91A. doi:10.1103/PhysRevLett.49.91.

[27] C. H. Bennett and G. Brassard. "Quantum cryptography: Public key distribution and coin tossing". In *Proceedings of IEEE International Conference on Computers, Systems and Signal Processing*, volume 175, page 8. New York, 1984. http://researcher.watson.ibm.com/researcher/files/us-bennetc/BB84highest.pdf

[28] Ekert, A.K. (1991). "Quantum cryptography based on Bell's theorem". *Phys. Rev. Lett.* (APS) **67** (6): 661–663. Bibcode:1991PhRvL..67..661E. doi:10.1103/PhysRevLett.67.661. ISSN 0031-9007. PMID 10044956. (subscription required (help)).

[29] Asher Peres, *Quantum Theory, Concepts and Methods*, Kluwer, 1993; ISBN 0-7923-2549-4 p. 115.

[30] I. Gerhardt, Q. Liu, A. Lamas-Linares, J. Skaar, V. Scarani, V. Makarov, C. Kurtsiefer (2011), "Experimentally faking the violation of Bell's inequalities", *Phys. Rev. Lett.* **107** (17): 170404, arXiv:1106.3224, Bibcode:2011PhRvL.107q0404G, doi:10.1103/PhysRevLett.107.170404

[31] Santos, E (2004). "The failure to perform a loophole-free test of Bell's Inequality supports local realism". *Foundations of Physics* **34**: 1643–1673. doi:10.1007/s10701-004-1308-z.

[32] H. Zbinden; et al. (2001). "Experimental test of nonlocal quantum correlations in relativistic configurations". *Phys. Rev. A* **63** (2): 22111. arXiv:quant-ph/0007009. Bibcode:2001PhRvA..63b2111Z. doi:10.1103/PhysRevA.63.022111.

[33] Some of the history of both referenced Zbinden, et al. experiments is provided in Gilder, L., *The Age of Entanglement*, Vintage Books, 2008, pp. 321-324.

[34] Cirel'son, B. S. (1980). "Quantum generalizations of Bell's inequality". *Letters in Mathematical Physics* **4** (2): 93–100. Bibcode:1980LMaPh...4...93C. doi:10.1007/BF00417500.

[35] Xiao-song Ma, Stefan Zotter, Johannes Kofler, Rupert Ursin, Thomas Jennewein, Časlav Brukner & Anton Zeilinger; Zotter; Kofler; Ursin; Jennewein; Brukner; Zeilinger (26 April 2012). "Experimental delayed-choice entanglement swapping". *Nature Physics* **8** (6): 480–485. arXiv:1203.4834. Bibcode:2012NatPh...8..480M. doi:10.1038/nphys2294.

[36] Megidish, E.; Halevy, A.; Shacham, T.; Dvir, T.; Dovrat, L.; Eisenberg, H. S. (2013). "Entanglement Swapping between Photons that have Never Coexisted". *Physical Review Letters* **110** (21). doi:10.1103/physrevlett.110.210403.

[37] "Classical carrier could create entanglement". physicsworld.com. Retrieved 2014-06-14.

[38] "Entangled photons make a picture from a paradox". *Nature News & Comment*. Retrieved 13 October 2014.

[39] "[1310.4691] Time from quantum entanglement: an experimental illustration". *Physical Review A* **89**. arXiv:1310.4691. Bibcode:2014PhRvA..89e2122M. doi:10.1103/PhysRevA.89.052122. Retrieved 13 October 2014.

[40] "Entangled toy universe shows time may be an illusion". Retrieved 13 October 2014.

[41] David Deutsch, The Beginning of infinity. Page 299

[42] "Quantum Experiment Shows How Time 'Emerges' from Entanglement". *Medium*. Retrieved 13 October 2014.

[43] "New Quantum Theory Could Explain the Flow of Time". *WIRED*. Retrieved 13 October 2014.

[44] "The Einstein-Podolsky-Rosen Argument in Quantum Theory (Stanford Encyclopedia of Philosophy)". Plato.stanford.edu. Retrieved 2014-06-14. The Stanford encyclopedia says that Niels Bohr distinguished between "mechanical disturbances" and "an influence on the very conditions which define the possible types of predictions regarding the future behavior of [the other half of an entangled] system."

[45] Sidney Coleman (Apr 9, 1994). *Quantum Mechanics in Your Face* (Speech). New England sectional meeting of the American Physical Society.

[46] Rubin, Mark A. (2001). "Locality in the Everett Interpretation of Heisenberg-Picture Quantum Mechanics". *Found. Phys. Lett. ()* **14** (2001): 301–322. arXiv:quant-ph/0103079. Bibcode:2001quant.ph..3079R.

[47] Werner, R.F. (1989). "Quantum States with Einstein-Podolsky-Rosen correlations admitting a hidden-variable model". *Physical Review A* **40** (8): 4277–4281. Bibcode:1989PhRvA..40.4277W. doi:10.1103/PhysRevA.40.4277. PMID 9902666.

[48] Jaeger G, Shimony A, Vaidman L; Shimony; Vaidman (1995). "Two Interferometric Complementarities". *Phys. Rev.* **51** (1): 54–67. Bibcode:1995PhRvA..51...54J. doi:10.1103/PhysRevA.51.54.

[49] Nielsen, Michael A.; Chuang, Isaac L. (2000). *Quantum Computation and Quantum Information*. Cambridge University Press. pp. 112–113. ISBN 0-521-63503-9.

[50] Laloe, Franck (2012), *Do We Really Understand Quantum Mechanics*, Cambridge University Press, ISBN 978-1-107-02501-1

[51] Gurvits L (2003). "Classical deterministic complexity of Edmonds' Problem and quantum entanglement". *Proceedings of the thirty-fifth annual ACM symposium on Theory of computing*: 10. doi:10.1145/780542.780545. ISBN 1-58113-674-9.

[52] Horodecki M, Horodecki P, Horodecki R; Horodecki; Horodecki (1996). "Separability of mixed states: necessary and sufficient conditions". *Physics Letters A* **223**: 210. arXiv:quant-ph/9605038. Bibcode:1996PhLA..223....1H. doi:10.1016/S0375-9601(96)00706-2.

[53] Dirac, P. A. M. (2008). "Note on Exchange Phenomena in the Thomas Atom". *Mathematical Proceedings of the Cambridge Philosophical Society* **26** (3): 376. Bibcode:1930PCPS...26..376D. doi:10.1017/S0305004100016108.

[54] Fan, H; Korepin V; Roychowdhury V (2004-11-26). "Entanglement in a Valence-Bond Solid State". *Physical Review Letters* **93** (22): 227203. arXiv:quant-ph/0406067. Bibcode:2004PhRvL..93v7203F. doi:10.1103/PhysRevLett.93.227203. PMID 15601113.

[55] Franchini, F.; Its, A. R.; Korepin, V. E.; Takhtajan, L. A. (2010). "Spectrum of the density matrix of a large *block of* spins of the XY model in one dimension". *Quantum Information Processing* **10** (3): 325–341. arXiv:1002.2931. doi:10.1007/s11128-010-0197-7.

[56] Cerf, Nicolas J.; Cleve, Richard. "Information-theoretic interpretation of quantum error-correcting codes" (PDF).

[57] Plenio; Virmani (2007). "An introduction to entanglement measures". *Quant. Inf. Comp.* **1**: 1–51. arXiv:quant-ph/0504163. Bibcode:2005quant.ph..4163P.

[58] Wolchover, Natalie (25 April 2014). "New Quantum Theory Could Explain the Flow of Time". *www.wired.com* (Quanta Magazine). Retrieved 27 April 2014.

[59] Huang, Yichen (21 March 2014). "Computing quantum discord is NP-complete". *New Journal of Physics* **16** (3): 033027. arXiv:1305.5941. Bibcode:2014NJPh...16c3027H. doi:10.1088/1367-2630/16/3/033027.

[60] Bouwmeester, Dik; Pan, Jian-Wei; Mattle, Klaus; Eibl, Manfred; Weinfurter, Harald & Zeilinger, Anton (1997). "Experimental Quantum Teleportation" (PDF). *Nature* **390** (6660): 575–579. Bibcode:1997Natur.390..575B. doi:10.1038/37539.

[61] Richard Jozsa; Noah Linden (2002). "On the role of entanglement in quantum computational speed-up". *Proceedings of the Royal Society A: Mathematical, Physical and Engineering Sciences* **459** (2036): 2011–2032. arXiv:quant-ph/0201143. Bibcode:2003RSPSA.459.2011J. doi:10.1098/rspa.2002.1097.

[62] Ekert, Artur K. (1991). "Quantum cryptography based on Bell's theorem". *Physical Review Letters* **67** (6): 661–663. Bibcode:1991PhRvL..67..661E. doi:10.1103/PhysRevLett.67.661. PMID 10044956.

[63] Karol Horodecki; Michal Horodecki; Pawel Horodecki; Ryszard Horodecki; Marcin Pawlowski; Mohamed Bourennane (2010). "Contextuality offers device-independent security". arXiv:1006.0468 [quant-ph].

[64] Pezze, Luca & Smerzi, Augusto (2009). "Entanglement, Nonlinear Dynamics, and the Heisenberg Limit" (PDF). *Phys. Rev. Lett.* **102** (10): 100401. arXiv:0711.4840. Bibcode:2009PhRvL.102j0401P. doi:10.1103/PhysRevLett.102.100401. PMID 19392092.

[65] Database error - Qwiki

[66] Kitagawa, Masahiro; Ueda, Masahito (1993). "Squeezed Spin States". *Phys. Rev. A* **47**: 5138–5143. doi:10.1103/physreva.47.5138.

[67] Wineland, D. J.; Bollinger, J. J.; Itano, W. M.; Moore, F. L.; Heinzen, D. J. "Spin squeezing and reduced quantum noise in spectroscopy". *Phys. Rev. A* **46**: R6797–R6800. doi:10.1103/PhysRevA.46.R6797.

[68] "Phys. Rev. Lett. 71, 1355 (1993): Interferometric detection of optical phase shifts at the Heisenberg limit". *Physical Review Letters*. Retrieved 13 October 2014.

[69] Horodecki R, Horodecki P, Horodecki M, Horodecki K; Horodecki; Horodecki; Horodecki (2007). "Quantum entanglement". *Rev. Mod. Phys.* **81** (2): 865–942. arXiv:quant-ph/0702225. Bibcode:2009RvMP...81..865H. doi:10.1103/RevModPhys.81.865.

[70] Gurvits, L., Classical deterministic complexity of Edmonds' problem and quantum entanglement, in Proceedings of the 35th ACM Symposium on Theory of Computing, ACM Press, New York, 2003.

[71] Sevag Gharibian, Strong NP-Hardness of the Quantum Separability Problem, Quantum Information and Computation, Vol. 10, No. 3&4, pp. 343-360, 2010. arXiv: 0810.4507.

[72] "Geometrical aspects of entanglement", Physical Review A 74, 012313 (2006)

[73] Frank Jensen: *Introduction to Computational Chemistry*. Wiley, 2007, ISBN 978-0-470-01187-4.

[74] Berkeley Lab Press Release: *Untangling the Quantum Entanglement Behind Photosynthesis: Berkeley scientists shine new light on green plant secrets.*

[75] Mohan Sarovar, Akihito Ishizaki, Graham R. Fleming, K. Birgitta Whaley: *Quantum entanglement in photosynthetic light harvesting complexes.* arXiv:0905.3787

20.9 Further reading

- Bengtsson I; Życzkowski K (2006). "Geometry of Quantum States". *An Introduction to Quantum Entanglement*. Cambridge: Cambridge University Press.
- Cramer, JG (2015). *The Quantum Handshake: Entanglement, Nonlocality and Transactions*. Springer Verlag. ISBN 978-3-319-24642-0.
- Gühne, O.; Tóth, G. (2009). "Entanglement detection". *Physics Reports* **474**: 1–75. arXiv:0811.2803. Bibcode:2009PhR...474....1G. doi:10.1016/j.physrep.2009.02.004.
- Horodecki R, Horodecki P, Horodecki M, Horodecki K; Horodecki; Horodecki; Horodecki (2009). "Quantum entanglement". *Rev. Mod. Phys.* **81** (2): 865–942. arXiv:quant-ph/0702225. Bibcode:2009RvMP...81..865H. doi:10.1103/RevModPhys.81.865.
- Jaeger G (2009). *Entanglement, Information, and the Interpretation of Quantum Mechanics*. Heildelberg: Springer. ISBN 978-3-540-92127-1.
- Plenio MB, Virmani S; Virmani (2007). "An introduction to entanglement measures". *Quant. Inf. Comp.* **1** (7): 151. arXiv:quant-ph/0504163. Bibcode:2005quant.ph..4163P.
- Shadbolt PJ, Verde MR, Peruzzo A, Politi A, Laing A, Lobino M, Matthews JCF, Thompson MG, O'Brien JL; Verde; Peruzzo; Politi; Laing; Lobino; Matthews; Thompson; O'Brien (2012). "Generating, manipulating and measuring entanglement and mixture with a reconfigurable photonic circuit". *Nature Photonics* **6**: 45–59. arXiv:1108.3309. Bibcode:2012NaPho...6...45S. doi:10.1038/nphoton.2011.283.
- Steward EG (2008). *Quantum Mechanics: Its Early Development and the Road to Entanglement*. Imperial College Press. ISBN 978-1-86094-978-4.

20.10 External links

- The original EPR paper
- Quantum Entanglement at Stanford Encyclopedia of Philosophy
- How to entangle photons experimentally (subscription required)
- A creative interpretation of Quantum Entanglement
- Albert's chest: entanglement for lay persons
- How Quantum Entanglement Works
- Explanatory video by Scientific American magazine
- Hanson Lab - Loophole-free Bell test 'Spooky action at a distance', no cheating.
- Two Diamonds Linked by Strange Quantum Entanglement
- Entanglement experiment with photon pairs - interactive
- Multiple entanglement and quantum repeating
- Quantum Entanglement and Bell's Theorem at MathPages
- Audio - Cain/Gay (2009) Astronomy Cast Entanglement
- Recorded research seminars at Imperial College relating to quantum entanglement
- Quantum Entanglement and Decoherence: 3rd International Conference on Quantum Information (ICQI)
- Ion trapping quantum information processing
- IEEE Spectrum On-line: *The trap technique*
- Was Einstein Wrong?: A Quantum Threat to Special Relativity
- Citizendium: Entanglement
- Spooky Actions At A Distance?: Oppenheimer Lecture, Prof. David Mermin (Cornell University) Univ. California, Berkeley, 2008. Non-mathematical popular lecture on YouTube, posted Mar 2008
- "StateSeparator" web-app

Chapter 21

Quantum neural network

Quantum neural networks (**QNNs**) are neural network models which are based on the principles of quantum mechanics. There are two different approaches to QNN research, one exploiting quantum information processing to improve existing neural network models (sometimes also vice versa), and the other one searching for potential quantum effects in the brain.

21.1 Artificial quantum neural networks

In the computational approach to quantum neural network research,[1][2] scientists try to combine artificial neural network models (which are widely used in machine learning for the important task of pattern classification) with the advantages of quantum information in order to develop more efficient algorithms (for a review, see [3]). One important motivation for these investigations is the difficulty to train classical neural networks, especially in big data applications. The hope is that features of quantum computing such as quantum parallelism or the effects of interference and entanglement can be used as resources. Since the technological implementation of a quantum computer is still in a premature stage, such quantum neural network models are mostly theoretical proposals that await their full implementation in physical experiments.

Quantum neural network research is still in its infancy, and a conglomeration of proposals and ideas of varying scope and mathematical rigor have been put forward. Most of them are based on the idea of replacing classical binary or McCulloch-Pitts neurons with a qubit (which can be called a "quron"), resulting in neural units that can be in a superposition of the state 'firing' and 'resting'.

21.1.1 Historical notion

The first ideas on neural computation have been published by Subhash Kak,[4] who discusses the similarity of the neural activation function with the quantum mechanical Eigenvalue equation. Kak also discussed the application of these ideas to the study of brain function[5] and the limitations of this approach.[6] Ajit Narayanan and Tammy Menneer proposed a photonic implementation of a quantum neural network model that is based on the many-universe theory and "collapses" into the desired model upon measurement.[7] Since then, more and more articles have been published in journals of computer science as well as quantum physics in order to find a superior quantum neural network model.

21.1.2 Quantum perceptrons

A lot of proposals attempt to find a quantum equivalent for the perceptron unit from which neural nets are constructed. A problem is that nonlinear activation functions do not immediately correspond to the mathematical structure of quantum theory, since a quantum evolution is described by linear operations and leads to probabilistic observation. Ideas to imitate the perceptron activation function with a quantum mechanical formalism reach from special measurements [8][9] to postulating non-linear quantum operators (a mathematical framework that is disputed) [.[10][11] A direct implementation of the activation function using the circuit-based model of quantum computation has recently been proposed by Schuld, Sinayskiy and Petruccione based on the quantum phase estimation algorithm.[12]

21.1.3 Fuzzy logic

A substantial amount of interest has been given to a "quantum-inspired" model that uses ideas from quantum theory to implement a neural network based on fuzzy logic.[13]

21.1.4 Quantum networks

Some contributions reverse the approach and try to exploit the insights from neural network research in order to obtain powerful applications for quantum computing, such as quantum algorithmic design supported by machine learning.[14] An example is the work of Elizabeth Behrman and Jim Steck,[15] who propose a quantum computing setup that consists of a number of qubits with tunable mutual interactions. Following the classical backpropagation rule, the strength of the interactions are learned from a training set of desired input-output relations, and the quantum network thus 'learns' an algorithm.

21.1.5 Quantum associative memory

The quantum associative memory algorithm [16] has been introduced by Dan Ventura and Tony Martinez in 1999. The authors do not attempt to translate the structure of artificial neural network models into quantum theory, but propose an algorithm for a circuit-based quantum computer that simulates associative memory. The memory states (in Hopfield neural networks saved in the weights of the neural connections) are written into a superposition, and a Grover-like quantum search algorithm retrieves the memory state closest to a given input. An advantage lies in the exponential storage capacity of memory states, however the question remains whether the model has significance regarding the initial purpose of Hopfield models as a demonstration of how simplified artificial neural networks can simulate features of the brain.

21.1.6 Quantum learning

Most learning algorithms follow the classical model of training an artificial neural network to learn the input-output function of a given training set and use a classical feedback loops to update parameters of the quantum system until they converge to an optimal configuration. Learning as a parameter optimisation problem has also been approached by adiabatic models of quantum computing.[17]

21.1.7 Biological quantum neural networks

Although many quantum neural network researchers explicitly limit their scope to a computational perspective, the field is closely connected to investigations of potential quantum effects in biological neural networks.[18][19] Models of cognitive agents and memory based on quantum collectives have been proposed by Subhash Kak,[20] but he also points to specific problems of limits on observation and control of these memories due to fundamental logical reasons.[21] The combination of quantum physics and neuroscience also nourishes a vivid debate beyond the borders of science, an illustrative example being journals such as NeuroQuantology [22] or the healing method of Quantum Neurology.[23] However, also in the scientific sphere theories of how the brain might harvest the behavior of particles on a quantum level are controversially debated.[24][25] The fusion of biology and quantum physics recently gained momentum by the discovery of signs for efficient energy transport in photosynthesis due to quantum effects. However, there is no widely accepted evidence for the 'quantum brain' yet.

21.2 See also

- Holographic associative memory

21.3 References

[26] [27]

[1] da Silva, Adenilton J.; Ludermir, Teresa B.; de Oliveira, Wilson R. "Quantum perceptron over a field and neural network architecture selection in a quantum computer". *Neural Networks* **76**: 55–64. doi:10.1016/j.neunet.2016.01.002.

[2] Panella, Massimo; Martinelli, Giuseppe. "Neural networks with quantum architecture and quantum learning". *International Journal of Circuit Theory and Applications* **39**: 61–77. doi:10.1002/cta.619.

[3] M. Schuld, I. Sinayskiy, F. Petruccione: The quest for a Quantum Neural Network, Quantum Information Processing 13, 11 , pp. 2567-2586 (2014)

[4] S. Kak, On quantum neural computing, Advances in Imaging and Electron Physics 94, 259 (1995)

[5] S. Kak, The three languages of the brain: quantum, reorganizational, and associative. In Learning as Self- Organization, K. Pribram and J. King (editors). Lawrence Erlbaum Associates, Mahwah, NJ, 185-219 (1996)

[6] A. Gautam and S. Kak, Symbols, meaning, and origins of mind. Biosemiotics (Springer Verlag) 6: 301-310 (2013)

[7] A. Narayanan and T. Menneer: Quantum artificial neural network architectures and components, Information Sciences 128, 231-255 (2000)

[8] M. Perus: Neural Networks as a basis for quantum associative memory, Neural Network World 10 (6), 1001 (2000)

[9] M. Zak, C.P. Williams: Quantum Neural Nets, International Journal of Theoretical Physics 37(2), 651 (1998)

[10] S. Gupta, R. Zia: Quantum Neural Networks, Journal of Computer and System Sciences 63(3), 355 (2001)

[11] J. Faber, G.A. Giraldi: Quantum Models for Artificial Neural Network (2002), Electronically available: http: //arquivosweb. lncc.br/pdfs/QNN-Review. pdf

[12] M. Schuld, I. Sinayskiy, F. Petruccione: Simulating a perceptron on a quantum computer ArXiv:1412.3635 (2014)

[13] G. Purushothaman, N. Karayiannis: Quantum Neural Networks (QNN's): Inherently Fuzzy Feedforward Neural Networks, IEEE Transactions on Neural Networks, 8(3), 679 (1997)

[14] J. Bang et al. : A strategy for quantum algorithm design assisted by machine learning, New Journal of Physics 16 073017 (2014)

[15] E.C. Behrman, J.E. Steck, P. Kumar, K.A. Walsh: Quantum Algorithmic design using dynamic learning, Quantum Information and Computation, vol. 8, No. 1&2, pp. 12-29 (2008)

[16] D. Ventura, T. Martinez: A quantum associative memory based on Grover's algorithm, Proceedings of the International Conference on Artificial Neural Networks and Genetics Algorithms, pp. 22-27 (1999)

[17] H. Neven et al.: Training a Binary Classifier with the Quantum Adiabatic Algorithm, arXiv:0811.0416v1 (2008)

[18] W. Loewenstein: Physics in mind. A quantum view of the brain, Basic Books (2013)

[19] H. Stapp: Mind Matter and Quantum Mechanics, Springer, Heidelberg (2009)

[20] S. Kak, Biological memories and agents as quantum collectives. NeuroQuantology 11: 391-398 (2013)

[21] S. Kak, Observability and computability in physics, Quantum Matter 3: 172-176 (2014)

[22] http://www.neuroquantology.com/index.php/journal

[23] http://quantumneurology.com/

[24] S. Hameroff: Quantum computation in brain microtubules? The Penrose-Hameroff 'Orch-OR' model of consciousness, Philosophical Transactions Royal Society of London Series A, 356 1743 1869 (1998)

[25] E. Pessa, G. Vitiello: Bioelectrochemistry and Bioenergetics, 48 2 339 (1999)

[26] Neukart, Florian (2013). "On Quantum Computers and Artificial Neural Networks". *Signal Processing Research* **2** (1).

[27] Neukart, Florian (2014). "Operations on Quantum Physical Artificial Neural Structures". *Procedia Engineering* **2** (1): 1509–1517.

21.4 External links

- Recent review of quantum neural networks by M. Schuld, I. Sinayskiy and F. Petruccione
- Review of quantum neural networks by Wei
- Article by P. Gralewicz on the plausibility of quantum computing in biological neural networks
- Training a neural net to recognize images

Chapter 22

Quantum t-design

A **Quantum t-design** is a probability distribution over pure quantum states which can duplicate properties of the probability distribution over the Haar measure for polynomials of degree t or less. Specifically, the average of any polynomial function of degree t over the design is exactly the same as the average over Haar measure. Here the Haar measure is a uniform probability distribution over all quantum states. Quantum t-designs are so called because they are analogous to t-designs in classical statistics, which arose historically in connection with the problem of design of experiments. Quantum t-designs are usually unique, and thus almost always calculable. Two particularly important types of t-designs in quantum mechanics are spherical and unitary t-designs.

Spherical t-designs are designs where points of the design (i.e. the points being used for the averaging process) are points on a unit sphere. Spherical t-designs and variations thereof have been considered lately and found useful in quantum information theory,[1] quantum cryptography and other related fields.

Unitary designs are analogous to spherical designs in that they approximate the entire unitary group via a finite collection of unitary matrices. Unitary designs have been found useful in information theory[2] and quantum computing. Unitary designs are especially useful in quantum computing since most operations are represented by unitary operators.

22.1 Motivation

In a d-dimensional Hilbert space when averaging over all quantum pure states the natural group is SU(d), the special unitary group of dimension d. The Haar measure is, by definition, the unique group-invariant measure, so it is used to average properties that are not unitarily invariant over all states, or over all unitaries.

A particularly widely used example of this is the spin $\frac{1}{2}$ system. For this system the relevant group is SU(2) which is the group of all 2x2 unitary operators. Since every 2x2 unitary operator is a rotation of the Bloch sphere, the Haar measure for spin-1/2 particles is invariant under all rotations of the Bloch sphere. This implies that the Haar measure is *the* rotationally invariant measure on the Bloch sphere, which can be thought of as a constant density distribution over the surface of the sphere.

Another recent application is the fact that a symmetric informationally complete POVM is also a spherical 2-design. Also, since a 2-design must have more than d^2 elements, a SIC-POVM is a **minimal** 2-design.

22.2 Spherical Designs

Complex projective (t,t)-designs have been studied in quantum information theory as quantum 2-designs, and in t-designs of vectors in the unit sphere in $\mathbb{R}^N$ which, when transformed to vectors in $\mathbb{C}^{N/2}$ become complex projective (t/2,t/2)-designs.

Formally, we define[3] a complex projective (t,t)-design as a probability distribution over quantum states $(p_i, |\phi_i\rangle)$ if

$\sum_i p_i(|\phi_i\rangle\langle\phi_i|)^{\otimes t} = \int_\psi (|\psi\rangle\langle\psi|)^{\otimes t} d\psi$

Here, the integral over states is taken over the Haar measure on the unit sphere in $\mathbb{C}^N$

Exact t-designs over quantum states cannot be distinguished from the uniform probability distribution over all states when using t copies of a state from the probability distribution. However in practice even t-designs may be difficult to compute. For this reason approximate t-designs are useful.

Approximate (t,t)-designs are most useful due to their ability to be efficiently implemented. i.e. it is possible to generate a quantum state $|\phi\rangle$ distributed according to the probability distribution $p_i|\phi_i\rangle$ in $O(\log^c N)$ time. This efficient construction also implies that the POVM of the operators $Np_i|\phi_i\rangle\langle\phi_i|$ can be implemented in $O(\log^c N)$ time.

The technical definition of an approximate (t,t)-design is:

If $\sum_i p_i|\phi_i\rangle\langle\phi_i| = \int_\psi |\psi\rangle\langle\psi| d\psi$

and $(1-\epsilon)\int_\psi (|\psi\rangle\langle\psi|)^{\otimes t} d\psi \leq \sum_i p_i(|\phi_i\rangle\langle\phi_i|)^{\otimes t} \leq (1+\epsilon)\int_\psi (|\psi\rangle\langle\psi|)^{\otimes t} d\psi$

then $(p_i, |\phi_i\rangle)$ is an ϵ -approximate (t,t)-design.

It is possible, though perhaps inefficient, to find an ϵ - approximate (t,t) design consisting of quantum pure states for a fixed t.

22.2.1 Construction

For convenience N is assumed to be a power of 2.

Using the fact that for any N there exists a set of N^d functions {0,...,N-1} $\rightarrow$ {0,...,N-1} such that for any distinct $k_1, ..., k_d \in$ {0,...,N-1} the image under f, where f is chosen at random from S, is exactly the uniform distribution over tuples of d elements of {0,...,N-1}.

Let $|\psi\rangle = \sum_{i=1}^{N} \alpha|i\rangle$ be drawn from the Haar measure. Let P_n be the probability distribution of α_n and let $P = \lim_{N\to\infty} \sqrt{N}P_N$. Finally let α be drawn from P. If we define $X = |\alpha|$ with probability $\frac{1}{2}$ and $X = -|\alpha|$ with probability $\frac{1}{2}$ then: $E[X^j] = 0$ for odd j and $E[X^j] = (\frac{j}{2})!$ for even j.

Using this and Gaussian quadrature we can construct $p_{f,g} = \frac{\sum_{i=1}^{N} a_{f,i}^2}{|S_1||S_2|}$ so that $p_{f,g}|\psi_{f,g}\rangle$ is an approximate (t,t)-design.

22.3 Unitary Designs

Elements of the unitary design are elements of the unitary group, U(d), the group of $d \times d$ unitary matrices. A t-design of unitary operators will generate a t-design of states.

Suppose U_k is your unitary design (i.e. a set of unitary operators). Then for *any* pure state $|\psi\rangle$ let $|\psi_k\rangle = U_k|\psi\rangle$. Then $|\psi_k\rangle$ will always be a t-design for states.

Formally define[4] a *unitary t-design*, X, if

$\frac{1}{|X|}\sum_{U\in X} U^{\otimes t} \otimes (U^*)^{\otimes t} = \int_{U(d)} U^{\otimes t} \otimes (U^*)^{\otimes t} dU$

Observe that the space linearly spanned by the matrices $U^{\otimes r} \otimes (U^*)^{\otimes s} dU$ over all choices of U is identical to the restriction $U \in X$ and $r + s = t$ This observation leads to a conclusion about the duality between unitary designs and unitary codes.

Using the permutation maps it is possible[3] to verify directly that a set of unitary matrices forms a t-design.[5]

One direct result of this is that for any finite $X \subseteq U(d)$

$\frac{1}{|X|^2}\sum_{U,V\in X} |tr(U * V)|^{2t} \geq \int_{U(d)} |tr(U * V)|^{2t} dU$

With equality if and only if X is a t-design.

1 and 2-designs have been examined in some detail and absolute bounds for the dimension of X, |X|, have been derived.[6]

22.3.1 Bounds for unitary designs

Define $Hom(U(d), t, t)$ as the set of functions homogeneous of degree t in U and homogeneous of degree t in U^* , then if for every $f \in Hom(U(d), t, t)$:

$\frac{1}{|X|}\sum_{U\in X} f(U) = \int_{U(d)} f(U)dU$

then X is a unitary t-design.

We further define the inner product for functions f and g on $U(d)$ as the average value of $\bar{f}g$ as:

$\langle f, g\rangle := \int_{U(d)} \bar{f(U)}g(U)dX$

and $\langle f, g\rangle_X$ as the average value of $\bar{f}g$ over any finite subset $X \subset U(d)$.

it follows that X is a unitary t-design iff $\langle 1, f\rangle_X = \langle 1, f\rangle \quad \forall f$.

From the above it is demonstrable that if X is a t-design then $|X| \geq dim(Hom(U(d), \lceil\frac{t}{2}\rceil, \lfloor\frac{t}{2}\rfloor))$ is an **absolute bound** for the design. This imposes an upper bound on the size of a unitary design. This bound is **absolute** meaning it depends only on the strength of the design or the degree of the code, and not the distances in the subset, X.

A unitary code is a finite subset of the unitary group in which a few inner product values occur between elements. Specifically, a unitary code is defined as a finite subset $X \subset U(d)$ if for all $U \neq M$ in X $|tr(U^*M)|^2$ takes only distinct values.

It follows that $|X| \leq dim(Hom(U(d), s, s))$ and if U and M are orthogonal: $|X| \leq dim(Hom(U(d), s, s-1))$

22.4 Notes

[1] A. Hayashi, T. Hashimoto, M. Horibe. Reexamination of optimal quantum state estimation of pure states. Phys. Rev. A, 72: 032325, 2006. Also quant-ph/0410207.

[2] C. Dankert, R. Cleve, J. Emerson, and E. Livine, Exact and approximate unitary 2-designs: constructions and applications, (2006).

[3] [quant-ph/0701126] Quantum t-designs: t-wise independence in the quantum world

[4] [0809.3813] Unitary designs and codes

[5] B. Collins and P. ´ Sniady, Integration with respect to the Haar measure on unitary, orthogonal and symplectic group, Comm. Math. Phys.,264 (2006), 773–795.

[6] D. Gross, K. Audenaert, and J. Eisert, Evenly distributed unitaries: on the structure of unitary designs, J. Math. Phys., 48 (2007),052104, 22.

Chapter 23

Quantum threshold theorem

In quantum computing, the (**quantum**) **threshold theorem** (or **quantum fault-tolerance theorem**), proved by Michael Ben-Or and Dorit Aharonov (along with other groups), states that a quantum computer with noise can quickly and accurately simulate an ideal quantum computer, provided the level of noise is below a certain threshold. Practically, the Threshold Theorem implies that the error in quantum computers can be controlled as the number of qubits scales up.

23.1 See also

- Quantum error correction

23.2 References

- http://arxiv.org/abs/1006.4941
- http://arxiv.org/abs/quant-ph/0703230
- http://arxiv.org/abs/quant-ph/9705031

23.3 External links

- Gil Kalai. "Perpetual Motion of The 21st Century?".
- Scott Aaronson. "PHYS771 Lecture 14: Skepticism of Quantum Computing": *«The entire content of the Threshold Theorem is that you're correcting errors faster than they're created. That's the whole point, and the whole non-trivial thing that the theorem shows. That's the problem it solves.»*

Chapter 24

Quantum bus

A **quantum bus** is a device which can be used to store or transfer information between independent qubits in a quantum computer, or combine two qubits into a superposition. The concept was first demonstrated by researchers at Yale University and the National Institute of Standards and Technology (NIST) in 2007.[1][2][3] Prior to this experimental demonstration, the quantum bus had been described by scientists at NIST as one of the possible cornerstone building blocks in quantum computer architecture.[4]

24.1 References

[1] J. Majer; J. M. Chow, J. M. Gambetta, Jens Koch, B. R. Johnson, J. A. Schreier, L. Frunzio, D. I. Schuster, A. A. Houck, A. Wallraff, A. Blais, M. H. Devoret, S. M. Girvin & R. J. Schoelkopf (2007-09-27). "Coupling superconducting qubits via a cavity bus". *Nature* **449** (7161): 443–447. arXiv:0709.2135. Bibcode:2007Natur.449..443M. doi:10.1038/nature06184. PMID 17898763. Cite uses deprecated parameter |coauthors= (help)

[2] M. A. Sillanpää; J. I. Park; R. W. Simmonds (2007-09-27). "Coherent quantum state storage and transfer between two phase qubits via a resonant cavity". *Nature* **449** (7161): 438–42. arXiv:0709.2341. Bibcode:2007Natur.449..438S. doi:10.1038/nature06124. PMID 17898762.

[3] "All Aboard the Quantum 'Bus'". 2007-09-27. Retrieved 2008-12-12.

[4] G.K. Brennen; D. Song; C.J. Williams (2003). "Quantum-computer architecture using nonlocal interactions". *Physical Review A* **67** (5): 050302. arXiv:quant-ph/0301012. Bibcode:2003PhRvA..67e0302B. doi:10.1103/PhysRevA.67.050302.

Chapter 25

Quantum spin model

A **quantum spin model** is a quantum Hamiltonian model that describes a system which consists of spins either interacting or not and are an active area of research in the fields of strongly correlated electron systems, quantum information theory, and quantum computing. The physical observables in these quantum models are actually operators in a Hilbert space acting on state vectors as opposed to the physical observables in the corresponding classical spin models - like the Ising model - which are commutative variables.

25.1 References

- Michael Nielsen and Isaac Chuang (2000). *Quantum Computation and Quantum Information*. Cambridge: Cambridge University Press. ISBN 0-521-63503-9. OCLC 174527496.

Chapter 26

Quantum channel

In quantum information theory, a **quantum channel** is a communication channel which can transmit quantum information, as well as classical information. An example of quantum information is the state of a qubit. An example of classical information is a text document transmitted over the Internet.

More formally, quantum channels are completely positive (CP) trace-preserving maps between spaces of operators. In other words, a quantum channel is just a quantum operation viewed not merely as the reduced dynamics of a system but as a pipeline intended to carry quantum information. (Some authors use the term "quantum operation" to also include trace-decreasing maps while reserving "quantum channel" for strictly trace-preserving maps.[1])

26.1 Memoryless quantum channel

We will assume for the moment that all state spaces of the systems considered, classical or quantum, are finite-dimensional.

The **memoryless** in the section title carries the same meaning as in classical information theory: the output of a channel at a given time depends only upon the corresponding input and not any previous ones.

26.1.1 Schrödinger picture

Consider quantum channels that transmit only quantum information. This is precisely a quantum operation, whose properties we now summarize.

Let H_A and H_B be the state spaces (finite-dimensional Hilbert spaces) of the sending and receiving ends, respectively, of a channel. $L(H_A)$ will denote the family of operators on H_A . In the Schrödinger picture, a purely quantum channel is a map Φ between density matrices acting on H_A and H_B with the following properties:

1. As required by postulates of quantum mechanics, Φ needs to be linear.

2. Since density matrices are positive, Φ must preserve the cone of positive elements. In other words, Φ is a positive map.

3. If an ancilla of arbitrary finite dimension n is coupled to the system, then the induced map $I_n \otimes \Phi$, where *In* is the identity map on the ancilla, must also be positive. Therefore it is required that $I_n \otimes \Phi$ is positive for all n. Such maps are called completely positive.

4. Density matrices are specified to have trace 1, so Φ has to preserve the trace.

The adjectives **completely positive and trace preserving** used to describe a map are sometimes abbreviated **CPTP**. In the literature, sometimes the fourth property is weakened so that Φ is only required to be not trace-increasing. In this article, it will be assumed that all channels are CPTP.

26.1.2 Heisenberg picture

Density matrices acting on *HA* only constitute a proper subset of the operators on *HA* and same can be said for system *B*. However, once a linear map Φ between the density matrices is specified, a standard linearity argument, together with the finite-dimensional assumption, allow us to extend Φ uniquely to the full space of operators. This leads to the adjoint map Φ^*, which describes the action of Φ in the Heisenberg picture:

The spaces of operators *L*(*HA*) and *L*(*HB*) are Hilbert spaces with the Hilbert–Schmidt inner product. Therefore, viewing $\Phi : L(H_A) \to L(H_B)$ as a map between Hilbert spaces, we obtain its adjoint Φ^* given by

$$\langle A, \Phi(\rho)\rangle = \langle \Phi^*(A), \rho\rangle.$$

While Φ takes states on *A* to those on *B*, Φ^* maps observables on system *B* to observables on *A*. This relationship is same as that between the Schrödinger and Heisenberg descriptions of dynamics. The measurement statistics remain unchanged whether the observables are considered fixed while the states undergo operation or vice versa.

It can be directly checked that if Φ is assumed to be trace preserving, Φ^* is unital, that is, $\Phi^*(I) = I$. Physically speaking, this means that, in the Heisenberg picture, the trivial observable remains trivial after applying the channel.

26.1.3 Classical information

So far we have only defined quantum channel that transmits only quantum information. As stated in the introduction, the input and output of a channel can include classical information as well. To describe this, the formulation given so far needs to be generalized somewhat. A purely quantum channel, in the Heisenberg picture, is a linear map Ψ between spaces of operators:

$$\Psi : L(H_B) \to L(H_A)$$

that is unital and completely positive (**CP**). The operator spaces can be viewed as finite-dimensional C*-algebras. Therefore we can say a channel is a unital CP map between C*-algebras:

$$\Psi : \mathcal{B} \to \mathcal{A}.$$

Classical information can then be included in this formulation. The observables of a classical system can be assumed to be a commutative C*-algebra, i.e. the space of continuous functions $C(X)$ on some set X. We assume X is finite so $C(X)$ can be identified with the n-dimensional Euclidean space $\mathbb{R}^n$ with entry-wise multiplication.

Therefore, in the Heisenberg picture, if the classical information is part of, say, the input, we would define $\mathcal{B}$ to include the relevant classical observables. An example of this would be a channel

$$\Psi : L(H_B) \otimes C(X) \to L(H_A).$$

Notice $L(H_B) \otimes C(X)$ is still a C*-algebra. An element a of a C*-algebra $\mathcal{A}$ is called positive if $a = x^*x$ for some x. Positivity of a map is defined accordingly. This characterization is not universally accepted; the quantum instrument is sometimes given as the generalized mathematical framework for conveying both quantum and classical information. In axiomatizations of quantum mechanics, the classical information is carried in a Frobenius algebra or Frobenius category.

26.2 Examples

26.2.1 States

A state, viewed as a mapping from observables to their expectation values, is an immediate example of a channel.

26.2.2 Time evolution

For a purely quantum system, the time evolution, at certain time t, is given by

$$\rho \to U \rho U^*,$$

where $U = e^{-iHt/\hbar}$ and H is the Hamiltonian and t is the time. Clearly this gives a CPTP map in the Schrödinger picture and is therefore a channel. The dual map in the Heisenberg picture is

$$A \to U^* A U.$$

26.2.3 Restriction

Consider a composite quantum system with state space $H_A \otimes H_B$. For a state

$$\rho \in H_A \otimes H_B,$$

the reduced state of ϱ on system A, ϱ^A, is obtained by taking the partial trace of ϱ with respect to the B system:

$$\rho^A = \mathrm{Tr}_B\ \rho.$$

The partial trace operation is a CPTP map, therefore a quantum channel in the Schrödinger picture. In the Heisenberg picture, the dual map of this channel is

$$A \to A \otimes I_B,$$

where A is an observable of system A.

26.2.4 Observable

An observable associates a numerical value $f_i \in \mathbb{C}$ to a quantum mechanical *effect* F_i . F_i 's are assumed to be positive operators acting on appropriate state space and $\sum F_i = I$. (Such a collection is called a POVM.) In the Heisenberg picture, the corresponding *observable map* Ψ maps a classical observable

$$f = \begin{bmatrix} f_1 \\ \vdots \\ f_n \end{bmatrix} \in C(X)$$

to the quantum mechanical one

$$\Psi(f) = \sum_i f_i F_i.$$

In other words, one integrate f against the POVM to obtain the quantum mechanical observable. It can be easily checked that Ψ is CP and unital.

The corresponding Schrödinger map Ψ^* takes density matrices to classical states:

$$\Psi(\rho) = \begin{bmatrix} \langle F_1, \rho \rangle \\ \vdots \\ \langle F_n, \rho \rangle \end{bmatrix}$$

,where the inner product is the Hilbert–Schmidt inner product. Furthermore, viewing states as normalized functionals, and invoking the Riesz representation theorem, we can put

$$\Psi(\rho) = \begin{bmatrix} \rho(F_1) \\ \vdots \\ \rho(F_n) \end{bmatrix}.$$

26.2.5 Instrument

The observable map, in the Schrödinger picture, has a purely classical output algebra and therefore only describe measurement statistics. To take the state change into account as well, we define what is called an quantum instrument. Let $\{F_1, \cdots, F_n\}$ be the effects (POVM) associated to an observable. In the Schrödinger picture, an instrument is a map Φ with pure quantum input $\rho \in L(H)$ and with output space $C(X) \otimes L(H)$:

$$\Phi(\rho) = \begin{bmatrix} \rho(F_1) \cdot F_1 \\ \vdots \\ \rho(F_n) \cdot F_n \end{bmatrix}.$$

Let

$$f = \begin{bmatrix} f_1 \\ \vdots \\ f_n \end{bmatrix} \in C(X).$$

The dual map in the Heisenberg picture is

$$\Psi(f \otimes A) = \begin{bmatrix} f_1 \Psi_1(A) \\ \vdots \\ f_n \Psi_n(A) \end{bmatrix}$$

where Ψ_i is defined in the following way: Factor $F_i = M_i^2$ (this can always be done since elements of a POVM are positive) then $\Psi_i(A) = M_i A M_i$. We see that Ψ is CP and unital.

Notice that $\Psi(f \otimes I)$ gives precisely the observable map. The map

$$\tilde{\Psi}(A) = \sum_i \Psi_i(A) = \sum_i M_i A M_i$$

describes the overall state change.

26.2.6 Separable channel

A separable channel is an example of local operation and classical communication (LOCC). Suppose two parties *A* and *B* wish to communicate in the following manner: *A* performs measurement on an observable and communicates the measurement outcome to *B* classically. According to the message he receives, *B* prepares his (quantum) system in a state that is previously agreed upon by both parties. In the Schrödinger picture, the first part of the channel Φ_1 simply consists of *A* making a measurement, i.e. it is the observable map:

$$\Phi_1(\rho) = \begin{bmatrix} \rho(F_1) \\ \vdots \\ \rho(F_n) \end{bmatrix}.$$

If, in the event of the *i*-th measurement outcome, *B* prepares his system in state *Ri*, the second part of the channel Φ_2 takes the above classical state to the density matrix

$$\Phi_2 \left(\begin{bmatrix} \rho(F_1) \\ \vdots \\ \rho(F_n) \end{bmatrix} \right) = \sum_i \rho(F_i) R_i.$$

The total operation is the composition

$$\Phi(\rho) = \Phi_2 \circ \Phi_1(\rho) = \sum_i \rho(F_i) R_i.$$

Channels of this form are called *separable* or in Holevo form.

In the Heisenberg picture, the dual map $\Phi^* = \Phi_1^* \circ \Phi_2^*$ is defined by

$$\Phi^*(A) = \sum_i R_i(A) F_i.$$

A separable channel can not be the identity map. This is precisely the statement of the no teleportation theorem, which says classical teleportation (not to be confused with entanglement-assisted teleportation) is impossible. In other words, a quantum state can not be measured reliably.

In the channel-state duality, a channel is separable if and only if the corresponding state is separable. Several other characterizations of separable channels are known, notably that a channel is separable if and only if it is entanglement-breaking.

26.2.7 Pure channel

Consider the case of a purely quantum channel Ψ in the Heisenberg picture. With the assumption that everything is finite-dimensional, Ψ is a unital CP map between spaces of matrices

$$\Psi : \mathbb{C}^{n\times n} \to \mathbb{C}^{m\times m}.$$

By Choi's theorem on completely positive maps, Ψ must take the form

$$\Psi(A) = \sum_{i=1}^{N} K_i A K_i^*$$

where $N \leq nm$. The matrices Ki are called **Kraus operators** of Ψ (after the German physicist Karl Kraus, who introduced them). The minimum number of Kraus operators is call the Kraus rank of Ψ. A channel with Kraus rank 1 is called **pure**. The time evolution is one example of a pure channel. This terminology again comes from the channel-state duality. A channel is pure if and only if its dual state is a pure state. Since this duality preserves the extremal points, the extremal points in the convex set of channels are precisely the pure channels.

26.2.8 Teleportation

In quantum teleportation, a sender wishes to transmit an arbitrary quantum state of a particle to a possibly distant receiver. Consequently, the teleportation process is a quantum channel. The apparatus for the process itself requires a quantum channel for the transmission of one particle of an entangled-state to the receiver. Teleportation occurs by a joint measurement of the sent particle and the remaining entangled particle. This measurement results in classical information which must be sent to the receiver to complete the teleportation. Importantly, the classical information can be sent after the quantum channel has ceased to exist.

26.3 In the experimental setting

Experimentally, a simple implementation of a quantum channel is fiber optic (or free-space for that matter) transmission of single photons. Single photons can be transmitted up to 100 km in standard fiber optics before losses dominate. The photon's time-of-arrival (*time-bin entanglement*) or polarization are used as a basis to encode quantum information for purposes such as quantum cryptography. The channel is capable of transmitting not only basis states (e.g. |0>, |1>) but also superpositions of them (e.g. |0>+|1>). The coherence of the state is maintained during transmission through the channel. Contrast this with the transmission of electrical pulses through wires (a classical channel), where only classical information (e.g. 0s and 1s) can be sent.

26.4 Channel capacity

26.4.1 The cb-norm of a channel

Before giving the definition of channel capacity, the preliminary notion of the **norm of complete boundedness**, or **cb-norm** of a channel needs to be discussed. When considering the capacity of a channel Φ, we need to compare it with an "ideal channel" Λ. For instance, when the input and output algebras are identical, we can choose Λ to be the identity map. Such a comparison requires a metric between channels. Since a channel can be viewed as a linear operator, it is tempting to use the natural operator norm. In other words, the closeness of Φ to the ideal channel Λ can be defined by

$$\|\Phi - \Lambda\| = \sup\{\|(\Phi - \Lambda)(A)\| \mid \|A\| \leq 1\}.$$

However, the operator norm may increase when we tensor Φ with the identity map on some ancilla.

To make the operator norm even a more undesirable candidate, the quantity

$$\|\Phi \otimes I_n\|$$

may increase without bound as $n \to \infty$. The solution is to introduce, for any linear map Φ between C*-algebras, the cb-norm

$$\|\Phi\|_{cb} = \sup_n \|\Phi \otimes I_n\|.$$

26.4.2 Definition of channel capacity

The mathematical model of a channel used here is same as the classical one.

Let $\Psi : \mathcal{B}_1 \to \mathcal{A}_1$ be a channel in the Heisenberg picture and $\Psi_{id} : \mathcal{B}_2 \to \mathcal{A}_2$ be a chosen ideal channel. To make the comparison possible, one needs to encode and decode Φ via appropriate devices, i.e. we consider the composition

$$\hat{\Psi} = D \circ \Phi \circ E : \mathcal{B}_2 \to \mathcal{A}_2$$

where E is an encoder and D is a decoder. In this context, E and D are unital CP maps with appropriate domains. The quantity of interest is the *best case scenario*:

$$\Delta(\hat{\Psi}, \Psi_{id}) - \inf_{E,D} \|\hat{\Psi} - \Psi_{id}\|_{cb}$$

with the infimum being taken over all possible encoders and decoders.

To transmit words of length n, the ideal channel is to be applied n times, so we consider the tensor power

$$\Psi_{id}^{\otimes n} = \Psi_{id} \otimes \cdots \otimes \Psi_{id}.$$

The $\otimes$ operation describes n inputs undergoing the operation Ψ_{id} independently and is the quantum mechanical counterpart of concatenation. Similarly, *m invocations of the channel* corresponds to $\hat{\Psi}^{\otimes m}$.

The quantity

$$\Delta(\hat{\Psi}^{\otimes m}, \Psi_{id}^{\otimes n})$$

is therefore a measure of the ability of the channel to transmit words of length n faithfully by being invoked m times.

This leads to the following definition:

> An a non-negative real number r is an **achievable rate of Ψ with respect to Ψ_{id}** if
>
> For all sequences $\{n_\alpha\}, \{m_\alpha\} \subset \mathbb{N}$ where $m_\alpha \to \infty$ and $\limsup_\alpha (n_\alpha / m_\alpha) < r$, we have

$$\lim_\alpha \Delta(\hat{\Psi}^{\otimes m_\alpha}, \Psi_{id}^{\otimes n_\alpha}) = 0.$$

A sequence $\{n_\alpha\}$ can be viewed as representing a message consisting of possibly infinite number of words. The limit supremum condition in the definition says that, in the limit, faithful transmission can be achieved by invoking the channel no more than r times the length of a word. One can also say that r is the number of letters per invocation of the channel that can be sent without error.

The **channel capacity of Ψ with respect to Ψ_{id}** , denoted by $C(\Psi, \Psi_{id})$ is the supremum of all achievable rates.

From the definition, it is vacuously true that 0 is an achievable rate for any channel.

26.4.3 Important examples

As stated before, for a system with observable algebra $\mathcal{B}$, the ideal channel Ψ_{id} is by definition the identity map $I_{\mathcal{B}}$. Thus for a purely n dimensional quantum system, the ideal channel is the identity map on the space of $n \times n$ matrices $\mathbb{C}^{n \times n}$. As a slight abuse of notation, this ideal quantum channel will be also denoted by $\mathbb{C}^{n \times n}$. Similarly for a classical system with output algebra $\mathbb{C}^m$ will have an ideal channel denoted by the same symbol. We can now state some fundamental channel capacities.

The channel capacity of the classical ideal channel $\mathbb{C}^m$ with respect to a quantum ideal channel $\mathbb{C}^{n \times n}$ is

$$C(\mathbb{C}^m, \mathbb{C}^{n \times n}) = 0.$$

This is equivalent to the no-teleportation theorem: it is impossible to transmit quantum information via a classical channel.

Moreover, the following equalities hold:

$$C(\mathbb{C}^m, \mathbb{C}^n) = C(\mathbb{C}^{m \times m}, \mathbb{C}^{n \times n})$$
$$== C(\mathbb{C}^{m \times m}, \mathbb{C}^{\,n}) == \frac{\log n}{\log m}.$$

The above says, for instance, an ideal quantum channel is no more efficient at transmitting classical information than an ideal classical channel. When $n = m$, the best one can achieve is *one bit per qubit.*

It is relevant to note here that both of the above bounds on capacities can be broken, with the aid of entanglement. The entanglement-assisted teleportation scheme allows one to transmit quantum information using a classical channel. Superdense coding. achieves *two bit per qubit.* These results indicate the significant role played by entanglement in quantum communication.

26.4.4 Classical and quantum channel capacities

Using the same notation as the previous subsection, the **classical capacity** of a channel Ψ is

$$C(\Psi, \mathbb{C}^2),$$

that is, it is the capacity of Ψ with respect to the ideal channel on the classical one-bit system $\mathbb{C}^2$.

Similarly the **quantum capacity** of Ψ is

$$C(\Psi, \mathbb{C}^{2 \times 2}),$$

where the reference system is now the one qubit system $\mathbb{C}^{2 \times 2}$.

26.5 Channel fidelity

Another measure of how well a quantum channel preserves information is called **channel fidelity**, and it arises from fidelity of quantum states.

26.6 Quantum channel with memory

26.7 See also

- No-communication theorem
- Amplitude damping channel

26.8 References

- M. Keyl and R.F. Werner, *How to Correct Small Quantum Errors*, Lecture Notes in Physics Volume 611, Springer, 2002.
- Mark M. Wilde, "From Classical to Quantum Shannon Theory", arXiv:1106.1445.

[1] C. Weedbrook at al., "Gaussian quantum information", *Rev. Mod. Phys.* **84**, 621 (2012).

Chapter 27

Quantum depolarizing channel

A **quantum depolarizing channel** is a model for noise in quantum systems. The d-dimensional depolarizing channel can be viewed as a completely positive trace-preserving map Δ_λ , depending on one parameter λ , which maps a state ρ onto a linear combination of itself and the maximally mixed state:

$$\Delta_\lambda(\rho) = \lambda\rho + \frac{1-\lambda}{d} I$$

The condition of complete positivity requires λ to satisfy the bounds:

$$-\frac{1}{d^2-1} \leq \lambda \leq 1$$

27.1 Classical capacity

The HSW theorem states that the classical capacity of a quantum channel Ψ can be characterized as its regularized Holevo information:

$$\lim_{n\to\infty} \frac{1}{n} \chi\left(\Psi^{\otimes n}\right)$$

This quantity is difficult to compute and this reflects our ignorance on quantum channels. However, if the Holevo information is additive for a channel Ψ , i.e.,

$$\chi\left(\Psi \otimes \Psi\right) = \chi\left(\Psi\right) + \chi\left(\Psi\right)$$

Then we can get its classical capacity by computing the Holevo information of the channel.

The additivity of Holevo information for all channels was a famous open conjecture in quantum information theory, but it is now known that this conjecture doesn't hold in general. This was proved by showing that the additivity of minimum output entropy for all channels doesn't hold,[1] which is an equivalent conjecture.

Nonetheless, the additivity of the Holevo information is shown to hold for the quantum depolarizing channel,[2] and an outline of the proof is given below. As a consequence, entanglement across multiple uses of the channel cannot increase the classical capacity. In this sense, the channel behaves like a classical channel. To achieve the optimal rate of communication, it suffices to choose an orthonormal basis to encode the message, and perform measurements that project onto to the same basis at the receiving end.

27.1.1 Outline of the proof of the additivity of Holevo information

The additivity of Holevo information for the depolarizing channel was proved by Christopher King.[2] He showed that the maximum output p-norm of the depolarizing channel is multiplicative, which implied the additivity of the minimum output entropy, which is equivalent to the additivity of the Holevo information.

A stronger version of the additivity of the Holevo information is shown for the depolarizing channel Δ_λ . For any channel Ψ :

$$\chi\left(\Delta_\lambda \otimes \Psi\right) = \chi\left(\Delta_\lambda\right) + \chi\left(\Psi\right)$$

This is implied by the following multiplicativity of maximum output p-norm (denoted as v_p):

$$v_p\left(\Delta_\lambda \otimes \Psi\right) = v_p\left(\Delta_\lambda\right) v_p\left(\Psi\right)$$

The greater than or equal to direction of the above is trivial, it suffices to take the tensor product the states that achieve the maximum p-norm for Δ_λ and Ψ respectively, and input the product state into the product channel to get the output p-norm $v_p(\Delta_\lambda)v_p(\Psi)$. The proof for the other direction is more involved

The main idea of the proof is to rewrite the depolarizing channel as a convex combination of simpler channels, and use properties of those simpler channels to get the multiplicativity of the maximum output p-norm for the depolarizing channel.

It turns out that we can write the depolarizing channel as follows:

$$\Delta_\lambda(\rho) = \sum_{n=1}^{2d^2(d+1)} c_n U_n^* \Phi_\lambda^{(n)}(\rho) Un$$

where c_n 's are positive numbers, U_n 's are unitary matrices, $\Phi_\lambda^{(n)}$'s are some dephasing channels and ρ is an arbitrary input state.

Therefore, the product channel can be written as:

$$(\Delta_\lambda \otimes \Psi)(\rho) = \sum_{n=1}^{2d^2(d+1)} c_n (U_n^* \otimes I) \left(\Phi_\lambda^{(n)} \otimes \Psi\right)(\rho)(U_n \otimes I)$$

By the convexity and the unitary invariance of the p-norm, it suffices to show the simpler bound:

$$\| \left(\Phi_\lambda^{(n)} \otimes \Psi\right)(\rho) \|_p \leq v_p(\Delta_\lambda) v_p(\Psi)$$

One important mathematical tool used in the proof of this bound is the Lieb–Thirring inequality, which provides a bound for p-norm of a product of positive matrices. The details and the calculations of the proof are skipped, interested readers are referred to the paper of C. King mentioned above.

27.1.2 Discussion

The main technique used in this proof, namely rewriting the channel of interest as a convex combination of other simpler channels, is a generalization of the method used earlier to prove similar results for unital qubit channels.[3]

The fact that the classical capacity of the depolarizing channel is equal to the Holevo information of the channel means that we can't really use quantum effects such as entanglement to improve the transmission rate of classical information. In this sense, the depolarizing channel can be treated as a classical channel.

However the fact that the additivity of Holevo information doesn't hold in general proposes some areas of future work, namely finding channels that violates the additivity, in other words, channels that can exploit quantum effects to improve the classical capacity beyond its Holevo information.

27.2 Notes

[1] Hastings 2009.

[2] King 2003.

[3] C. King, *Additivity for unital qubit channels*

27.3 References

- King, C. (14 January 2003), "The capacity of the quantum depolarizing channel", *IEEE Transactions on Information Theory* **49** (1): 221–229, arXiv:quant-ph/0204172v2, doi:10.1109/TIT.2002.806153
- Hastings, M. B. (15 March 2009), "Superadditivity of communication capacity using entangled inputs", *Nature Physics* **5** (4): 255–257, arXiv:0809.3972v4, Bibcode:2009NatPh...5..255H, doi:10.1038/nphys1224

Chapter 28

Quantum capacity

In the theory of quantum communication, the **quantum capacity** is the highest rate at which quantum information can be communicated over many independent uses of a noisy quantum channel from a sender to a receiver. It is also equal to the highest rate at which entanglement can be generated over the channel, and forward classical communication cannot improve it. The quantum capacity theorem is important for the theory of quantum error correction, and more broadly for the theory of quantum computation. The theorem giving a lower bound on the quantum capacity of any channel is colloquially known as the LSD theorem, after the authors Lloyd,[1] Shor,[2] and Devetak[3] who proved it with increasing standards of rigor.

28.1 Hashing Bound for Pauli Channels

The LSD theorem states that the coherent information of a quantum channel is an achievable rate for reliable quantum communication. For a Pauli channel, the coherent information has a simple form and the proof that it is achievable is particularly simple as well. We prove the theorem for this special case by exploiting random stabilizer codes and correcting only the likely errors that the channel produces.

Theorem (Hashing Bound). There exists a stabilizer quantum error-correcting code that achieves the hashing limit $R = 1 - H(\mathbf{p})$ for a Pauli channel of the following form:

$$\rho \mapsto p_I \rho + p_X X \rho X + p_Y Y \rho Y + p_Z Z \rho Z,$$

where $\mathbf{p} = (p_I, p_X, p_Y, p_Z)$ and $H(\mathbf{p})$ is the entropy of this probability vector.

Proof. We consider correcting only the typical errors. That is, consider defining the typical set of errors as follows:

$$T_\delta^{\mathbf{p}^n} \equiv \left\{ a^n : \left| -\frac{1}{n} \log_2 \left(\Pr\left\{ E_{a^n} \right\} \right) - H(\mathbf{p}) \right| \leq \delta \right\},$$

where a^n is some sequence consisting of the letters $\{I, X, Y, Z\}$ and $\Pr\{E_{a^n}\}$ is the probability that an IID Pauli channel issues some tensor-product error $E_{a^n} \equiv E_{a_1} \otimes \cdots \otimes E_{a_n}$. This typical set consists of the likely errors in the sense that

$$\sum_{a^n \in T_\delta^{\mathbf{p}^n}} \Pr\left\{ E_{a^n} \right\} \geq 1 - \epsilon,$$

for all $\epsilon > 0$ and sufficiently large n . The error-correcting conditions[4] for a stabilizer code $\mathcal{S}$ in this case are that $\{E_{a^n} : a^n \in T_\delta^{\mathbf{p}^n}\}$ is a correctable set of errors if

$$E_{a^n}^{\dagger} E_{b^n} \notin N(\mathcal{S}) \backslash \mathcal{S},$$

for all error pairs E_{a^n} and E_{b^n} such that $a^n, b^n \in T_\delta^{\mathbf{p}^n}$ where $N(\mathcal{S})$ is the normalizer of $\mathcal{S}$. Also, we consider the expectation of the error probability under a random choice of a stabilizer code.

We proceed as follows:

$$\mathbb{E}_{\mathcal{S}}\left\{ p_e \right\} = \mathbb{E}$$

$$\mathcal{S}\left\{ \sum_{a^n} \Pr\left\{ E_{a^n} \right\} \mathcal{I}\left(E_{a^n} \text{ under uncorrectable is } \mathcal{S} \right) \right\}$$

$$\leq \mathbb{E}_{\mathcal{S}}$$

$$\left\{ \sum_{a^n \in T_\delta^{\mathbf{p}^n}} \Pr\left\{ E_{a^n} \right\} \mathcal{I}\left(E_{a^n} \text{ under uncorrectable is } \mathcal{S} \right) \right\} + \epsilon$$

$$= \sum_{a^n \in T_\delta^{\mathbf{p}^n}} \Pr\left\{ E_{a^n} \right\} \mathbb{E}_{\mathcal{S}} \left\{ \mathcal{I}\left(E_{a^n} \text{ under uncorrectable is } \mathcal{S} \right) \right\} + \epsilon$$

$$= \sum_{a^n \in T_\delta^{\mathbf{p}^n}} \Pr\left\{ E_{a^n} \right\} \Pr_{\mathcal{S}} \left\{ E_{a^n} \text{ under uncorrectable is } \mathcal{S} \right\} + \epsilon.$$

The first equality follows by definition— $\mathcal{I}$ is an indicator function equal to one if E_{a^n} is uncorrectable under $\mathcal{S}$ and equal to zero otherwise. The first inequality follows, since we correct only the typical errors because the atypical error set has negligible probability mass. The second equality follows by exchanging the expectation and the sum. The third equality follows because the expectation of an indicator function is the probability that the event it selects occurs. Continuing, we have

$$= \sum_{a^n \in T_\delta^{\mathbf{p}^n}} \Pr\{E_{a^n}\} \Pr_{\mathcal{S}} \left\{ \exists E_{b^n} : b^n \in T_\delta^{\mathbf{p}^n},\ b^n / = a^n,\ E_{a^n}^\dagger E_{b^n} \in N(\mathcal{S}) \backslash \mathcal{S} \right\}$$

$$\leq \sum_{a^n \in T_\delta^{A^n}} \Pr\{E_{a^n}\} \Pr_{\mathcal{S}} \left\{ \exists E_{b^n} : b^n \in T_\delta^{\mathbf{p}^n},\ b^n \neq an,\ E_{a^n} E_{b^n}^\dagger \in N(\mathcal{S}) \right\}$$

$$= \sum_{a^n \in T_\delta^{\mathbf{p}^n}} \Pr\{E_{a^n}\} \Pr_{\mathcal{S}} \left\{ \bigcup_{b^n \in T_\delta^{\mathbf{p}^n},\ b^n \neq a^n} E_{a^n}^\dagger E_{b^n} \in N(\mathcal{S}) \right\}$$

$$\leq \sum_{a^n, b^n \in T_\delta^{\mathbf{p}^n},\ b^n \neq a^n} \Pr\{E_{a^n}\} \Pr_{\mathcal{S}} \left\{ E_{a^n}^\dagger E_{b^n} \in N(\mathcal{S}) \right\}$$

$$\leq \sum_{a^n, b^n \in T_\delta^{\mathbf{p}^n},\ b^n \neq a^n} \Pr\{E_{a^n}\} 2^{-(n-k)}$$

$$\leq 2^{2n[H(\mathbf{p})+\delta]} 2^{-n[H(\mathbf{p})+\delta]} 2^{-(n-k)}$$

$$= 2^{-n[1-H(\mathbf{p})-k/n-3\delta]}.$$

The first equality follows from the error-correcting conditions for a quantum stabilizer code, where $N(\mathcal{S})$ is the normalizer of $\mathcal{S}$. The first inequality follows by ignoring any potential degeneracy in the code—we consider an error uncorrectable if it lies in the normalizer $N(\mathcal{S})$ and the probability can only be larger because $N(\mathcal{S}) \backslash \mathcal{S} \in N(\mathcal{S})$. The second equality follows by realizing that the probabilities for the existence criterion and the union of events are equivalent. The second inequality follows by applying the union bound. The third inequality follows from the fact that the probability for a fixed operator $E_{a^n}^\dagger E_{b^n}$ not equal to the identity commuting with the stabilizer operators of a random stabilizer can be upper bounded as follows:

$$\Pr_{\mathcal{S}} \left\{ E_{a^n}^\dagger E_{b^n} \in N(\mathcal{S}) \right\} = \frac{2^{n+k}-1}{2^{2n}-1} \leq 2^{-(n-k)}.$$

The reasoning here is that the random choice of a stabilizer code is equivalent to fixing operators Z_1 , ..., Z_{n-k} and performing a uniformly random Clifford unitary. The probability that a fixed operator commutes with Z_1 , ..., Z_{n-k} is then just the number of non-identity operators in the normalizer ($2^{n+k}-1$) divided by the total number of non-identity operators ($2^{2n}-1$). After applying the above bound, we then exploit the following typicality bounds:

$$\forall a^n \in T_\delta^{\mathbf{p}^n} : \Pr\{E_{a^n}\} \leq 2^{-n[H(\mathbf{p})+\delta]},$$

$$\left| T_\delta^{\mathbf{p}^n} \right| \leq 2^{n[H(\mathbf{p})+\delta]}.$$

We conclude that as long as the rate $k/n = 1 - H(\mathbf{p}) - 4\delta$, the expectation of the error probability becomes arbitrarily small, so that there exists at least one choice of a stabilizer code with the same bound on the error probability.

28.2 References

[1] Seth Lloyd (1997). "Capacity of the noisy quantum channel". *Physical Review A* **55** (3): 1613–1622. arXiv:quant-ph/9604015. Bibcode:1997PhRvA..55.1613L. doi:10.1103/PhysRevA.55.1613.

[2] Peter Shor (2002). "The quantum channel capacity and coherent information" (pdf). *Lecture Notes, MSRI Workshop on Quantum Computation.*

[3] Igor Devetak (2005). "The private classical capacity and quantum capacity of a quantum channel". *IEEE Transactions on Information Theory* **51**: 44–55. arXiv:quant-ph/0304127. doi:10.1109/TIT.2004.839515.

[4] Nielsen, Michael A.; Chuang, Isaac L. (2000), *Quantum Computation and Quantum Information*, Cambridge University Press, ISBN 9780521635035.

28.3 Further reading

- Mark M. Wilde, "From Classical to Quantum Shannon Theory", arXiv:1106.1445.

Chapter 29

Quantum cognition

Quantum cognition is an emerging field which applies the mathematical formalism of quantum theory to model cognitive phenomena such as information processing by the human brain, decision making, human memory, concepts and conceptual reasoning, human judgment, and perception.[1][2] [3][4] The field clearly distinguishes itself from the quantum mind as it is not reliant on the hypothesis that there is something micro-physical quantum mechanical about the brain. Quantum cognition is based on the quantum-like paradigm[5][6] or generalized quantum paradigm [7] or quantum structure paradigm [8] that information processing by complex systems such as the brain, taking into account contextual dependence of information and probabilistic reasoning, can be mathematically described in the framework of quantum information and quantum probability theory.

Quantum cognition uses the mathematical formalism of quantum theory to inspire and formalize models of cognition that aim to be an advance over models based on traditional classical probability theory. The field focuses on modeling phenomena in cognitive science that have resisted traditional techniques or where traditional models seem to have reached a barrier (e.g., human memory [9]), and modeling preferences in decision theory that seem paradoxical from a traditional rational point of view (e.g., preference reversals [10]). Since the use of a quantum-theoretic framework is for modeling purposes, the identification of quantum structures in cognitive phenomena does not presuppose the existence of microscopic quantum processes in the human brain.[11]

29.1 Main subjects of research

29.1.1 Quantum-like models of information processing ("quantum-like brain")

The brain is definitely a macroscopic physical system operating on the scales (of time, space, temperature) which differ crucially from the corresponding quantum scales. (The macroscopic quantum physical phenomena such as e.g. the Bose-Einstein condensate are also characterized by the special conditions which are definitely not fulfilled in the brain.) In particular, the brain is simply too hot to be able perform the real quantum information processing, i.e., to use the quantum carriers of information such as photons, ions, electrons. As is commonly accepted in brain science, the basic unit of information processing is a neuron. It is clear that a neuron cannot be in the superposition of two states: firing and non-firing. Hence, it cannot produce superposition playing the basic role in the quantum information processing. Superpositions of mental states are created by complex neural networks of neurons (and these are classical neural networks). Quantum cognition community states that the activity of such neural networks can produce effects which are formally described as interference (of probabilities) and entanglement. In principle, the community does not try to create the concrete models of quantum (-like) representation of information in the brain.[12]

The quantum cognition project is based on the observation that various cognitive phenomena are more adequately described by quantum information theory and quantum probability than by the corresponding classical theories, see examples below. Thus the quantum formalism is considered as an operational formalism describing nonclassical processing of probabilistic data. Recent derivations of the complete quantum formalism from simple operational principles for representation of information supports the foundations of quantum cognition. The subjective probability viewpoint on quantum probability which was developed by C. Fuchs and collaborators [13] also supports the quantum cognition approach, especially using of quantum probabilities to describe the process of decision making.

Although at the moment we cannot present the concrete neurophysiological mechanisms of creation of the quantum-like representation of information in the brain, we can present general informational considerations supporting the idea that information processing in the brain matches with quantum information and probability. Here, contextuality is the key word, see the monograph of Khrennikov [1] for detailed representation of this viewpoint. Quantum mechanics is fundamentally contextual.[14] Quantum systems do not have objective properties which can be defined independently of measurement context. (As was pointed by N. Bohr, the whole experimental arrangement must be taken into account.) Contextuality implies existence of incompatible mental variables, violation of the classical law of total probability and (constructive and destructive) interference effects. Thus the quantum cognition approach can be considered as an attempt to formalize contextuality of mental processes by using the mathematical apparatus of quantum mechanics.

29.1.2 Decision making

Suppose a person is given an opportunity to play two rounds of the following gamble: a coin toss will determine whether the subject wins $200 or loses $100. Suppose the subject has decided to play the first round, and does so. Some subjects are then given the result (win or lose) of the first round, while other subjects are not yet given any information about the results. The experimenter then asks whether the subject wishes to play the second round. Performing this experiment with real subjects gives the following results:

1) When subjects believe they won the first round, the majority of subjects choose to play again on the second round.

2) When subjects believe they lost the first round, the majority of subjects choose to play again on the second round.

Given these two separate choices, according to the *sure thing* principle of rational decision theory, they should also play the second round even if they don't know or think about the outcome of the first round.[15] But, experimentally, when subjects are not told the results of the first round, the majority of them decline to play a second round.[16] This finding violates the law of total probability, yet it can be explained as a quantum interference effect in a manner similar to the explanation for the results from double-slit experiment in quantum physics.[2][17]

The above deviations from classical rational expectations in agents' decisions under uncertainty produce well known paradoxes in behavioral economics, that is, the Allais, Ellsberg and Machina paradoxes.[18][19][20] These deviations can be explained if one assumes that the overall conceptual landscape influences the subject's choice in a neither predictable nor controllable way. A decision process is thus an intrinsically contextual process, hence it cannot be modeled in a single Kolmogorovian probability space, which justifies the employment of quantum probability models in decision theory. More explicitly, the paradoxical situations above can be represented in a unified Hilbert space formalism where human behavior under uncertainty is explained in terms of genuine quantum aspects, namely, superposition, interference, contextuality and incompatibility.[21][22][23]

29.1.3 Human probability judgments

Quantum probability provides a new way to explain human probability judgment errors including the conjunction and disjunction errors.[24] A conjunction error occurs when a person judges the probability of a likely event L *and* an unlikely event U to be greater than the unlikely event U; a disjunction error occurs when a person judges the probability of a likely event L to be greater than the probability of the likely event L *or* an unlikely event U. Quantum probability theory is a generalization of Bayesian probability theory because it is based on a set of von Neumann axioms that relax some of the classic Kolmogorov axioms. The quantum model introduces a new fundamental concept to cognition—the compatibility versus incompatibility of questions and the effect this can have on the sequential order of judgments. Quantum probability provides a simple account of conjunction and disjunction errors as well as many other findings such as order effects on probability judgments.[25][26][27]

The liar paradox - The contextual influence of a human subject on the truth behavior of a cognitive entity is explicitly exhibited by the so-called liar paradox, that is, the truth value of a sentence like "this sentence is false". One can show that the true-false state of this paradox is represented in a complex Hilbert space, while the typical oscillations between true and false are dynamically described by the Schrödinger equation.[28][29]

29.1.4 Knowledge representation

Concepts are basic cognitive phenomena, which provide the content for inference, explanation, and language understanding. Cognitive psychology has researched different approaches for understanding concepts including exemplars, prototypes, and neural networks, and different fundamental problems have been identified, such as the experimentally tested non classical behavior for the conjunction and disjunction of concepts, more specifically the Pet-Fish problem or guppy effect,[30] and the overextension and underextension of typicality and membership weight for conjunction and disjunction.[31][32] By and large, quantum cognition has drawn on quantum theory in three ways to model concepts.

1. Exploit the contextuality of quantum theory to account for the contextuality of concepts in cognition and language and the phenomenon of emergent properties when concepts combine [11][33][34][35][36]

2. Use quantum entanglement to model the semantics of concept combinations in a non-decompositional way, and to account for the emergent properties/associates/inferences in relation to concept combinations[37]

3. Use quantum superposition to account for the emergence of a new concept when concepts are com-

bined, and as a consequence put forward an explanatory model for the Pet-Fish problem situation, and the overextension and underextension of membership weights for the conjunction and disjunction of concepts.[25][33][34]

The large amount of data collected by Hampton [31][32] on the combination of two concepts can be modeled in a specific quantum-theoretic framework in Fock space where the observed deviations from classical set (fuzzy set) theory, the above-mentioned over- and under- extension of membership weights, are explained in terms of contextual interactions, superposition, interference, entanglement and emergence.[25][38][39][40] And, more, a cognitive test on a specific concept combination has been performed which directly reveals, through the violation of Bell's inequalities, quantum entanglement between the component concepts.[41][42]

29.1.5 Human memory

The hypothesis that there may be something quantum-like about the human mental function was put forward with the quantum entanglement formula which attempted to model the effect that when a word's associative network is activated during study in memory experiment, it behaves like a quantum-entangled system.[9] Models of cognitive agents and memory based on quantum collectives have been proposed by Subhash Kak.[43][44] But he also points to specific problems of limits on observation and control of these memories due to fundamental logical reasons.[45]

29.1.6 Semantic analysis and information retrieval

The research in (iv) had a deep impact on the understanding and initial development of a formalism to obtain semantic information when dealing with concepts, their combinations and variable contexts in a corpus of unstructured documents. This conundrum of natural language processing (NLP) and information retrieval (IR) on the web – and data bases in general – can be addressed using the mathematical formalism of quantum theory. As basic steps, (a) the seminal book "The Geometry of Information Retrieval" by K. Van Rijsbergen[46] introduced a quantum structure approach to IR, (b) Widdows and Peters utilised a quantum logical negation for a concrete search system,[36][47] and Aerts and Czachor identified quantum structure in semantic space theories, such as latent semantic analysis.[48] Since then, the employment of techniques and procedures induced from the mathematical formalisms of quantum theory – Hilbert space, quantum logic and probability, non-commutative algebras, etc. – in fields such as IR and NLP, has produced significant results.

29.1.7 Human Perception

Bi-stable perceptual phenomena is a fascinating topic in the area of perception. If a stimulus has an ambiguous interpretation, such as a Necker cube, the interpretation tends to oscillate across time. Quantum models have been developed to predict the time period between oscillations and how these periods change with frequency of measurement.[49] Quantum theory has also been used for modeling Gestalt perception, to account for interference effects obtained with measurements of ambiguous figures (see next section).[50][51][52][53]

Gestalt perception

There are apparent similarities between Gestalt perception and quantum theory. In an article discussing the application of Gestalt to chemistry, Anton Amann writes: "Quantum mechanics does *not* explain Gestalt perception, of course, but in quantum mechanics and Gestalt psychology there exist almost isomorphic conceptions and problems:

- Similarly as with the Gestalt concept, the shape of a quantum object does *not* a priori exist but it depends on the interaction of this quantum object with the environment (for example: an observer or a measurement apparatus).
- Quantum mechanics and Gestalt perception are organized in a holistic way. Subentities do *not* necessarily exist in a distinct, individual sense.
- In quantum mechanics and Gestalt perception *objects have to be created* by elimination of holistic correlations with the 'rest of the world'."[54]

Amann comments: "The structural similarities between Gestalt perception and quantum mechanics are on a level of a parable, but even parables can teach us something, for example, that quantum mechanics is more than just production of numerical results or that the Gestalt concept is more than just a silly idea, incompatible with atomistic conceptions."[54]

A totally different position is that one of the theoretical physicist Elio Conte who for the first time has produced experimental results related to theoretical studies on quantum cognition. The position of this scientist is that quantum mechanics has a basic role at the perceptive and cognitive level of human functions. Elio Conte profoundly disagrees with the position of researchers who only use quantum mechanics as an instrumental method. They often use the term quantum-like within this instrumental approach with the justification that in some applications (by means of psychological tests) the use of probabilistic calculus seems to provide a better description than the classic one based on classical probabilistic calculation. This author argues that the subsistence of quantum mechanics to the mental level is demonstrated and in this regard he has constructed a large number of experiments that aim to highlight two peculiar features of quantum mechanics. The first is the so-called phenomenon of quantum interference. The second is the proof that starting with experimental data obtained by posing subsequent and incompatible tasks A and B to subjects, it is possible to reconstruct a posteriori the wave function of quantum mechanics that is the quantum entity representing the knowledge factor characterizing the mental condition of the subject. He started his studies on application of quantum mechanics in 1972 and derived the first basic foundations of his approach in 1986 . Starting in 2003 until today he has given the first experimental confirmations of quantum interference effect and the existence of wave function at the perceptive-cognitive level in human beings using ambiguous figures, Stroop effect, cognitive anomalies such as the conjunction fallacy, priming, emotive-cognitive conflict, observation of ambiguous figures following a cognitive task, evidencing in particular the basic quantum properties of our consciousness, which articulates itself on the basis of the founding quantum principle of the superposition of the states in quantum mechanics. In some experiments he has also proven violation of Bell inequalities at the cognitive level. One basic feature of the theory of this scientist is his demonstration of the logical origins of quantum mechanics that follows the celebrated thesis "it from bit" of John Wheeler, of the logic of Orlov and of Deutsch. Elio Conte has in fact reformulated the whole body of quantum mechanics by using Clifford algebra. In this framework he has also given proof of von Neumann postulates on quantum measurement and wave function collapse. Recently, he has also given convincing arguments against the question of order effect in quantum cognition (if tasks A and B are posed in one order and in reversed order, generally subjects respond with different results) evidencing that quantum mechanics is an intrinsic time symmetric theory but on the other hand in contrast with such feature as law-like, time asymmetry follows instead as fact-like. Quantum cognitive models based on time symmetry were elaborated by this scientist beginning in 1981. Recently, in collaboration with Alelù Paz Raul and Ignazio Licata he has extended his research on quantum interference effects also at the neurological level. Rich Norman has recently elaborated upon Conte's quantum cognitive theory with applications in psychology.

29.1.8 Quantum-like models of cognition in economics and finances

The assumption that information processing by the agents of the market follows the laws of quantum information theory and quantum probability was actively explored by many authors, e.g., E. Haven, O. Choustova, A. Khrennikov, see the book of E. Haven and A. Khrennikov,[55] for detailed bibliography. We can mention, e.g., the Bohmian model of dynamics of prices of shares in which the quantum(-like) potential is generated by expectations of agents of the financial market and, hence, it has the mental nature. This approach can be used to model real financial data, see the book of E. Haven and A. Khrennikov (2012).

29.1.9 Application of theory of open quantum systems to decision making and "cell's cognition"

An isolated quantum system is an idealized theoretical entity. In reality interactions with environment have to be taken into account. This is the subject of theory of open quantum systems. Cognition is also fundamentally contextual. The brain is a kind of (self-)observer which makes context dependent decisions. Mental environment plays a crucial role in information processing. Therefore, it is natural to apply theory of open quantum systems to describe the process of decision making as the result of quantum-like dynamics of the mental state of a system interacting with an environment. The description of the process of decision making is mathematically equivalent to the description of the process of decoherence. This idea was explored in a series of works of the multidisciplinary group of researchers at Tokyo University of Science.[56] .[57]

Since in the quantum-like approach the formalism of quantum mechanics is considered as a purely operational formalism, it can be applied to the description of information processing by any biological system, i.e., not only by human beings.

Operationally it is very convenient to consider e.g. a cell as a kind of decision maker processing information in the quantum information framework. This idea was explored in a series of papers of the Swedish-Japanese research group using the methods of theory of open quantum systems: genes expressions were modeled as decision making in the process of interaction with environment.[58]

29.2 History of quantum cognition

Here is a short history of applying the formalisms of quantum theory to topics in psychology. Ideas for applying quantum formalisms to cognition first appeared in the 1990s by Diederik Aerts and his co-authors Jan Broekaert and Sonja Smets, by Harald Atmanspacher, Robert Bordley, and Andrei Khrennikov. A special issue on *Quantum Cognition and Decision* appeared in the Journal of Mathematical Psychology (2009, vol 53.), which planted a flag for the field. A few books related to quantum cognition have been published including those by Khrennikov (2004, 2010), Ivancivic and Ivancivic (2010), Busemeyer and Bruza (2012), E. Conte (2012). The first Quantum Interaction workshop was held at Stanford in 2007 organized by Peter Bruza, William Lawless, C. J. van Rijsbergen, and Don Sofge as part of the 2007 AAAI Spring Symposium Series. This was followed by workshops at Oxford in 2008, Saarbrücken in 2009, at the 2010 AAAI Fall Symposium Series held in Washington, D.C., 2011 in Aberdeen, 2012 in Paris, and 2013 in Leicester. Tutorials also were presented annually beginning in 2007 until 2013 at the annual meeting of the Cognitive Science Society. A *Special Issue on Quantum models of Cognition* appeared in 2013 *Topics in Cognitive Science.*

29.2.1 Related theories

It was suggested by theoretical physicists David Bohm and Basil Hiley that mind and matter both emerge from an "implicate order".[59] Bohm and Hiley's approach to mind and matter is supported by philosopher Paavo Pylkkänen.[60] Pylkkänen underlines "unpredictable, uncontrollable, indivisible and non-logical" features of conscious thought and draws parallels to a philosophical movement some call "post-phenomenology", in particular to Pauli Pylkkö's notion of the "aconceptual experience", an unstructured, unarticulated and pre-logical experience.[61]

The mathematical techniques of both Conte's group and Hiley's group involve the use of Clifford algebras. These algebras account for "non-commutativity" of thought processes (for an example, *see:* noncommutative operations in everyday life).

Elio Conte has applied quantum mechanics to human biological dynamics (primarily the human cognitive level).[62]

However, an area that needs to be investigated is the concept lateralised brain functioning. Some studies in marketing have related lateral influences on cognition and emotion in processing of attachment related stimuli.

29.3 See also

- Holonomic brain theory
- Quantum Bayesianism

29.4 References

[1] Khrennikov, A. "Ubiquitous Quantum Structure: from Psychology to Finances". Springer, 2010.

[2] Busemeyer, J., Bruza, P. (2012), Quantum Models of Cognition and Decision, Cambridge University Press, Cambridge.

[3] Pothos, E. M., & Busemeyer, J. R. (2013). Can quantum probability provide a new direction for cognitive modeling. Behavioral and Brain Sciences,36,255-274.

[4] Wang, Z., Busemeyer, J. R., Atmanspacher, H., & Pothos, E. M. (2013). The potential of using quantum theory to build models of cognition. Topics in Cognitive Science, 5(4), 672-688.

[5] Khrennikov, A. 2006. Quantum-like brain: "Interference of minds" Biosystems , vol. 84, no. 3, pp. 225-241

[6] Khrennikov, A. Information Dynamics in Cognitive, Psychological, Social, and Anomalous Phenomena (Fundamental Theories of Physics) (Volume 138), Kluwer, 2004.

[7] Atmanspacher, H., Römer, H., & Walach, H. (2002). Weak quantum theory: Complementarity and entanglement in physics and beyond. Foundations of Physics, 32(3), 379-406.

[8] Aerts, D. & Aerts, S. (1994) Applications of quantum statistics in psychological studies of decision processes. Foundations of Science, 1, 85-97.

[9] Bruza, P., Kitto, K., Nelson, D., & McEvoy, C. (2009). Is there something quantum-like about the human mental lexicon?. *Journal of Mathematical Psychology,* 53(5), 362-377.

[10] Lambert Mogiliansky, A., Zamir, S., & Zwirn, H. (2009). Type indeterminacy: A model of the KT (Kahneman–Tversky)-man. Journal of Mathematical Psychology, 53(5), 349-361.

[11] de Barros, J. A., Suppes, P. (2009). Quantum mechanics, interference, and the brain. *Journal of Mathematical Psychology 53* (5), 306-313.

[12] Khrennikov, A. 2008. The Quantum-Like Brain on the Cognitive and Subcognitive Time Scales. Journal of Consciousness Studies, vol. 15, no.7

[13] Caves, C. M., Fuchs, C. A., & Schack, R. (2002). Quantum probabilities as Bayesian probabilities. Physical review A, 65(2), 022305.

[14] Khrennikov, A., "Contextual Approach to Quantum Formalism" (Fundamental Theories of Physics 160), Springer, 2009.

[15] Savage, L. J. (1954). *The Foundations of Statistics.* John Wiley & Sons.

[16] Tversky, A., Shafir, E. (1992). The disjunction effect in choice under uncertainty. *Psychological Science 3*, 305-309.

[17] Pothos, E. M., & Busemeyer, J. R. (2009). A quantum probability explanation for violations of 'rational'decision theory. Proceedings of the Royal Society B: Biological Sciences, 276(1665), 2171-2178.

[18] Allais, M. (1953) Le comportement de l'homme rationnel devant le risque: Critique des postulats et axiomes de l'ecole Americaine. *Econometrica 21*, 503-546.

[19] Ellsberg, D. (1961). Risk, ambiguity, and the Savage axioms. *Quarterly Journal of Economics 75*, 643-669.

[20] Machina, M. J. (2009). Risk, ambiguity, and the dark-dependence axioms. *American Econonomical Review 99*, 385-392.

[21] Aerts, D., Sozzo, S., Tapia, J. (2012). A quantum model for the Ellsberg and Machina paradoxes. In *Quantum Interaction 2012*, Busemeyer, J., Dubois, F., Lambert-Mogilansky, A., editors, 48-59, LNCS 7620 (Springer, Berlin).

[22] Aerts, D., Sozzo, S., Tapia, J. (2013). Identifying quantum structures in the Ellsberg paradox. *ArXiv: 1302.3850v1 [physics.soc-ph].*

[23] La Mura, P. (2009). Projective expected utility. Journal of Mathematical Psychology, 53(5), 408-414.

[24] Tversky, A., Kahneman, D. (1983). Extensional versus intuitive reasoning: The conjunction fallacy in probability judgment. *Psychological Review 90*, 293-315.

[25] Aerts D. (2009a). Quantum structure in cognition. *Journal of Mathematical Psychology 53*, 314-348.

[26] Busemeyer, J. R., Pothos, E., Franco, R., Trueblood, J. S. (2011). A quantum theoretical explanation for probability judgment 'errors'. *Psychological Review 118*, 193-218.

[27] Trueblood, J. S., & Busemeyer, J. R. (2011). A quantum probability account of order effects in inference. Cognitive science, 35(8), 1518-1552.

[28] Aerts, D., Broekaert, J., Smets, S. (1999). The liar paradox in a quantum mechanical perspective. *Foundations of Science 4*, 115-132.

[29] Aerts, D., Aerts, S., Broekaert, J., Gabora, L. (2000). The violation of Bell inequalities in the macroworld. *Foundations of Physics 30*, 1387-1414.

[30] Osherson, D. N., Smith, E. E. (1981) On the adequacy of prototype theory as a theory of concepts. Cognition 9, 35–58

[31] Hampton, J. A. (1988a). Overextension of conjunctive concepts: Evidence for a unitary model for concept typicality and class inclusion. *Journal of Experimental Psychology: Learning, Memory, and Cognition 14*, 12–32

[32] Hampton, J. A. (1988b). Disjunction of natural concepts. *Memory & Cognition 16*, 579-591.

[33] Aerts, D., Gabora, L. (2005). A state-context-property model of concepts and their combinations I: The structure of the sets of contexts and properties. *Kybernetes 34* (1&2), 167-191.

[34] Aerts, D., Gabora, L. (2005). A state-context-property model of concepts and their combinations II: A Hilbert space representation. *Kybernetes 34*(1&2), 192-221.

[35] Gabora, L., Aerts, D. (2002). Contextualizing concepts using a mathematical generalization of the quantum formalism. *Journal of Experimental and Theoretical Artificial Intelligence 14* (4), 327-358.

[36] Widdows, D., Peters, S. (2003). Word Vectors and Quantum Logic: Experiments with negation and disjunction. *Eighth Mathematics of Language Conference*, 141-154.

[37] Bruza, P. D., Cole, R. J. (2005). Quantum logic of semantic space: An exploratory investigation of context effects in practical reasoning. In S. Artemov, H. Barringer, A. S. d'Avila Garcez, L.C. Lamb, J. Woods (eds.) *We Will Show Them: Essays in Honour of Dov Gabbay*. College Publications.

[38] Aerts, D. (2009b). Quantum particles as conceptual entities: A possible explanatory framework for quantum theory. *Foundations of Science 14*, 361-411.

[39] Aerts, D., Broekaert, J., Gabora, L., Sozzo, S. (2013). Quantum structure and human thought. *Behavioral and Brain Sciences 36* (3), 274-276.

[40] Aerts, D., Gabora, L., Sozzo, S. (2013). Concepts and their dynamics: A quantum-theoretic modeling of human thought. *Topics in Cognitive Science*, in print. *ArXiv: 1206.1069v1 [cs.AI].*

[41] Aerts, D., Sozzo, S. (2012). Quantum structures in cognition: Why and how concepts are entangled. In *Quantum Interaction 2011*, Song, D., Melucci, M., Frommholz, I., editors, 118-1299, LNCS 7052 (Springer, Berlin).

[42] Aerts, D., Sozzo, S. (2013). Quantum entanglement in concept combinations. Accepted in *International Journal of Theoretical Physics. ArXiv: 1302.3831v1 [cs.Ai].*

[43] Kak, S. The three languages of the brain: quantum, reorganizational, and associative. In Learning as Self-Organization, Karl Pribram and J. King (editors). Lawrence Erlbaum Associates, Mahwah, NJ, 1996, pp. 185-219.

[44] Kak, S. Biological memories and agents as quantum collectives. NeuroQuantology 11: 391-398, 2013.

[45] Kak, S. Observability and computability in physics, Quantum Matter 3: 172-176, 2014.

[46] Van Rijsbergen, K. (2004). *The Geometry of Information Retrieval*. Cambridge.

[47] Widdows, D. (2006). Geometry and meaning. *CSLI Publications*, University of Chicago Press.

[48] Aerts, D., Czachor, M. (2004). Quantum aspects of semantic analysis and symbolic artificial intelligence. *Journal of Physics A 37*, L123-L132.

[49] Atmanspacher, H., Filk, T., Romer, H. (2004). Quantum zeno features of bi-stable perception. *Biological Cybernetics 90*, 33-40.

[50] Conte, E., Todarello, O., Federici, A., Vitiello, F., Lopane, M., Khrennikov, A., Zbilut, J. P. (2007). Some remarks on an experiment suggesting quantum-like behavior of cognitive entities and formulation of an abstract quantum mechanical formalism to describe cognitive entity and its dynamics. *Chaos, Solitons & Fractals 31* (5), 1076–1088 doi:10.1016/j.chaos.2005.09.061, arXiv:0710.5092 (submitted 26 October 2007).

[51] Conte, E., Khrennikov, A., Todarello, O., Federici, A., Zbilut, J. P. (2009). Mental states follow quantum mechanics during perception and cognition of ambiguous figures. *Open Systems and Information Dynamics 16*, 1–17.

[52] Conte, E., Khrennikov A., Todarello, O., De Robertis, R., Federici, A., Zbilut, J. P. (2011). On the possibility that we think in a quantum mechanical manner: An experimental verification of existing quantum interference effects in cognitive anomaly of Conjunction Fallacy. *Chaos and Complexity Letters 4*, 123-136.

[53] Conte, E., Santacroce, N., Laterza, V., Conte, S., Federici A., Todarello, O. (2012). The brain knows more than it admits: A quantum model and its experimental confirmation. *Electronic Journal of Theoretical Physics 9*, 72-110.

[54] Anton Amann: The Gestalt Problem in Quantum Theory: Generation of Molecular Shape by the Environment, Synthese, vol. 97, no. 1 (1993), pp. 125-156, jstor 20117832

[55] Haven E. and Khrennikov A. Quantum Social Science, Cambridge University Press, 2012.

[56] Asano, M., Ohya, M., Tanaka, Y., Basieva, I., Khrennikov, A., 2011. Quantum-like model of brain's functioning: Decision making from decoherence. Journal of Theoretical Biologyvol. 281, no. 1, pp. 56-64.

[57] Asano, M., Basieva, I., Khrennikov, A., Ohya, M.,Yamato, I. 2013. Non-Kolmogorovian Approach to the Context-Dependent Systems Breaking the Classical Probability Law Foundations of Physics, vol. 43, no 7, pp. 895-911.

[58] Asano, M., Basieva, I., Khrennikov, A., Ohya, M., Tanaka, Y. Yamato, I. 2012. Quantum-like model for the adaptive dynamics of the genetic regulation of E. coli's metabolism of glucose/lactose. System Synthetic Biology vol. 6(1-2) pp.1–7.

[59] B.J. Hiley: *Particles, fields, and observers*, Volume I The Origins of Life, Part 1 Origin and Evolution of Life, Section II The Physical and Chemical Basis of Life, pp. 87–106 (PDF)

[60] Basil J. Hiley, Paavo Pylkkänen: *Naturalizing the mind in a quantum framework*. In Paavo Pylkkänen and Tere Vadén (eds.): Dimensions of conscious experience, Advances in Consciousness Research, Volume 37, John Benjamins B.V., 2001, ISBN 90-272-5157-6, pages 119-144

[61] Paavo Pylkkänen. "Can quantum analogies help us to understand the process of thought?" (PDF). *Mind & Matter* **12** (1): 61–91. p. 83–84.

[62] CONTE E (2012). On a simple derivation of the effect of repeated measurements on quantum unstable systems by using the regularized incomplete beta-function. ADVANCED STUDIES IN THEORETICAL PHYSICS, vol. 6, p. 1207-1213, CONTE E, SANTACROCE N, FEDERICI A (2012). A Possible Quantum Model of Consciousness Interfaced with a Non-Lipschitz Chaotic Dynamics of Neural Activity (Part I) and (Part II))

29.5 External links

- http://mypage.iu.edu/~{}jbusemey/quantum/Quantum%20Cognition%20Notes.htm
- http://www.vub.ac.be/CLEA/aerts/
- http://www.le.ac.uk/ulsm/research/qdt/index.html
- http://www.quantum-cognition.de/
- http://www.quantuminteraction.org/
- https://people.ok.ubc.ca/lgabora/research.htm
- http://www.saistmp.com/

29.6 Additional Reading

- Busemeyer, J. R. & Bruza, P. D. (2012). Quantum models of cognition and decision. Cambridge University Press.
- Conte, E. (2012) Advances in application of quantum mechanics in neuroscience and psychology: a Clifford algebraic approach, Nova Science Publishers.
- Ivancevic, V. and Ivancevic, T. (2010) *Quantum Neural Computation*. Springer.

Chapter 30

Quantum catalyst

In quantum information theory, a **quantum catalyst** is a special ancillary quantum state whose presence enables certain local transformations that would otherwise by impossible.[1][2]

30.1 References

[1] Jonathan, D.; Plenio, M. B. (1999). "Entanglement-Assisted Local Manipulation of Pure Quantum States". *Physical Review Letters* **83** (17): 3566. doi:10.1103/PhysRevLett.83.3566.

[2] Duarte, Cristhiano; Drumond, Raphael C.; Marcelo Terra Cunha (2015). "Self-catalytic conversion of pure quantum states". arXiv:1504.06364 [quant-ph].

Chapter 31

Quantum complex network

Being part of network science the study of quantum complex networks aims to explore the impact of complexity science and network architectures in quantum systems.[1][2][3] According to quantum information theory it is possible to improve communication security and data transfer rates by taking advantage of quantum mechanics.[4][5] In this context the study of quantum complex networks is motivated by the possibility of quantum communications being used on a massive scale in the future.[2] In such case it is likely that quantum communication networks will acquire non trivial features as its common in the exiting communication networks today.[3][6]

31.1 Motivation

It is theoretically possible to take an advantage of quantum mechanics to create secure and faster communications, namely, quantum key distribution is an application of quantum cryptography that allows for theoretical completely secure communications,[4] and quantum teleportation that can be used to transfer data at higher rate than using only classic channels.[5]

The successful quantum teleportation experiments in 1998[7] followed by the development of first quantum communication networks in 2004,[8] opened the possibility of quantum communication being used in a large scale in the future. According to findings in network science the topology of the networks is, in most cases, extremely important, and the exiting large scale communication networks today tend to have non-trivial topologies and traits, like small world effect, community structure and scale free properties.[6] The Study the of networks with quantum properties and complex network topologies, can help us not only to better understand such networks but also how to use the network topology to improve the efficience of communication networks in the future.

31.2 Important concepts

31.2.1 Qubits

In quantum information Qubits are the equivalent to bits in classical systems. A qubit is quantum objects with only two states that is used to transmit information.[4] The polarization of a photon or the nuclear spin are examples of two state systems that can be used as qubits.[4]

31.2.2 Entanglement

Quantum entanglement is a physical phenomenon characterized by a correlation between the quantum states of two or more particles.[4] While entangled particle do not interact in the classical sense, the quantum state of those particle can not be described independently. Particles can be entangle in different degrees, and the maximally entangled state are the ones the maximize the entropy of entanglement.[9][10] In the context of quantum communication, quantum entanglement qubits are used as a quantum channel capable of transmitting information when combined with a classical chanel.[4]

31.2.3 Bell measurement

Bell measurement is joint quantum-mechanical measurement of two qubits, so that after the measurement the two qubits will be maixmailly entangle.[4][10]

31.2.4 Entanglement swapping

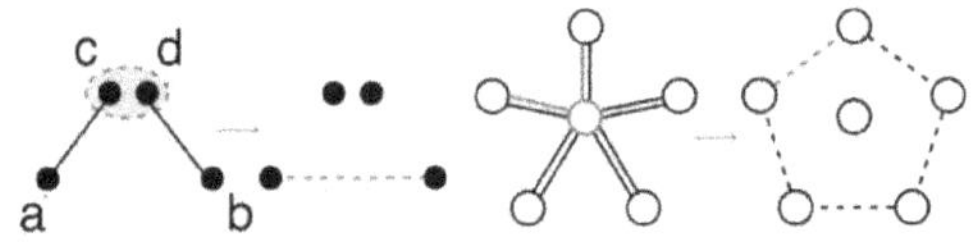

2 different examples of entanglement swapping. Dots represent qubits and dashed and solid lines represent entangled states.[11](Edited and simplified)

Entanglement swapping is a frequent strategy used in quantum networks that allows the connections in the network to change.[1][11] Lets us suppose that we have 4 qubits, A B C and D, C and D belong to the same station, while A and C belong to two different stations. Qubit A is entangled with qubit C and qubit B is entangled with qubit D. By performing a bell measurement in qubits A and B, not only the qubits A and B will be entangled but it is also possible to create an entanglement state between qubit C and qubit D, despite the fact that there was never an interactions between them. Following this process the entanglement between qubits A and C, and qubits B and D will be lost. This strategy can be use to shape the connection on the network.[1][11][12]

31.3 Network structure

While not all models for quantum complex network follow exactly the same structure, usually nodes represent a set of qubits in the same station were operation like bell measurements and entanglement swapping can be applied. In the other hand, a link between a node i and j means that a qubit in node i is entangled to a quibit in node j , but those two qubits are in different places, thus physical interactions between them are not possible.[1][11]

31.3.1 Notation

Each node in the network is composed by a set of qubits that can be in different states. The most convenient representation for the quantum state of the qubits is the dirac notation and represent the two state of the qubits as $|0\rangle$ and $|1\rangle$.[1][11] Two particle are entangled if the joint wave function, $|\psi_{ij}\rangle$, can not be decomposed as,[4][10]

$$|\psi_{ij}\rangle = |\phi\rangle_i \otimes |\phi\rangle_j,$$

where $|\phi\rangle_i$ represents the quantum state of the qubit at node i and $|\phi\rangle_j$ represents the quantum state of the qubit at node j. Another important concept is maximally entangled states. For the four states that maximize the entropy of entanglement can be written as[4][10]

$$|\Phi^+_{ij}\rangle = \frac{1}{\sqrt{2}}(|0\rangle_i \otimes |0\rangle_j + |1\rangle_i \otimes |1\rangle_j),$$

$$|\Phi^-_{ij}\rangle = \frac{1}{\sqrt{2}}(|0\rangle_i \otimes |0\rangle_j - |1\rangle_i \otimes |1\rangle_j),$$

$$|\Psi^+_{ij}\rangle = \frac{1}{\sqrt{2}}(|0\rangle_i \otimes |1\rangle_j + |1\rangle_i \otimes |0\rangle_j),$$

$$|\Psi^-_{ij}\rangle = \frac{1}{\sqrt{2}}(|0\rangle_i \otimes |1\rangle_j - |1\rangle_i \otimes |0\rangle_j).$$

31.4 Models

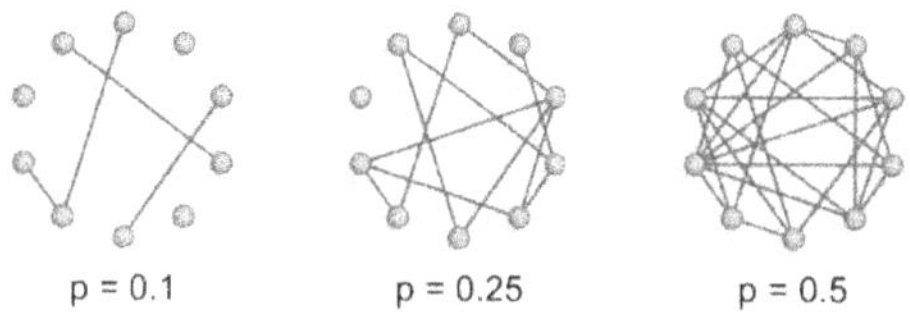

FIG. 1: Evolution process of a classical random graph with $N = 10$ nodes: starting from isolated nodes, we randomly add edges with increasing probability p, to eventually get the complete graph K_{10} for $p = 1$.

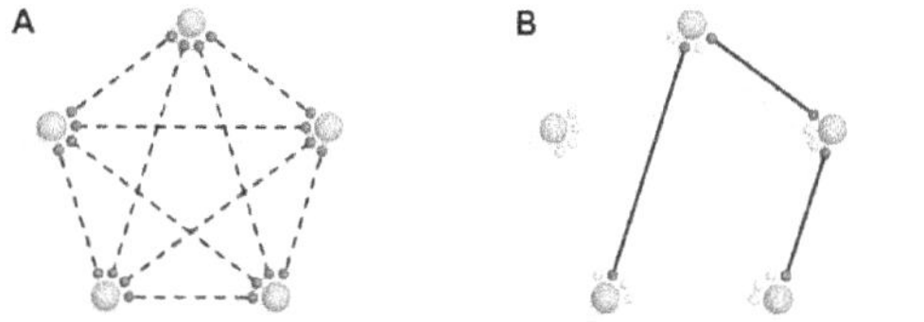

FIG. 2: An example of a quantum random graph on five nodes. **(A)** Each node is in possession of four qubits which are entangled with qubits belonging to the other nodes. All the connections are identical and pure but non-maximally entangled pairs. **(B)** Imperfect pairs can be converted into maximally entangled ones with some probability of success p (here $p = 0.25$): this strategy mimics the behavior of classical random graphs.

[1]

31.4.1 Quantum random networks

The quantum random network model proposed by Perseguers et al.[1] can be thought as a quantum version of the Erdős–Rényi model. Instead of the typical links used in to represent other complex networks, in the quantum random network model each pair of nodes is connected trough an pair of entangled qubits. In this case each node contains $N-1$ quibits, one for each other node. In quantum random network the degree of entanglement between two pairs of nodes represented by p , plays a similar role to the parameter p in the Erdős–Rényi model. While in the Erdős–Rényi model two nodes form a connection with probability p , in the context of quantum random networks p means the probability of an entangled pair of qubits being successful converted to a maximally entangled state using only local operations and classical communications, called LOCC operations.[13] We can think of maximally entangled qubits as the true links between nodes.

Using the notation introduced previously, we can represent a pair of entangle qubits connecting the nodes i and j , as

$$|\psi_{ij}\rangle = \sqrt{1-p/2}|0\rangle_i \otimes |0\rangle_j + \sqrt{p/2}|1\rangle_i \otimes |1\rangle_j,$$

For $p = 0$ the two qubits are not entangled,

$$|\psi_{ij}\rangle = |0\rangle_i \otimes |0\rangle_j,$$

and for $p = 1$ we obtain the maximally entangled state,

given by

$$|\psi_{ij}\rangle = \sqrt{1/2}(|0\rangle_i \otimes |0\rangle_j + |1\rangle_i \otimes |1\rangle_j)$$

For intermediate values of p , $0 < p < 1$, any entangle state can be, with probability p , successfully converted to the maximally entangled entangled state using LOCC operations.[13]

One of the main features that distinguish this model from its classic version is the fact the in quantum random networks links are only truly established after measurements in the networks being made, and It is possible to take advantage of this fact to shape final shape of the network. Considering an initial quantum complex network with an infinity number of nodes, Perseguers et al.[1] showed that, by doing the right measurements and entanglement swapping, it is possible to collapsed the initial network to a network containing any finite subgraph, provided that p scales with N as,

$$p \sim N^Z,$$

were $Z \geq -2$. This results is contrary to what we find in classic graph theory were the type of subgraphs contained in a network is bounded by the value of z .[14]

31.4.2 Entanglement Percolation

The goal of entanglement percolation models is to determine if a quantum network is capable of establishing a connection between two arbitrary nodes trough entanglement, and to find best the strategies to create those same connections.[11][15] In a model proposed by Cirac et al.[15] and applied to complex networks by Cuquet et al.,[11] nodes ares distributed in a lattice,[15] or in a complex network,[11] and each pair of neighbors share two pairs of entangled qubits that can be converted to a maximally entangle qubit pair with probability p . We can think of maximally entangled qubits as the true links between nodes. According to classic percolation theory, considering a probability p of two neighbors being connected, there is a critical p designed by p_c , so that if $p > p_c$ there is a finite probability of existing a path between two random selected node, and for $p < p_c$ the probability of existing a path between two random selected nodes goes to zero.[16] p_c depends only on the topology of the network.[16] A similar phenomena was found in the model proposed by Cirac et al.,[15] where the probability of a forming a maximally entangled state between two random selected nodes is zero if $p < p_c$ and finite if $p > p_c$. The main difference between classic and entangled percolation is that in quantum networks it is possible to change the links in the network, in a way changing the effective topology of the network, as a consequence p_c will depend on the strategy used to convert partial entangle qubits to maximally connected qubits.[11][15] A naive approach yields that p_c for a quantum network is equal to p_c for a classic network with the same topology.[15] Nevertheless, it was shown that is possible to take advantage of quantum swamping to lower that value, both in regular lattices[15] and complex networks.[11]

31.5 See also

- Quantum key distribution
- Quantum teleportation
- Erdős–Rényi model

31.6 References

[1] Perseguers, S.; Lewenstein, M.; Acín, A.; Cirac, J. I. (16 May 2010) [19 July 2009]. "Quantum random networks" [Quantum complex networks]. *Nature Physics* **6** (7): 539–543. arXiv:0907.3283. doi:10.1038/nphys1665.

[2] Huang, Liang; Lai, Ying C. (2011). "Cascading dynamics in complex quantum networks". *Chaos: An Interdisciplinary Journal of Nonlinear Science* **21** (2). doi:10.1063/1.3598453.

[3] Cuquet, Martí; Calsamiglia, John (2009). "Entanglement Percolation in Quantum Complex Networks". *Physical Review Letters* **103** (24). doi:10.1103/physrevlett.103.240503.

[4] Nielsen, Michael A.; Chuang, Isaac L. (1 January 2004). *Quantum Computation and Quantum Information*. Cambridge University Press. ISBN 978-1-107-00217-3.

[5] Takeda, Shuntaro; Mizuta, Takahiro; Fuwa, Maria; Loock, Peter van; Furusawa, Akira (14 August 2013). "Deterministic quantum teleportation of photonic quantum bits by a hybrid technique". *Nature* **500** (7462): 315. doi:10.1038/nature12366.

[6] Dorogovtsev, S.N.; Mendes, J.F.F. (2003). *Evolution of Networks: From biological networks to the Internet and WWW*. Oxford University Press. ISBN 0-19-851590-1.

[7] Boschi, D.; Branca, S.; De Martini, F.; Hardy, L.; Popescu, S. "Experimental Realization of Teleporting an Unknown Pure Quantum State via Dual Classical and Einstein-Podolsky-Rosen Channels". *Physical Review Letters* **80**: 1121–1125. doi:10.1103/physrevlett.80.1121.

[8] Elliott, Chip; Colvin, Alexander; Pearson, David; Pikalo, Oleksiy; Schlafer, John; Yeh, Henry (17 March 2005). "Current status of the DARPA Quantum Network". arXiv:quant-ph/0503058.

[9] Eisert, J.; Cramer, M.; Plenio, M. B. (February 2010). "Colloquium: Area laws for the entanglement entropy". *Reviews of Modern Physics* **82** (1): 277–306. doi:10.1103/RevModPhys.82.277.

[10] Chandra, Naresh; Ghosh, Rama (2013). *Quantum Entanglement in Electron Optics: Generation, Characterization, and Applications*. Springer Series on Atomic, Optical, and Plasma Physics **67**. Springer. p. 43. ISBN 3642240704.

[11] Cuquet, M.; Calsamiglia, J. (10 December 2009) [6 June 2009]. "Entanglement percolation in quantum complex networks". *Physical Review Letters* **103** (24). arXiv:0906.2977. doi:10.1103/physrevlett.103.240503.

[12] Coecke, Bob (2003). "The logic of entanglement". Department of Computer Science, University of Oxford. arXiv:quant-ph/0402014.

[13] Werner, Reinhard F. (15 Oct 1989). "Quantum states with Einstein-Podolsky-Rosen correlations admitting a hidden-variable model". *Physical Review A* **40** (8): 4277. doi:10.1103/physreva.40.4277.

[14] Albert, Réka; Barabási, Albert L. (Jan 2002). "Statistical mechanics of complex networks". *Reviews of Modern Physics* **74** (1): 47–97. doi:10.1103/revmodphys.74.47.

[15] Acin, Antonio; Cirac, J. Ignacio; Lewenstein, Maciej (25 February 2007). "Entanglement percolation in quantum networks". *Nature Physics* **3** (4): 256–259.

[16] Stauffer, Dietrich; Aharony, Anthony (1994). *Introduction to Percolation Theory* (2nd ed.). CRC Press. ISBN 978-0-7484-0253-3.

Chapter 32

Quantum LC circuit

An LC circuit can be quantized using the same methods as for the quantum harmonic oscillator. An **LC circuit** is a variety of resonant circuit, and consists of an inductor, represented by the letter L, and a capacitor, represented by the letter C. When connected together, an electric current can alternate between them at the circuit's resonant frequency:

$$\omega = \sqrt{\frac{1}{LC}}$$

where **L** is the inductance in henries, and **C** is the capacitance in farads. The angular frequency ω has units of radians per second. A capacitor stores energy in the electric field between the plates, which can be written as follows:

$$U_C = \frac{1}{2}CV^2 = \frac{Q^2}{2C}$$

Where Q is the net charge on the capacitor, calculated as

$$Q(t) = \int_{-\infty}^{t} I(\tau)d\tau$$

Likewise, an inductor stores energy in the magnetic field depending on the current, which can be written as follows:

$$U_L = \frac{1}{2}LI^2 = \frac{\phi^2}{2L}$$

Where ϕ is the branch flux, defined as

$$\phi(t) \equiv \int_{-\infty}^{t} V(\tau)d\tau$$

Since charge and flux are canonically conjugate variables, one can use canonical quantization to rewrite the classical hamiltonian in the quantum formalism, by identifying

$$\phi \to \hat{\phi}$$

$$q \to \hat{q}$$

$$H \to \hat{H} = \frac{\hat{\phi}^2}{2L} + \frac{\hat{q}^2}{2C}$$

and enforcing the canonical commutation relation

$$[\phi, q] = i\hbar$$

32.1 One-dimensional harmonic oscillator

32.1.1 Hamiltonian and energy eigenstates

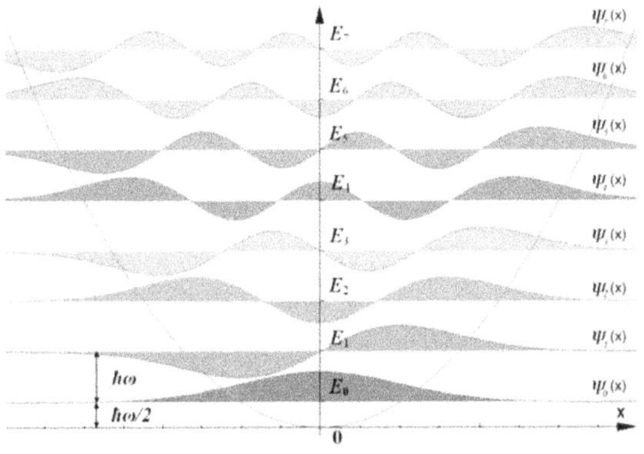

Wavefunction representations for the first eight bound eigenstates, n = *0 to 7. The horizontal axis shows the position* x. *The graphs are not normalised*

Like the one-dimensional harmonic oscillator problem, an LC circuit can be quantized by either solving the Schrödinger equation or using creation and annihilation operators. The energy stored in the inductor can be looked at as a "kinetic energy term" and the energy stored in the capacitor can be looked at as a "potential energy term".

The Hamiltonian of such a system is:

$$H = \frac{\phi^2}{2L} + \frac{1}{2}L\omega^2 Q^2$$

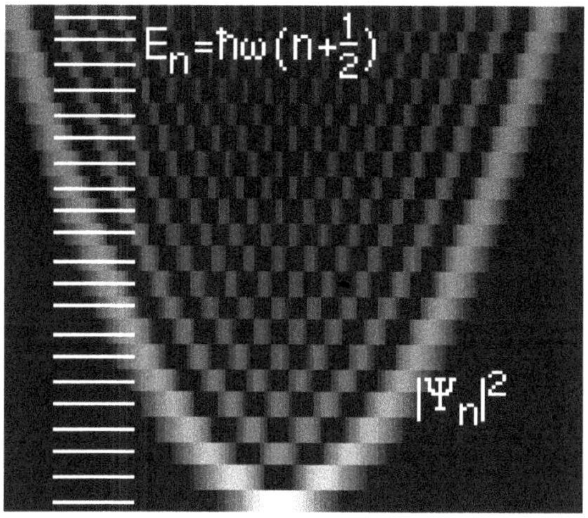

Probability densities $|\psi_n(x)|^2$ for the bound eigenstates, beginning with the ground state (n = 0) at the bottom and increasing in energy toward the top. The horizontal axis shows the position x, and brighter colors represent higher probability densities.

where Q is the charge operator, and ϕ is the magnetic flux operator. The first term represents the energy stored in an inductor, and the second term represents the energy stored in a capacitor. In order to find the energy levels and the corresponding energy eigenstates, we must solve the time-independent Schrödinger equation,

$$H|\psi >= E|\psi >$$

$$E\psi = -\frac{\hbar^2}{2L}\nabla^2\psi + \frac{1}{2}L\omega^2 Q^2\psi$$

Since an LC circuit really is an electrical analog to the harmonic oscillator, solving the Schrödinger equation yields a family of solutions (the Hermite polynomials).

$$\langle Q|\psi_n\rangle = \sqrt{\frac{1}{2^n\, n!}}\cdot\left(\frac{L\omega}{\pi\hbar}\right)^{1/4}\cdot\exp\left(-\frac{L\omega Q^2}{2\hbar}\right)\cdot H_n\left(\sqrt{\frac{L\omega}{\hbar}}Q\right)$$

$$n = 0, 1, 2, \ldots$$

32.2 Magnetic Flux as a Conjugate Variable

A completely equivalent solution can be found using magnetic flux as the conjugate variable where the conjugate "momentum" is equal to capacitance times the time derivative of magnetic flux. The conjugate "momentum" is really the charge.

$$\pi = C\frac{d\phi}{dt}$$

Using Kirchhoff's Junction Rule, the following relationship can be obtained:

$$C\frac{dV}{dt} + \frac{1}{L}\int_0^t V\,dt = 0$$

Since $V = \frac{d\phi}{dt}$, the above equation can be written as follows:

$$C\frac{d^2\phi}{dt^2} + \frac{1}{L}\phi = 0$$

Converting this into a Hamiltonian, one can develop a Schrödinger equation as follows:

$i\hbar\frac{d\psi}{dt} = -\frac{\hbar^2}{2C}\nabla^2\psi + \frac{\phi^2}{2L}\psi$ where ψ is a function of magnetic flux

32.3 Quantization of coupled LC circuits

Two inductively coupled LC circuits have a non-zero mutual inductance. This is equivalent to a pair of harmonic oscillators with a kinetic coupling term.

The Lagrangian for an inductively coupled pair of LC circuits is as follows:

$$L = \frac{1}{2}L_1\frac{dQ_1}{dt}^2 + \frac{1}{2}L_2\frac{dQ_2}{dt}^2 + m\frac{dQ_1}{dt}\frac{dQ_2}{dt} - \frac{Q_1^2}{2C_1} - \frac{Q_2^2}{2C_2}$$

As usual, the Hamiltonian is obtained by a Legendre transform of the Lagrangian.

$$H = \frac{1}{2}L_1\frac{dQ_1}{dt}^2 + \frac{1}{2}L_2\frac{dQ_2}{dt}^2 + m\frac{dQ_1}{dt}\frac{dQ_2}{dt} + \frac{Q_1^2}{2C_1} + \frac{Q_2^2}{2C_2}$$

Promoting the observables to quantum mechanical operators yields the following Schrödinger equation.

$$E\psi = -\frac{\hbar^2}{2L_1}\frac{d^2\psi}{dQ_1^2} - \frac{\hbar^2}{2L_2}\frac{d^2\psi}{dQ_2^2} - \frac{\hbar^2}{m}\frac{d^2\psi}{dQ_1 dQ_2} + \frac{1}{2}L_1\omega^2 Q_1^2\psi + \frac{1}{2}L_2\omega^2 Q_2^2\psi$$

One cannot proceed further using the above coordinates because of the coupled term. However, a coordinate transformation from the wave function as a function of both charges to the wave function as a function of the charge difference Q_d , where $Q_d = Q_1 - Q_2$ and a coordinate Q_c (somewhat analogous to a "Center-of-Mass"), the above Hamiltonian can be solved using the Separation of Variables technique.

The CM coordinate is as seen below:

$$Q_c = \frac{L_1 Q_1 + L_2 Q_2}{L_1 + L_2}$$

The Hamiltonian under the new coordinate system is as follows:

$$E\psi = -\frac{\hbar^2(1-\lambda)}{2(L_1+L_2)}\frac{d^2\psi}{dQ_c^2} - \frac{\hbar^2(1-\lambda)}{2\mu}\frac{d^2\psi}{dQ_d^2} + \frac{1}{2}\mu\omega^2 Q_d^2\psi$$

In the above equation λ is equal to $\frac{2m}{L_1+L_2}$ and μ equals the reduced inductance.

The separation of variables technique yields two equations, one for the "CM" coordinate that is the differential equation of a free particle, and the other for the charge difference coordinate, which is the Schrödinger equation for a harmonic oscillator.

$$E\psi_c = -\frac{\hbar^2(1-\lambda)}{2(L_1+L_2)}\frac{d^2\psi_c}{dQ_c^2}$$

$$E\psi_d = -\frac{\hbar^2(1-\lambda)}{2\mu}\frac{d^2\psi_d}{dQ_d^2} + \frac{1}{2}\mu\omega^2 Q_d^2\psi_d$$

The solution for the first differential equation once the time dependence is appended resembles a plane wave, while the solution of the second differential equation is seen above.

32.4 Hamiltonian mechanics

32.4.1 Classical case

Stored energy (Hamiltonian) for classical LC circuit:

$$\mathcal{H} = \frac{q^2(t)}{2C} + \frac{p^2(t)}{2L}$$

Hamiltonian's equations:

$$\frac{\partial\mathcal{H}(q,p)}{\partial q} = \frac{q(t)}{C} = -\dot{p}(t)$$

$$\frac{\partial\mathcal{H}(q,p)}{\partial p} = \frac{p(t)}{L} = -\dot{q}(t)$$

where $q(t) = Cv(t)$ stored capacitor charge (or electric flux) and $p(t) = Li(t)$ magnetic momentum (magnetic flux), $v(t)-$ capacitor voltage and $i(t)-$ inductance current, $t-$ time variable.

Nonzero initial conditions: At $q(0), p(0)$ we shall have oscillation frequency:

$$\omega = \frac{1}{\sqrt{LC}}$$

and wave impedance of the LC circuit (without dissipation):

$$\rho = \sqrt{\frac{L}{C}}$$

Hamiltonian's equations solutions: At $t \geq 0$ we shall have the following values of charges, magnetic flux and energy:

$$\mathbf{q} = q(0) + j\frac{p(0)}{\omega L}$$

$$< q(t) = Re[\mathbf{q}e^{-j\omega t}]$$

$$p(t) = Im[\omega L\mathbf{q}e^{-j\omega t}]$$

$$\mathcal{H} = \frac{|\mathbf{q}|^2}{2C} = constant$$

Definition of the Phasor

In the general case the wave amplitudes can be defined in the complex space

$$a(t) = a_1(t) + ja_2(t)$$

where $j = \sqrt{-1}$.

$a_1(t) = \frac{q(t)}{q(0)}$,

where $q(0) = D(0)S_C = \sqrt{\frac{2\hbar}{\rho}}$ - electric charge at zero time, S_C- capacitance area.

$a_2(t) = \frac{p(t)}{p(0)}$,

where $p(0) = \sqrt{2\hbar\rho}$ - magnetic flux at zero time, S_L- inductance area. Note that, at the equal area elements

$$S_C = S_L = S_q$$

we shall have the following relationship for the wave impedance:

$$\rho = \sqrt{\frac{L}{C}} = \frac{q(0)}{p(0)}$$

Wave amplitude and energy could be defined as:

$$a(t) = ae^{-j\omega t}$$

$$\mathcal{H} = \hbar\omega[a_1^2(t) + a_2^2(t)] = \hbar\omega|a|^2$$

32.4.2 Quantum case

In the quantum case we have the following definition for momentum operator:

$$\hat{p} = -j\hbar\frac{\partial}{\partial q}$$

Momentum and charge operators produce the following commutator:

$$[\hat{q}, \hat{p}] = j\hbar$$

Amplitude operator can be defined as:

$$\hat{a} = \hat{a_1} + j\hat{a_2} = \frac{\hat{q}}{q_0} + j\frac{\hat{p}}{p_0}$$

and phazor:

$$\hat{a(t)} = \hat{a}e^{-j\omega t}$$

Hamilton's operator will be:

$$\hat{\mathcal{H}}\hbar\omega[\hat{a}_1^2(t) + \hat{a}_2^2(t)] = \hbar\omega[\hat{a}\hat{a}^\dagger + 1/2]$$

Amplitudes commutators:

$$[\hat{a}_1(t), \hat{a}_2(t)] = j/2$$

$$[\hat{a}(t), \hat{a}^\dagger(t)] = 1$$

Heisenberg uncertainty principle:

$$\langle\Delta\hat{a}_1^2(t)\rangle\langle\Delta\hat{a}_2^2(t)\rangle \geq \frac{1}{16}$$

Wave impedance of free space

When wave impedance of quantum LC circuit takes the value of free space

$$\rho_0 = \sqrt{\frac{L_0}{C_0}} = \sqrt{\frac{\mu_0}{\epsilon_0}} = 2\alpha\frac{h}{e^2}$$

where $e-$ electron charge and $\alpha-$ fine structure constant, then "electric" and "magnetic" fluxes at zero time point will be:

$$q_0 = \sqrt{\frac{2\hbar}{\rho_0}} = \frac{e}{\sqrt{2\pi\alpha}}$$

$$p_0 = \sqrt{2\hbar\rho_0} = \phi_0\sqrt{\frac{2\alpha}{\pi}}$$

where $\phi_0 = \frac{h}{e}-$ magnetic flux quantum.

32.5 Quantum LC circuit paradox

32.5.1 General formulation

In the classical case the energy of LC circuit will be:

$$W_{LC} = W_C + W_L,$$

where $W_C = 0.5CV_C^2-$ capacitance energy, and $W_L = 0.5LI_L^2-$ inductance energy. Furthermore, there are the following relationships between charges (electric or magnetic) and voltages or currents:

$$Q_C = CV_C$$

$$\Phi_L = LI_L.$$

Therefore, the maximal values of capacitance and inductance energies will be:

$$W_{max} = W_{LC} = \frac{Q_{C0}^2}{2C} + \frac{\Phi_{L0}^2}{2L}.$$

Note that the resonance frequency $\omega_0 = 1/\sqrt{LC}$ has nothing to do with the energy in the classical case. But it has the following relationship with energy in the quantum case:

$$W_0 = \frac{\hbar\omega_0}{2} = \frac{\hbar}{2\sqrt{LC}}.$$

So, in the quantum case, by filling capacitance with the one electron charge:

$$Q_{C0} = e = CV_C \text{ and } W_C = \frac{e^2}{2C}.$$

The relationship between capacitance energy and the ground state oscillator energy will then be:

$$\xi_C = \frac{W_C}{W_0} = \frac{2\pi}{R_H}\sqrt{\frac{L}{C}} = 2\pi \cdot \frac{\rho_q}{R_H}.$$

where $\rho_q = \sqrt{L/C}$ quantum impedance of LC circuit. The quantum impedance of the quantum LC circuit could be in practice of the two types:

$$\rho_q = \sqrt{\frac{L}{C}} = \begin{cases} \rho_w = 2\alpha R_H, & \text{- wave impedance} \\ \rho_{DOS} = R_H, & \text{- DOS impedance} \end{cases}$$

So, the energy relationships will be:

$$\xi_C = \frac{W_C}{W_0} = 2\pi\frac{\rho_q}{R_H} = \begin{cases} 4\pi\alpha, & \text{at } \rho_w \\ 2\pi, & \text{at } \rho_{DOS} \end{cases}$$

and that is the main problem of the quantum LC circuit: *energies stored on capacitance and inductance are not equal to the ground state energy of the quantum oscillator*. This energy problem produces the quantum LC circuit paradox (QLCCP).

32.5.2 Possible solution

Some simple solution of the QLCCP could be found in the following way. Yakymakha (1989) [1](eqn.30) proposed the following DOS quantum impedance definition:

$$\rho_{DOS}^{ij} = \frac{\Delta\Phi_j}{\Delta Q_i} = \frac{i}{j} R_H,$$

where $\Delta\Phi_j = j\Phi_0-$ magnetic flux, and $\Delta Q_i = ie-$ electric flux, $i, j = integer$.

So, there are no electric or magnetic charges in the quantum LC circuit, but electric and magnetic fluxes only. Therefore, not only in the DOS LC circuit, but in the other LC circuits too, there are only the electromagnetic waves. Thus, the quantum LC circuit is the minimal geometrical-topological value of the quantum waveguide, in which there are no electric or magnetic charges, but electromagnetic waves only. Now one should consider the quantum LC circuit as a "black wave box" (BWB), which has no electric or magnetic charges, but waves. Furthermore, this BWB could be "closed" (in Bohr atom or in the vacuum for photons), or "open" (as for QHE and Josephson junction). So, the quantum LC circuit should has BWB and "input - output" supplements. The total energy balance should be calculated with considering of "input" and "output" devices. Without "input - output" devices, the energies "stored" on capacitances and inductances are virtual or "characteristics", as in the case of characteristic impedance (without dissipation). Very close to this approach now are Devoret (2004),[2] which consider Josephson junctions with quantum inductance, Datta impedance of Schrödinger waves (2008) and Tsu (2008),[3] which consider quantum wave guides.

32.5.3 Explanation for DOS quantum LC circuit

As presented below, the resonance frequency for QHE is:

$$\omega_Q = \sqrt{\frac{1}{L_{QA}C_{QA}}} = \frac{\omega_B}{2\pi},$$

where $\omega_B = eB/m-$ cyclotron frequency, $L_{QA} = \frac{4\pi R_H}{\omega_B}$ and $C_{QA} = \frac{4\pi}{R_H\omega_B}$. The scaling current for QHE will be:

$$I_B = \frac{e\omega_B}{4\pi}.$$

Therefore, the inductance energy will be:

$$W_L = \frac{L_{QA}I_B^2}{2} = \frac{\hbar\omega_B}{4}.$$

So for quantum magnetic flux $\Phi_0 = h/e$, inductance energy is half as much as the ground state oscillation energy. This is due to the spin of electron (there are two electrons on Landau level on the same quantum area element). Therefore, the inductance/capacitance energy considers the total Landau level energy per spin.

32.5.4 Explanation for "wave" quantum LC circuit

By analogy to the DOS LC circuit, we have

$$W_0 = \frac{1}{2}\cdot\frac{W_C}{2\pi\alpha} = \frac{\gamma_{BY}W_C}{2}$$

two times lesser value due to the spin. But here there is the new dimensionless fundamental constant:

$$\gamma_{BY} = \frac{1}{2\pi\alpha}$$

which considers topological properties of the quantum LC circuit. This fundamental constant first appeared in the Bohr atom for Bohr radius:

$$a_B = \gamma_{BY}\cdot\lambda_0,$$

where $\lambda_0 = h/m_0c-$ Compton wavelength of electron.

Thus, the wave quantum LC circuit has no charges in it, but electromagnetic waves only. So capacitance or inductance "characteristic energies" are $\gamma_{BY}-$ times less than the total energy of the oscillator. In other words, charges "disappear" at the "input" and "generate" at the "output" of the wave LC circuit, adding energies to keep balance.

32.6 Total energy of quantum LC circuit

Energy stored on the quantum capacitance:

$$W_C = \frac{Q_C^2}{2C} = 2\pi\alpha W_{LC}.$$

Energy stored on the quantum inductance:

$$W_L = \frac{\Phi_L^2}{2L} = 2\pi\alpha W_{LC}.$$

Resonance energy of the quantum LC circuit:

$$W_{LC} = \hbar\omega_{LC} = \frac{\hbar}{\sqrt{LC}}.$$

Thus, the total energy of the quantum LC circuit should be:

$$W_{tot} = W_{LC} + W_C + W_L.$$

In the general case, resonance energy W_{LC} could be due to the "rest mass" of electron, energy gap for Bohr atom, etc. However, energy stored on capacitance W_C is due to electric charge. Actually, for free electron and Bohr atom LC circuits we have quantized electric fluxes, equal to the electronic charge, e .

Furthermore, energy stored on inductance W_L is due to magnetic momentum. Actually, for Bohr atom we have Bohr Magneton:

$$\mu_B = \frac{e\hbar}{2m_0} = 0.5e\nu_B S_B = \frac{ea_B^2}{\sqrt{L_B C_B}}.$$

In the case of free electron, Bohr Magneton will be:

$$\mu_e = 0.5e\nu_e S_e = 0.5e\frac{m_0 c^2}{h}\frac{\lambda_0^2}{2\pi} = \frac{e\hbar}{2m_0},$$

the same, as for Bohr atom.

32.7 Applications

32.7.1 Electron as LC circuit

Electron capacitance could be presented as the spherical capacitor:

$$C_e = \frac{4\pi\epsilon_0}{\frac{1}{r_e} - \frac{1}{r_e+\lambda_0}} = \frac{\epsilon_0\lambda_0}{2\pi},$$

where $r_e = \frac{\lambda_0}{2\sqrt{2\pi}}-$ electron radius and λ_0- Compton wavelength.

Note, that this electron radius is consistent with the standard definition of the spin. Actually, rotating momentum of electron is:

$$l_e = m_0\omega_e r_e^2 = \hbar/2,$$

where $\omega_e = m_0 c^2/\hbar$ is considered.

Spherical inductance of electron:

$$L_e = \frac{\mu_0\lambda_0}{2\pi}.$$

Characterictic impedance of electron:

$$\rho_e = \sqrt{\frac{L_e}{C_e}} = \sqrt{\frac{\mu_0}{\epsilon_0}} = \rho_0 = 2\alpha R_H.$$

Resonance frequency of electron LC circuit:

$$\omega_e = \sqrt{\frac{1}{L_e C_e}} = \frac{2\pi c}{\lambda_0} = \frac{m_0 c^2}{\hbar}.$$

Induced electric flux on electron capacitance:

$$Q_e = C_e V_e.$$

Energy, stored on electron capacitance:

$$W_{Ce} = \frac{C_e V_e^2}{2} = \frac{Q_e^2}{2C_e} = 2\pi\alpha W_0,$$

where $W_0 = m_0 c^2-$ is the "rest energy" of electron. So, induced electric flux will be:

$$Q_e = \sqrt{2\alpha m_0 c^2\epsilon_0\lambda_0} = e.$$

Thus, through electron capacitance we have quantized electric flux, equal to the electron charge.

Magnetic flux through inductance:

$$\Phi_e = L_e I_e.$$

Magnetic energy, stored on inductance:

$$W_{Le} = \frac{L_e I_e^2}{2} = \frac{\Phi_e^2}{2L_e} = 2\pi\alpha W_0.$$

So, induced magnetic flux will be:

$$\Phi_e = \sqrt{2\mu_0 hc\alpha} = 2\alpha\Phi_0.$$

where $\Phi_0 = h/e-$ magnetic flux quantum. Thus, through electron inductance there are no quantization of magnetic flux.

32.7.2 Bohr atom as LC circuit

Bohr radius:

$$a_B = \frac{\lambda_0}{2\pi\alpha}$$

where $\lambda_0 = \frac{h}{m_0 c}-$ Compton wavelength of electron, $\alpha-$ fine structure constant.

Bohr atomic surface:

$$S_B = 4\pi a_B^2$$

Bohr inductance:

$$L_B = \frac{\mu_0}{\lambda_0} \cdot S_B$$

Bohr capacitance:

$$C_B = \frac{\epsilon_0}{\lambda_0} \cdot S_B$$

Bohr wave impedance:

$$\rho_B = \sqrt{\frac{L_B}{C_B}} = \sqrt{\frac{\mu_0}{\epsilon_0}} = \rho_0.$$

Bohr angular frequency:

$$\omega_B = \sqrt{\frac{1}{L_B C_B}} = \frac{\alpha^2}{2} \cdot \frac{m_0 c^2}{\hbar} = \frac{2\pi c}{\lambda_B},$$

where $\lambda_B = \frac{4\pi a_B}{\alpha}-$ Bohr wavelength for the first energy level.

Induced electric flux of the Bohr first energy level:

$$Q_B = C_B V_B.$$

Energy, stored on the Bohr capacitance:

$$W_C B = \frac{C_B V_B^2}{2} = \frac{Q_B^2}{2C_B} = 2\pi\alpha W_B,$$

where $W_B = \hbar\omega_B-$ is the Bohr energy. So, induced electric flux will be:

$$Q_B = \sqrt{2\pi\alpha^3 m_0 c^2 C_B} = e.$$

Thus, through the Bohr capacitance we have quantized electric flux, equal to the electron charge.

Magnetic flux through the Bohr inductance:

$$W_L B = \frac{L_B I_B^2}{2} = \frac{\Phi_B^2}{2L_B} = 2\pi\alpha W_0.$$

So, induced magnetic flux will be:

$$\Phi_B = \frac{\pi\alpha^2 ec}{\lambda_0} L_B = 2\alpha\Phi_0.$$

Thus, through the Bohr inductance there are no quantization of magnetic flux.

32.7.3 Photon as LC circuit

Photon "resonant angular frequency":

$$\omega_w = \sqrt{\frac{1}{L_w C_w}}.$$

Photon "wave impedance":

$$\rho_w = \sqrt{\frac{L_w}{C_w}} = \sqrt{\frac{\mu_0}{\epsilon_0}} = \rho_0.$$

Photon "wave inductance":

$$L_w = \frac{\rho_0}{\omega_w}.$$

Photon "wave capacitance":

$$C_w = \frac{1}{\rho_0 \omega_w}.$$

Photon "magnetic flux quantum":

$$\phi_w = L_w I_w = \phi_0 = \frac{h}{e}.$$

Photon "wave current":

$$I_w = \frac{h}{eL_w} = \frac{e\omega_w}{2\alpha}.$$

32.7.4 Quantum Hall effect as LC circuit

In the general case 2D- density of states (DOS) in a solid could be defined by the following:

$$D_{2D} = \frac{m^*}{\pi\hbar^2}$$

where $m^* = \xi m_0-$ current carriers effective mass in a solid, m_0- electron mass, and $\xi-$ dimensionless parameter, which considers band structure of a solid. So, the quantum inductance can be defined as follows:

$$L_{QL} = \phi_0^2 \cdot D_{2D} = \xi \cdot L_{Q0}$$

where $L_{Q0} 8\pi\beta \cdot L_{QY}$ - the "ideal value" of quantum inductance at $\xi = 1$ and another ideal quantum inductance:

$$L_{QY} = \frac{\mu_0}{\lambda_0} = H/m^2$$

where μ_0- magnetic constant, $\beta = \frac{1}{4\alpha}-$ magnetic "fine structure constant"[4](p. 62), $\alpha-$ fine structure constant and λ_0- Compton wavelength of electron, first defined by Yakymakha (1994)[5] in the spectroscopic investigations of the silicon MOSFETs.

Since defined above quantum inductance is per unit area, therefore its absolute value will be in the QHE mode:

$$L_{QA} = \frac{L_{QL}}{n_B}$$

where the carrier concentration is:

$$n_B = \frac{eB}{h}$$

and $h-$ is the Planck constant. By analogically, the absolute value of the quantum capacitance will be in the QHE mode:

$$C_{QA} = \frac{C_{QL}}{n_B}$$

where

$$C_{QL} = e^2 \cdot D_{2D} = \xi \cdot C_{Q0}$$

is DOS definition of the quantum capacitance according to Luryi,[6] $C_{Q0} = 8\pi\alpha \cdot C_{QY}$ - quantum capacitance "ideal value" at $\xi = 1$, and other quantum capacitance:

$$C_{QY} = \frac{\epsilon_0}{\lambda_0} = 3.6492417 F/m^2$$

where ϵ_0- dielectric constant, first defined by Yakymakha (1994)[5] > in the spectroscopic investigations of the silicon MOSFETs. The standard wave impedance definition for the QHE LC circuit could be presented as:

$$\rho_Q = \sqrt{\frac{L_{QA}}{C_{QA}}} = \sqrt{\frac{\phi_0^2}{e^2}} = \frac{h}{e^2} = R_H$$

where $R_H = \frac{h}{e^2} = 25.812813 k\Omega$ von Klitzing constant for resistance.

The standard resonant frequency definition for the QHE LC circuit could be presented as:

$$\omega_Q = \frac{1}{\sqrt{L_{QA} C_{QA}}} = \frac{\hbar\omega_c}{\phi_0 e} = \frac{\omega_c}{2\pi}$$

where $\omega_c = \frac{eB}{m^*}-$ standard cyclotron frequency in the magnetic field B.

Hall scaling current quantum will be

$$I_H = \frac{h}{e L_{QA}} = \frac{e\omega_B}{4\pi}$$

where $\omega_B = \frac{eB}{m^*}-$ Hall angular frequency.

32.7.5 Josephson junction as LC circuit

Electromagnetic induction (Faraday) low:

$$V_{ind} = \frac{\partial \Phi}{\partial t} = -L\frac{\partial I}{\partial t},$$

where $\Phi-$ magnetic flux, $L-$ Josephson junction quantum inductance and $I-$ Josephson junction current. DC Josephson equation for current:

$$I = I_J \cdot \sin\phi,$$

where I_J- Josephson scale for current, $\phi-$ phase difference between superconductors. Current derivative on time variable will be:

$$\frac{\partial I}{\partial t} = I_J \cos\phi \cdot \frac{\partial \phi}{\partial t}.$$

AC Josephson equation:

$$\frac{\partial \phi}{\partial t} = \frac{q}{\hbar}V = \frac{2\pi}{\Phi_0}V,$$

where $\hbar-$ reduced Planck constant, $\Phi_0 = h/2e-$ Josephson magnetic flux quantum, $q = 2e$ and $e-$ electron charge. Combining equations for derivatives yields junction voltage:

$$V = \frac{\Phi_0}{2\pi I_J} \cdot \frac{1}{\cos\phi} \cdot \frac{\partial I}{\partial t} = L_J \cdot \frac{\partial I}{\partial t},$$

where

$$L_J = \frac{\Phi_0}{2\pi I_J} \cdot \frac{1}{\cos\phi}$$

is the Devoret (1997) [7] quantum inductance.

AC Josephson equation for angular frequency:

$$\omega_J = \frac{q}{\hbar} \cdot V.$$

Resonance frequency for Josephson LC circuit:

$$\omega_J = \sqrt{\frac{1}{L_J C_J}}.$$

where $C_J -$ is the Devoret quantum capacitance, that can be defined as:

$$C_J = \frac{1}{L_J \omega_J^2} = \frac{\Phi_0 I_J}{V_0^2} \cdot \frac{\cos\phi}{2\pi}.$$

Quantum wave impedance of Josephson junction:

$$\rho_J = \sqrt{\frac{L_J}{C_J}} = \frac{V_0}{I_J} \cdot \frac{1}{\sqrt{\cos\phi}}.$$

For $V_0 = 0,1$ mV and $I_J = 0,2\mu$ A wave impedance will be $\rho_J = 500\Omega$.

32.7.6 Flat Atom as LC circuit

Quantum capacitance of *Flat Atom* (FA):

$$C_{F0} = \frac{\epsilon_0}{\lambda_0} \cdot S_{F0} = 5.1805 \cdot 10^{-7}$$

where $\lambda_0 = \frac{h}{m_0 c}$.

Quantum inductance of FA:

$$L_{F0} = \frac{\mu_0}{\lambda_0} \cdot S_{F0} = 7.3524 \cdot 10^{-2}$$

Quantum area element of FA:

$$S_{F0} = \frac{\lambda_0 c}{\omega_{F0}} = \frac{h}{m_0 \omega_{F0}} = 1.4196 \cdot 10^{-7} \text{ m}^2.$$

Resonance frequency of FA:

$$\omega_{F0} = \sqrt{\frac{1}{L_{F0} C_{F0}}} = 5123.9$$

Characteristic impedunce of FA:

$$\rho_{F0} = \sqrt{\frac{L_{F0}}{C_{F0}}} = \rho_0 - 2\alpha R_H,$$

where ρ_0 is the impedance of free space.

Total electric charge on the first energy level of FA:

$$Q_{F1} = e\sqrt{\frac{S_{F0}}{S_B}} = 2 \cdot 10^6 e$$

where $S_B = 4\pi a_B^2 -$ Bohr quantum area element. First FA was discovered by Yakymakha (1994) [5] as very low frequency resonance on the p- channel MOSFETs. Contrary to the spherical Bohr atom, the FA has gyperbolic dependence on the number of energy level (n) [8]

$$\omega_{F0n} = \frac{\omega_{F0}}{n}.$$

32.8 See also

- LC circuit
- Harmonic oscillator
- Quantum harmonic oscillator
- Quantum Electromagnetic Resonator

32.9 References

[1] Yakymakha O.L.(1989). *High Temperature Quantum Galvanomagnetic Effects in the Two- Dimensional Inversion Layers of MOSFET's* (In Russian). Kyiv: Vyscha Shkola. p. 91. ISBN 5-11-002309-3. djvu</

[2] Devoret M.H., Martinis J.M. (2004). "Implementing Qubits with Superconducting Integrated Circuits". Quantum Information Processing, v.3, N1. Pdf

[3] Raphael Tsu and Timir Datta (2008) "Conductance and Wave Impedance of Electrons". Progress In Electromagnetics Research Symposium, Hangzhou, China, March 24–28 Pdf

[4] Yakymakha O.L.(1989). *High Temperature Quantum Galvanomagnetic Effects in the Two- Dimensional Inversion Layers of MOSFET's* (In Russian). Kyiv: Vyscha Shkola. p.91. ISBN 5-11-002309-3. djvu

[5] Yakymakha O.L., Kalnibolotskij Y.M. (1994). "Very-low-frequency resonance of MOSFET amplifier parameters". *Solid- State Electronics* 37(10),1739-1751 Pdf

[6] Serge Luryi (1988). "Quantum capacitance device". *Appl.Phys.Lett.* 52(6). Pdf

[7] Devoret M.H. (1997). "Quantum Fluctuations". Amsterdam, Netherlands: Elsevier. pp.351-386. Pdf

[8] Yakymakha O.L., Kalnibolotskij Y.M., Solid- State Electronics, vol.38, No.3,1995.,pp.661-671 pdf

32.10 Sources

- W. H. Louisell, "Quantum Statistical Properties of Radiation" (Wiley, New York, 1973)
- Michel H.Devoret. Quantum Fluctuation in Electric Circuit.PDF
- Fan Hong-yi, Pan Xiao-yin. Chin.Phys.Lett. No9(1998)625.PDF
- Xu, Xing-Lei; Li, Hong-Qi; Wang, Ji-Suo Quantum fluctuations of mesoscopic damped double resonance RLC circuit with mutual capacitance inductance coupling in thermal excitation state. Chinese Physics, Volume 16, Issue 8, pp. 2462–2470 (2007).
- Hong-Qi Li, Xing-Lei Xu and Ji-Suo Wang. Quantum Fluctuations of the Current and Voltage in Thermal Vacuum State for Mesoscopic Quartz Piezoelectric Crystal.
- Boris Ya. Zel'dovich. Impedance and parametric excitation of oscillators. UFN, 2008, v. 178, No 5 PDF

Chapter 33

Quantum cryptography

Quantum cryptography is the science of exploiting quantum mechanical properties to perform cryptographic tasks. The best known example of quantum cryptography is quantum key distribution which offers an information-theoretically secure solution to the key exchange problem. Currently used popular public-key encryption and signature schemes (e.g., RSA and ElGamal) can be broken by quantum adversaries. The advantage of quantum cryptography lies in the fact that it allows the completion of various cryptographic tasks that are proven or conjectured to be impossible using only classical (i.e. non-quantum) communication (see below for examples). For example, it is impossible to copy data encoded in a quantum state and the very act of reading data encoded in a quantum state changes the state. This is used to detect eavesdropping in quantum key distribution.

33.1 History

Quantum cryptography was proposed first by Stephen Wiesner, then at Columbia University in New York, who, in the early 1970s, introduced the concept of quantum conjugate coding. His seminal paper titled "Conjugate Coding" was rejected by IEEE Information Theory Society, but was eventually published in 1983 in SIGACT News (15:1 pp. 78–88, 1983). In this paper he showed how to store or transmit two messages by encoding them in two "conjugate observables", such as linear and circular polarization of light, so that either, but not both, of which may be received and decoded. He illustrated his idea with a design of unforgeable bank notes. In 1984, building upon this work, Charles H. Bennett, of the IBM's Thomas J. Watson Research Center, and Gilles Brassard, of the Université de Montréal, proposed a method for secure communication based on Wiesner's "conjugate observables", which is now called BB84.[1] In 1991 Artur Ekert developed a different approach to quantum key distribution based on peculiar quantum correlations known as quantum entanglement.[2]

Random rotations of the polarization by both parties (usually called Alice and Bob) have been proposed in Kak's three-stage quantum cryptography protocol.[3] In principle, this method can be used for continuous, unbreakable encryption of data if single photons are used.[4] The basic polarization rotation scheme has been implemented.[5]

The BB84 method is at the basis of quantum key distribution methods. Companies that manufacture quantum cryptography systems include MagiQ Technologies, Inc. of Boston, ID Quantique of Geneva, Switzerland, QuintessenceLabs (Canberra, Australia) and SeQureNet (Paris).

33.2 Quantum key distribution

Main article: Quantum key distribution

The most well known and developed application of quantum cryptography is quantum key distribution (QKD), which is the process of using quantum communication to establish a shared key between two parties (Alice and Bob, for example) without a third party (Eve) learning anything about that key, even if Eve can eavesdrop on all communication between Alice and Bob. This is achieved by Alice encoding the bits of the key as quantum data and sending them to Bob; if Eve tries to learn these bits, the messages will be disturbed and Alice and Bob will notice. The key is then typically used for encrypted communication using classical techniques. For instance, the exchanged key could be used as the seed of the same random number generator both by Alice and Bob.

The security of QKD can be proven mathematically without imposing any restrictions on the abilities of an eavesdropper, something not possible with classical key distribution. This is usually described as "unconditional security", although there are some minimal assumptions required including that the laws of quantum mechanics apply and that Alice and Bob are able to authenticate each other, i.e. Eve should not be able to impersonate Alice or Bob as otherwise a man-in-the-middle attack would be possible.

One aspect of QKD is that it is secure against quantum computers, as its strength does not depend on mathematical complexity, like post-quantum cryptography, but on physical principles.

33.3 Quantum commitment

Following the discovery of quantum key distribution and its unconditional security, researchers tried to achieve other cryptographic tasks with unconditional security. One such task was commitment. A commitment scheme allows a party Alice to fix a certain value (to "commit") in such a way that Alice cannot change that value while at the same time ensuring that the recipient Bob cannot learn anything about that value until Alice decides to reveal it. Such commitment schemes are commonly used in cryptographic protocols. In the quantum setting, they would be particularly useful: Crépeau and Kilian showed that from a commitment and a quantum channel, one can construct an unconditionally secure protocol for performing so-called oblivious transfer.[6] Oblivious transfer, on the other hand, had been shown by Kilian to allow implementation of almost any distributed computation in a secure way (so-called secure multi-party computation).[7] (Notice that here we are a bit imprecise: The results by Crépeau and Kilian[6] and Kilian[7] together do not directly imply that given a commitment and a quantum channel one can perform secure multi-party computation. This is because the results do not guarantee "composability", that is, when plugging them together, one might lose security. Later works showed, however, how composability can be ensured in this setting.)

Unfortunately, early quantum commitment protocols[8] were shown to be flawed. In fact, Mayers showed that (unconditionally secure) quantum commitment is impossible: a computationally unlimited attacker can break any quantum commitment protocol.[9]

Yet, the result by Mayers does not preclude the possibility of constructing quantum commitment protocols (and thus secure multi-party computation protocols) under assumptions that they are much weaker than the assumptions needed for commitment protocols that do not use quantum communication. The bounded quantum storage model described below is an example for a setting in which quantum communication can be used to construct commitment protocols. A breakthrough in November 2013 offers "unconditional" security of information by harnessing quantum theory and relativity, which has been successfully demonstrated on a global scale for the first time.[10]

33.4 Bounded- and noisy-quantum-storage model

One possibility to construct unconditionally secure quantum commitment and quantum oblivious transfer (OT) protocols is to use the bounded quantum storage model (BQSM). In this model, we assume that the amount of quantum data that an adversary can store is limited by some known constant Q. We do not, however, impose any limit on the amount of classical (i.e., non-quantum) data the adversary may store.

In the BQSM, one can construct commitment and oblivious transfer protocols.[11] The underlying idea is the following: The protocol parties exchange more than Q quantum bits (qubits). Since even a dishonest party cannot store all that information (the quantum memory of the adversary is limited to Q qubits), a large part of the data will have to be either measured or discarded. Forcing dishonest parties to measure a large part of the data allows to circumvent the impossibility result by Mayers;[9] commitment and oblivious transfer protocols can now be implemented.

The protocols in the BQSM presented by Damgård, Fehr, Salvail, and Schaffner[11] do not assume that honest protocol participants store any quantum information; the technical requirements are similar to those in QKD protocols. These protocols can thus, at least in principle, be realized with today's technology. The communication complexity is only a constant factor larger than the bound Q on the adversary's quantum memory.

The advantage of the BQSM is that the assumption that the adversary's quantum memory is limited is quite realistic. With today's technology, storing even a single qubit reliably over a sufficiently long time is difficult. (What "sufficiently long" means depends on the protocol details. By introducing an artificial pause in the protocol, the amount of time over which the adversary needs to store quantum data can be made arbitrarily large.)

An extension of the BQSM is the noisy-storage model introduced by Wehner, Schaffner and Terhal.[12] Instead of considering an upper bound on the physical size of the adversary's quantum memory, an adversary is allowed to use imperfect quantum storage devices of arbitrary size. The level of imperfection is modelled by noisy quantum channels. For high enough noise levels, the same primitives as in the BQSM can be achieved [13] and the BQSM forms a special case of the noisy-storage model.

In the classical setting, similar results can be achieved when assuming a bound on the amount of classical (non-quantum) data that the adversary can store.[14] It was proven, however, that in this model also the honest parties have to use a large amount of memory (namely the square-root of the adversary's memory bound).[15] This makes these protocols impractical for realistic memory bounds. (Note that with today's technology such as hard disks, an adversary can cheaply store large amounts of classical data.)

33.5 Position-based quantum cryptography

The goal of position-based quantum cryptography is to use the *geographical location* of a player as its (only) credential. For example, one wants to send a message to a player at a specified position with the guarantee that it can only be read if the receiving party is located at that particular position. In the basic task of *position-verification*, a player Alice wants to convince the (honest) verifiers that she is located at a particular point. It has been shown by Chandran *et al.* that position-verification using classical protocols is impossible against colluding adversaries (who control all positions except the prover's claimed position).[16] Under various restrictions on the adversaries, schemes are possible.

Under the name of 'quantum tagging', the first position-based quantum schemes have been investigated in 2002 by Kent. A US-patent[17] was granted in 2006, but the results only appeared in the scientific literature in 2010.[18] After several other quantum protocols for position verification have been suggested in 2010,[19][20] Buhrman et al. were able to show a general impossibility result:[21] using an enormous amount of quantum entanglement (they use a doubly exponential number of EPR pairs, in the number of qubits the honest player operates on), colluding adversaries are always able to make it look to the verifiers as if they were at the claimed position. However, this result does not exclude the possibility of practical schemes in the bounded- or noisy-quantum-storage model (see above). Later Beigi and König improved the amount of EPR pairs needed in the general attack against position-verification protocols to exponential. They also showed that a particular protocol remains secure against adversaries who controls only a linear amount of EPR pairs.[22]

33.6 Device-independent quantum cryptography

Main article: Device-independent quantum cryptography

A quantum cryptographic protocol is **device-independent** if its security does not rely on trusting that the quantum devices used are truthful. Thus the security analysis of such a protocol needs to consider scenarios of imperfect or even malicious devices. Mayers and Yao[23] proposed the idea of designing quantum protocols using "self-testing" quantum apparatus, the internal operations of which can be uniquely determined by their input-output statistics. Subsequently, Roger Colbeck in his Thesis[24] proposed the use of Bell tests for checking the honesty of the devices. Since then, several problems have been shown to admit unconditional secure and device-independent protocols, even when the actual devices performing the Bell test are substantially "noisy," i.e., far from being ideal. These problems include quantum key distribution,[25][26] randomness expansion,[26][27] and randomness amplification.[28]

33.7 Post-quantum cryptography

Main article: Post-quantum cryptography

Quantum computers may become a technological reality; it is therefore important to study cryptographic schemes used against adversaries with access to a quantum computer. The study of such schemes is often referred to as post-quantum cryptography. The need for post-quantum cryptography arises from the fact that many popular encryption and signature schemes (such as RSA and its variants, and schemes based on elliptic curves) can be broken using Shor's algorithm for factoring and computing discrete logarithms on a quantum computer. Examples for schemes that are, as of today's knowledge, secure against quantum adversaries are McEliece and lattice-based schemes. Surveys of post-quantum cryptography are available.[29][30]

There is also research into how existing cryptographic techniques have to be modified to be able to cope with quantum adversaries. For example, when trying to develop zero-knowledge proof systems that are secure against quantum adversaries, new techniques need to be used: In a classical setting, the analysis of a zero-knowledge proof system usually involves "rewinding", a technique that makes it necessary to copy the internal state of the adversary. In a quantum setting, copying a state is not always possible (no-cloning theorem); a variant of the rewinding technique has to be used.[31]

Post quantum algorithms are also called "quantum resistant", because – unlike QKD – it is not known or provable that there will not be potential future quantum attacks against them. Even though they are not vulnerable to Shor's algorithm the NSA are announcing plans to transition to quantum resistant algorithms.[32]

33.8 References

[1] Bennett, C.H. and G. Brassard. Quantum cryptography: Public key distribution and coin tossing. In Proceedings of IEEE International Conference on Computers, Systems and Signal Processing, volume 175, page 8. New York, 1984.

[2] Ekert. A. Physical Review Letters, 67, pp.661-663, (1991)

[3] Kak, S., A three-stage quantum cryptography protocol. Foundations of Physics Letters, vol. 19, pp.293-296, 2006.

[4] Chen, Y. et al., Embedded security framework for integrated classical and quantum cryptography in optical burst switching networks. Security and Communication Networks, vol. 2, pp. 546-554, 2009.

[5] http://www.kurzweilai.net/ a-multi-photon-approach-to-quantum-cryptography

[6] Crépeau, Claude; Joe, Kilian (1988). *Achieving Oblivious Transfer Using Weakened Security Assumptions (Extended Abstract)*. FOCS 1988. IEEE. pp. 42–52.

[7] Kilian, Joe (1988). *Founding cryptography on oblivious transfer*. STOC 1988. ACM. pp. 20–31.

[8] Brassard, Gilles; Claude, Crépeau; Jozsa, Richard; Langlois, Denis (1993). *A Quantum Bit Commitment Scheme Provably Unbreakable by both Parties*. FOCS 1993. IEEE. pp. 362–371.

[9] Mayers, Dominic (1997). "Unconditionally Secure Quantum Bit Commitment is Impossible". *Physical Review Letters* (APS) **78** (17): 3414–3417. arXiv:quant-ph/9605044. Bibcode:1997PhRvL..78.3414M. doi:10.1103/PhysRevLett.78.3414. Preprint at arXiv:quant-ph/9605044v2

[10] "Experimental Bit Commitment Based on Quantum Communication and Special Relativity".

[11] Damgård, Ivan; Fehr, Serge; Salvail, Louis; Schaffner, Christian (2005). *Cryptography In the Bounded Quantum-Storage Model*. FOCS 2005. IEEE. pp. 449–458. A full version is available at arXiv:quant-ph/0508222.

[12] Wehner, Stephanie; Schaffner, Christian; Terhal, Barbara M. (2008). "Cryptography from Noisy Storage". *Physical Review Letters* (APS) **100** (22): 220502. arXiv:0711.2895. Bibcode:2008PhRvL.100v0502W. doi:10.1103/PhysRevLett.100.220502. PMID 18643410. A full version is available at arXiv:0711.2895.

[13] Koenig, Robert; Wehner, Stephanie; Wullschleger, Juerg. "Unconditional security from noisy quantum storage". A full version is available at arXiv:0906.1030.

[14] Cachin, Christian; Crépeau, Claude; Marcil, Julien (1998). *Oblivious Transfer with a Memory-Bounded Receiver*. FOCS 1998. IEEE. pp. 493–502.

[15] Dziembowski, Stefan; Ueli, Maurer (2004). *On Generating the Initial Key in the Bounded-Storage Model*. Eurocrypt 2004. LNCS. Springer. pp. 126–137. Preprint available at .

[16] Chandran, Nishanth; Moriarty, Ryan; Goyal, Vipul; Ostrovsky, Rafail (2009). *Position-Based Cryptography*. A full version is available at IACR eprint:2009/364.

[17] US 7075438, issued 2006-07-11

[18] Kent, Adrian; Munro, Bill; Spiller, Tim (2010). "Quantum Tagging with Cryptographically Secure Tags". A full version is available at arXiv:1008.2147.

[19] Lau, Hoi-Kwan; Lo, Hoi-Kwong (2010). "Insecurity of position-based quantum-cryptography protocols against entanglement attacks". *Physical Review A* (APS) **83**: 012322. arXiv:1009.2256. Bibcode:2011PhRvA..83a2322L. doi:10.1103/PhysRevA.83.012322. A full version is available at arXiv:1009.2256.

[20] Malaney, Robert A. (2010). "Location-dependent communications using quantum entanglement". *Physical Review A* **81**: 042319. arXiv:1003.0949. Bibcode:2010PhRvA..81d2319M. doi:10.1103/PhysRevA.81.042319.

[21] Buhrman, Harry; Chandran, Nishanth; Fehr, Serge; Gelles, Ran; Goyal, Vipul; Ostrovsky, Rafail; Schaffner, Christian (2010). "Position-Based Quantum Cryptography: Impossibility and Constructions". A full version is available at arXiv:1009.2490.

[22] Beigi, Salman; König, Robert (2011). "Simplified instantaneous non-local quantum computation with applications to position-based cryptography". arXiv:1101.1065.

[23] Mayers, Dominic; Yao, Andrew C.-C. (1998). *Quantum Cryptography with Imperfect Apparatus*. IEEE Symposium on Foundations of Computer Science (FOCS). arXiv:quant-ph/9809039. horizontal tab character in |conference= at position 43 (help)

[24] Colbeck, Roger (December 2006). "Chapter 5". *Quantum And Relativistic Protocols For Secure Multi-Party Computation* (Thesis). University of Cambridge.

[25] Vazirani, Umesh; Vidick, Thomas (2014). "Fully Device-Independent Quantum Key Distribution". *Physical Review Letters* **113**: 140501. arXiv:1403.3830. Bibcode:2014PhRvL.113b0501A. doi:10.1103/PhysRevLett.113.020501.

[26] Miller, Carl; Shi, Yaoyun (2014). "Robust protocols for securely expanding randomness and distributing keys using untrusted quantum devices". arXiv:1402.0489.

[27] Miller, Carl; Shi, Yaoyun (2015). "Universal security for randomness expansion". arXiv:1411.6608.

[28] Chung, Kai-Min; Shi, Yaoyun; Wu, Xiaodi (2014). "Physical Randomness Extractors: Generating Random Numbers with Minimal Assumptions". arXiv:1402.4797.

[29] "Post-quantum cryptography". Retrieved 29 August 2010.

[30] Bernstein, Daniel J.; Buchmann, Johannes; Dahmen, Erik, eds. (2009). *Post-quantum cryptography*. Springer. ISBN 978-3-540-88701-0.

[31] Watrous, John (2009). "Zero-Knowledge against Quantum Attacks". *SIAM J. Comput.* **39** (1): 25–58. doi:10.1137/060670997.

[32] "NSA Suite B Cryptography". Retrieved 29 December 2015.

Chapter 34

One-way quantum computer

The **one-way** or **measurement based quantum computer** (**MBQC**) is a method of quantum computing that first prepares an entangled *resource state*, usually a cluster state or graph state, then performs single qubit measurements on it. It is "one-way" because the resource state is destroyed by the measurements.

The outcome of each individual measurement is random, but they are related in such a way that the computation always succeeds. In general the choices of basis for later measurements need to depend on the results of earlier measurements, and hence the measurements cannot all be performed at the same time.

34.1 Equivalence to quantum circuit model

Any one-way computation can be made into a quantum circuit by using quantum gates to prepare the resource state. For cluster and graph resource states, this requires only one two-qubit gate per bond, so is efficient.

Conversely, any quantum circuit can be simulated by a one-way computer using a two-dimensional cluster state as the resource state, by laying out the circuit diagram on the cluster; Z measurements ($\{|0\rangle, |1\rangle\}$ basis) remove physical qubits from the cluster, while measurements in the X-Y plane ($|0\rangle \pm e^{i\theta}|1\rangle$ basis) teleport the logical qubits along the "wires" and perform the required quantum gates.[1] This is also polynomially efficient, as the required size of cluster scales as the size of the circuit (qubits x timesteps), while the number of measurement timesteps scales as the number of circuit timesteps.

34.2 Topological cluster state quantum computer

Measurement-based computation on a periodic 3D lattice cluster state can be used to implement topological quantum error correction.[2] Topological cluster state computation is closely related to Kitaev's toric code, as the 3D topological cluster state can be constructed and measured over time by a repeated sequence of gates on a 2D array.[3]

34.3 Implementations

One-way quantum computation has been demonstrated by running the 2 qubit Grover's algorithm on a 2x2 cluster state of photons.[4][5] A linear optics quantum computer based on one-way computation has been proposed.[6]

Cluster states have also been created in optical lattices,[7] but were not used for computation as the atom qubits were too close together to measure individually.

34.4 AKLT state as a resource

It has been shown that the (spin $\frac{3}{2}$) AKLT state on a 2D Honeycomb lattice can be used as a resource for MBQC.[8][9] More recently it has been shown that a spin-mixture AKLT state can be used as a resource.[10]

34.5 References

[1] R. Raussendorf, D. E. Browne, and H. J. Briegel (2003). "Measurement based Quantum Computation on Cluster States". *Phys. Rev. A* **68** (2): 022312. arXiv:quant-ph/0301052. Bibcode:2003PhRvA..68b2312R. doi:10.1103/PhysRevA.68.022312.

[2] Robert Raussendorf, Jim Harrington, Kovid Goyal (2007). "Topological fault-tolerance in cluster state quantum computation". *New Journal of Physics* **9**: 199. arXiv:quant-ph/0703143. Bibcode:2007NJPh....9..199R. doi:10.1088/1367-2630/9/6/199.

[3] Robert Raussendorf, Jim Harrington (2007). "Fault-tolerant quantum computation with high threshold in two dimensions". *Phys. Rev. Lett.* **98**: 190504. doi:10.1103/physrevlett.98.190504.

[4] P. Walther, K. J. Resch, T. Rudolph, E. Schenck, H. Weinfurter, V. Vedral, M. Aspelmeyer and A. Zeilinger (2005). "Experimental one-way quantum

computing". *Nature* **434** (7030): 169–76. arXiv:quant-ph/0503126. Bibcode:2005Natur.434..169W. doi:10.1038/nature03347. PMID 15758991.

[5] Robert Prevedel, Philip Walther, Felix Tiefenbacher, Pascal Böhi, Rainer Kaltenbaek, Thomas Jennewein and Anton Zeilinger (2007). "High-speed linear optics quantum computing using active feed-forward". *Nature* **445** (7123): 65–69. arXiv:quant-ph/0701017. Bibcode:2007Natur.445...65P. doi:10.1038/nature05346. PMID 17203057.

[6] Daniel E. Browne, Terry Rudolph (2005). "Resource-efficient linear optical quantum computation". *Physical Review Letters* **95** (1): 010501. arXiv:quant-ph/0405157. Bibcode:2005PhRvL..95a0501B. doi:10.1103/PhysRevLett.95.010501. PMID 16090595.

[7] Olaf Mandel, Markus Greiner, Artur Widera, Tim Rom, Theodor W. Hänsch and Immanuel Bloch (2003). "Controlled collisions for multi-particle entanglement of optically trapped atoms". *Nature* **425** (6961): 937–40. arXiv:quant-ph/0308080. Bibcode:2003Natur.425..937M. doi:10.1038/nature02008. PMID 14586463.

[8] Tzu-Chieh Wei, Ian Affleck, and Robert Raussendorf (2012). "Two-dimensional Affleck-Kennedy-Lieb-Tasaki state on the honeycomb lattice is a universal resource for quantum computation". *PRA* **86** (032328). arXiv:1009.2840. doi:10.1103/PhysRevA.86.032328.

[9] Akimasa Miyake (2011). "Quantum computational capability of a 2D valence bond solid phase". *Annals of Physics* **236** (7): 1656–1671. arXiv:1009.3491. doi:10.1016/j.aop.2011.03.006.

[10] Tzu-Chieh Wei, Poya Haghnegahdar, Robert Raussendorf. "Spin mixture AKLT states for universal quantum computation".

General

- R. Raussendorf and H. J. Briegel (2001). "A One-Way Quantum Computer". *Physical Review Letters* **86** (22): 5188–91. Bibcode:2001PhRvL..86.5188R. doi:10.1103/PhysRevLett.86.5188. PMID 11384453.

- D. Gross, J. Eisert, N. Schuch, D. Perez-Garcia (2007). "Measurement-based quantum computation beyond the one-way model". *Physical Review A* **76** (5): 052315. arXiv:0706.3401. Bibcode:2007PhRvA..76e2315G. doi:10.1103/PhysRevA.76.052315. Non-cluster resource states

- A. Trisetyarso and R. Van Meter (2010). "Circuit Design for A Measurement-Based Quantum Carry-Lookahead Adder". *International Journal of Quantum Information* **8** (05): 843–867. arXiv:0903.0748. doi:10.1142/S0219749910006496. Measurement-based quantum computation, quantum carry-lookahead adder

Chapter 35

Kane quantum computer

The Kane quantum computer is a proposal for a scalable quantum computer proposed by Bruce Kane in 1998,[1] who was then at the University of New South Wales. Often thought of as a hybrid between quantum dot and nuclear magnetic resonance (NMR) quantum computers, the Kane computer is based on an array of individual phosphorus donor atoms embedded in a pure silicon lattice. Both the nuclear spins of the donors and the spins of the donor electrons participate in the computation.

Unlike many quantum computation schemes, the Kane quantum computer is in principle scalable to an arbitrary number of qubits. This is possible because qubits may be individually addressed by electrical means.

35.1 Description

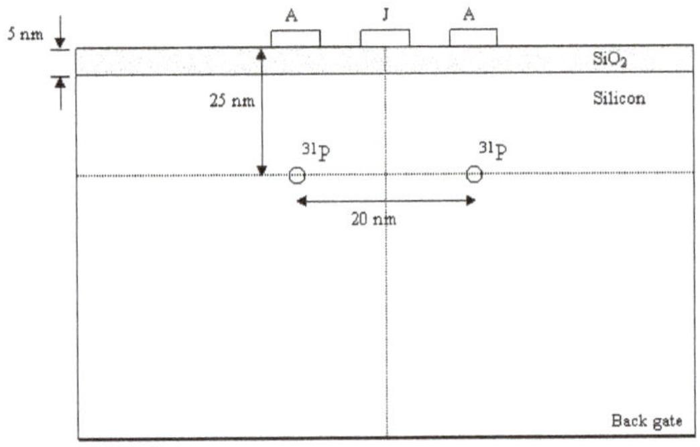

The original proposal calls for phosphorus donors to be placed in an array with a spacing of 20 nm, approximately 20 nm below the surface. An insulating oxide layer is grown on top of the silicon. Metal **A gates** are deposited on the oxide above each donor, and **J gates** between adjacent donors.

The phosphorus donors are isotopically pure ^{31}P, which have a nuclear spin of 1/2. The silicon substrate is isotopically pure ^{28}Si which has nuclear spin 0. Using the nuclear spin of the P donors as a method to encode qubits has two major advantages. Firstly, the state has an extremely long decoherence time, perhaps on the order of 10^{18} seconds at millikelvin temperatures. Secondly, the qubits may be manipulated by applying an oscillating magnetic field, as in typical NMR proposals. By altering the voltage on the A gates, it should be possible to alter the Larmor frequency of individual donors. This allows them to be addressed individually, by bringing specific donors into resonance with the applied oscillating magnetic field.

Nuclear spins alone will not interact significantly with other nuclear spins 20 nm away. Nuclear spin is useful to perform single-qubit operations, but to make a quantum computer, two-qubit operations are also required. This is the role of electron spin in this design. Under A-gate control, the spin is transferred from the nucleus to the donor electron. Then, a potential is applied to the J gate, drawing adjacent donor electrons into a common region, greatly enhancing the interaction between the neighbouring spins. By controlling the J gate voltage, two-qubit operations are possible.

Kane's proposal for readout was to apply an electric field to encourage spin-dependent tunneling of an electron to transform two neutral donors to a D^+–D^- state, that is, one where two electrons orbit the same donor. The charge excess is then detected using a single-electron transistor. This method has two major difficulties. Firstly, the D^- state has strong coupling with the environment and hence a short decoherence time. Secondly and perhaps more importantly, it's not clear that the D^- state has a sufficiently long lifetime to allow for readout—the electron tunnels into the conduction band.

35.2 Development

Since Kane's proposal, under the guidance of Robert Clark and now Michelle Simmons, pursuing realisation of the Kane quantum computer has become the primary quantum computing effort in Australia.[2] Theorists have put forward a number of proposals for improved readout. Experimentally, atomic-precision deposition of phosphorus atoms has been demonstrated, using an scanning tunneling microscope (STM) technique. Detection of the movement of single electrons between small, dense clusters of phosphorus donors has also been achieved. The group remains optimistic that a practical large-scale quantum computer can be built. Other groups believe that the idea needs to be modified.[3]

35.3 References

[1] Kane, B.E. (1998)"A silicon-based nuclear spin quantum computer ", *Nature*, **393**, p133

[2] Centre for Quantum Computation & Communication Technology

[3] O'Gorman, J. A silicon-based surface code quantum computer. http://arxiv.org/pdf/1406.5149.pdf 2014

Chapter 36

Quantum technology

Quantum technology is a new field of physics and engineering, which transitions some of the properties of quantum mechanics, especially quantum entanglement, quantum superposition and quantum tunnelling, into practical applications such as quantum computing, quantum sensing, quantum cryptography, quantum simulation, quantum metrology and quantum imaging.

36.1 Applications

36.1.1 Sensing

Quantum superposition states can be very sensitive to a number of external effects, such as electric, magnetic and gravitational fields; rotation, acceleration and time, and t2 herefore can used to make very accurate sensors. There are many experimental demonstrations of quantum sensing devices, such as the experiments carried out by the nobel laureate William D. Phillips on using cold atom interferometer systems to measure gravity and the atomic clock which is used by many national standards agencies around the world to define the second.

Recent efforts are being made to engineer quantum sensing devices, so that they are cheaper, easier to use, more portable, lighter and consume less power. It is believed that if these efforts are successful, it will lead to multiple commercial markets, such as for the monitoring of oil and gas deposits, or in construction.

36.1.2 Secure communications

Quantum secure communication are methods which are expected to be 'quantum safe' in the advent of a quantum computing systems that could break current cryptography systems. One significant component of a quantum secure communication systems is expected to be Quantum key distribution, or 'QKD': a method of transmitting information using entangled light in a way that makes any interception of the transmission obvious to the user.

36.1.3 Computing

Quantum computers are the ultimate quantum network, combining 'quantum bits' or 'qubit' which are devices which can store and process quantum data (as opposed to binary data) with links that can transfer quantum information between quits. In doing this, quantum computers are predicted to calculate certain algorithms significantly faster than even the largest classical computer available today.

Quantum computers are expected to have a number of significant uses in computing fields such as optimisation and machine learning. They are famous for their expected ability to carry out 'Shor's Algorithm', which can be used to factorise large numbers which are mathematically important to secure data transmission.

36.2 The first and second quantum revolutions

There are many devices available today which are fundamentally reliant on the effects of quantum mechanics. These include: laser systems, transistors and semiconductor devices and other devices, such as MRI imagers. These devices are often referred to belonging to the 'first quantum revolution'; the UK Defence Science and Technology Laboratory (Dstl) grouped these devices as 'quantum 1.0',[1] that is devices which rely on the effects of quantum mechanics. Quantum technologies are often described as the 'second quantum revolution' or 'quantum 2.0'. These are generally regarded as a class of device that actively create, manipulate and read out quantum states of matter, often using the quantum effects of superposition and entanglement.

36.3 History

The field of quantum technology was first outlined in a 1997 book by Gerard J. Milburn,[2] which was then followed by a 2003 article by Jonathan P. Dowling and Gerard J. Milburn,[3][4] as well as a 2003 article by

David Deutsch.[5] The field of quantum technology has benefited immensely from the influx of new ideas from the field of quantum information processing, particularly quantum computing. Disparate areas of quantum physics, such as quantum optics, atom optics, quantum electronics, and quantum nanomechanical devices, have been unified under the search for a quantum computer and given a common language, that of quantum information theory.

36.4 National programmes

From 2010 onwards, multiple governments have established programmes to explore quantum technologies, such as the UK National Quantum Technologies Programme, which created four quantum 'hubs', the Centre for Quantum Technologies in Singapore, and QuTech a Dutch centre to develop a topological quantum computer.[6]

In the private sector, there have been multiple investments into quantum technologies made by large companies. Examples include Google's partnership with the John Martinis group at UCSB,[7] multiple partnerships with the Canadian quantum computing company D-wave systems, and investment by many UK companies within the UK quantum technologies programme.

36.5 See also

- Quantum nanoscience
- Atomic engineering

36.6 References

[1]

[2] *Schrödinger's Machines*, G.J.Milburn, W H Freeman & Co. (1997) Archived August 30, 2007, at the Wayback Machine.

[3] "Quantum Technology: The Second Quantum Revolution,"J.P.Dowling and G.J.Milburn, Phil. Trans. R. Soc. A 361, 3655 (2003)

[4] "Quantum Technology: The Second Quantum Revolution," J.P.Dowling and G.J.Milburn, arXiv:quant-ph/0206091v1

[5] "Physics, Philosophy, and Quantum Technology," D.Deutsch in the Proceedings of the Sixth International Conference on Quantum Communication, Measurement and Computing, Shapiro, J.H. and Hirota, O., Eds. (Rinton Press, Princeton, NJ. 2003)

[6] 'A little bit, better' The Economist, 18th June 2015

[7] The man who will build Google's elusive quantum computer; Wired, 09.05.14

36.7 External links

- "National Strategy for Quantum Technologies" UK Quantum Technologies strategy
- "Gadgets from the Quantum Spookhouse," Science News, Vol. 160, No. 23, Dec. 8, 2001, p. 364.
- "Spooky Timing: Quantum-linked photons coordinate clock ticks," Science News, Vol. 166, No. 13, Sept. 25, 2004, p. 196.
- "Kittens Catch Phase," Jonathan P. Dowling, Nature 450, 362-363 (15 November 2007).
- "Quantum-enhanced positioning and clock synchronization," Nature 412, 417-419 (26 July 2001).
- B. Bylicka, D. Chruściński, S. Maniscalco Non-Markovianity as a Resource for Quantum Technologies arXiv:1301.2585
- G.J. Milburn, M.J. Woolley, «Quantum nanoscience» Contemporary Physics, Vol. 49, No. 6, (2008) 413—433.
- V.E. Tarasov, «Quantum Nanotechnology» International Journal of Nanoscience. Vol.8. No.4-5. (2009) 337—344.
- Quantum Feedback Control and Metrology with Cold Atoms
- Quantum Atomic Gravity Gradiometer
- Real World Quantum Effects Demonstrated
- EPJ Quantum Technology Springer journal

Chapter 37

Bennett's laws

Bennett's laws of quantum information are:

1. 1 qubit $\geqslant$ 1 bit (classical)
2. 1 qubit $\geqslant$ 1 ebit (entanglement bit)
3. 1 ebit + 1 qubit $\geqslant$ 2 bits (i.e. superdense coding)
4. 1 ebit + 2 bits $\geqslant$ 1 qubit (i.e. quantum teleportation)

where $\geqslant$ indicates 'can do the job of.'

These principles were formulated around 1993 by Charles H. Bennett.

37.1 References

- *Quantum Mechanics: The Physics of the Microscopic World*, Benjamin Schumacher, The Teaching Company, lecture 21

Chapter 38

Bistochastic quantum channel

In quantum information science, a **bistochastic quantum channel** is a quantum channel $\phi(\rho)$ which is unital,[1] i.e. $\phi(I) = I$.

38.1 References

[1] John A. Holbrook, David W. Kribs, and Raymond Laflamme. "Noiseless Subsystems and the Structure of the Commutant in Quantum Error Correction." *Quantum Information Processing*. Volume 2, Number 5, p. 381-419. Oct 2003.

Chapter 39

Channel-state duality

In quantum information theory, the **channel-state duality** refers to the correspondence between quantum channels and quantum states (described by density matrices). Phrased differently, the duality is the isomorphism between completely positive maps (channels) from A to $\mathbf{C}^{n \times n}$, where A is a C*-algebra and $\mathbf{C}^{n \times n}$ denotes the $n \times n$ complex entries, and positive linear functionals (states) on the tensor product

$$\mathbb{C}^{n \times n} \otimes A.$$

39.1 Details

Let H_1 and H_2 be (finite-dimensional) Hilbert spaces. The family of linear operators acting on Hi will be denoted by $L(Hi)$. Consider two quantum systems, indexed by 1 and 2, whose states are density matrices in $L(Hi)$ respectively. A quantum channel, in the Schrödinger picture, is a completely positive (CP for short) linear map

$$\Phi : L(H_1) \to L(H_2)$$

that takes a state of system 1 to a state of system 2. Next we describe the dual state corresponding to Φ.

Let $Ei\,j$ denote the matrix unit whose ij-th entry is 1 and zero elsewhere. The (operator) matrix

$$\rho_\Phi = (\Phi(E_{ij}))_{ij} \in L(H_1) \otimes L(H_2)$$

is called the *Choi matrix* of Φ. By Choi's theorem on completely positive maps, Φ is CP if and only if $\varrho\Phi$ is positive (semidefinite). One can view $\varrho\Phi$ as a density matrix, and therefore the state dual to Φ.

The duality between channels and states refers to the map

$$\Phi \to \rho_\Phi,$$

a linear bijection. This map is also called **Jamiołkowski isomorphism** or **Choi–Jamiołkowski isomorphism**.

Chapter 40

Classical capacity

In quantum information theory, the **classical capacity** of a quantum channel is the maximum rate at which classical data can be sent over it error-free in the limit of many uses of the channel. Holevo, Schumacher, and Westmoreland proved the following lower bound on the classical capacity of any quantum channel $\mathcal{N}$:

$$\chi(\mathcal{N}) = \max_{\rho^{XA}} I(X;B)_{\mathcal{N}(\rho)}$$

where ρ^{XA} is a classical-quantum state of the following form:

$$\rho^{XA} = \sum_x p_X(x)|x\rangle\langle x|^X \otimes \rho_x^A,$$

$p_X(x)$ is a probability distribution, and each ρ_x^A is a density operator that can be input to the channel $\mathcal{N}$.

40.1 Achievability using sequential decoding

We briefly review the HSW coding theorem (the statement of the achievability of the Holevo information rate $I(X;B)$ for communicating classical data over a quantum channel). We first review the minimal amount of quantum mechanics needed for the theorem. We then cover quantum typicality, and finally we prove the theorem using a recent sequential decoding technique.

40.2 Review of Quantum Mechanics

In order to prove the HSW coding theorem, we really just need a few basic things from quantum mechanics. First, a quantum state is a unit trace, positive operator known as a density operator. Usually, we denote it by ρ , σ , ω , etc. The simplest model for a quantum channel is known as a classical-quantum channel:

$$x \mapsto \rho_x.$$

The meaning of the above notation is that inputting the classical letter x at the transmitting end leads to a quantum state ρ_x at the receiving end. It is the task of the receiver to perform a measurement to determine the input of the sender. If it is true that the states ρ_x are perfectly distinguishable from one another (i.e., if they have orthogonal supports such that Tr $\{\rho_x \rho_{x'}\} = 0$ for $x \neq x'$), then the channel is a noiseless channel. We are interested in situations for which this is not the case. If it is true that the states ρ_x all commute with one another, then this is effectively identical to the situation for a classical channel, so we are also not interested in these situations. So, the situation in which we are interested is that in which the states ρ_x have overlapping support and are non-commutative.

The most general way to describe a quantum measurement is with a positive operator-valued measure (POVM). We usually denote the elements of a POVM as $\{\Lambda_m\}_m$. These operators should satisfy positivity and completeness in order to form a valid POVM:

$$\Lambda_m \geq 0 \quad \forall m$$
$$\sum_m \Lambda_m = I.$$

The probabilistic interpretation of quantum mechanics states that if someone measures a quantum state ρ using a measurement device corresponding to the POVM $\{\Lambda_m\}$, then the probability $p(m)$ for obtaining outcome m is equal to

$$p(m) = \text{Tr}\{\Lambda_m \rho\},$$

and the post-measurement state is

$$\rho'_m = \frac{1}{p(m)} \sqrt{\Lambda_m} \rho \sqrt{\Lambda_m},$$

if the person measuring obtains outcome m . These rules are sufficient for us to consider classical communication schemes over cq channels.

40.3 Quantum Typicality

The reader can find a good review of this topic in the article about the typical subspace.

40.4 Gentle Operator Lemma

The following lemma is important for our proofs. It demonstrates that a measurement that succeeds with high probability on average does not disturb the state too much on average:

Lemma: [Winter] Given an ensemble $\{p_X(x), \rho_x\}$ with expected density operator $\rho \equiv \sum_x p_X(x) \rho_x$, suppose that an operator Λ such that $I \geq \Lambda \geq 0$ succeeds with high probability on the state ρ :

$$\mathrm{Tr}\{\Lambda\rho\} \geq 1 - \epsilon.$$

Then the subnormalized state $\sqrt{\Lambda}\rho_x\sqrt{\Lambda}$ is close in expected trace distance to the original state ρ_x :

$$\mathbb{E}_X\left\{\left\|\sqrt{\Lambda}\rho_X\sqrt{\Lambda} - \rho_X\right\|_1\right\} \leq 2\sqrt{\epsilon}.$$

(Note that $\|A\|_1$ is the nuclear norm of the operator A so that $\|A\|_1 \equiv \mathrm{Tr}\left\{\sqrt{A^\dagger A}\right\}$.)

The following inequality is useful for us as well. It holds for any operators ρ , σ , Λ such that $0 \leq \rho, \sigma, \Lambda \leq I$:

The quantum information-theoretic interpretation of the above inequality is that the probability of obtaining outcome Λ from a quantum measurement acting on the state ρ is upper bounded by the probability of obtaining outcome Λ on the state σ summed with the distinguishability of the two states ρ and σ .

40.5 Non-Commutative Union Bound

Lemma: [Sen's bound] The following bound holds for a subnormalized state σ such that $0 \leq \sigma$ and $Tr\{\sigma\} \leq 1$ with Π_1 , ... , Π_N being projectors: $\mathrm{Tr}\{\sigma\} - \mathrm{Tr}\{\Pi_N \cdots \Pi_1\, \sigma\, \Pi_1 \cdots \Pi_N\} \leq 2\sqrt{\sum_{i=1}^N \mathrm{Tr}\{(I - \Pi_i)\,\sigma\}}$,

We can think of Sen's bound as a "non-commutative union bound" because it is analogous to the following union bound from probability theory:

$$\Pr\{(A_1 \cap \cdots \cap A_N)^c\} = \Pr\{A_1^c \cup \cdots \cup A_N^c\} \leq \sum_{i=1}^N \Pr\{A_i^c\},$$

where A_1 , \ldots, A_N are events. The analogous bound for projector logic would be

$$\mathrm{Tr}\{(I - \Pi_1 \cdots \Pi_N \cdots \Pi_1)\,\rho\} \leq \sum_{i=1}^N \mathrm{Tr}\{(I - \Pi_i)\,\rho\},$$

if we think of $\Pi_1 \cdots \Pi_N$ as a projector onto the intersection of subspaces. Though, the above bound only holds if the projectors Π_1 , ..., Π_N are commuting (choosing $\Pi_1 = |+\rangle\langle+|$, $\Pi_2 = |0\rangle\langle 0|$, and $\rho = |0\rangle\langle 0|$ gives a counterexample). If the projectors are non-commuting, then Sen's bound is the next best thing and suffices for our purposes here.

40.6 HSW Theorem with the non-commutative union bound

We now prove the HSW theorem with Sen's non-commutative union bound. We divide up the proof into a few parts: codebook generation, POVM construction, and error analysis.

Codebook Generation. We first describe how Alice and Bob agree on a random choice of code. They have the channel $x \to \rho_x$ and a distribution $p_X(x)$. They choose M classical sequences x^n according to the IID\ distribution $p_{X^n}(x^n)$. After selecting them, they label them with indices as $\{x^n(m)\}_{m \in [M]}$. This leads to the following quantum codewords:

$$\rho_{x^n(m)} = \rho_{x_1(m)} \otimes \cdots \otimes \rho_{x_n(m)}.$$

The quantum codebook is then $\left\{\rho_{x^n(m)}\right\}$. The average state of the codebook is then

where $\rho = \sum_x p_X(x)\, \rho_x$.

POVM Construction . Sens' bound from the above lemma suggests a method for Bob to decode a state that Alice transmits. Bob should first ask "Is the received state in the average typical subspace?" He can do this operationally by performing a typical subspace measurement corresponding to $\left\{\Pi^n_{\rho,\delta}, I - \Pi^n_{\rho,\delta}\right\}$. Next, he asks in sequential order, "Is the received codeword in the mth conditionally typical subspace?" This is in some sense equivalent to the question, "Is the received codeword the mth transmitted codeword?" He can ask these questions operationally by performing the measurements corresponding to the conditionally typical projectors $\left\{\Pi_{\rho_{x^n(m)},\delta}, I - \Pi_{\rho_{x^n(m)},\delta}\right\}$.

Why should this sequential decoding scheme work well? The reason is that the transmitted codeword lies in the typical subspace on average:

$$\mathbb{E}_{X^n}\left\{\mathrm{Tr}\left\{\Pi_{\rho,\delta}\,\rho_{X^n}\right\}\right\} = \mathrm{Tr}\left\{\Pi_{\rho,\delta}\,\mathbb{E}_{X^n}\left\{\rho_{X^n}\right\}\right\}$$
$$= \mathrm{Tr}\left\{\Pi_{\rho,\delta}\,\rho^{\otimes n}\right\}$$
$$\geq 1-\epsilon,$$

where the inequality follows from (\ref{eq: 1st-typ-prop}). Also, the projectors $\Pi_{\rho_{x^n(m)},\delta}$ are "good detectors" for the states $\rho_{x^n(m)}$ (on average) because the following condition holds from conditional quantum typicality:

$$\mathbb{E}_{X^n}\left\{\mathrm{Tr}\left\{\Pi_{\rho_{X^n},\delta}\,\rho_{X^n}\right\}\right\} \geq 1-\epsilon.$$

Error Analysis . The probability of detecting the mth codeword correctly under our sequential decoding scheme is equal to

$$\mathrm{Tr}\Big\{\Pi_{\rho_{X^n(m)},\delta}\hat{\Pi}_{\rho_{X^n(m-1)},\delta}\cdots \hat{\Pi}_{\rho_{X^n(1)},\delta}\,\Pi^n_{\rho,\delta}\,\rho_{x^n(m)}\,\Pi^n_{\rho,\delta}\,\hat{\Pi}_{\rho_{X^n(1)},\delta}\cdots\hat{\Pi}_{\rho_{X^n(m-1)},\delta}\Pi_{\rho_{X^n(m)},\delta}\Big\},$$

where we make the abbreviation $\Pi \equiv I - \Pi$. (Observe that we project into the average typical subspace just once.) Thus, the probability of an incorrect detection for the mth codeword is given by

$$1-\mathrm{Tr}\Big\{\Pi_{\rho_{X^n(m)},\delta}\hat{\Pi}_{\rho_{X^n(m-1)},\delta}\cdots \hat{\Pi}_{\rho_{X^n(1)},\delta}\,\Pi^n_{\rho,\delta}\,\rho_{x^n(m)}\,\Pi^n_{\rho,\delta}\,\hat{\Pi}_{\rho_{X^n(1)},\delta}\cdots\hat{\Pi}_{\rho_{X^n(m-1)},\delta}\Pi_{\rho_{X^n(m)},\delta}\Big\},$$

and the average error probability of this scheme is equal to

$$1-\frac{1}{M}\sum_m \mathrm{Tr}\Big\{\Pi_{\rho_{X^n(m)},\delta}\hat{\Pi}_{\rho_{X^n(m-1)},\delta}\cdots \hat{\Pi}_{\rho_{X^n(1)},\delta}\,\Pi^n_{\rho,\delta}\,\rho_{x^n(m)}\,\Pi^n_{\rho,\delta}\,\hat{\Pi}_{\rho_{X^n(1)},\delta}\cdots\hat{\Pi}_{\rho_{X^n(m-1)},\delta}\Pi_{\rho_{X^n(m)},\delta}\Big\}.$$

Instead of analyzing the average error probability, we analyze the expectation of the average error probability, where the expectation is with respect to the random choice of code:

Our first step is to apply Sen's bound to the above quantity. But before doing so, we should rewrite the above expression just slightly, by observing that

$$1=\mathbb{E}_{X^n}\left\{\frac{1}{M}\sum_m \mathrm{Tr}\left\{\rho_{X^n(m)}\right\}\right\}$$
$$=\mathbb{E}_{X^n}\left\{\frac{1}{M}\sum_m \mathrm{Tr}\left\{\Pi^n_{\rho,\delta}\rho_{X^n(m)}\right\} + \mathrm{Tr}\left\{\hat{\Pi}^n_{\rho,\delta}\rho_{X^n(m)}\right\}\right\}$$
$$=\mathbb{E}_{X^n}\left\{\frac{1}{M}\sum_m \mathrm{Tr}\left\{\Pi^n_{\rho,\delta}\rho_{X^n(m)}\Pi^n_{\rho,\delta}\right\}\right\} + \frac{1}{M}\sum_m \mathrm{Tr}\left\{\hat{\Pi}^n_{\rho,\delta}\mathbb{E}_{X^n}\left\{\rho_{X^n(m)}\right\}\right\}$$
$$=\mathbb{E}_{X^n}\left\{\frac{1}{M}\sum_m \mathrm{Tr}\left\{\Pi^n_{\rho,\delta}\rho_{X^n(m)}\Pi^n_{\rho,\delta}\right\}\right\} + \mathrm{Tr}\left\{\hat{\Pi}^n_{\rho,\delta}\rho^{\otimes n}\right\}$$
$$\leq \mathbb{E}_{X^n}\left\{\frac{1}{M}\sum_m \mathrm{Tr}\left\{\Pi^n_{\rho,\delta}\rho_{X^n(m)}\Pi^n_{\rho,\delta}\right\}\right\} + \epsilon$$

Substituting into (**3**) (and forgetting about the small ϵ term for now) gives an upper bound of

$$\mathbb{E}_{X^n}\left\{\frac{1}{M}\sum_m \mathrm{Tr}\left\{\Pi^n_{\rho,\delta}\rho_{X^n(m)}\Pi^n_{\rho,\delta}\right\}\right\}$$
$$-\mathbb{E}_{X^n}\Big\{\frac{1}{M}\sum \mathrm{Tr}\Big\{\Pi_{\rho_{X^n(m)},\delta}\hat{\Pi}_{\rho_{X^n(m-1)},\delta}\cdots \hat{\Pi}_{\rho_{X^n(1)},\delta}\,\Pi^n_{\rho,\delta}\,\rho_{X^n(m)}\,\Pi^n_{\rho,\delta}\,\hat{\Pi}_{\rho_{X^n(1)},\delta}\cdots\hat{\Pi}_{\rho_{X^n(m-1)},\delta}\Pi_{\rho_{X^n(m)},\delta}\Big\}\Big\}.$$

We then apply Sen's bound to this expression with $\sigma = \Pi^n_{\rho,\delta}\rho_{X^n(m)}\Pi^n_{\rho,\delta}$ and the sequential projectors as $\Pi_{\rho_{X^n(m)},\delta}$, $\hat{\Pi}_{\rho_{X^n(m-1)},\delta}$, ..., $\hat{\Pi}_{\rho_{X^n(1)},\delta}$. This gives the upper bound

$$\mathbb{E}_{X^n}\left\{\frac{1}{M}\sum_m 2\left[\mathrm{Tr}\left\{\left(I-\Pi_{\rho_{X^n(m)},\delta}\right)\Pi^n_{\rho,\delta}\rho_{X^n(m)}\Pi^n_{\rho,\delta}\right\} + \sum_{i=1}^{m-1}\mathrm{Tr}\left\{\Pi_{\rho_{X^n(i)},\delta}\Pi^n_{\rho,\delta}\rho_{X^n(m)}\Pi^n_{\rho,\delta}\right\}\right]^{1/2}\right\}.$$

Due to concavity of the square root, we can bound this expression from above by

$$2\left[\mathbb{E}_{X^n}\left\{\frac{1}{M}\sum_m \mathrm{Tr}\left\{\left(I-\Pi_{\rho_{X^n(m)},\delta}\right)\Pi^n_{\rho,\delta}\rho_{X^n(m)}\Pi^n_{\rho,\delta}\right\}\right.\right.$$
$$\leq 2\left[\mathbb{E}_{X^n}\left\{\frac{1}{M}\sum_m \mathrm{Tr}\left\{\left(I-\Pi_{\rho_{X^n(m)},\delta}\right)\Pi^n_{\rho,\delta}\rho_{X^n(m)}\Pi^n_{\rho,\delta}\right\} + \sum_{i\neq m}\mathrm{Tr}\left\{\Pi_{\rho_{X^n(i)},\delta}\Pi^n_{\rho,\delta}\rho_{X^n(m)}\Pi^n_{\rho,\delta}\right\}\right\}\right]^{1/2},$$

where the second bound follows by summing over all of the codewords not equal to the mth codeword (this sum can only be larger).

We now focus exclusively on showing that the term inside the square root can be made small. Consider the first term:

$$\mathbb{E}_{X^n}\left\{\frac{1}{M}\sum_m \mathrm{Tr}\left\{\left(I-\Pi_{\rho_{X^n(m)},\delta}\right)\Pi^n_{\rho,\delta}\rho_{X^n(m)}\Pi^n_{\rho,\delta}\right\}\right\}$$
$$\leq \mathbb{E}_{X^n}\left\{\frac{1}{M}\sum_m \mathrm{Tr}\left\{\left(I-\Pi_{\rho_{X^n(m)},\delta}\right)\rho_{X^n(m)}\right\} + \left\|\rho_{X^n(m)} - \Pi^n_{\rho,\delta}\rho_{X^n(m)}\Pi^n_{\rho,\delta}\right\|_1\right\}$$
$$\leq \epsilon + 2\sqrt{\epsilon}.$$

where the first inequality follows from (**1**) and the second inequality follows from the Gentle Operator Lemma and the properties of unconditional and conditional typicality. Consider now the second term and the following chain of inequalities:

$$\sum_{i\neq m}\mathbb{E}_{X^n}\left\{\mathrm{Tr}\left\{\Pi_{\rho_{X^n(i)},\delta}\,\Pi^n_{\rho,\delta}\,\rho_{X^n(m)}\,\Pi^n_{\rho,\delta}\right\}\right\}$$

$$= \sum_{i \neq m} \text{Tr}\left\{\mathbb{E}_{X^n}\left\{\Pi_{\rho_{X^n(i)},\delta}\right\} \Pi^n_{\rho,\delta}\, \mathbb{E}_{X^n}\left\{\rho_{X^n(m)}\right\} \Pi^n_{\rho,\delta}\right\}$$

$$= \sum_{i \neq m} \text{Tr}\left\{\mathbb{E}_{X^n}\left\{\Pi_{\rho_{X^n(i)},\delta}\right\} \Pi^n_{\rho,\delta}\, \rho^{\otimes n}\, \Pi^n_{\rho,\delta}\right\}$$

$$\leq \sum_{i \neq m} 2^{-n[H(B)-\delta]}\, \text{Tr}\left\{\mathbb{E}_{X^n}\left\{\Pi_{\rho_{X^n(i)},\delta}\right\} \Pi^n_{\rho,\delta}\right\}$$

The first equality follows because the codewords $X^n(m)$ and $X^n(i)$ are independent since they are different. The second equality follows from (**2**). The first inequality follows from (\ref{eq:3rd-typ-prop}). Continuing, we have

$$\leq \sum_{i \neq m} 2^{-n[H(B)-\delta]}\, \mathbb{E}_{X^n}\left\{\text{Tr}\left\{\Pi_{\rho_{X^n(i)},\delta}\right\}\right\}$$

$$\leq \sum_{i \neq m} 2^{-n[H(B)-\delta]}\, 2^{n[H(B|X)+\delta]}$$

$$= \sum_{i \neq m} 2^{-n[I(X;B)-2\delta]}$$

$$\leq M\, 2^{-n[I(X;B)-2\delta]}.$$

The first inequality follows from $\Pi^n_{\rho,\delta} \leq I$ and exchanging the trace with the expectation. The second inequality follows from (\ref{eq:2nd-cond-typ}). The next two are straightforward.

Putting everything together, we get our final bound on the expectation of the average error probability:

$$1-\mathbb{E}_{X^n}\left\{\frac{1}{M}\sum_{m} \text{Tr}\left\{\Pi_{\rho_{X^n(m)},\delta}\hat{\Pi}_{\rho_{X^n(m-1)},\delta}\cdots\hat{\Pi}_{\rho_{X^n(1)},\delta}\,\Pi^n_{\rho,\delta}\,\rho_{X^n(m)}\,\Pi^n_{\rho,\delta}\,\hat{\Pi}_{\rho_{X^n(1)},\delta}\cdots\hat{\Pi}_{\rho_{X^n(m-1)},\delta}\Pi_{\rho_{X^n(m)},\delta}\right\}\right\}$$

$$\leq \epsilon + 2\left[\left(\epsilon + 2\sqrt{\epsilon}\right) + M\, 2^{-n[I(X;B)-2\delta]}\right]^{1/2}.$$

Thus, as long as we choose $M = 2^{n[I(X;B)-3\delta]}$, there exists a code with vanishing error probability.

40.7 See also

- Quantum capacity
- Entanglement-assisted classical capacity
- Typical subspace
- Quantum information theory

40.8 References

- Holevo, Alexander S. (1998), "The Capacity of Quantum Channel with General Signal States", *IEEE Transactions on Information Theory* **44** (1): 269–273, arXiv:quant-ph/9611023, doi:10.1109/18.651037.
- Schumacher, Benjamin; Westmoreland, Michael (1997), "Sending classical information via noisy quantum channels", *Phys. Rev. A* **56**: 131–138, Bibcode:1997PhRvA..56..131S, doi:10.1103/PhysRevA.56.131.
- Wilde, Mark M. (2013), *Quantum Information Theory*, Cambridge University Press, arXiv:1106.1445, Bibcode:2011arXiv1106.1445W
- Sen, Pranab (2012), "Achieving the Han-Kobayashi inner bound for the quantum interference channel by sequential decoding", *IEEE International Symposium on Information Theory Proceedings (ISIT 2012)*, pp. 736–740, arXiv:1109.0802, doi:10.1109/ISIT.2012.6284656.
- Guha, Saikat; Tan, Si-Hui; Wilde, Mark M. (2012), "Explicit capacity-achieving receivers for optical communication and quantum reading", *IEEE International Symposium on Information Theory Proceedings (ISIT 2012)*, pp. 551–555, arXiv:1202.0518, doi:10.1109/ISIT.2012.6284251.

Chapter 41

Coherent information

Coherent information is an entropy measure used in quantum information theory. It is a property of a quantum state ρ and a quantum channel $\mathcal{N}$; intuitively, it attempts to describe how much of the quantum information in the state will remain after the state goes through the channel. In this sense, it is intuitively similar to the mutual information of classical information theory. The coherent information is written $I(\rho, \mathcal{N})$.

41.1 Definition

The coherent information is defined as $I(\rho, \mathcal{N}) \stackrel{\text{def}}{=} S(\mathcal{N}\rho) - S(\mathcal{N}, \rho)$ where $S(\mathcal{N}\rho)$ is the von Neumann entropy of the output and $S(\mathcal{N}, \rho)$ is the entropy exchange between the state and the channel.

41.2 History

The coherent information was introduced by Benjamin Schumacher and Michael A. Nielsen in a 1996 paper *Quantum data processing and error correction*, which appeared in Physical Review A.

41.3 References

- Nielsen, Michael A. and Isaac L. Chuang (2000). *Quantum Computation and Quantum Information*, Cambridge University Press, ISBN 0-521-63503-9
- Nielsen, Michael A. and Benjamin Schumacher (1996). Quantum data processing and error correction. *Physical Review A.*, **54** (4), 2629-2635.

Chapter 42

Entanglement witness

In quantum information theory, an **entanglement witness** is a functional which distinguishes a specific entangled state from separable ones. Entanglement witnesses can be linear or nonlinear functionals of the density matrix. If linear, then they can also be viewed as observables for which the expectation value of the entangled state is strictly outside the range of possible expectation values of any separable state.

42.1 Details

Let a composite quantum system have state space $H_A \otimes H_B$. A mixed state ρ is then a trace-class positive operator on the state space which has trace 1. We can view the family of states as a subset of the real Banach space generated by the Hermitian trace-class operators, with the trace norm. A mixed state ρ is separable if it can be approximated, in the trace norm, by states of the form

$$\xi = \sum_{i=1}^{k} p_i \, \rho_i^A \otimes \rho_i^B,$$

where ρ_i^A 's and ρ_i^B 's are pure states on the subsystems *A* and *B* respectively. So the family of separable states is the closed convex hull of pure product states. We will make use of the following variant of Hahn–Banach theorem:

Theorem Let S_1 and S_2 be disjoint convex closed sets in a real Banach space and one of them is compact, then there exists a bounded functional *f* separating the two sets.

This is a generalization of the fact that, in real Euclidean space, given a convex set and a point outside, there always exists an affine subspace separating the two. The affine subspace manifests itself as the functional *f*. In the present context, the family of separable states is a convex set in the space of trace class operators. If ρ is an entangled state (thus lying outside the convex set), then by theorem above, there is a functional *f* separating ρ from the separable states. It is this functional *f*, or its identification as an operator, that we call an **entanglement witness**. There are more than one hyperplane separating a closed convex set and a point lying outside of it. So for an entangled state there are more than one entanglement witnesses. Recall the fact that the dual space of the Banach space of trace-class operators is isomorphic to the set of bounded operators. Therefore we can identify *f* with a Hermitian operator *A*. Therefore, modulo a few details, we have shown the existence of an entanglement witness given an entangled state:

Theorem For every entangled state ρ, there exists a Hermitian operator A such that $\mathrm{Tr}(A\,\rho) < 0$, and $\mathrm{Tr}(A\,\sigma) \geq 0$ for all separable states σ.

When both H_A and H_B have finite dimension, there is no difference between trace-class and Hilbert–Schmidt operators. So in that case *A* can be given by Riesz representation theorem. As an immediate corollary, we have:

Theorem A mixed state σ is separable if and only if

$$\mathrm{Tr}(A\,\sigma) \geq 0$$

for any bounded operator A satisfying $\mathrm{Tr}(A \cdot P \otimes Q) \geq 0$, for all product pure state $P \otimes Q$.

If a state is separable, clearly the desired implication from the theorem must hold. On the other hand, given an entangled state, one of its entanglement witnesses will violate the given condition.

Thus if a bounded functional *f* of the trace-class Banach space and *f* is positive on the product pure states, then *f*, or its identification as a Hermitian operator, is an entanglement witness. Such a *f* indicates the entanglement of some state.

Using the isomorphism between entanglement witnesses and non-completely positive maps, it was shown (by the Horodecki's) that

Theorem A mixed state $\sigma \in L(H_A) \otimes L(H_B)$ is separable if for every positive map Λ from bounded operators on H_B to bounded operators on H_A, the operator $(I_A \otimes \Lambda)(\sigma)$ is positive, where I_A is the identity map on $L(H_A)$, the bounded operators on H_A.

42.2 References

- Terhal, Barbara M. (2000). "Bell inequalities and the separability criterion". *Physics Letters A* **271** (5-6): 319–326. arXiv:quant-ph/9911057. Bibcode:2000PhLA..271..319T. doi:10.1016/S0375-9601(00)00401-1. ISSN 0375-9601. Also available at quant-ph/9911057
- R.B. Holmes. *Geometric Functional Analysis and Its Applications*, Springer-Verlag, 1975.
- M. Horodecki, P. Horodecki, R. Horodecki, *Separability of Mixed States: Necessary and Sufficient Conditions*, Physics Letters A 223, 1 (1996) and arXiv:quant-ph/9605038
- Z. Ficek, "Quantum Entanglement Processing with Atoms", Appl. Math. Inf. Sci. 3, 375–393 (2009).
- Barry C. Sanders and Jeong San Kim, "Monogamy and polygamy of entanglement in multipartite quantum systems", Appl. Math. Inf. Sci. 4, 281–288 (2010).
- Gühne, O.; Tóth, G. (2009). "Entanglement detection". *Phys. Rep.* **474**: 1–75. arXiv:0811.2803. Bibcode:2009PhR...474....1G. doi:10.1016/j.physrep.2009.02.004.

Chapter 43

Greenberger–Horne–Zeilinger state

In physics, in the area of quantum information theory, a **Greenberger–Horne–Zeilinger state** is a certain type of entangled quantum state which involves at least three subsystems (particles). It was first studied by Daniel Greenberger, Michael Horne and Anton Zeilinger in 1989.[1] They have noticed the extremely non-classical properties of the state.

43.1 Definition

The **GHZ state** is an entangled quantum state of $M > 2$ subsystems. In the case of each of the subsystems being two-dimensional, that is for qubits, it reads

$$|\mathrm{GHZ}\rangle = \frac{|0\rangle^{\otimes M} + |1\rangle^{\otimes M}}{\sqrt{2}}.$$

In simple words it is a quantum superposition of all subsystems being in state 0 with all of them being in state 1 (states 0 and 1 of a single subsystem are fully distinguishable).

The simplest one is the 3-qubit GHZ state:

$$|\mathrm{GHZ}\rangle = \frac{|000\rangle + |111\rangle}{\sqrt{2}}.$$

A different form of tripartite entanglement is given by the W state. The GHZ state and the W state cannot be transformed into one-another; they are distinct. The W state is, in a certain sense "less entangled" than the GHZ state; however, that entanglement is, in a sense, more robust against single-particle measurements, in that, for an N-qubit W state, an entangled (N-1) qubit state remains after a single particle measurement. By contrast, certain measurements on the GHZ state collapse it into a mixture or a pure state.

43.2 Properties

There is no standard measure of multi-partite entanglement because different types of multi-partite entanglement exist which are not mutually convertible. Nonetheless, many measures define the GHZ to be maximally entangled.

Another important property of the GHZ state is that when we trace over one of the three systems we get

$$\mathrm{Tr}_3\big((|000\rangle+|111\rangle)(\langle 000|+\langle 111|)\big) = \frac{(|00\rangle\langle 00| + |11\rangle\langle 11|)}{2}$$

which is an unentangled mixed state. It has certain two-particle (qubit) correlations, but these are of a classical nature.

On the other hand, if we were to measure one of the subsystems, in such a way that the measurement distinguishes between the states 0 and 1, we will leave behind either $|00\rangle$ or $|11\rangle$ which are unentangled pure states. This is unlike the W state which leaves bipartite entanglements even when we measure one of its subsystems.

The GHZ state leads to striking non-classical correlations (1989). Particles prepared in this state lead to a version of Bell's theorem, which shows the internal inconsistency of the notion of elements-of-reality introduced in the famous Einstein–Podolsky–Rosen paper. The first laboratory observation of GHZ correlations was by the group of Anton Zeilinger (1998). Many, more accurate observations followed. The correlations can be utilized in some quantum information tasks. These include multipartner quantum cryptography (1998) and communication complexity tasks (1997, 2004).

43.3 Pairwise entanglment

Although a naive measurement of the third particle of the GHZ state results in an unentangled pair, a more clever measurement, along an orthogonal direction, can leave behind a maximally entangled Bell state. This is illustrated below. The lesson to be drawn from this is that pairwise entanglement in the GHZ is more subtle than it naively appears: measurements along the privileged Z-direction destroy pair-wise entanglement, but other measurements (along different axes) do not.

The GHZ state can be written as

$$|000\rangle + |111\rangle = (|00\rangle + |11\rangle) \otimes |L\rangle + (|00\rangle - |11\rangle) \otimes |R\rangle$$

where the third particle ("Wigner's friend"[2]) is written as a superposition in the X-basis (as opposed to the Z-basis) as $|0\rangle = |L\rangle + |R\rangle$ and $|1\rangle = |L\rangle - |R\rangle$.

A measurement of the GHZ state along the X-basis for the third particle then yields either $|00\rangle + |11\rangle$, if $|L\rangle$ was measured, or $|00\rangle - |11\rangle$, if $|R\rangle$ was measured. In the later case, the phase can be rotated by applying a Z-quantum gate, to give $|00\rangle + |11\rangle$; while, in the former case, no additional transformations are applied. In either case, the end result of the operations is a maximally entangled Bell state.

The point of this example is that it illustrates that the pairwise entanglement of the GHZ state is more subtle than it first appears: a judicious measurement along an orthogonal direction, along with the application of a quantum transform depending on the measurement outcome, can leave behind a maximally entangled state.

43.4 See also

- Bell's theorem
- Bell state
- GHZ experiment
- Local hidden variable theory
- Quantum entanglement
- Qubit
- Measurement in quantum mechanics

43.5 References

[1] Daniel M. Greenberger, Michael A. Horne, Anton Zeilinger (2007), *Going beyond Bell's Theorem*, arXiv:0712.0921, Bibcode:2007arXiv0712.0921G

[2] The other two particles are Wigner and the cat; the three together form a GHZ state, of seeing a dead cat or not.

Chapter 44

Holevo's theorem

Holevo's theorem is an important limitative theorem in quantum computing, an interdisciplinary field of physics and computer science. It is sometimes called **Holevo's bound**, since it establishes an upper bound to the amount of information which can be known about a quantum state (accessible information). It was published by Alexander Holevo in 1973.

44.1 Accessible Information

As for several concepts in quantum information theory, accessible information is best understood in terms of a 2-party communication. So we introduce two parties, Alice and Bob. Alice has a *classical* random variable X, which can take the values $\{1, 2, ..., n\}$ with corresponding probabilities $\{p_1, p_2, ..., pn\}$. Alice then prepares a quantum state, represented by the density matrix ϱX chosen from a set $\{\varrho_1, \varrho_2, ... \varrho n\}$, and gives this state to Bob. Bob's goal is to find the value of X, and in order to do that, he performs a measurement on the state ϱX, obtaining a classical outcome, which we denote with Y. In this context, the amount of accessible information, that is, the amount of information that Bob can get about the variable X, is the maximum value of the mutual information $I(X : Y)$ between the random variables X and Y over all the possible measurements that Bob can do.[1]

There is currently no known formula to compute the accessible information. There are however several upper bounds, the best-known of which is the Holevo bound, which is specified in the following theorem.[1]

44.2 Statement of the theorem

Let $\{\varrho_1, \varrho_2, ..., \varrho n\}$ be a set of mixed states and let ϱX be one of these states drawn according to the probability distribution $P = \{p_1, p_2, ..., pn\}$.

Then, for any measurement described by POVM elements $\{EY\}$ and performed on $\rho = \sum_X p_X \rho_X$, the amount of accessible information about the variable X knowing the outcome Y of the measurement is bounded from above as follows:

$$I(X : Y) \leq S(\rho) - \sum_i p_i S(\rho_i)$$

where $\rho = \sum_i p_i \rho_i$ and $S(\cdot)$ is the von Neumann entropy.

The quantity on the right hand side of this inequality is called the **Holevo information** or **Holevo χ quantity**:

$$\chi := S(\rho) - \sum_i p_i S(\rho_i)$$

44.3 Proof

The proof can be given using three quantum systems, called P, Q, M . P can be intuitively thought as the *preparation*, Q can be thought as the quantum state prepared by Alice and given to Bob, and M can be thought as Bob's measurement apparatus.

The compound system $P \otimes Q \otimes M$ at the beginning is in the state

$$\rho^{PQM} := \sum_x p_x |x\rangle\langle x| \otimes \rho_x \otimes |0\rangle\langle 0|$$

This can be thought as Alice having the value x for the random variable X . Then the *preparation state* is the mixed state described by the density matrix $\sum_x p_x |x\rangle\langle x|$, and the quantum state given to Bob is $\sum_x p_x \rho_x$, and Bob's *measurement apparatus* is in its *initial* or *rest* state $|0\rangle$. Using known results of quantum information theory it can be shown that

$$S(P'; M') \leq S(P; Q)$$

which, after some algebraic manipulation, can be shown to be equivalent to the statement of the theorem.[1]

44.4 Comments and remarks

In essence, the Holevo bound proves that given n qubits, although they can "carry" a larger amount of (classical) information (thanks to quantum superposition), the amount of classical information that can be *retrieved*, i.e. *accessed*, can be only up to n classical (non-quantum encoded) bits. This is surprising, for two reasons: (1) quantum computing is so often more powerful than classical computing, that results which show it to be only as good or inferior to conventional techniques are unusual, and (2) because it takes $2^n - 1$ complex numbers to encode the qubits which represent a mere n bits.

44.5 Footnotes

[1] Nielsen & Chuang (2000)

44.6 See also

- Superdense coding

44.7 References

- Holevo, Alexander S. (1973). "Bounds for the quantity of information transmitted by a quantum communication channel". *Problems of Information Transmission* **9**: 177–183.
- Nielsen, Michael A.; Chuang, Isaac L. (2000). *Quantum Computation and Quantum Information*. Cambridge, UK: Cambridge University Press. ISBN 978-0-521-63235-5. OCLC 43641333. (see page 531, subsection 12.1.1 - equation (12.6))
- Wilde, Mark M. (2011). "From Classical to Quantum Shannon Theory". arXiv:1106.1445v2.. See in particular Section 11.6 and following. Holevo's theorem is presented as exercise 11.9.1 on page 288.

44.8 External links

- Holevo's theorem and its implications for quantum communication and computation, talk by Ashwin Nayak at the Mathematical Sciences Research Institute, 2000

Chapter 45

Joint quantum entropy

The **joint quantum entropy** generalizes the classical joint entropy to the context of quantum information theory. Intuitively, given two quantum states ρ and σ , represented as density operators that are subparts of a quantum system, the joint quantum entropy is a measure of the total uncertainty or entropy of the joint system. It is written $S(\rho,\sigma)$ or $H(\rho,\sigma)$, depending on the notation being used for the von Neumann entropy. Like other entropies, the joint quantum entropy is measured in bits, i.e. the logarithm is taken in base 2.

In this article, we will use $S(\rho,\sigma)$ for the joint quantum entropy.

45.1 Background

In information theory, for any classical random variable X , the classical Shannon entropy $H(X)$ is a measure of how uncertain we are about the outcome of X . For example, if X is a probability distribution concentrated at one point, the outcome of X is certain and therefore its entropy $H(X) = 0$. At the other extreme, if X is the uniform probability distribution with n possible values, intuitively one would expect X is associated with the most uncertainty. Indeed such uniform probability distributions have maximum possible entropy $H(X) = \log_2(n)$.

In quantum information theory, the notion of entropy is extended from probability distributions to quantum states, or density matrices. For a state ρ , the von Neumann entropy is defined by

$$-\operatorname{Tr}\rho\log\rho.$$

Applying the spectral theorem, or Borel functional calculus for infinite dimensional systems, we see that it generalizes the classical entropy. The physical meaning remains the same. A maximally mixed state, the quantum analog of the uniform probability distribution, has maximum von Neumann entropy. On the other hand, a pure state, or a rank one projection, will have zero von Neumann entropy. We write the von Neumann entropy $S(\rho)$ (or sometimes $H(\rho)$.

45.2 Definition

Given a quantum system with two subsystems *A* and *B*, the term **joint quantum entropy** simply refers to the von Neumann entropy of the combined system. This is to distinguish from the entropy of the subsystems. In symbols, if the combined system is in state ρ^{AB} ,

the joint quantum entropy is then

$$S(\rho^A,\rho^B) = S(\rho^{AB}) = -\operatorname{Tr}(\rho^{AB}\log(\rho^{AB})).$$

Each subsystem has it own entropy. The state of the subsystems are given by the partial trace operation.

45.3 Properties

The classical joint entropy is always at least equal to the entropy of each individual system. This is not the case for the joint quantum entropy. If the quantum state ρ^{AB} exhibits quantum entanglement, then the entropy of each subsystem may be larger than the joint entropy. This is equivalent to the fact that the conditional quantum entropy may be negative, while the classical conditional entropy may never be.

Consider a maximally entangled state such as a Bell state. If ρ^{AB} is a Bell state, say,

$$|\Psi\rangle = \frac{1}{\sqrt{2}}\left(|00\rangle + |11\rangle\right),$$

then the total system is a pure state, with entropy 0, while each individual subsystem is a maximally mixed state, with maximum von Neumann entropy $\log 2 = 1$. Thus the joint entropy of the combined system is less than that of subsystems. This is because for entangled states, definite states cannot be assigned to subsystems, resulting in positive entropy.

Notice that the above phenomenon cannot occur if a state is a separable pure state. In that case, the reduced states of the subsystems are also pure. Therefore all entropies are zero.

45.4 Relations to other entropy measures

The joint quantum entropy $S(\rho^{AB})$ can be used to define of the conditional quantum entropy:

$$S(\rho^A|\rho^B) \stackrel{\text{def}}{=} S(\rho^A,\rho^B) - S(\rho^B)$$

and the quantum mutual information:

$$I(\rho^A:\rho^B) \stackrel{\text{def}}{=} S(\rho^A) + S(\rho^B) - S(\rho^A,\rho^B)$$

These definitions parallel the use of the classical joint entropy to define the conditional entropy and mutual information.

45.5 See also

- Quantum relative entropy
- Quantum mutual information

45.6 References

- Nielsen, Michael A. and Isaac L. Chuang, *Quantum Computation and Quantum Information*. Cambridge University Press, 2000. ISBN 0-521-63235-8

Chapter 46

Lieb-Robinson bounds

The **Lieb-Robinson bound** is a theoretical upper limit on the speed at which information can propagate in non-relativistic quantum systems. It demonstrates that information cannot travel instantaneously in quantum theory, even when the relativity limits of the speed of light are ignored.

In the study of quantum systems such as quantum optics, quantum information theory, atomic physics, and condensed matter physics, it is important to know that there is a finite speed with which information can propagate. The theory of relativity shows that no information, or anything else for that matter, can travel faster than the speed of light. When non-relativistic mechanics is considered, however, (Newton's equations of motion or Schrödinger's equation of quantum mechanics) it had been thought that there is then no limitation to the speed of propagation of information. This is not so for certain kinds of quantum systems of atoms arranged in a lattice, often called quantum spin systems. This is important conceptually and practically, because it means that, for short periods of time, distant parts of a system act independently.

The surprising existence of such a finite limit to the speed of propagation, up to exponentially small error terms, was discovered mathematically in 1972.[1] It turns the locality properties of physical systems into the existence of an upper bound for this speed. This bound is known as the Lieb-Robinson bound and the speed is known as the **Lieb-Robinson velocity**. The velocity is not universal, because it depends on the details of the system under consideration, but, for each system, there is a finite velocity.

One of the practical applications of Lieb-Robinson bounds is quantum computing. Current proposals to construct quantum computers built out of atomic-like units mostly rely on the existence of this finite speed of propagation to protect against too rapid dispersal of information.

Review articles can be found in the following references, for example,[2][3][4]

46.1 Set up

To define the bound, it is necessary to first describe basic facts about quantum mechanical systems composed of several units, each with a finite dimensional Hilbert space.

Lieb-Robinson bounds are considered on a d -dimensional lattice ($d = 1, 2$ or 3) such as the square lattice $\Gamma = \mathbb{Z}^d$.

A Hilbert space of states $\mathcal{H}_x$ is associated with each point $x \in \Gamma$. The dimension of this space is finite, but this was generalized in 2008 (see below). This is called *quantum spin system*.

For every finite subset of the lattice, $X \subset \Gamma$, the associated Hilbert space is given by the tensor product

$$\mathcal{H}_X = \otimes_{x \in X} \mathcal{H}_x$$

$\mathcal{H}_X$ is a subspace of $\mathcal{H}_Y$ if $X \subset Y$.

An observable A supported on (i.e., depends only on) a finite set $X \subset \Gamma$ is a linear operator on the Hilbert space $\mathcal{H}_X$.

When $\mathcal{H}_x$ is finite dimensional choose a finite basis of operators that span the set of linear operators on $\mathcal{H}_x$. Then any observable on $\mathcal{H}_x$ can be written as a sum of basis operators on $\mathcal{H}_x$.

The Hamiltonian of the system is described by an interaction $\Phi(\cdot)$. The *interaction* is a function from the finite sets $X \subset \Gamma$ to self-adjoint observables $\Phi(X)$ supported in X . The interaction is assumed to be finite range (meaning that $\Phi(X) = 0$ if the size of X exceeds a certain prescribed size) and translation invariant. These requirements were lifted later, see:[5][6]

Although translation invariance is usually assumed, it is not necessary to do so. It is enough to assume that the interaction is bounded above and below on its domain. Thus, the bound is quite robust in the sense that it is tolerant of changes of the Hamiltonian. A finite range *is* essential, however. An interaction is said to be of finite range if there is a finite number R such that for any set X with diameter greater than R the interaction is zero, i.e., $\Phi(X) = 0$.

The Hamiltonian of the system with interaction Φ is defined formally by:

$$H_\Phi = \sum_{X \subset \Gamma} \Phi(X)$$

The laws of quantum mechanics say that corresponding to every physically observable quantity there is a self-adjoint operator A . For every observable A with a finite support the Hamiltonian defines a continuous one-parameter group τ_t of transformations of the observables τ_t given by

$$\tau_t(A) = e^{itH_\Phi} A e^{-itH_\Phi}.$$

Here, t has the physical meaning of time. (Technically speaking, this time evolution is defined by a power-series expansion that is known to be a norm-convergent series $\tau_t(A) = A + it[H, A] + \frac{(it)^2}{2!}[H, [H, A]] + \cdots$, see,[7] Theorem 7.6.2, which is an adaptation from.[8] More rigorous details can be found in.[11])

The bound in question was proved in [1] and is the following: For any observables A and B with finite supports $X \subset \Gamma$ and $Y \subset \Gamma$, respectively, and for any time $t \in \mathbb{R}$ the following holds for some positive constants a, c and v :

where $d(X, Y)$ denotes the distance between the sets X and Y . The operator $[A, B] = AB - BA$ is called the commutator of the operators A and B , while the symbol $\|O\|$ denotes the norm, or size, of an operator O . It is very important to note that the bound has nothing to do with the *state* of the quantum system, but depends only on the Hamiltoninan governing the dynamics. Once this operator bound is established it necessarily carries over to any state of the system.

A positive constant c depends on the norms of the observables A and B , the sizes of the supports X and Y , the interaction, the lattice structure and the dimension of the Hilbert space $\mathcal{H}_x$. A positive constant v depends on the interaction and the lattice structure only. The number $a > 0$ can be chosen at will provided $d(X, Y)/v|t|$ is chosen sufficiently large. In other words, the further out one goes on the light cone, $d(X, Y) - v|t|$, the sharper the exponential decay rate is. (In later works authors tended to regard a as a fixed constant.) The constant v is called the **group velocity** or **Lieb-Robinson velocity**.

The bound (**1**) is presented slightly differently from the equation in the original paper.[1] This more explicit form (**1**) can be seen from the proof of the bound [1]

Lieb-Robinson bound shows that for times $|t| < d(X, Y)/v$ the norm on the right-hand side is exponentially small. This is the exponentially small error mentioned above.

The reason for considering the commutator on the left-hand side of the Lieb-Robinson bounds is the following:

The commutator between observables A and B is zero if their supports are disjoint.

The converse is also true: if observable A is such that its commutator with any observable B supported outside some set X is zero, then A has a support inside set X .

This statement is also approximately true in the following sense:[9] suppose that there exists some $\epsilon > 0$ such that $\|[A, B]\| \le \epsilon \|B\|$ for some observable A and any observable B that is supported outside the set X . Then there exists an observable $A(\epsilon)$ with support inside set X that approximates an observable A , i.e. $\|A - A(\epsilon)\| \le \epsilon$.

Thus, Lieb-Robinson bounds say that the time evolution of an observable A with support in a set X is supported (up to exponentially small errors) in a δ -neighborhood of set X , where $\delta > v|t|$ with v being the Lieb-Robinson velocity. Outside this set there is no influence of A . In other words, this bounds assert that the speed of propagation of perturbations in quantum spin systems is bounded.

46.2 Improvements of the Lieb-Robinson bounds

In [10] Robinson generalized the bound (**1**) by considering exponentially decaying interactions (that need not be translation invariant), i.e., for which the strength of the interaction decays exponentially with the diameter of the set. This result is discussed in detail in,[11] Chapter 6. No great interest was shown in the Lieb-Robinson bounds until 2004 when Hastings [12] applied them to the Lieb–Schultz–Mattis theorem. Subsequently Nachtergaele and Sims [13] extended the results of [10] to include models on vertices with a metric and to derive exponential decay of correlations. From 2005–2006 interest in Lieb–Robinson bounds strengthened with additional applications to exponential decay of correlations (see [5][6][14] and the sections below). New proofs of the bounds were developed and, in particular, the constant in (**1**) was improved making it independent of the dimension of the Hilbert space.

Several further improvements of the constant c in (**1**) were made.[15] In 2008 the Lieb-Robinson bound was extended to the case in which each H_x is infinite dimensional.[16] In [16] it was shown that on-site unbounded perturbations do not change the Lieb-Robinson bound. That is, Hamiltonians of the following form can be considered on a finite subset $\Lambda \subset \Gamma$:

$$H_\Lambda = \sum_{x \in \Lambda} H_x + \sum_{X \subset \Lambda} \Phi(X),$$

where H_x is a self-adjoint operator over $\mathcal{H}_x$, which needs not to be bounded.

46.2.1 Harmonic and Anharmonic Hamiltonians

The Lieb-Robinson bounds were extended to certain continuous quantum systems, that is to a general harmonic Hamiltonian,[16] which, in a finite volume $\Gamma_L = (-L, L)^d \cap \mathbb{Z}^d$, , where L, d are positive integers, takes the form:

$$\sum_{x\in\Gamma_L} p_x^2 + \omega^2 q_x^2 + \sum_{x\in\Gamma_L} \sum_{j=1}^{\nu} \lambda_j (q_x - q_{x+e_j})^2,$$

where the periodic boundary conditions are imposed and $\lambda_j \geq 0$, $\omega > 0$. Here $\{e_j\}$ are canonical basis vectors in $\mathbb{Z}^d$.

Anharmonic Hamiltonians with on-site and multiple-site perturbations were considered and the Lieb–Robinson bounds were derived for them,[16][17] Further generalizations of the harmonic lattice were discussed,[18][19]

46.2.2 Irreversible dynamics

Another generalization of the Lieb–Robinson bounds was made to the irreversible dynamics, in which case the dynamics has a Hamiltonian part and also a dissipative part. The dissipative part is described by terms of Lindblad form, so that the dynamics τ_t satisfies the Lindblad-Kossakowski master equation.

Lieb-Robinson bounds for the irreversible dynamics were considered by [14] in the classical context and by [20] for a class of quantum lattice systems with finite-range interactions. Lieb-Robinson bounds for lattice models with a dynamics generated by both Hamiltonian and dissipative interactions with suitably fast decay in space, and that may depend on time, were proved by,[21] where they also proved the existence of the infinite dynamics as a strongly continuous cocycle of unit preserving completely positive maps.

46.3 Some applications

Lieb–Robinson bounds are used in many areas of mathematical physics. Among the main applications of the bound there is the existence of the thermodynamic limit, the exponential decay of correlations and the Lieb–Schultz–Mattis theorem.

46.3.1 Thermodynamic limit of the dynamics

One of the important properties of any model meant to describe properties of bulk matter is the existence of the thermodynamic limit. This says that intrinsic properties of the system should be essentially independent of the size of the system which, in any experimental setup, is finite.

The static thermodynamic limit from the equilibrium point of view was settled much before the Lieb–Robinson bound was proved, see [7] for example. In certain cases one can use a Lieb–Robinson bound to establish the existence of a thermodynamic limit of the *dynamics*, τ_t^Γ , for an infinite lattice Γ as the limit of finite lattice dynamics. The limit is usually considered over an increasing sequence of finite subsets $\Lambda_n \subset \Gamma$, i.e. such that for $n < m$, there is an inclusion $\Lambda_n \subset \Lambda_m$. In order to prove the existence of the infinite dynamics τ_t^Γ as a strongly continuous, one-parameter group of automorphisms, it was proved that $\{\tau_t^{\Lambda_n}\}_n$ is a Cauchy sequence and consequently is convergent. By elementary considerations, the existence of the thermodynamic limit then follows. A more detailed discussion of the thermodynamic limit can be found in [22] section 6.2.

Robinson was the first to show the existence of the thermodynamic limit for exponentially decaying interactions.[10] Later, Nachtergaele et al.[6][17][21] showed the existence of the infinite volume dynamics for almost every type of interaction described in the section "Improvements of Lieb–Robinson bounds" above.

46.3.2 Exponential decay of correlations

Let $< A >_\Omega$ denote the expectation value of the observable A with respect to a state Ω . The correlation function between two observables A and B is defined as $< AB >_\Omega - < A >_\Omega < B >_\Omega$.

Lieb–Robinson bounds are used to show that the correlations decay exponentially in distance for a system with an *energy gap above a non-degenerate ground state* Ω , see.[5][13] In other words, the inequality

$$|< AB >_\Omega - < A >_\Omega < B >_\Omega | \leq K\|A\|\|B\| \min(|X|, |Y|)\, e^{-a\, d(X,Y)},$$

holds for observables A and B with support in the sets X and Y respectively. Here K and a are some constants.

Alternatively the state Ω can be taken as a product state, in which case correlations decay exponentially without assuming the energy gap above the ground state.[6]

Such a decay was long known for relativistic dynamics, but only guessed for Newtonian dynamics. The Lieb–Robinson bounds succeed in replacing the relativistic symmetry by local estimates on the Hamiltonian.

46.3.3 Lieb-Schultz-Mattis theorem

Lieb-Schultz-Mattis theorem implies that the ground state of the Heisenberg antiferromagnet on a bipartite lattice with isomorphic sublattices, is non-degenerate, i.e., unique, but the gap can be very small.[23]

For one-dimensional and quasi-one-dimensional systems of even length and with half-integral spin Affleck and Lieb,[24] generalizing the original result by Lieb, Schultz, and Mattis,[25] proved that the gap γ_L in the spectrum above the ground state is bounded above by

$$\gamma_L \leq c/L,$$

where L is the size of the lattice and c is a constant. Many attempts were made to extend this result to *higher dimensions*, $d > 1$,

The Lieb–Robinson bound was utilized by Hastings [12] and by Nachtergaele-Sims [26] in a proof of the Lieb–Schultz–Mattis Theorem for higher-dimensional cases. The following bound on the gap was obtained:

$$\gamma_L \leq c \log(L)/L.$$

46.3.4 Discretisation of the Continuum via Gauss-Quadrature Rules

In 2015, it was shown that the Lieb-Robinson bound can also have applications outside of the context of local Hamiltonians as we now explain. The Spin-Boson model describes the dynamics of a spin coupled to a continuum of oscillators. It has been studied in great detail and explains quantum dissipative effects in a wide range of quantum systems. Let H denote the Hamiltonian of the Spin-Boson model with a continuum bosonic bath, and H_L denote the Spin-Boson model who's bath has been discretised to include $L \in \mathbb{N}^+$ harmonic oscillators with frequencies chosen according to Gauss Quadrature Rules. For all observables A on the Spin Hamiltonian, the error on the expectation value of A induced by discretising the Spin-Boson model according to the above discretisation scheme is bounded by [27]

where c, a are positive constants and v is the Lieb-Robinson velocity which in this case is directly proportional to ω_{max} , the maximum frequency of the bath in the Spin-Boson model. Here, the number of discrete modes L play the role of a distance $d(X, Y)$ mentioned below Eq. (**1**). One can also bound the error induced by local Fock space truncation of the harmonic oscillators [28]

46.4 Experiments

The first experimental observation of the Lieb–Robinson velocity was done by Cheneau et al.[29]

46.5 References

[1] E. Lieb, D. Robinson, The finite group velocity of quantum spin systems, Commun. Math. Phys. 28, 251–257, (1972)

[2] B. Nachtergaele, R. Sims, Much Ado About Something: Why Lieb-Robinson bounds are useful, IAMP News Bulletin, October 2010, 22–29, (2010)

[3] M. Kliesch, C. Gogolin, J. Eisert, Lieb-Robinson bounds and the simulation of time evolution of local observables in lattice systems, arXiv:1306.0716, (2013)

[4] M. B. Hastings, Locality in quantum systems, arXiv:1008.5137

[5] M. Hastings, T. Koma, Spectral Gap and Exponential Decay of Correlations, Commun. Math. Phys. 256, 781, (2006)

[6] B. Nachtergaele, Y. Ogata, R. Sims, Propagation of Correlations in Quantum Lattice Systems, J. Stat. Phys. 124, 1–13, (2006)

[7] D. Ruelle, Statistical mechanics. Rigorous results, Benjamin, New York, 1969

[8] D. W. Robinson, Statistical mechanics of quantum spin systems II. Comm. Math. Phys. 7, 337–348, (1968)

[9] S. Bachmann, S. Michalakis, B. Nachtergaele, R. Sims, Automorphic Equivalence within Gapped Phases of Quantum Lattice Systems, Commun. Math. Phys. 309, 835–871, (2012)

[10] D. W. Robinson, Properties of propagation of quantum spin systems, J. Austral. Math. Soc. 19 (Series B), 387–399, (1976)

[11] O. Bratteli, D. W. Robinson, Operator algebras and quantum statistical mechanics, 1ed., vol. 2, Springer-Verlag, 1981 and 2 ed., vol. 2, Springer-Verlag, 1997

[12] M. Hastings, Lieb–Schultz–Mattis in higher dimensions, Phys. Rev. B 69, 104431–10444, (2004)

[13] B. Nachtergaele, R. Sims, Lieb-Robinson bounds and the exponential clustering theorem, Commun. Math. Phys., 265, 119–130, (2006)

[14] M. Hastings, Locality in quantum and Markov dynamics on lattices and networks, Phys. Rev. Lett. 93, 140402, (2004)

[15] B. Nachtergaele, R. Sims. Locality Estimates for Quantum Spin Systems, Sidoravicius, Vladas (Ed.), New Trends in Mathematical Physics. Selected contributions of the XVth International Congress on Mathematical Physics, Springer Verlag, 591–614, (2009)

[16] B. Nachtergaele, H. Raz, B. Schlein, R. Sims, Lieb-Robinson bounds for harmonic and anharmonic lattice systems, Commun. Math. Phys. 286, 1073–1098, (2009)

[17] B. Nachtergaele, B. Schlein, R. Sims, S. Starr, V. Zagrebnov, On the existence of the dynamics for anharmonic quantum oscillator systems, Rev. Math. Phys., 22, 207–231, (2010)

[18] M. Cramer, A. Serafini, J. Eisert, Locality of dynamics in general harmonic quantum systems, arXiv:0803.0890, (2008)

[19] J. Juenemann, A. Cadarso, D. Perez-Garcia, A. Bermudez, J. J. Garcia-Ripoll, Lieb–Robinson bounds for spin-boson lattice models and trapped ions, arXiv:1307.1992, (2013)

[20] D. Poulin, Lieb–Robinson bound and locality for general Markovian quantum dynamics, Phys. Rev. Lett. 104, 190401, (2010)

[21] B. Nachtergaele, A. Vershynina, V. Zagrebnov, Lieb-Robinson bounds and Existence of the thermodynamic limit for a class of irreversible quantum dynamics, AMS Contemporary Mathematics, 552, 161–175, (2011)

[22] O. Bratteli, D. W. Robinson, Operator algebras and quantum statistical mechanics, 2 ed., vol. 2, Springer Verlag, 1997

[23] E. Lieb, D. Mattis, Ordering energy levels in interacting spin chains, Journ. Math. Phys. 3, 749–751, (1962)

[24] I. Affleck, E.H. Lieb, A proof of part of Haldane's conjecture on quantum spin chains, Lett. Math. Phys. 12, 57–69, (1986)

[25] E. Lieb, T. Schultz, D. Mattis, Two soluble models of an antiferromagnetic chain, Ann. Phys. (N.Y.) 16, 407–466, (1961)

[26] B. Nachtergaele, R. Sims, A multi-dimensional Lieb–Schultz–Mattis theorem, Commun. Math. Phys. 276, 437-472, (2007)

[27] M.P. Woods & M.B. Plenio, Dynamical error bounds for continuum discretisation via Gauss quadrature rules, -- A Lieb-Robinson bound approach, J. Math. Phys. 57, 022105 (2016), ArXiv

[28] M.P. Woods, M. Cramer & M.B. Plenio, Simulation Bosonic Baths with Error bars, Phys. Rev. Lett. 115, 130401 (2015) ArXiv

[29] M. Cheneau, P. Barmettler, D. Poletti, M. Endres, P. Schauß, T. Fukuhara, C. Gross, I. Bloch, C. Kollath, S. Kuhr, Light-cone-like spreading of correlations in a quantum many-body system, Nature 481, 484–487, (2012)

Chapter 47

Mutually unbiased bases

In quantum information theory, **mutually unbiased bases** in Hilbert space $\mathbf{C}^d$ are two orthonormal bases $\{|e_1\rangle, \ldots, |e_d\rangle\}$ and $\{|f_1\rangle, \ldots, |f_d\rangle\}$ such that the square of the magnitude of the inner product between any basis states $|e_j\rangle$ and $|f_k\rangle$ equals the inverse of the dimension *d*:[1]

$$|\langle e_j|f_k\rangle|^2 = \frac{1}{d}, \quad \forall j,k \in \{1,\ldots,d\}.$$

These bases are *unbiased* in the following sense: if a system is prepared in a state belonging to one of the bases, then all outcomes of the measurement with respect to the other basis will occur with equal probabilities.

47.1 Overview

The notion of mutually unbiased bases was first introduced by Schwinger in 1960,[2] and the first person to consider applications of mutually unbiased bases was Ivanovic[3] in the problem of quantum state determination.

Another area where mutually unbiased bases can be applied is quantum key distribution, more specifically in secure quantum key exchange.[4] Mutually unbiased bases are used in many protocols since the outcome is random when a measurement is made in a basis unbiased to that in which the state was prepared. When two remote parties share two non-orthogonal quantum states, attempts by an eavesdropper to distinguish between these by measurements will affect the system and this can be detected. While many quantum cryptography protocols have relied on 1-qubit technologies, employing higher-dimensional states, such as qutrits, allows for better security against eavesdropping.[4] This motivates the study of mutually unbiased bases in higher-dimensional spaces.

Other uses of mutually unbiased bases include quantum state reconstruction,[5] quantum error correction codes,[6][7] detection of quantum entanglement,[8] and the so-called "mean king's problem".[9][10]

47.2 Existence problem

Let $\mathfrak{M}(d)$ denote the maximum number of mutually unbiased bases in the d-dimensional Hilbert space $\mathbf{C}^d$. It is an open question[11] how many mutually unbiased bases, $\mathfrak{M}(d)$, one can find in $\mathbf{C}^d$, for arbitrary *d*.

In general, if

$$d = p_1^{n_1} p_2^{n_2} \cdots p_k^{n_k}$$

is the prime-power factorization of *d*, where

$$p_1^{n_1} < p_2^{n_2} < \cdots < p_k^{n_k}$$

then the maximum number of mutually unbiased bases which can be constructed satisfies[1]

$$p_1^{n_1} + 1 \le \mathfrak{M}(d) \le d + 1.$$

It follows that if the dimension of a Hilbert space *d* is an integer power of a prime number, then it is possible to find *d* + 1 mutually unbiased bases. This can be seen in the previous equation, as the prime number decomposition of *d* simply is $d = p^n$. Therefore,

$$\mathfrak{M}(p^n) = p^n + 1.$$

Thus, the maximun number of mutually unbiased bases is known when *d* is an integer power of a prime number, but it is not known for arbitrary *d*.

47.3 Examples of sets of mutually unbiased bases

47.3.1 Example for *d* = 2

The three bases

$$M_0 = \{|0\rangle, |1\rangle\}$$

$$M_1 = \left\{\frac{|0\rangle + |1\rangle}{\sqrt{2}}, \frac{|0\rangle - |1\rangle}{\sqrt{2}}\right\}$$

$$M_2 = \left\{\frac{|0\rangle + i|1\rangle}{\sqrt{2}}, \frac{|0\rangle - i|1\rangle}{\sqrt{2}}\right\}$$

provide the simplest example of mutually unbiased bases in $\mathbf{C}^2$. The above bases are composed of the eigenvectors of the Pauli spin matrices σ_x, σ_z and their product $\sigma_x\sigma_z$.

47.3.2 Example for d = 4

For d = 4, an example of d + 1 = 5 mutually unbiased bases where each basis is denoted by Mj, $0 \le j \le 4$, is given as follows:[12]

$$M_0 = \{(1,0,0,0),(0,1,0,0),(0,0,1,0),(0,0,0,1)\}$$

$$M_1 = \left\{\frac{1}{2}(1,1,1,1), \frac{1}{2}(1,1,-1,-1), \frac{1}{2}(1,-1,-1,1), \frac{1}{2}(1,-1,1,-1)\right\}$$

$$M_2 = \left\{\frac{1}{2}(1,-1,-i,-i), \frac{1}{2}(1,-1,i,i), \frac{1}{2}(1,1,i,-i), \frac{1}{2}(1,1,-i,i)\right\}$$

$$M_3 = \left\{\frac{1}{2}(1,-i,-i,-1), \frac{1}{2}(1,-i,i,1), \frac{1}{2}(1,i,i,-1), \frac{1}{2}(1,i,-i,1)\right\}$$

$$M_4 = \left\{\frac{1}{2}(1,-i,-1,-i), \frac{1}{2}(1,-i,1,i), \frac{1}{2}(1,i,-1,i), \frac{1}{2}(1,i,1,-i)\right\}$$

47.4 Methods for finding mutually unbiased bases

47.4.1 Weyl group method[1]

Let $\hat{X}$ and $\hat{Z}$ be two unitary operators in the Hilbert space $\mathbf{C}^d$ such that

$$\hat{Z}\hat{X} = \omega\hat{X}\hat{Z}$$

for some phase factor ω . If ω is a primitive root of unity, for example $\omega \equiv e^{\frac{2\pi i}{d}}$ then the eigenbases of $\hat{X}$ and $\hat{Z}$ are mutually unbiased.

By choosing the eigenbasis of $\hat{Z}$ to be the standard basis, we can generate another basis unbiased to it using a Fourier matrix. The elements of the Fourier matrix are given by

$$F_{ab} = \omega^{ab}, 0 \le a, b \le N - 1$$

Other bases which are unbiased to both the standard basis and the basis generated by the Fourier matrix can be generated using Weyl groups.[1] The dimension of the Hilbert space is important when generating sets of mutually unbiased bases using Weyl groups. When d is a prime number, then the usual d + 1 mutually unbiased bases can be generated using Weyl groups. When d is not a prime number, then it is possible that the maximal number of mutually unbiased bases which can be generated using this method is 3.

47.4.2 Unitary operators method using finite fields[13]

When $d = p$ is prime, we define the unitary operators $\hat{X}$ and $\hat{Z}$ by

$$\hat{X} = \sum_{k=0}^{d-1} |k+1\rangle\langle k|$$

$$\hat{Z} = \sum_{k=0}^{d-1} \omega^k |k\rangle\langle k|$$

where $\{|k\rangle | 0 \le j \le d-1\}$ is the standard basis and $\omega = e^{\frac{2\pi i}{d}}$ is a root of unity.

Then the eigenbases of the following d + 1 operators are mutually unbiased:[13]

$$\hat{X}, \hat{Z}, \hat{X}\hat{Z}, \hat{X}\hat{Z}^2 ... \hat{X}\hat{Z}^{d-1}$$

When $d = p^r$ is a power of a prime, we make use of the finite field $\mathbb{F}_d$ to construct a maximal set of d + 1 mutually unbiased bases. We label the elements of the computational basis of $\mathbf{C}^d$ using the finite field: $\{|a\rangle | a \in \mathbb{F}_d\}$.

We define the operators $\hat{X}_a$ and $\hat{Z}_b$ in the following way

$$\hat{X}_a = \sum_{c \in \mathbb{F}_d} |c + a\rangle\langle c|$$

$$\hat{Z}_b = \sum_{c \in \mathbb{F}_d} \chi(bc) |c\rangle\langle c|$$

where

$$\chi(\theta) = \exp\left[\frac{2\pi i}{p}\left(\theta + \theta^p + \theta^{p^2} + \cdots + \theta^{p^{r-1}}\right)\right],$$

is an additive character over the field and the addition and multiplication in the kets and $\chi(\cdot)$ is that of $\mathbb{F}_d$.

Then we form d + 1 sets of commuting unitary operators:

$\{\hat{Z}_s | s \in \mathbb{F}_d\}$ and $\{\hat{X}_s \hat{Z}_{sr} | s \in \mathbb{F}_d\}$ for each $r \in \mathbb{F}_d$

The joint eigenbases of the operators in one set are mutually unbiased to that of any other set.[13] We thus have d + 1 mutually unbiased bases.

47.4.3 Hadamard matrix method[1]

Given that one basis in a Hilbert space is the standard basis, then all bases which are unbiased with respect to this basis can be represented by the columns of a complex Hadamard matrix multiplied by a normalization factor. For d = 3 these matrices would have the form

$$U = \frac{1}{\sqrt{d}} \begin{bmatrix} 1 & 1 & 1 \\ e^{i\phi_{10}} & e^{i\phi_{11}} & e^{i\phi_{12}} \\ e^{i\phi_{20}} & e^{i\phi_{21}} & e^{i\phi_{22}} \end{bmatrix}$$

The problem of finding a set of k+1 mutually unbiased bases therefore corresponds to finding k mutually unbiased complex Hadamard matrices.

An example of a one parameter family of Hadamard matrices in a 4-dimensional Hilbert space is

$$H_4(\phi) = \frac{1}{2} \begin{bmatrix} 1 & 1 & 1 & 1 \\ 1 & e^{i\phi} & -1 & -e^{i\phi} \\ 1 & -1 & 1 & -1 \\ 1 & -e^{i\phi} & -1 & e^{i\phi} \end{bmatrix}$$

47.5 The problem of finding a maximal set of MUBs when d = 6

The smallest dimension that is not an integer power of a prime is d = 6. This is also the smallest dimension for which the number of mutually unbiased bases is not known. The methods used to determine the number of mutually unbiased bases when d is an integer power of a prime number cannot be used in this case. Searches for a set of four mutually unbiased bases when d = 6, both by using Hadamard matrices[1] and numerical methods[14][15] have been unsuccessful. The general belief is that the maximum number of mutually unbiased bases for d = 6 is $\mathfrak{M}(6) = 3$.[1]

47.6 Entropic uncertainty relations and MUBs

There is an alternative characterization of mutually unbiased bases that considers them in terms of uncertainty relations.[16]

Entropic uncertainty relations are analogous to the Heisenberg uncertainty principle, and Maassen and Uffink[17] found that for any two bases $B_1 = \{|a_i\rangle_{i=1}^d\}$ and $B_2 = \{|b_j\rangle_{j=1}^d\}$:

$$H_{B_1} + H_{B_2} \geq -2 \log c.$$

where $c = \max |\langle a_j | b_k \rangle|$ and H_{B_1} and H_{B_2} is the respective entropy of the bases B_1 and B_2 , when measuring a given state.

Entropic uncertainty relations are often preferable[18] to the Heisenberg uncertainty principle, as they are not phrased in terms of the state to be measured, but in terms of c.

In scenarios such as quantum key distribution, we aim for measurement bases such that full knowledge of a state with respect to one basis implies minimal knowledge of the state with respect to the other bases. This implies a high entropy of measurement outcomes, and thus we call these *strong* entropic uncertainty relations.

For two bases, the lower bound of the uncertainty relation is maximized when the measurement bases are mutually unbiased, since mutually unbiased bases are *maximally incompatible*: the outcome of a measurement made in a basis unbiased to that in which the state is prepared in is completely random. In fact, for a d-dimensional space, we have:[19]

$$H_{B_1} + H_{B_2} \geq \log(d)$$

for any pair of mutually unbiased bases B_1 and B_2 . This bound is *optimal*:[20] If we measure a state from one of the bases then the outcome has entropy 0 in that basis and an entropy of $\log(d)$ in the other.

If the dimension of the space is a prime power, we can construct d + 1 MUBs, and then it has been found that[21]

$$\sum_{k=1}^{d+1} H_{B_k} \geq \frac{d+1}{2} \log\left(\frac{d+1}{2}\right)$$

which is stronger than the relation we would get from pairing up the sets and then using the Maassen and Uffink equation. Thus we have a characterization of d + 1 mutually unbiased bases as those for which the uncertainty relations are strongest.

Although the case for two bases, and for d + 1 bases is well studied, very little is known about uncertainty relations for mutually unbiased bases in other circumstances.[21][22]

When considering more than two, and less than $d + 1$ bases it is known that large sets of mutually unbiased bases exist which exhibit very little uncertainty.[23] This means merely being mutually unbiased does not lead to high uncertainty, except when considering measurements in only two bases. Yet there do exist other measurements that are very uncertain.[21][24]

47.7 Mutually unbiased bases in infinite dimension Hilbert spaces

While there has been investigation into mutually unbiased bases in infinite dimension Hilbert space, their existence remains an open question. It is conjectured that in a continuous Hilbert space, two orthonormal bases $|\psi^b_s\rangle$ and $|\psi^{b'}_{s'}\rangle$ are said to be mutually unbiased if[25]

$$|\langle\psi^b_s|\psi^{b'}_{s'}\rangle|^2 = k > 0, s, s' \in \mathbb{R}$$

For the generalized position and momentum eigenstates $|q\rangle, q \in \mathbb{R}$ and $|p\rangle, p \in \mathbb{R}$, the value of *k* is

$$|\langle q|p\rangle|^2 = \frac{1}{2\pi\hbar}$$

The existence of mutually unbiased bases in a continuous Hilbert space remains open for debate, as further research in their existence is required before any conclusions can be reached.

Position states $|q\rangle$ and momentum states $|p\rangle$ are eigenvectors of Hermitian operators $\hat{x}$ and $-i\frac{\partial}{\partial x}$, respectively. Weigert and Wilkinson[25] were first to notice that also a linear combination of these operators have eigenbases, which have some features typical for the mutually unbiased bases. An operator $\alpha\hat{x} - i\beta\frac{\partial}{\partial x}$ has eigenfunctions proportional to $\exp(i(ax^2 + bx))$ with $\alpha + 2\beta a = 0$ and the corresponding eigenvalues $b\beta$. If we parametrize α and β as $\cos\theta$ and $\sin\theta$, the overlap between any eigenstate of the linear combination and any eigenstate of the position operator (both states normalized to the Dirac delta) is constant, but dependent on β :

$$|\langle x_\theta|x\rangle|^2 = \frac{1}{2\pi|\sin\theta|},$$

where $|x\rangle$ and $|x_\theta\rangle$ stand for eigenfunctions of $\hat{x}$ and $\cos\theta\hat{x} - i\sin\theta\frac{\partial}{\partial x}$.

47.8 References

[1] I. Bengtsson, Three ways to look at mutually unbiased bases, http://arxiv.org/abs/quant-ph/0610216.

[2] Schwinger, J. (1960). "Unitary Operator Bases, Harvard University". *Proc. Natl. Acad. Sci. U.S.A.* **46**: 570–9. doi:10.1073/pnas.46.4.570. PMC 222876. PMID 16590645.

[3] Ivanovic, I. D. (1981). "Geometrical description of quantal state determination". *J. Phys. A.* **14**: 3241–3245. Bibcode:1981JPhA...14.3241I. doi:10.1088/0305-4470/14/12/019.

[4] M. Planat et al, A Survey of Finite Algebraic Geometrical Structures Underlying Mutually Unbiased Quantum Measurements, http://hal.ccsd.cnrs.fr/docs/00/07/99/18/PDF/MUB_FP.pdf.

[5] Wootters, W. K.; Fields, B. D. (1989). "Optimal State-Determination by Mutually Unbiased Measurements". *Ann. Phys.* **191**: 363–381. Bibcode:1989AnPhy.191..363W. doi:10.1016/0003-4916(89)90322-9.

[6] Gottesman, D. (1996). "Class of quantum error-correcting codes saturating the quantum Hamming bound". *Phys. Rev. A* **54**: 1862–1868. arXiv:quant-ph/9604038. Bibcode:1996PhRvA..54.1862G. doi:10.1103/physreva.54.1862.

[7] Calderbank, A. R.; et al. (1997). ", Quantum Error Correction and Orthogonal Geometry". *Phys. Rev. Lett.* **78**: 405–408. arXiv:quant-ph/9605005. Bibcode:1997PhRvL..78..405C. doi:10.1103/physrevlett.78.405.

[8] Spengler, C.; Huber, M.; Brierley, S.; Adaktylos, T.; Hiesmayr, B. C. (2012). "Entanglement detection via mutually unbiased bases". *Phys. Rev. A* **86**: 022311. arXiv:1202.5058. Bibcode:2012PhRvA..86b2311S. doi:10.1103/physreva.86.022311.

[9] Vaidman, L.; et al. (1987). "How to ascertain the values of σ_x, σ_y, and σ_z of a spin-1/2 particle". *Phys. Rev. Lett.* **58**: 1385–1387. Bibcode:1987PhRvL..58.1385V. doi:10.1103/PhysRevLett.58.1385.

[10] Englert, B.-G.; Aharonov, Y. (2001). "The mean king's problem: prime degrees of freedom". *Phys. Lett. A* **284**: 1–5. arXiv:quant-ph/0101134. Bibcode:2001PhLA..284....1E. doi:10.1016/s0375-9601(01)00271-7.

[11] Durt, T.; Englert, B.-G.; Bengtsson, I.; Życzkowski, K. (2010). "On mutually unbiased bases". *Int. J. Quantum Information* **8**: 535–640. arXiv:1004.3348. doi:10.1142/s0219749910006502.

[12] A. Klappenecker, M. Roetteler, Constructions of Mutually Unbiased Bases, 2003, http://arxiv.org/abs/quant-ph/0309120.

[13] S. Bandyopadhyay, P. O. Boykin, V. Roychowdhury, F. Vatan, A new proof for the existence of mutually unbiased bases, 2001, http://arxiv.org/abs/quant-ph/0103162.

[14] P. Butterley, W. Hall "Numerical evidence for the maximum number of mutually unbiased bases in dimension six, 2007, http://arxiv.org/abs/quant-ph/0701122.

[15] Brierley, S.; Weigert, S. (2008). "Maximal sets of mutually unbiased quantum states in dimension six". *Phys. Rev. A* **78**: 042312. arXiv:0808.1614. Bibcode:2008PhRvA..78d2312B. doi:10.1103/physreva.78.042312.

[16] Hirschman, I.I.; Jr. "A note on entropy". *American Journal of Mathematics* **1957**: 152–156. doi:10.2307/2372390.

[17] H. Maassen, J.B.M. Uffink: Generalized entropic uncertainty relations: Phys. Rev. Lett. 60, 1103–1106 (1988).

[18] I. Damgard, S. Fehr, R. Renner, L. Salvail, C. Schaner(2006), http://arxiv.org/abs/quant-ph/0612014.

[19] Deutsch, D. (1982). "Uncertainty in Quantum Measurements". *Physical Review Letters* **50** (9): 631–633. Bibcode:1983PhRvL..50..631D. doi:10.1103/physrevlett.50.631.

[20] A. Ambainis, Limits on entropic uncertainty relations for 3 and more MUBs, http://arxiv.org/abs/0909.3720.

[21] S. Wehner and A. Winter, 2010 New J. Phys. 12 025009: http://iopscience.iop.org/1367-2630/12/2/025009/.

[22] Wu, S.; Yu, S.; Mølmer, K. (2009). "Entropic uncertainty relation for mutually unbiased bases". *Phys. Rev. A* **79**: 022104. arXiv:0811.2298. doi:10.1103/physreva.79.022104.

[23] Ballester, M.; S. Wehner (2007). "Entropic uncertainty relations and locking: tight bounds for mutually unbiased bases". *Physical Review A* **75**: 022319. arXiv:0704.1506. Bibcode:2007PhRvA..75a2319C. doi:10.1103/PhysRevA.75.012319.

[24] Wehner, S.; A. Winter (2008). "Higher entropic uncertainty relations for anti-commuting observables". *Journal of Mathematical Physics* **49**: 062105. arXiv:0710.1185. Bibcode:2008JMP....49f2105W. doi:10.1063/1.2943685.

[25] S. Weigert, M. Wilkinson, Mutually Unbiased Bases for Continuous Variables, Phys. Rev. A 78, 020303(R) (2008), http://arxiv.org/abs/0802.0394.

Chapter 48

No-teleportation theorem

In quantum information theory, the **no-teleportation theorem** states that an arbitrary quantum state cannot be converted into a sequence of classical bits (or even an infinite number of such bits); nor can such bits be used to reconstruct the original state, thus "teleporting" it by merely moving classical bits around. Put another way, it states that the unit of quantum information, the qubit, cannot be exactly, precisely converted into classical information bits. This should not be confused with quantum teleportation, which does allow a quantum state to be destroyed in one location, and an exact replica to be created at a different location.

In crude terms, the no-teleportation theorem stems from the Heisenberg uncertainty principle and the EPR paradox: although a qubit $|\psi\rangle$ can be imagined to be a specific direction on the Bloch sphere, that direction cannot be measured precisely, for the general case $|\psi\rangle$; for if it could, the results of that measurement would be describable with words, i.e. classical information.

The no-teleportation theorem is implied by the no-cloning theorem: if it were possible to convert a qubit into classical bits, then a qubit would be easy to copy (since classical bits are trivially copyable).

48.1 Formulation

The term *quantum information* refers to information stored in the state of a quantum system. Two quantum states ϱ_1 and ϱ_2 are identical if the measurement results of any physical observable have the same expectation value for ϱ_1 and ϱ_2. Thus measurement can be viewed as an information channel with quantum input and classical output, that is, performing measurement on a quantum system transforms quantum information into classical information. On the other hand, preparing a quantum state takes classical information to quantum information.

In general, a quantum state is described by a density matrix. Suppose one has a quantum system in some mixed state ϱ. Prepare an ensemble, of the same system, as follows:

1. Perform a measurement on ϱ.
2. According to the measurement outcome, prepare a system in some pre-specified state.

The no-teleportation theorem states that the result will be different from ϱ, irrespective of how the preparation procedure is related to measurement outcome. A quantum state cannot be determined via a single measurement. In other words, if a quantum channel measurement is followed by preparation, it cannot be the identity channel. Once converted to classical information, quantum information cannot be recovered.

In contrast, perfect transmission is possible if one wishes to convert classical information to quantum information then back to classical information. For classical bits, this can be done by encoding them in orthogonal quantum states, which can always be distinguished.

48.2 See also

Among other no-go theorems in quantum information are:

- No-communication theorem. Entangled states cannot be used to transmit classical information.
- No-cloning theorem. Quantum states cannot be copied.
- No-broadcast theorem. A generalization of the no cloning theorem, to the case of mixed states.
- No-deleting theorem. A result dual to the no-cloning theorem: copies cannot be deleted.

With the aid of shared entanglement, quantum states can be teleported, see

- Quantum teleportation

48.3 References

- Jozef Gruska, Iroshi Imai, "Power, Puzzles and Properties of Entanglment" (2001) pp 25–68, appearing in *Machines, Computations, and Universality: Third International Conference.* edited by Maurice Margenstern, Yurii Rogozhin. (see p 41)

- Anirban Pathak, *Elements of Quantum Computation and Quantum Communication* (2013) CRC Press. (see p. 128)

Chapter 49

Peres–Horodecki criterion

The **Peres–Horodecki criterion** is a necessary condition, for the joint density matrix ρ of two quantum mechanical systems A and B , to be separable. It is also called the **PPT** criterion, for *positive partial transpose*. In the 2x2 and 2x3 dimensional cases the condition is also sufficient. It is used to decide the separability of mixed states, where the Schmidt decomposition does not apply.

In higher dimensions, the test is inconclusive, and one should supplement it with more advanced tests, such as those based on entanglement witnesses.

49.1 Definition

If we have a general state ρ which acts on $\mathcal{H}_A \otimes \mathcal{H}_B$

$$\rho = \sum_{ijkl} p^{ij}_{kl} |i\rangle\langle j| \otimes |k\rangle\langle l|$$

Its partial transpose (with respect to the B party) is defined as

$$\rho^{T_B} := I \otimes T(\rho) = \sum_{ijkl} p^{ij}_{kl} |i\rangle\langle j| \otimes (|k\rangle\langle l|)^T =$$

$$\rho = \sum_{ijkl} p^{ij}_{kl} |i\rangle\langle j| \otimes |l\rangle\langle k|$$

Note that the *partial* in the name implies that only part of the state is transposed. More precisely, $I \otimes T(\rho)$ is the identity map applied to the A party and the transposition map applied to the B party.

This definition can be seen more clearly if we write the state as a block matrix:

$$\rho = \begin{pmatrix} A_{11} & A_{12} & \dots & A_{1n} \\ A_{21} & A_{22} & & \\ \vdots & & \ddots & \\ A_{n1} & & & A_{nn} \end{pmatrix}$$

Where $n = \dim \mathcal{H}_A$, and each block is a square matrix of dimension $m = \dim \mathcal{H}_B$. Then the partial transpose is

$$\rho^{T_B} = \begin{pmatrix} A^T_{11} & A^T_{12} & \dots & A^T_{1n} \\ A^T_{21} & A^T_{22} & & \\ \vdots & & \ddots & \\ A^T_{n1} & & & A^T_{nn} \end{pmatrix}$$

The criterion states that if ρ is separable, ρ^{T_B} has non-negative eigenvalues. In other words, if ρ^{T_B} has a negative eigenvalue, ρ is guaranteed to be entangled. If the eigenvalues are non-negative, and the dimension is larger than 6, the test is inconclusive.

The result is independent of the party that was transposed, because $\rho^{T_A} = (\rho^{T_B})^T$.

49.2 Example

Consider this 2-qubit family of Werner states:

$$\rho = p|\Psi^-\rangle\langle\Psi^-| + (1-p)\frac{I}{4}$$

It can be regarded as the convex combination of $|\Psi^-\rangle$, a maximally entangled state, and identity, the maximally mixed state.

Its density matrix is

$$\rho = \frac{1}{4}\begin{pmatrix} 1-p & 0 & 0 & 0 \\ 0 & p+1 & -2p & 0 \\ 0 & -2p & p+1 & 0 \\ 0 & 0 & 0 & 1-p \end{pmatrix}$$

and the partial transpose

$$\rho^{T_B} = \frac{1}{4}\begin{pmatrix} 1-p & 0 & 0 & -2p \\ 0 & p+1 & 0 & 0 \\ 0 & 0 & p+1 & 0 \\ -2p & 0 & 0 & 1-p \end{pmatrix}$$

Its least eigenvalue is $(1-3p)/4$. Therefore, the state is entangled for $p > 1/3$.

49.3 Demonstration

If ρ is separable, it can be written as

$$\rho = \sum p_i \rho_i^A \otimes \rho_i^B$$

In this case, the effect of the partial transposition is trivial:

$$\rho^{T_B} = I \otimes T(\rho) = \sum p_i \rho_i^A \otimes (\rho_i^B)^T$$

As the transposition map preserves eigenvalues, the spectrum of ρ^{T_B} is the same as the spectrum of ρ , and in particular ρ^{T_B} must still be positive semidefinite. This proves the necessity of the PPT criterion.

Showing that being PPT is also sufficient for the 2 X 2 and 3 X 2 (equivalently 2 X 3) cases is more involved. It was shown by the Horodeckis that for every entangled state there exists an entanglement witness. This is a result of geometric nature and invokes the Hahn–Banach theorem (see reference below).

From the existence of entanglement witnesses, one can show that $I \otimes \Lambda(\rho)$ being positive for all positive maps Λ is a necessary and sufficient condition for the separability of ρ, where Λ maps $B(\mathcal{H}_B)$ to $B(\mathcal{H}_A)$

Furthermore, every positive map from $B(\mathcal{H}_B)$ to $B(\mathcal{H}_A)$ can be decomposed into a sum of completely positive and completely copositive maps, when $\dim(\mathcal{H}_B) = 2$ and $\dim(\mathcal{H}_A) = 2$ or 3 . In other words, every such map Λ can be written as

$$\Lambda = \Lambda_1 + \Lambda_2 \circ T,$$

where Λ_1 and Λ_2 are completely positive and T is the transposition map. This follows from the Størmer-Woronowicz theorem.

Loosely speaking, the transposition map is therefore the only one that can generate negative eigenvalues in these dimensions. So if ρ^{T_B} is positive, $I \otimes \Lambda(\rho)$ is positive for any Λ. Thus we conclude that the Peres–Horodecki criterion is also sufficient for separability when $\dim(\mathcal{H}_A \otimes \mathcal{H}_B) \leq 6$.

In higher dimensions, however, there exist maps that can't be decomposed in this fashion, and the criterion is no longer sufficient. Consequently, there are entangled states which have a positive partial transpose. Such states have the interesting property that they are bound entangled, i.e. they can not be distilled for quantum communication purposes.

49.4 Continuous variable systems

The Peres–Horodecki criterion has been extended to continuous variable systems. Simon [1] formulated a particular version of the PPT criterion in terms of the second-order moments of canonical operators and showed that it is necessary and sufficient for $1 \oplus 1$ -mode Gaussian states (see Ref.[2] for a seemingly different but essentially equivalent approach). It was later found [3] that Simon's condition is also necessary and sufficient for $1 \oplus n$ -mode Gaussian states, but no longer sufficient for $2 \oplus 2$ -mode Gaussian states. Simon's condition can be generalized by taking into account the higher order moments of canonical operators [4] or by using entropic measures.[5]

49.5 References

[1] Simon, R. "Peres-Horodecki Separability Criterion for Continuous Variable Systems". *Physical Review Letters* **84** (12): 2726–2729. arXiv:quant-ph/9909044. Bibcode:2000PhRvL..84.2726S. doi:10.1103/PhysRevLett.84.2726.

[2] Duan, Lu-Ming; Giedke, G.; Cirac, J. I.; Zoller, P. "Inseparability Criterion for Continuous Variable Systems". *Physical Review Letters* **84** (12): 2722–2725. arXiv:quant-ph/9908056. Bibcode:2000PhRvL..84.2722D. doi:10.1103/PhysRevLett.84.2722.

[3] Werner, R. F.; Wolf, M. M. "Bound Entangled Gaussian States". *Physical Review Letters* **86** (16): 3658–3661. arXiv:quant-ph/0009118. Bibcode:2001PhRvL..86.3658W. doi:10.1103/PhysRevLett.86.3658.

[4] Shchukin, E.; Vogel, W. "Inseparability Criteria for Continuous Bipartite Quantum States". *Physical Review Letters* **95** (23). arXiv:quant-ph/0508132. Bibcode:2005PhRvL..95w0502S. doi:10.1103/PhysRevLett.95.230502. Hillery, Mark; Zubairy, M. Suhail. "Entanglement Conditions for Two-Mode States". *Physical Review Letters* **96** (5). arXiv:quant-ph/0507168. Bibcode:2006PhRvL..96e0503H. doi:10.1103/PhysRevLett.96.050503.

[5] Walborn, S.; Taketani, B.; Salles, A.; Toscano, F.; de Matos Filho, R. "Entropic Entanglement Criteria for Continuous Variables". *Physical Review Letters* **103** (16). arXiv:0909.0147. Bibcode:2009PhRvL.103p0505W. doi:10.1103/PhysRevLett.103.160505. Huang, Yichen. "Entanglement Detection: Complexity and Shannon Entropic Criteria". *IEEE Transactions on Information Theory* **59** (10): 6774–6778. doi:10.1109/TIT.2013.2257936.

- Asher Peres, *Separability Criterion for Density Matrices*, Phys. Rev. Lett. **77**, 1413–1415 (1996)
- Michał Horodecki, Paweł Horodecki, Ryszard Horodecki, *Separability of Mixed States: Necessary and Sufficient Conditions*, Physics Letters A **223**, 1-8 (1996)

- Karol Życzkowski and Ingemar Bengtsson, *Geometry of Quantum States*, Cambridge University Press, 2006
- S. L. Woronowicz, Positive maps of low dimensional matrix algebras, *Rep. Math. Phys.* **10** (1976), 165–183.

Chapter 50

POVM

In functional analysis and quantum measurement theory, a **positive-operator valued measure** (**POVM**) is a measure whose values are non-negative self-adjoint operators on a Hilbert space, and whose integral is the identity operator. It is the most general formulation of a measurement in the theory of quantum physics. The need for the POVM formalism arises from the fact that projective measurements on a larger system, by which we mean measurements that are performed mathematically by a *projection-valued measure* (PVM), will act on a subsystem in ways that cannot be described by a PVM on the subsystem alone. POVMs are used in the field of quantum information.

In rough analogy, a POVM is to a PVM what a density matrix is to a pure state. Density matrices are needed to specify the state of a subsystem of a larger system, even when the larger system is in a pure state (see purification of quantum state); analogously, POVMs on a physical system are used to describe the effect of a projective measurement performed on a larger system.

Historically, the term **probability-operator measure** (**POM**) has been used as a synonym for POVM,[1] although this usage is now rare.

50.1 Definition

In the simplest case, a POVM is a set of Hermitian positive semidefinite operators $\{F_i\}$ on a Hilbert space $\mathcal{H}$ that sum to the identity operator,

$$\sum_{i=1}^{n} F_i = \mathrm{I}_H .$$

This formula is a generalization of the decomposition of a (finite-dimensional) Hilbert space by a set of orthogonal projectors, $\{E_i\}$, defined for an orthogonal basis $\{|\phi_i\rangle\}$ by:

$$\sum_{i=1}^{N} E_i = \mathrm{I}_H, \quad E_i E_j = \delta_{ij} E_i, \quad E_i = |\phi_i\rangle \langle\phi_i| .$$

An important difference is that the elements of a POVM are not necessarily orthogonal, with the consequence that the number of elements in the POVM, n, can be larger than the dimension, N, of the Hilbert space they act in.

In general, POVMs can be defined in situations where the outcomes of measurements take values in a non-discrete space. The relevant fact is that measurement determines a probability measure on the outcome space:

Definition. Let (X, M) be measurable space; that is M is a σ-algebra of subsets of X. A **POVM** is a function F defined on M whose values are bounded non-negative self-adjoint operators on a Hilbert space H such that F(X) = IH and for every $\xi \in H$,

$$E \mapsto \langle F(E)\xi \mid \xi\rangle$$

is a non-negative countably additive measure on the σ-algebra M.

This definition should be contrasted with that of the projection-valued measure, which is similar, except that for projection-valued measures, the values of F are required to be projection operators.

50.2 Neumark's dilation theorem

Main article: Neumark's dilation theorem

> *Note: An alternate spelling of this is "Naimark's Theorem"*

Neumark's dilation theorem is a result that expresses POVMs in terms of projection-valued measures. It states that a POVM can be "lifted" by an operator map of the form $V^*(\cdot)V$ to a projection-valued measure. In the physical context, this means that the measurements accomplished by a POVM consisting of a weighted sum of n rank-one operators acting on an N-dimensional Hilbert space (where one may typically have $n > N$) can equally well be achieved by performing a projective measurement on a Hilbert space of dimension n.

So, for example, as in the theory of projective measurement, the probability that the outcome associated with measurement of operator F_i occurs

$$P(i) = \mathrm{tr}(\rho F_i),$$

where ρ is the density matrix representing the mixed state of the measured system.

Such a measurement can be carried out by doing a projective measurement in a larger Hilbert space. Let us extend the Hilbert space H_A to $H_A \oplus H_A^\perp$ and perform the measurement defined by the projection operators $\{\bar{\pi}_i\}$. The probability of the outcome associated with $\bar{\pi}_i$ is

$$P(i) = \mathrm{tr}(\rho\bar{\pi}_i) = \mathrm{tr}(\rho\bar{\pi}_A\bar{\pi}_i\bar{\pi}_A),$$

where $\bar{\pi}_A$ is the orthogonal projection taking $H_A \oplus H_A^\perp$ to H_A . In the original Hilbert space H_A , this is a POVM with operators given by $F_i = \bar{\pi}_A\bar{\pi}_i\bar{\pi}_A$. Neumark's dilation theorem guarantees that any POVM can be implemented in this manner.

In practice, POVMs are usually performed by coupling the original system to an ancilla. For an ancilla prepared in a pure state $|0\rangle_B$, this is a special case of the above; the Hilbert space is extended by the states $|\phi\rangle_A \otimes |\psi\rangle_B$ where $\langle\psi|0\rangle_B = 0$.

50.2.1 Post-measurement state

Consider the case where the ancilla is initially a pure state $|0\rangle_B$. We entangle the ancilla with the system, taking

$$|\psi\rangle_A|0\rangle_B \to \sum_i M_i|\psi\rangle_A|i\rangle_B,$$

and perform a projective measurement on the ancilla in the $\{|i\rangle_B\}$ basis. The operators of the resulting POVM are given by

$$F_i = M_i^\dagger M_i \,.$$

Since the M_i are not required to be positive, there are an infinite number of solutions to this equation. This means that there are infinite different experimental apparatuses that give the same probabilities for the outcomes. Since the post-measurement state of the system

$$\rho' = \frac{M_i\rho M_i^\dagger}{\mathrm{tr}(M_i\rho M_i^\dagger)}$$

depends on the M_i , in general it cannot be inferred from the POVM alone.

Another difference from the projective measurements is that a POVM is not repeatable. If ρ' is subjected to the same measurement, the new state is

$$\rho'' = \frac{M_i\rho' M_i^\dagger}{\mathrm{tr}(M_i\rho' M_i^\dagger)} = \frac{M_iM_i\rho M_i^\dagger M_i^\dagger}{\mathrm{tr}(M_iM_i\rho M_i^\dagger M_i^\dagger)}$$

which is equal to ρ' iff $M_i^2 = M_i$, that is, if the POVM reduces to a projective measurement.

This gives rises to many interesting effects, amongst them the quantum anti-Zeno effect.

50.3 Quantum properties of measurements

A recent work by T. Amri[2] makes the claim that the properties of a measurement are not revealed by the POVM element corresponding to the measurement, but by its pre-measurement state. This one is the main tool of the retrodictive approach of quantum physics in which we make predictions about state preparations leading to a measurement result. We show,[2][3] that this state simply corresponds to the normalized POVM element:

$$\hat{\rho}_{\text{retr}}^{[n]} = \frac{\hat{\Pi}_n}{\mathrm{Tr}\{\hat{\Pi}_n\}}.$$

We can make predictions about preparations leading to the result 'n' by using an expression similar to Born's rule:

$$\Pr(m|n) = \mathrm{Tr}\{\hat{\rho}_{\text{retr}}^{[n]}\hat{\Theta}_m\},$$

in which $\hat{\Theta}_m$ is a hermitian and positive operator corresponding to a proposition about the state of the measured system just after its preparation in some a state $\hat{\rho}_m$.[2] Such an approach allows us to determine in which kind of states the system was prepared for leading to the result 'n'.

Thus, the **non-classicality of a measurement** corresponds to the **non-classicality of its pre-measurement state**, for which such a notion can be measured by different signatures of non-classicality. The projective character of a measurement can be measured by its **projectivity** π_n which is the purity of its pre-measurement state:

$$\pi_n = \mathrm{Tr}\left[\left(\hat{\rho}_{\text{retr}}^{[n]}\right)^2\right].$$

The measurement is **projective** when its pre-measurement state is a pure quantum state $|\psi_n\rangle(\pi_n = 1)$. Thus, the corresponding POVM element is given by:

$$\hat{\Pi}_n = \eta_n|\psi_n\rangle\langle\psi_n|,$$

where $\eta_n = \mathrm{Tr}\{\Pi_n\}$ is in fact the detection efficiency of the state $|\psi_n\rangle$, since Born's rule leads to $\Pr(n|\psi_n) = \eta_n$. Therefore, the measurement can be projective but non-ideal, which is an important distinction with the usual definition of projective measurements.

50.4 An example: Unambiguous quantum state discrimination

Let us suppose that a quantum system (which we call the input) is known to be in a state drawn randomly from a given set of pure states. The task of unambiguous quantum state discrimination (UQSD) is to discern conclusively, at least sometimes, which state the system was in. The impossibility of perfectly discriminating between a set of non-orthogonal states is the basis for quantum information protocols such as quantum cryptography, quantum coin-flipping, and quantum money.

We will give a 2-dimensional example in which using a POVM strategy has a higher success probability for achieving UQSD than any possible projective measurement.

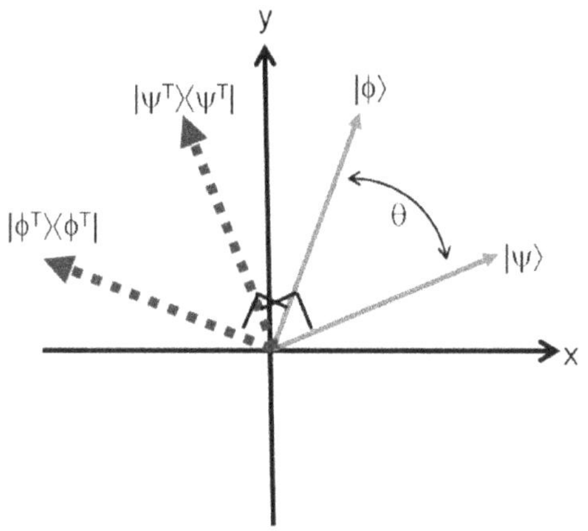

The projective measurement strategy for unambiguously discriminating between nonorthogonal states (at least sometimes).

First, consider a trivial case. Take a set consisting of two orthogonal states $|\psi\rangle$ and $|\psi^T\rangle$. A projective measurement whose corresponding Hermitian operator has the form

$$\hat{A} = a|\psi^T\rangle\langle\psi^T| + b|\psi\rangle\langle\psi|,$$

will result in eigenvalue *a* only when the system is in $|\psi^T\rangle$ and eigenvalue *b* only when the system is in $|\psi\rangle$. In addition, the measurement *always* discriminates between the two states (i.e. with 100% probability). So we can achieve UQSD every single time. This is impossible for anything but orthogonal states.

Now consider a set that consists of two states $|\psi\rangle$ and $|\phi\rangle$ in two-dimensional Hilbert space that are not orthogonal. i.e.,

$$|\langle\phi|\psi\rangle| = \cos(\theta),$$

for $\theta > 0$. These could be states of a system such as the spin of spin-1/2 particle (e.g. an electron), or the polarization of a photon.

In order to make a quantitative comparison between different strategies, we make the *a-priori assumption* that the system has an *equal likelihood* of being in each of these two permitted states. Then the best strategy for UQSD using only projective measurement is to perform each of the following measurements,

$$\hat{\pi}_{\psi^T} = |\psi^T\rangle\langle\psi^T|,$$

$$\hat{\pi}_{\phi^T} = |\phi^T\rangle\langle\phi^T|,$$

50% of the time. Here the "T" indicates a vector orthogonal to the given vector. Being projections, these observables have possible outcomes of 0 or 1. If the measurement $\hat{\pi}_{\psi^T}$ is performed and results in a value of 1, then it is certain that the state was in $|\phi\rangle$. However, a result of 0 is inconclusive since this can come from the system being in either of the two states in the set. Similarly, a result of 1 for the measurement $\hat{\pi}_{\phi^T}$ indicates conclusively that the system was in $|\psi\rangle$ and a result of 0 is inconclusive. The probability that this strategy returns a conclusive result is then,

$$P_{\text{proj}} = \frac{1 - |\langle\phi|\psi\rangle|^2}{2}.$$

As we shall see, a strategy based on POVMs has a greater probability of success given by,

$$P_{\text{POVM}} = 1 - |\langle\phi|\psi\rangle|.$$

This is the minimum allowed by the rules of quantum indeterminacy and the uncertainty principle. This strategy is based on a POVM consisting of,

$$\hat{F}_\psi = \frac{1 - |\phi\rangle\langle\phi|}{1 + |\langle\phi|\psi\rangle|}$$

$$\hat{F}_\phi = \frac{1 - |\psi\rangle\langle\psi|}{1 + |\langle\phi|\psi\rangle|}$$

$$\hat{F}_{\text{inconcl.}} = 1 - \hat{F}_\psi - \hat{F}_\phi,$$

where the result associated with $\hat{F}_i$ indicates the system is in state i with certainty.

These POVMs can be created by extending the two-dimensional Hilbert space. This can be visualized as follows: The two states fall in the x-y plane with an angle of θ between them and the space is extended in the z-direction. (The total space is the direct sum of spaces defined by the z-direction and the x-y plane.) The measurement first unitarily rotates the states towards the z-axis so that $|\psi\rangle$ has no component along the y-direction and $|\phi\rangle$

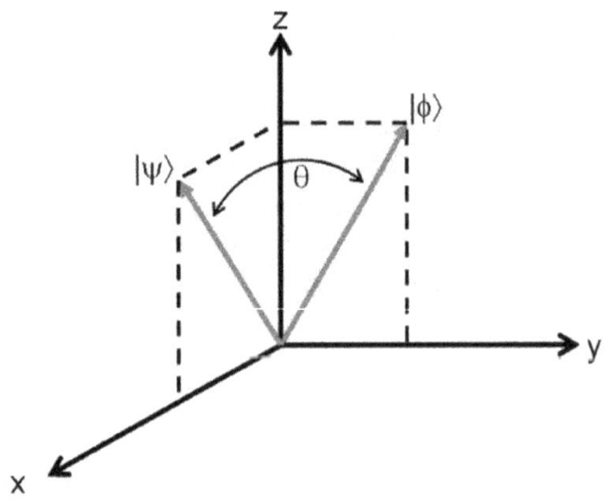

The POVM strategy for unambiguously discriminating between nonorthogonal states (at least sometimes, but a better sometimes).

has no component along the x-direction. At this point, the three elements of the POVM correspond to projective measurements along x-direction, y-direction and z-direction, respectively.

For a specific example, take a stream of photons, each of which is polarized along either the horizontal direction or at 45 degrees. On average there are equal numbers of horizontal and 45 degree photons. The projective strategy corresponds to passing the photons through a polarizer in either the vertical direction or -45 degree direction. If the photon passes through the vertical polarizer it must have been at 45 degrees and vice versa. The success probability is $(1-1/2)/2 = 25\%$. The POVM strategy for this example is more complicated and requires another optical mode (known as an ancilla). It has a success probability of $1-1/\sqrt{2} = 29.3\%$.

50.5 SIC-POVM

Main article: SIC-POVM

Quantum t-designs have been recently introduced to POVMs and symmetric, informationally-complete POVM's (SIC-POVM's) as a means of providing a simple and elegant formulation of the field in a general setting, since a SIC-POVM is a type of spherical t-design.[4]

50.6 See also

- Quantum measurement
- Mathematical formulation of quantum mechanics
- Quantum logic
- Density matrix
- Quantum operation
- Projection-valued measure
- Vector measure

50.7 References

[1] Carl W. Helstrom, (1976). *Quantum Detection and Estimation Theory*. Academic Press, Inc. ISBN 0123400503.

[2] Taoufik Amri, Quantum behavior of measurement apparatus, arXiv:1001.3032 (2010).

[3] S. M. Barnett et al. arXiv:0106139 (2001).

[4] http://arxiv.org/abs/quant-ph/0310075

- POVMs
  - J. Preskill, Lecture Notes for Physics: Quantum Information and Computation, http://www.theory.caltech.edu/people/preskill/ph229/#lecture
  - K. Kraus, States, Effects, and Operations, Lecture Notes in Physics 190, Springer (1983).
  - E.B.Davies, Quantum Theory of Open Systems, Academic Press (1976).
  - A.S. Holevo, Probabilistic and statistical aspects of quantum theory, North-Holland Publ. Cy., Amsterdam (1982).
- POVMs and measurement
  - M. Nielsen and I. Chuang, Quantum Computation and Quantum Information, Cambridge University Press, (2000)
- Neumark's theorem
  - A. Peres. Neumark's theorem and quantum inseparability. Foundations of Physics, 12:1441–1453, 1990.
  - A. Peres. Quantum Theory: Concepts and Methods. Kluwer Academic Publishers, 1993.
  - I. M. Gelfand and M. A. Neumark, On the embedding of normed rings into the ring of operators in Hilbert space, Rec. Math. [Mat. Sbornik] N.S. 12(54) (1943), 197–213.
- Unambiguous quantum state-discrimination
  - I. D. Ivanovic, Phys. Lett. A 123 257 (1987).
  - D. Dieks, Phys. Lett. A 126 303 (1988).
  - A. Peres, Phys. Lett. A 128 19 (1988).
- Review articles on quantum state-discrimination

- A. Chefles, Quantum State Discrimination, Contemp. Phys. 41, 401 (2000), http://arxiv.org/abs/quant-ph/0010114v1
- J.A. Bergou, U. Herzog, M. Hillery, Discrimination of Quantum States, Lect. Notes Phys. 649, 417–465 (2004)

Chapter 51

Schmidt decomposition

In linear algebra, the **Schmidt decomposition** (named after its originator Erhard Schmidt) refers to a particular way of expressing a vector in the tensor product of two inner product spaces. It has numerous applications in quantum information theory, for example in entanglement characterization and in state purification, and plasticity.

51.1 Theorem

Let H_1 and H_2 be Hilbert spaces of dimensions n and m respectively. Assume $n \geq m$. For any vector w in the tensor product $H_1 \otimes H_2$, there exist orthonormal sets $\{u_1, \ldots, u_n\} \subset H_1$ and $\{v_1, \ldots, v_m\} \subset H_2$ such that $w = \sum_{i=1}^{m} \alpha_i u_i \otimes v_i$, where the scalars α_i are real, non-negative, and, as a (multi-)set, uniquely determined by w .

51.1.1 Proof

The Schmidt decomposition is essentially a restatement of the singular value decomposition in a different context. Fix orthonormal bases $\{e_1, \ldots, e_n\} \subset H_1$ and $\{f_1, \ldots, f_m\} \subset H_2$. We can identify an elementary tensor $e_i \otimes f_j$ with the matrix $e_i f_j^T$, where f_j^T is the transpose of f_j . A general element of the tensor product

$$v = \sum_{1 \leq i \leq n, 1 \leq j \leq m} \beta_{ij} e_i \otimes f_j$$

can then be viewed as the $n \times m$ matrix

$$M_v = (\beta_{ij})_{ij}.$$

By the singular value decomposition, there exist an $n \times n$ unitary U, $m \times m$ unitary V, and a positive semidefinite diagonal $m \times m$ matrix Σ such that

$$M_v = U \begin{bmatrix} \Sigma \\ 0 \end{bmatrix} V^*.$$

Write $U = \begin{bmatrix} U_1 & U_2 \end{bmatrix}$ where U_1 is $n \times m$ and we have

$$M_v = U_1 \Sigma V^*.$$

Let $\{u_1, \ldots, u_m\}$ be the first m column vectors of U_1 , $\{v_1, \ldots, v_m\}$ the column vectors of V, and $\alpha_1, \ldots, \alpha_m$ the diagonal elements of Σ. The previous expression is then

$$M_v = \sum_{k=1}^{m} \alpha_k u_k v_k^*,$$

Then

$$v = \sum_{k=1}^{m} \alpha_k u_k \otimes v_k,$$

which proves the claim.

51.2 Some observations

Some properties of the Schmidt decomposition are of physical interest.

51.2.1 Spectrum of reduced states

Consider a vector w of the tensor product

$$H_1 \otimes H_2$$

in the form of Schmidt decomposition

$$w = \sum_{i=1}^{m} \alpha_i u_i \otimes v_i.$$

Form the rank 1 matrix $\varrho = w\,w^*$. Then the partial trace of ϱ, with respect to either system A or B, is a diagonal matrix whose non-zero diagonal elements are $|\alpha i\,|^2$. In other words, the Schmidt decomposition shows that the reduced state of ϱ on either subsystem have the same spectrum.

51.2.2 Schmidt rank and entanglement

The strictly positive values α_i in the Schmidt decomposition of *w* are its **Schmidt coefficients**. The number of Schmidt coefficients of w , counted with multiplicity, is called its **Schmidt rank**, or **Schmidt number**.

If *w* can be expressed as a product

$u \otimes v$

then *w* is called a separable state. Otherwise, *w* is said to be an entangled state. From the Schmidt decomposition, we can see that *w* is entangled if and only if *w* has Schmidt rank strictly greater than 1. Therefore, two subsystems that partition a pure state are entangled if and only if their reduced states are mixed states.

51.2.3 Von Neumann entropy

A consequence of the above comments is that, for bipartite pure states, the von Neumann entropy of the reduced states is a well-defined measure of entanglement. For the von Neumann entropy of both reduced states of ϱ is $-\sum_i |\alpha_i|^2 \log |\alpha_i|^2$, and this is zero if and only if ϱ is a product state (not entangled).

51.3 Crystal plasticity

In the field of plasticity, crystalline solids such as metals deform plastically primarily along crystal planes. Each plane, defined by its normal vector ν can "slip" in one of several directions, defined by a vector μ. Together a slip plane and direction form a slip system which is described by the Schmidt tensor $P = \mu \otimes \nu$. The velocity gradient is a linear combination of these across all slip systems where the scaling factor is the rate of slip along the system.

51.4 See also

- Singular value decomposition
- Purification of quantum state

51.5 Further reading

- Pathak, Anirban (2013). *Elements of Quantum Computation and Quantum Communication*. London: Taylor & Francis. pp. 92–98. ISBN 978-1-4665-1791-2.

Chapter 52

SCOP formalism

52.1 State COntext Property (SCOP) formalism

Our minds are able to construct a multitude of imaginary, hypothetical, or counterfactual deviations from the more prototypical states of particular concept, and the State COntext Property (SCOP) can model this. The SCOP formalism was inspired by the need to incorporate the effect of context into the formal description of a concept. It builds on an operational approach in the foundations of quantum mechanics in which a physical system is determined by the mathematical structure of its set of states, set of properties, the possible (measurement) contexts which can be applied to this entity, and the relations between these sets. The SCOP formalism is part of a longstanding effort to develop an operational approach to quantum mechanics known as the Geneva-Brussels approach.[1] With SCOP it is possible to describe situations with any degree of contextuality. In fact, classical an quantum come out as special cases: quantum at the one end of extreme contextuality and classical at the other end of extreme lack of contextuality.[2] The SCOP formalism permits one to describe not only physical or conceptual entities, but also potential entities of a more abstract nature,[3] which means that SCOP aims at a very general description of how the interaction between context and the state of an entity plays a fundamental role in its evolution.

52.2 SCOP entities

The description of SCOP entities seeks for a general description of an *observable*entity that evolves with time. Thus, the description of the entity needs to consider the different *states* that the entity can assume. In order to establish the differences among the states, we need to consider the *properties* that the states can hold. Note that a complete description of the states in terms of their properties requires that each state must hold a different properties, but in principle this is not the case. In order to *observe* the entity, we need a mechanism that permits us to measure properties on the states, i.e. there must exist a set of useful measurements or *contexts* that permits us to *observe* what properties are held by the current state the entity. However, the context can affect the state of the entity, and change its state (this is well known as the observer effect).

Formally, a SCOP entity consists of a 5-tuple $(\Sigma, \mathrm{M}, L, \mu, \nu)$, where Σ represents the set of *states* that the entity can assume, M represents a set of *contexts* (measurements), L represents a set of properties that the entity can hold, $\mu : \Sigma \times \mathrm{M} \times \Sigma \to [0,1]$, $(p,e,q) \mapsto \mu(p,e,q)$ is a *state-transition probability function* that represents the likelihood to transition from the state p to the state q under the influence of the context e , and $\nu : \Sigma \times L \to [0,1]$, $(p,a) \mapsto [0,1]$ is an *property-applicability function* that estimates how applicable is the property a to the state p of the entity.

52.3 Special states and contexts

It is possible to identify relations among the states and contexts, that recall the basic elements of the quantum formalism:

52.3.1 Unitary context and ground state

It is possible that the entity is in a situation of *no contextual influence*. We identify such situation by the *unitary context*, denoted by $\mathbf{1}$. Moreover, the state of the entity in this situation is identified by the *ground state* $\hat{p}$. We have that $\mu(\hat{p},\mathbf{1},\hat{p}) = 1$, and thus $\mu(p,\mathbf{1},\hat{p}) = 1$ for all $p \in \Sigma, p \neq \hat{p}$.

Thus, the interaction of the entity with any context different from the unitary context will lead to an evolutionary process of the state's entity.

52.3.2 Eigenstates and potentiality

If for some context e there is an state p such that $\mu(p,e,p) = 1$, we say p is an *eigenstate* for the context e . Any state q that is not an eigenstate, it is referred to as *potential state*.

52.4 Order theory and SCOP

It is possible to describe the elements of SCOP using order-theoretic structures. In[3] it has been shown how to obtain a pre-ordered set of states and properties. In[4] it is shown that the set of contexts and properties can be equipped with an orthocomplemented lattice structure. By imposing axioms on the order-theoretical structures of the former elements of a SCOP entity it is possible, via representation theoretical techniques, to obtain the Hilbert space description of the entity.[5]

52.5 SCOP concepts

The SCOP approach to concepts belongs to the emergent field of quantum cognition. In a SCOP model of a concept we are able to incorporate all of the possible contexts that could influence the state of a concept. The more states and contexts included, the richer the model becomes. The level of refinement is determined by the role the model is expected to play. It is outstanding that in SCOP, unlike other mathematical models of concepts, the potential to include this richness is present in the formalism, i.e., it can incorporate even improbable states, and largely but not completely irrelevant contexts. The SCOP formalism has been successfully applied to model conceptual entities.[4][6] It has been used shown how to solve the inconsistencies of other mathematical model of concepts,[7] and at the same time it permits to join different perspectives coming from psychology and phylosophy.[8]

52.5.1 Contextual dependence

Early concept theorists such Eleanor Rosch have noted that the context in which a concept is elicited plays a fundamental role in the meaning that it takes in natural reasoning tasks such as learning or planning. While in some theories, such as Gärdenfors or Nosofsky theories of concepts, the context is modeled as a weighting function across attributes or properties, in SCOP any effect of context occurs by way of its effect on the state.

52.5.2 Typicality, membership and similarity

Many researchers in concepts such as Hampton, Kamp and Partee, Osherson and Smith, among others, have noticed that measures of typicality and membership in concepts are not equivalent. Typicality refers to how common or representative is an instance of a concept. Membership rather than measure representativeness only measures the allegiance or inclusiveness of a conceptual instances in the category determined by the concept. It is well known that both measures are context-dependent, and they have been related to the notion of similarity of concepts, in that *concept-similarity* would be a more fundamental notion and will imply determine their values. But no satisfactory mathematical theory of concept-similarity has been developed yet. In SCOP, similarity, membership, typicality, and any other measure, is modeled as a *measurement-operator* that acts on the state of the concept, in the same way as context do. This general manner of approach the measurement of quantities that permits to differentiate states are called "experiment-contexts".

52.5.3 Concept combination and emergence

The emergence of meaning when concepts are combined is at the core of the drawbacks in concept theories. For example, it has been shown that *guppy* is not a typical instance neither of concept PET or concept FISH, but is a highly typical instance of the combined concept PET-FISH. It has been proven that no logical-based approach can explain the ways these effects in concept combination.[9] The SCOP-based approach to concepts has been shown to model the concept combination in a satisfactory manner, by embedding the states of the combined concept in tensor space formed by the Hilbert spaces representing each concept.[4][9]

52.6 References

[1] Piron, C.: Foundations of Quantum Physics. Benjamin, Reading, 1976.

[2] Aerts D. Classical theories and non classical theories as a special case of a more general theory, *Journal of Mathematical Physics*, 24, 2441 – 2453. 1983

[3] Aerts D. "Being and change: foundations of a realistic operational formalism", in *Probing the Structure of Quantum Mechanics: Nonlinearity, Nonlocality, Computation and Axiomatics.* eds. D. Aerts, M. Czachor and T. Durt, World Scientific, Singapore, 2002.

[4] Aerts D. and Gabora L. A state-context-property model of concepts and their combinations ii: A Hilbert space representation. *Kybernetes*, 34(1/2):176 – 204, 2005.

[5] D'Hooghe. B. A Possible Operational Motivation for the Orthocomplementation in Quantum Structures, *Found Phys.* 40: 1669–1680, 2010.

[6] Veloz T., Gabora L., Eyjolfson M., Aerts D., Toward a Formal Model of the Shifting Relationship between Concepts and Contexts during Associative Thought, Fifth International Symposium on Quantum Interaction, in press, 2011.

[7] Gabora L. and Aerts D. Contextualizing concepts using a mathematical generalization of the quantum formalism *Journal of Experimental and Theoretical Artificial Intelligence*, 14 (4), 327 – 358, 2002.

[8] Gabora L., Aerts D., A model of the emergence and evolution of integrated worldviews, *Journal of Mathematical Psychology*, 53, 434–451, 2009.

[9] Aerts D., Quantum structure in cognition, *Journal of Mathematical Psychology* 53, 314- 348, 2009.

Chapter 53

Superoperator

In physics, a **superoperator** is a linear operator acting on a vector space of linear operators.[1]

Sometimes the term refers more specially to a completely positive map which does not increase or preserve the trace of its argument. This specialized meaning is used extensively in the field of quantum computing, especially quantum programming, as they characterise mappings between density matrices.

The use of the **super-** prefix here is in no way related to its other use in mathematical physics. That is to say superoperators have no connection to supersymmetry and superalgebra which are extensions of the usual mathematical concepts defined by extending the ring of numbers to include Grassmann numbers. Since superoperators are themselves operators the use of the **super-** prefix is used to distinguish them from the operators upon which they act.

53.1 Example von Neumann Equation

In quantum mechanics the Schrödinger Equation, $i\hbar\frac{\partial}{\partial t}\Psi = \hat{H}\Psi$ expresses the time evolution of the state vector ψ by the action of the Hamiltonian $\hat{H}$ which is an operator mapping state vectors to state vectors.

In the more general formulation of John von Neumann, statistical states and ensembles are expressed by density operators rather than state vectors. In this context the time evolution of the density operator is expressed via the von Neumann equation in which density operator is acted upon by a **superoperator** $\mathcal{H}$ mapping operators to operators. It is defined by taking the commutator with respect to the Hamiltonian operator:

$i\hbar\frac{\partial}{\partial t}\rho = \mathcal{H}[\rho]$

where

$\mathcal{H}[\rho] = [\hat{H}, \rho] \equiv \hat{H}\rho - \rho\hat{H}$

As commutator brackets are used extensively in QM this explicit superoperator presentation of the Hamiltonian's action is typically omitted.

53.2 Example Derivatives of Functions on the Space of Operators

When considering an operator valued function of operators $\hat{H} = \hat{H}(\hat{P})$ as for example when we define the quantum mechanical Hamiltonian of a particle as a function of the position and momentum operators, we may (for whatever reason) define an "Operator Derivative" $\frac{\Delta\hat{H}}{\Delta\hat{P}}$ as a **superoperator** mapping an operator to an operator.

For example if $H(P) = P^3 = PPP$ then its operator derivative is the superoperator defined by:

$\frac{\Delta H}{\Delta P}[X] = XP^2 + PXP + P^2X$

This "operator derivative" is simply the Jacobian matrix of the function (of operators) where one simply treats the operator input and output as vectors and expands the space of operators in some basis. The Jacobian matrix is then an operator (at one higher level of abstraction) acting on that vector space (of operators).

53.3 See also

Lindblad superoperator

53.4 References

[1] John Preskill, Lecture notes for Quantum Computation course at Caltech, Ch. 3,

Chapter 54

Typical subspace

In quantum information theory, the idea of a **typical subspace** plays an important role in the proofs of many coding theorems (the most prominent example being Schumacher compression). Its role is analogous to that of the typical set in classical information theory.

54.1 Unconditional Quantum Typicality

Consider a density operator ρ with the following spectral decomposition:

$$\rho = \sum_{x} p_X(x) |x\rangle \langle x| .$$

The weakly typical subspace is defined as the span of all vectors such that the sample entropy $\overline{H}(x^n)$ of their classical label is close to the true entropy $H(X)$ of the distribution $p_X(x)$:

$$T_\delta^{X^n} \equiv \text{span}\left\{|x^n\rangle : \left|\overline{H}(x^n) - H(X)\right| \leq \delta\right\},$$

where

$$\overline{H}(x^n) \equiv -\frac{1}{n}\log(p_{X^n}(x^n)),$$

$$H(X) \equiv -\sum_x p_X(x)\log p_X(x) .$$

The projector $\Pi_{\rho,\delta}^n$ onto the typical subspace of ρ is defined as

$$\Pi_{\rho,\delta}^n \equiv \sum_{x^n \in T_\delta^{X^n}} |x^n\rangle \langle x^n| ,$$

where we have "overloaded" the symbol $T_\delta^{X^n}$ to refer also to the set of δ -typical sequences:

$$T_\delta^{X^n} \equiv \left\{x^n : \left|\overline{H}(x^n) - H(X)\right| \leq \delta\right\}.$$

The three important properties of the typical projector are as follows:

$$\text{Tr}\left\{\Pi_{\rho,\delta}^n \rho^{\otimes n}\right\} \geq 1 - \epsilon,$$

$$\text{Tr}\left\{\Pi_{\rho,\delta}^n\right\} \leq 2^{n[H(X)+\delta]},$$

$$2^{-n[H(X)+\delta]}\Pi_{\rho,\delta}^n \leq \Pi_{\rho,\delta}^n \rho^{\otimes n} \Pi_{\rho,\delta}^n \leq 2^{-n[H(X)-\delta]}\Pi_{\rho,\delta}^n,$$

where the first property holds for arbitrary $\epsilon, \delta > 0$ and sufficiently large n .

54.2 Conditional Quantum Typicality

Consider an ensemble $\{p_X(x), \rho_x\}_{x\in\mathcal{X}}$ of states. Suppose that each state ρ_x has the following spectral decomposition:

$$\rho_x = \sum_y p_{Y|X}(y|x) |y_x\rangle \langle y_x| .$$

Consider a density operator ρ_{x^n} which is conditional on a classical sequence $x^n \equiv x_1 \cdots x_n$:

$$\rho_{x^n} \equiv \rho_{x_1} \otimes \cdots \otimes \rho_{x_n}.$$

We define the weak conditionally typical subspace as the span of vectors (conditional on the sequence x^n) such that the sample conditional entropy $\overline{H}(y^n|x^n)$ of their classical labels is close to the true conditional entropy $H(Y|X)$ of the distribution $p_{Y|X}(y|x)\,p_X(x)$:

$$T_\delta^{Y^n|x^n} \equiv \text{span}\left\{|y_{x^n}^n\rangle : \left|\overline{H}(y^n|x^n) - H(Y|X)\right| \leq \delta\right\},$$

where

$$\overline{H}(y^n|x^n) \equiv -\frac{1}{n}\log\left(p_{Y^n|X^n}(y^n|x^n)\right),$$

$$H(Y|X) \equiv -\sum_x p_X(x) \sum_y p_{Y|X}(y|x) \log p_{Y|X}(y|x).$$

The projector $\Pi_{\rho_{x^n},\delta}$ onto the weak conditionally typical subspace of ρ_{x^n} is as follows:

$$\Pi_{\rho_{x^n},\delta} \equiv \sum_{y^n \in T_\delta^{Y^n|x^n}} |y^n_{x^n}\rangle \langle y^n_{x^n}|,$$

where we have again overloaded the symbol $T_\delta^{Y^n|x^n}$ to refer to the set of weak conditionally typical sequences:

$$T_\delta^{Y^n|x^n} \equiv \left\{ y^n : \left| \overline{H}(y^n|x^n) - H(Y|X) \right| \leq \delta \right\}.$$

The three important properties of the weak conditionally typical projector are as follows:

$$\mathbb{E}_{X^n}\left\{ \text{Tr}\left\{ \Pi_{\rho_{X^n},\delta} \rho_{X^n} \right\} \right\} \geq 1 - \epsilon,$$

$$\text{Tr}\left\{ \Pi_{\rho_{x^n},\delta} \right\} \leq 2^{n[H(Y|X)+\delta]},$$

$$2^{-n[H(Y|X)+\delta]} \, \Pi_{\rho_{x^n},\delta} \leq \Pi_{\rho_{x^n},\delta} \, \rho_{x^n} \, \Pi_{\rho_{x^n},\delta} \leq 2^{-n[H(Y|X)-\delta]} \, \Pi_{\rho_{x^n},\delta},$$

where the first property holds for arbitrary $\epsilon, \delta > 0$ and sufficiently large n , and the expectation is with respect to the distribution $p_{X^n}(x^n)$.

54.3 See also

- Classical capacity
- Quantum information theory

54.4 References

- Mark M. Wilde, "From Classical to Quantum Shannon Theory", arXiv:1106.1445.

Chapter 55

W state

The **W state** is an entangled quantum state of three qubits which has the following shape

$$|W\rangle = \frac{1}{\sqrt{3}}(|001\rangle + |010\rangle + |100\rangle)$$

and which is remarkable for representing a specific type of multipartite entanglement and for occurring in several applications in quantum information theory. Particles prepared in this state reproduce the properties of Bell's theorem which states that no classical theory of hidden variables can ever produce the predictions of quantum mechanics.

55.1 Properties

The W state is the representative of one of the two non-biseparable[1] classes of three-qubit states (the other being the GHZ state) which cannot be transformed (not even probabilistically) into each other by local quantum operations.[2] Thus $|W\rangle$ and $|\mathrm{GHZ}\rangle$ represent two very different kinds of tripartite entanglement.

This difference is, for example, illustrated by the following interesting property of the W state: if one of the three qubits is lost, the state of the remaining 2-qubit system is still entangled. This robustness of W-type entanglement contrasts strongly with the Greenberger-Horne-Zeilinger state which is fully separable after loss of one qubit.

The states in the W class can be distinguished from all other three-qubit states by means of multipartite entanglement measures. In particular, W states have non-zero entanglement across any bipartition[3] while the 3-tangle vanishes, which is also non-zero for GHZ-type states.[2]

55.2 Generalization

The notion of W state has been generalized for n qubits[2] and then refers to the quantum superpostion with equal expansion coefficients of all possible pure states in which exactly one of the qubits in an "excited state" $|1\rangle$, while all other ones are in the "ground state" $|0\rangle$

$$|W\rangle = \frac{1}{\sqrt{n}}(|100...0\rangle + |010...0\rangle + ... + |00...01\rangle)$$

Both the robustness against particle loss and the LOCC-inequivalence with the (generalized) GHZ state also hold for the n -qubit W state.

55.3 Applications

In systems in which a single qubit is stored in an ensemble of many two level systems the logical "1" is often represented by the W state while the logical "0" is represented by the state $|00...0\rangle$. Here the W state's robustness against particle loss is a very beneficial property ensuring good storage properties of these ensemble based quantum memories.[4]

55.4 References

[1] A pure state $|\psi\rangle$ of N parties is called *biseparable*, if one can find a partition of the parties in two disjoint subsets A and B with $A \cup B = \{1, ..., N\}$ such that $|\psi\rangle = |\phi\rangle_A \otimes |\gamma\rangle_B$, i.e. $|\psi\rangle$ is a product state with respect to the partition $A|B$.

[2] W. Dür, G. Vidal, and J.I. Cirac (2000). "Three qubits can be entangled in two inequivalent ways". *Phys. Rev.* A **62**: 062314. arXiv:quant-ph/0005115. Bibcode:2000PhRvA..62f2314D. doi:10.1103/PhysRevA.62.062314.

[3] A bipartition of the three qubits $1, 2, 3$ is any grouping $(12)3, 1(23)$ and $(13)2$ in which two qubits are considered to belong to the same party. The three qubit state can then be considered as a state on $\mathbb{C}^4 \otimes \mathbb{C}^2$ and studied with bipartite entanglement measures.

[4] M. Fleischhauer and M. D. Lukin (2002). "Quantum memory for photons: Dark-state polaritons". *Phys. Rev.* A **65**: 022314. arXiv:quant-ph/0106066. Bibcode:2002PhRvA..65b2314F. doi:10.1103/PhysRevA.65.022314.

Chapter 56

Institute for Quantum Computing

The **Institute for Quantum Computing**, or **IQC**, located in Waterloo, Ontario, is an affiliate scientific research institute of the University of Waterloo with a multidisciplinary approach to the field of quantum information processing. IQC was founded in 2002[1] primarily through a donation made by Mike Lazaridis and his wife Ophelia whose substantial donations have continued over the years.[2] The institute is now located in the Mike & Ophelia Lazaridis Quantum-Nano Centre and the Research Advancement Centre at the University of Waterloo.

It is led by co-founder and physicist, Raymond Laflamme with researchers based in 6 departments across 3 faculties at the University of Waterloo. In addition to theoretical and experimental research on quantum computing, IQC also hosts academic conferences and workshops, short courses for undergraduate and high school students, and scientific outreach events including open houses and tours for the public.

56.1 Mission

The IQC seeks to harness quantum mechanics to develop transformational technologies that will benefit society and become a new engine of economic development in the 21st century. It aims to develop and advance quantum information science and technology at the highest international level through the collaboration of computer scientists, engineers, mathematicians and physical scientists.[3]

The institute's three strategic objectives have been stated as:

1. To establish Waterloo as a world-class centre for research in quantum technologies and their applications.

2. To become a magnet for highly qualified personnel in the field of quantum information.

3. To establish IQC as the authoritative source of insight, analysis and commentary on quantum information.

56.2 History

The Institute for Quantum Computing was officially created in 2002, sparked by Research In Motion co-founder Mike Lazaridis and then-president of the University of Waterloo, David Johnston, for research into quantum information. Since inception, Lazaridis has provided more than $100 million in private funding for IQC. The institute is a collaboration between academia, the private sector, and the federal and provincial governments. Raymond Laflamme is the founding executive director and Michele Mosca is founding deputy director.[4]

At its establishment, the institute was composed of only a handful of researchers from the Departments of Computer Science and Physics. Ten years later, there are more than 200 researchers across six departments within the Faculties of Science, Mathematics, and Engineering at the University of Waterloo.

In 2008, IQC moved into the Research Advancement Centre 1 (RAC I) in the University of Waterloo's Research & Technology Park. In 2010, research operations expanded into the adjacent building, Research Advancement Centre 2 (RAC II).

In 2012, IQC expanded into the Mike & Ophelia Lazaridis Quantum-Nano Centre. The 285,000-square-foot facility is shared with the Waterloo Institute for Nanotechnology, and is built to stringent standards (controls for vibration, humidity, temperature, and electromagnetic radiation) for quantum and nanotechnology experiments. The building was designed by Toronto-based firm Kuwabara Payne McKenna Blumberg Architects (KPMB).[5]

56.3 Research

Research at IQC focuses on three main applications of quantum information science and technology using the physical sciences, mathematics and engineering from both theoretical and experimental perspectives. The three applications are quantum computing, which encompasses the manipulation and storage of quantum information; quantum communication, which is related to the transmission of quantum information; and quantum sensing, which is used to detect signals or stimuli that are present in the nanoscopic world.[6]

Areas of research currently studied at IQC include:

- Quantum information theory
- Quantum algorithms
- Quantum complexity
- Quantum error correction and fault tolerance
- Spin-based quantum information processing
- Nanoelectronics-based quantum information processing
- Optical quantum information processing
- Quantum cryptography

In collaboration with the University of Waterloo, IQC offers research positions and advanced courses in the foundations, applications, and implementation of quantum information processing for graduate students. In addition, IQC also offers an interdisciplinary graduate program in Quantum Information which leads to MMath, MSc, MASc, and PhD degrees.[7]

56.4 Scientific outreach

IQC's scientific outreach activities include annual workshops, short courses, public lectures, tours, and open houses. IQC shares many of these special events, including lectures and special interviews, with the online public through its YouTube channel, Flickr photostream, and Twitter feed. In the past, it has also played host to conferences and workshops including Women in Physics Canada,[8] Cross-Border Workshop on Laser Science, Quantum Information Processing with Spins and Superconductors (QISS2010), the AQuA Student Congress on Quantum Information & Computation, and Canadian Summer School on Quantum Information.

56.4.1 Public lectures

IQC has presented public lectures by notable researchers including David Cory, Joseph Emerson, Raymond Laflamme, and Michele Mosca.[9]

56.4.2 USEQIP

The Undergraduate School on Experimental Quantum Information Processing (USEQIP) is an annual two-week program held in May and June designed for undergraduate students completing the third year of their undergraduate education. The program aims to introduce 20 students to the field of quantum information processing through lectures on quantum information theory and experimental approaches to quantum devices, followed by hands-on exploration using the experimental facilities of IQC.[10]

56.4.3 QCSYS

The Quantum Cryptography School for Young Students (QCSYS) is an annual one-week summer program for 40 high school students aged 15 and older. The program is run by IQC in conjunction with the University of Waterloo. The selected students attend specialized lectures on quantum physics and cryptography, visit local research institutes, meet renowned researchers in these fields, and take a tour of quantum computing and quantum cryptography experiments.[11]

56.5 Facilities

IQC currently has offices and laboratories in both Research Advancement Centre I and II, located in the University of Waterloo's David Johnston Research & Technology Park.

On 9 June 2008, Mike and Ophelia Lazaridis, together with Ontario Premier Dalton McGuinty, University of Waterloo President David Johnston, and other guests officially broke ground on the project which will consist of three areas: one to house IQC, one for the Waterloo Institute for Nanotechnology, and a clean fabrication and metrology suite to be shared between the two institutes.[12] It will house offices, laboratory space, and areas for collaboration among researchers. The QNC opened September 21, 2012.[13]

56.6 People

As of 2014, IQC's research team consisted of 21 faculty members, 3 research assistant professors, over 40 postdoctoral fellows, and more than 100 students. The institute has expressed intentions to expand to include 33 faculty members, 50 post-doctoral fellows, and 125 students.[14]

IQC faculty members have appointments in the departments of Physics & Astronomy, Combinatorics & Optimization, Applied Mathematics, Electrical & Computer Engineering, Chemistry, and the David R. Cheriton School of Computer Science at the University of Waterloo. IQC faculty and postdoctoral fellows account for 10 of the 31 members of the Canadian Institute for Advanced Research's Quantum Information Processing Pro-

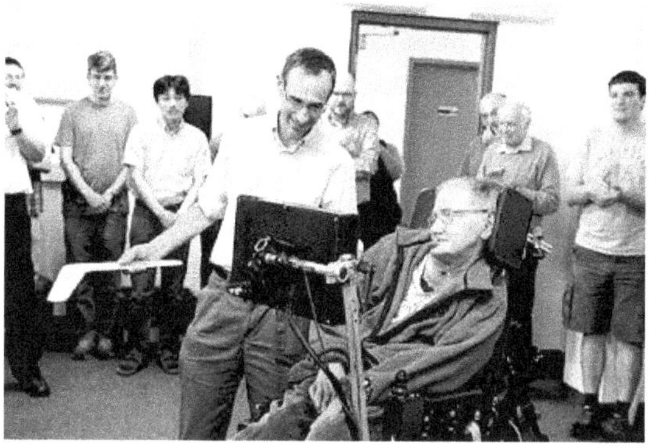

Stephen Hawking visits IQC on 21 June 2010 where Raymond Laflamme presents him with a boomerang to commemorate their work together.

gram. In addition, 3 faculty members have associate membership at the Perimeter Institute for Theoretical Physics and 11 are affiliate members.

Currently, 2 IQC faculty members hold Canada Research Chairs in various aspects of quantum information and 1 faculty member holds a Canada Excellence Research Chair.

56.6.1 Professors

- Michal Bajcsy
- Jonathan Baugh
- Andrew Childs
- Kyung Soo Choi
- Richard Cleve
- David Cory—Canada Excellence Research Chair in Quantum Information Processing
- Joseph Emerson
- Thomas Jennewein
- Robert Koenig
- Raymond Laflamme—Canada Research Chair in Quantum Information
- Debbie Leung—Canada Research Chair in Quantum Communications
- Adrian Lupascu
- Norbert Lütkenhaus
- Hamed Majedi
- Matteo Mariantoni
- Guo-Xing Miao
- Michele Mosca
- Ashwin Nayak
- Kevin Resch
- John Watrous
- Christopher Wilson

56.6.2 Notable visitors

- Sir Anthony Leggett—IQC Scientific Advisor and performs a guest lecture series annually
- Stephen Hawking—Visited June 2010, September 2012
- Seth Lloyd—Visited December 2010

56.7 See also

- Quantum computer
- Quantum cryptography
- Quantum information science
- Raymond Laflamme—director and professor at IQC
- Michele Mosca—deputy director and professor at IQC
- Anthony Leggett—winner of 2003 Nobel Prize in Physics and part-time faculty member at IQC

56.8 References

[1] "What Great Philanthropy Can Do". Institute for Quantum Computing. Retrieved 5 September 2012.

[2] no by-line.--> (2015). "Quick facts About the Institute". *University of Waterloo*. University of Waterloo. Retrieved 23 December 2015.

[3] "Strategic Direction". Institute for Quantum Computing. Retrieved 6 September 2012.

[4] "About the Institute". Institute for Quantum Computing. Retrieved 17 August 2012.

[5] "University of Waterloo Mike and Ophelia Lazaridis Quantum Nano Centre". Kuwabara Payne McKenna Blumberg Architects. Retrieved 17 August 2012.

[6] "Faculty & Research". Institute for Quantum Computing. Retrieved 6 September 2012.

[7] "Graduate Studies". Institute for Quantum Computing. Retrieved 6 September 2012.

[8] "Inaugural Women in Physics Canada Conference" (PDF). The Canadian Association of Physicists. Retrieved 6 September 2012.

[9] "Public Lectures". Institute for Quantum Computing. Retrieved 7 September 2012.

[10] "Undergraduate School on Experimental Quantum Information Processing 2012". Institute for Quantum Computing. Retrieved 6 September 2012.

[11] "Quantum Cryptography School for Young Students 2012". Institute for Quantum Computing. Retrieved 6 September 2012.

[12] "Groundbreaking for the Mike and Ophelia Lazaridis Quantum-Nano Centre". Institute for Quantum Computing. Retrieved 5 September 2012.

[13] "Mike & Ophelia Lazaridis Quantum-Nano Centre Grand Opening". University of Waterloo. Retrieved 5 September 2012.

[14] IQC Communications & Outreach, "IQC Annual Report 2012", 2012.

56.9 External links

56.10 Text and image sources, contributors, and licenses

56.10.1 Text

- **Quantum computing** *Source:* https://en.wikipedia.org/wiki/Quantum_computing?oldid=717539472 *Contributors:* AxelBoldt, LC~enwiki, CYD, Mav, Bryan Derksen, Robert Merkel, Danny, William Avery, Roadrunner, DavidLevinson, Heron, Stevertigo, Hfastedge, Edward, RTC, Michael Hardy, Tim Starling, Booyabazooka, Jarekadam, Oliver Pereira, Liftarn, Bobby D. Bryant, Dgrant, Card~enwiki, Looxix~enwiki, Cyp, Ronz, Stevenj, Aarchiba, Glenn, Cyan, AugPi, Marksuppes, Poor Yorick, Palfrey, Harry Potter, Epo~enwiki, Iseeaboar, Jengod, Charles Matthews, Timwi, Dcoetzee, Wikiborg, David Latapie, Dysprosia, Jitse Niesen, 4lex, Maximus Rex, Furrykef, Populus, Bevo, Pakaran, Jni, Phil Boswell, Gentgeen, Robbot, Wtanaka, Noldoaran, Chris 73, Jotomicron, Scott McNay, Sanders muc, RedWolf, Mattblack82, Nurg, Ojigiri~enwiki, Auric, Bkell, Alex R S, Hadal, Wereon, Fuelbottle, Asparagus, Mattflaschen, David Gerard, SimonMayer, Connelly, Giftlite, Smjg, DocWatson42, Lunkwill, DavidCary, Jao, Wolfkeeper, Tom harrison, Lupin, Sploo22, Anville, Millerc, Andris, Remy B, Matt Crypto, David Battle, Danko Georgiev, Antandrus, Beland, CSTAR, Togo~enwiki, Kevin B12, Simoneau, Sam Hocevar, Creidieki, Peter bertok, TJSwoboda, Robin klein, Kevyn, MementoVivere, Oneyd, Kate, AAAAA, MichaelMcGuffin, Indosauros, Discospinster, Rich Farmbrough, Pak21, Michal Jurosz, ArnoldReinhold, Bender235, Ben Standeven, Gauge, Fgrosshans, Pietzsche, MBisanz, El C, Susvolans, RoyBoy, WhiteTimberwolf, Kine, Bobo192, John Vandenberg, Marco de Mol~enwiki, Davidgothberg, Mjager, JavOs, Ultra megatron, Officiallyover, Hyperdivision, G Colyer, Gary, DavidB~enwiki, Keenan Pepper, Moment~enwiki, Andrewpmk, Axl, Sligocki, Scottcraig, Snowolf, Qcomp, CloudNine, DV8 2XL, Dan East, Tobyc75, Oleg Alexandrov, Revived, WilliamKF, Undecided, Simetrical, Woohookitty, Linas, Mindmatrix, RHaworth, The Belgain, Shoyer, Uncle G, Insurrectionist, Robert K S, Ruud Koot, Ajb, Wikiklrsc, GregorB, Isnow, Xiong Chiamiov, Eluchil, Turnstep, Graham87, BD2412, Qwertyus, Galwhaa, Drbogdan, Rjwilmsi, Koavf, Hulagutten, Ikh, Eyu100, X1011, Ligulem, NeonMerlin, Brighterorange, Muj0, Dar-Ape, Lotu, FlaBot, RobertG, Arnero, AndrewStuckey, Who, Mcleodm, Intgr, Edd Porter, Spasemunki, Roboto de Ajvol, Wavelength, Taejo, Foxxygirltamara, Archelon, Gaius Cornelius, Ihope127, Wimt, Hatethedj, Pagrashtak, Grafen, Vanished user 1029384756, Taed, Albedo, Brandon, Ravedave, Hyandat, Amcfreely, Voidxor, Amwebb, Durval, FoolsWar, Jeargle, Bjohnson00, Ripper234, Arthur Rubin, Mike1024, VodkaJazz, Caballero1967, MuncherOfSpleens, RG2, Rwwww, PaulCook, That Guy, From That Show!, Eigenlambda, SmackBot, David n m bond, Jrockley, Eaglizard, Edonovan, GaeusOctavius, Alsandro, Powo, GBL, Anwar saadat, KD5TVI, Chris the speller, Keegan, Jjalexand, Jon513, Tree Biting Conspiracy, Isaacsurh, The Rogue Penguin, Whispering, Colonies Chris, Sajendra, Dethme0w, V1adis1av, Onorem, Racklever, JonHarder, Justin Stafford, Wen D House, Fullstop, Speedplane, Lostart, Rajrajmarley, Pwjb, Bigmantonyd, -Ozone-, Snakeyes (usurped), DMacks, A5b, TenPoundHammer, ThurnerRupert, Vaspian, Squiggle, Harryboyles, Tomatoman, Kuru, MagnaMopus, Vincenzo.romano, Ksn, Mat8989, Nux, Count Caspian, Physis, Camilo Sanchez, SandyGeorgia, Dr.K., Elb2000, WindOwl, Supaman89, Norm mit, Dead3y3, JMK, TALlama, UncleDouggie, RekishiEJ, George100, Harold f, CRGreathouse, Ale jrb, Wafulz, CBM, Lighthead, JohnCD, Linus M., Green caterpillar, Jherm, Ispy1981, Abdullahazzam, Cydebot, Mblumber, Peterdjones, Cryptonaut, Tawkerbot4, Nol888, Manoliisfat, Headbomb, Electron9, Tellyaddict, Intestinalworms, ReallyMale, Hmrox, AntiVandalBot, Gioto, Widefox, Gnixon, Jj137, GaaraMsg, JAnDbot, Asmeurer, Husond, MER-C, Avaya1, Samuel Webster, IanOsgood, Theguyi26, Eurobas, Extropian314, Couchpotato99, Seraph 31, VoABot II, Martaen, Nyq, RJRocket53, Johannes Simon, Bubba hotep, Illspirit, David Eppstein, Beagel, Havanafreestone, Talon Artaine, Wim van Dam, B9 hummingbird hovering, RonanSandford, MartinBot, Goldsmitharmy, Crunkcar, Nzv8fan, Nikpapag, Subzbharti, Alsee, Brilliand, Jwoehr, J.delanoy, AstroHurricane001, Maurice Carbonaro, Manderso, 1mujin22, Octopus-Hands, Smite-Meister, Burgaz, Bond4154, DarkFalls, Wrdavenport, Tarotcards, Pyrospirit, AntiSpamBot, Captanpluto123, DuckFeather, Jorfer, Atropos235, Cometstyles, Onaillim, Ross Fraser, Scott Illini, Inwind, Ale2006, Turdus~enwiki, Zflood, Spin-Half, Pleasantville, Jeff G., Vrac, Gtg207u, DarkShroom, GimmeBot, Kannan karthik, Tomstdenis, MartinSieg, Selain03, Tricky Wiki44, Tre1234, Ndickson, Davidmenz, Ilia Kr., Bearian, Beeban~enwiki, Hanjabba, FKmailliW, Arcfrk, Mr. PIM, Scottywong, JRGregory, Steven Weston, SieBot, Mpassman, Moonriddengirl, Flyer22 Reborn, Bencoder, Iain David Stewart, Jdaloner, Techman224, Skippydo, AWeishaupt, Antlegs, Svick, RogueTeddy, CharlesGillingham, PatrickHoo, Jbw2, PerryTachett, Curtdbz, Denisarona, Wish wellingtons, Amir.tavasoli, Loren.wilton, Martarius, ClueBot, Avenged Eightfold, Fyyer, Alksentrs, EoGuy, Der Golem, Ammarsakaji, Daveagp, Symmetrysinger, Lartoven, Cenarium, Hans Adler, LunatikOwl, Pallinger, Troelssj, BumbleFootClown, Fattony77, HumphreyW, Bletchley, XLinkBot, Gumum, Frood, Kizeral, WikiDao, Shepelyansky, Tboonsun, Addbot, Phoneused, NotThatJames-Brown, Danielsc2, DOI bot, Jkasd, Bertrc, Mac Dreamstate, Enerjazzer, MrOllie, Favonian, Weekwhom, Peti610botH, Dmw47, Verbal, SPat, Gail, Mro, Narayan, Spikeuk14, Drpickem, Luckas-bot, Yobot, Ptbotgourou, Fraggle81, Bibliosapien, Pcap, Hannover.post, 4th-otaku, AnomieBOT, Steamturn, Greenbreen, Piano non troppo, HRV, Materialscientist, Chadkennedyonline, Citation bot, Bci2, Yongxiangu, Frankenpuppy, Xqbot, Sathimantha, Bihco, Smk65536, Stsang, REQC, Felipe Schenone, Ozhigov, Miym, GrouchoBot, Mario777Zelda, Omnipaedista, SassoBot, Sambarrows, CES1596, FrescoBot, ProtocolX, Sanpitch, Craig Pemberton, Citation bot 1, Rapsar, Jonesey95, Ekangas, WuTheFWasThat, RobinK, Xeworlebi, Sba479, DiaitaDoc, ErinM, Michael.brito, SkyMachine, Trappist the monk, Ale And Quail, LilyKitty, Leli Forte, Korepin, Murrayct, RjwilmsiBot, Becritical, EmausBot, WikitanvirBot, Beatnik8983, GoingBatty, Jmencisom, K6ka, Not enough names left, Stanford96, Basemajjan, Hasan.Abdeen, AManWithNoPlan, L0ngpar1sh, Timetraveler3.14, Glosser.ca, Qmtead, Zephyrus Tavvier, Zueignung, Mareacaspica, Rangoon11, MainFrame, ChuispastonBot, Xronon, TYelliot, ClueBot NG, Michaelmas1957, Tarpetes, This lousy T-shirt, Avonlode~enwiki, Qinqlinq345, Widr, Ojha.iiitm, Jorgenev, Helpful Pixie Bot, Martin Berka, J.Dong820, VanishedUser hjgjktyjhddgf, Frank.manus, Bibcode Bot, BG19bot, Virtualerian, JohnChrysostom, Copernicus01, Rolancito, Juuomaqk, Kaityo~enwiki, Lspiste, Tropcho, Chmarkine, Snow Blizzard, QuantumPhysicsPhD, Zedshort, Armine badalyan, V4711, Andrewayward, Twood1089, BattyBot, ArmorShieldA99, Toni 001, ChrisGualtieri, Mithoron, Sombra Corp., IjonTichyIjonTichy, Harsh 2580, SBareSSomErMig, Declaration1776, TwoTwoHello, Riverstogo, Frosty, Jamesx12345, Limit-theorem, Vetyu, Telfordbuck, Darvii, Wiki potal, Hunterrc95, ThorPorre, Myconix, LudicrousTripe, Joshvp99, Jwratner1, Ginsuloft, Martin Hovorka, GiantPeachTime, W. P. Uzer, Fedora99, Yllihp, Erudite Manatee, Anrnusna, Lyoova, Ajbilan, Linuxjava, JaconaFrere, I2000s, Wyn.junior, Lagoset, Monkbot, Ozdarka, Jaisb133, Carvalho1988, TopherDobson, Frankthetankk, Wikibaron666, Singularscribe, TheCoffeeAddict, PanoramicSequence, Ggf4t, Yogeshyvd, PAkeystone, ParrotOx, KasparBot, Nklirs, Renfredxh, Sjhessing-yale, SimonPIC, Jeamsid, Reetssydney, Pijushbhatta, Computerfixmeister, DoesThisShowUpOnHatnote, Scolombano, JKRLife, Yousifisalad and Anonymous: 692
- **Quantum finite automata** *Source:* https://en.wikipedia.org/wiki/Quantum_finite_automata?oldid=686944722 *Contributors:* Andris, Linas, Qwertyus, Rjwilmsi, SmackBot, Colonies Chris, Sct72, Cícero, Myasuda, Bongwarrior, David Eppstein, Fractional ideal, Sharp uzumaki, MagnesianPhoenix, Addbot, Yobot, LilHelpa, RobinK, Ashutosh y0078, John of Reading, BG19bot, Tremechus, DavidLeighEllis, Fuzzyfog and Anonymous: 13
- **Quantum information** *Source:* https://en.wikipedia.org/wiki/Quantum_information?oldid=715693327 *Contributors:* Seb, Stevertigo, Nealmcb, Michael Hardy, Dgrant, Cipapuc, Charles Matthews, Dcoetzee, Phys, Bearcat, Sanders muc, Naddy, Pengo, Antandrus,

Itchy~enwiki, CSTAR, Creidieki, Kipton, Sole Soul, Mwilde, The JPS, Linas, Isnow, Mandarax, BD2412, Margosbot~enwiki, J S Lundeen, Gene.arboit, Eliium, Robertvan1, Uukgoblin, SmackBot, Tracy Hall, Dave Kielpinski, Skatche, Pieterkonings~enwiki, Tim bates, CmdrObot, Mct mht, Alinihatekenwiki, Kilor, Widefox, Knotwork, DGG, Maurice Carbonaro, STBotD, Kenneth M Burke, VolkovBot, Ballhausflip, Dojarca, Guillaume2303, Ckwongb, Voorlandt, Jamelan, Billinghurst, Cnilep, Chemako0606, Flyer22 Reborn, KathrynLybarger, Skippydo, DFRussia, Ammarsakaji, Arjayay, Mastertek, Shishir0610, Shepelyansky, Addbot, Looie496, OrgasGirl, Ibayn, AnomieBOT, Materialscientist, 3malchio, FrescoBot, Sbalian, Adlerbot, Korepin, John of Reading, Quondum, Abdelaty, BG19bot, Todrobbins, Physicsch, Dexbot, Quantumjenny, I2000s, Velvel2, BooBoo314159, KasparBot and Anonymous: 60

- **Quantum mutual information** *Source:* https://en.wikipedia.org/wiki/Quantum_mutual_information?oldid=607162206 *Contributors:* PAR, Jheald, Linas, Wavelength, Mct mht, Avaya1, Cuzkatzimhut, ClueBot, Mild Bill Hiccup, SoxBot III, Addbot, Yobot, Reaper Eternal, ZéroBot, JurgenShang and Anonymous: 6
- **Quantum information science** *Source:* https://en.wikipedia.org/wiki/Quantum_information_science?oldid=684997215 *Contributors:* Jarekadam, Sanders muc, Liberatus, Mwilde, Linas, Quiddity, Margosbot~enwiki, Gene.arboit, CarlHewitt, NawlinWiki, Zwobot, SmackBot, Guntram~enwiki, Cícero, Trbdavies, Dbtfz, Mct mht, ST47, Bridgeplayer, Kostisl, Coppertwig, Julia Neumann, LokiClock, Eponyme13, Bender2k14, XLinkBot, Addbot, Danielidar, Steve Quinn, RA0808, YnnusOiramo, ClueBot NG, Jimbing, St.andyjkk, Quantumjenny, KasparBot, Mel12345678987654321 and Anonymous: 28
- **Quantum mechanics** *Source:* https://en.wikipedia.org/wiki/Quantum_mechanics?oldid=717607682 *Contributors:* AxelBoldt, Paul Drye, Chenyu, Derek Ross, CYD, Eloquence, Mav, The Anome, AstroNomer, Taral, Ap, Magnus~enwiki, Ed Poor, XJaM, Rgamble, Christian List, William Avery, Roadrunner, Ellmist, Mjb, Olivier, Stevertigo, Bdesham, Michael Hardy, Tim Starling, JakeVortex, Vudujava, Owl, Norm, Gabbe, Menchi, Ixfd64, Axlrosen, TakuyaMurata, Shanemac, Alfio, Looxix~enwiki, Mdebets, Ahoerstemeier, Cyp, Stevenj, J-Wiki, Theresa knott, Snoyes, Gyan, Nanobug, Cipapuc, Jebba, Александър, Glenn, Kyokpae~enwiki, Nikai, Dod1, Jouster, Mxn, Charles Matthews, Tantalate, Timwi, Stone, Jitse Niesen, Rednblu, Wik, Dtgm, PatrickOMoran, Tpbradbury, Nv8200pa, Phys, Bevo, Jecar, Fvw, Stormie, Sokane, Optim, Bcorr, Johnleemk, Jni, Rogper~enwiki, Robbot, Ke4roh, Midom, MrJones, Jaleho, Astronautics~enwiki, Fredrik, Chris 73, Moncrief, Goethean, Bkalafut, Lowellian, Centic, Gandalf61, StefanPernar, Academic Challenger, Rursus, Texture, Matty j, Moink, Hadal, Papadopc, Johnstone, Fuelbottle, Lupo, HaeB, Mcdutchie, Xanzzibar, Tea2min, David Gerard, Enochlau, Ancheta Wis, Decumanus, Giftlite, Donvinzk, DocWatson42, ScudLee, Awolf002, Barbara Shack, Harp, Fudoreaper, Lethe, Fastfission, Zigger, Monedula, Wwoods, Anville, Alison, Bensaccount, Tromer, Sukael, Andris, Jason Quinn, Gracefool, Solipsist, Nathan Hamblen, Foobar, SWAdair, Mckaysalisbury, AdamJacobMuller, Utcursch, CryptoDerk, Knutux, Yath, Amarvc, Pcarbonn, Stephan Leclercq, Antandrus, JoJan, Savant1984, Jossi, Karol Langner, CSTAR, Rdsmith4, APH, Anythingyouwant, Thincat, Aaron Einstein, Edsanville, Robin klein, Muijz, Zondor, Guybrush, Grunt, Lacrimosus, Chris Howard, L-H, Ta bu shi da yu, Freakofnurture, Sfngan, Venu62, Spiffy sperry, CALR, Ultratomio, KeyStroke, Noisy, Discospinster, Caroline Thompson, Rich Farmbrough, H0riz0n, FT2, Pj.de.bruin, Hidaspal, Pjacobi, Vsmith, Wk muriithi, Silence, Smyth, Phil179, Moogoo, WarEagleTH, Smear~enwiki, Paul August, Dmr2, Bender235, ESkog, Nabla, Dataphile, Dpotter, Floorsheim, El C, Lankiveil, Kross, Laurascudder, Edward Z. Yang, Shanes, Spearhead, RoyBoy, Femto, MPS, Bobo192, Army1987, John Vandenberg, AugustinMa, Geek84, GTubio, Clarkbhm, SpaceMonkey, Sjoerd visscher, I9Q79oL78KiL0QTFHgyc, Sriram sh, Matt McIrvin, Sasquatch, BM, Firewheel, MtB, Nsaa, Storm Rider, Alansohn, Gary, ChristopherWillis, Tek022, ZiggyZig, Keenan Pepper, La hapalo, Gpgarrettboast, Pippu d'Angelo, PAR, Batmanand, Hdeasy, Bart133, Snowolf, Wtmitchell, Tycho, Leoadec, Jon Cates, Mikeo, Dominic, Bsadowski1, W7KyzmJt, GabrielF, DV8 2XL, Alai, Nick Mks, KTC, Dan100, Chughtai, Falcorian, Oleg Alexandrov, Ashujo, Ott, Feezo, OwenX, Woohookitty, Linas, Superstring, Tripodics, Shoyer, StradivariusTV, Kzollman, Kosher Fan, JeremyA, Tylerni7, Pchov, GeorgeOrr, Mpatel, Adhalanay, Firien, Wikiklrsc, GregorB, AndriyK, SeventyThree, Wayward, Prashanthns, DL5MDA, Palica, Pfalstad, Graham87, Magister Mathematicae, Chun-hian, FreplySpang, Baker APS, JIP, RxS, Search4Lancer, Canderson7, Sjö, Saperaud~enwiki, Rjwilmsi, Jake Wartenberg, Linuxbeak, Tangotango, Bruce1ee, Darguz Parsilvan, Mike Peel, Pasky, HappyCamper, Ligulem, The wub, Ttwaring, Reinis, Hermione1980, Sango123, Oo64eva, St33lbird, Kevmitch, Titoxd, Das Nerd, Alejo2083, FlaBot, Moskvax, RobertG, Urbansky~enwiki, Arnero, Latka, Nihiltres, Pathoschild, Quuxplusone, Srleffler, Kri, Cpcheung, Phoenix2~enwiki, Chobot, DVdm, Gwernol, Niz, YurikBot, Wavelength, Paulraine, Arado, Loom91, Xihr, GLaDOS, Khatharr, Firas@user, Gaius Cornelius, Chaos, Rsrikanth05, Rodier, Wimt, Anomalocaris, Royalbroil, David R. Ingham, NawlinWiki, Grafen, NickBush24, RazorICE, Stephen e nelson, JocK, SCZenz, Randolf Richardson, Vb, E2mb0t~enwiki, Tony1, Syrthiss, SFC9394, DeadEyeArrow, Bota47, Kkmurray, Werdna, Bmju, Wknight94, WAS 4.250, FF2010, Donbert, Light current, Enormousdude, 21655, Zzuuzz, TheKoG, Lt-wiki-bot, Nielad, Closedmouth, Ketsuekigata, E Wing, Brina700, Modify, Dspradau, Netrapt, Petri Krohn, Badgettrg, Peter, Willtron, Mebden, RG2, GrinBot~enwiki, Mejor Los Indios, Sbyrnes321, CIreland, Luk, Itub, Hvitlys, SmackBot, Paulc1001, Moeron, Rex the first, InverseHypercube, KnowledgeOfSelf, Royalguard11, K-UNIT, Lagalag, Pgk, Jagged 85, Clpo13, Chairman S., Pxfbird, Grey Shadow, Delldot, Petgraveyard, Weiguxp, David Woolley, Lithium412, Philmurray, Yamaguchi??, Robbjedi, Gilliam, Slaniel, Betacommand, Skizzik, Dauto, Holy Ganga, JSpudeman, Modusoperandi, Amatulic, Stevenwagner, DetlevSchm, MK8, Jprg1966, MalafayaBot, Marks87, Silly rabbit, Complexica, Colonies Chris, Darth Panda, Sajendra, Warbirdadmiral, El Chupacabra, Zhinz, Can't sleep, clown will eat me, Physika~enwiki, Scott3, Scray, ApolloCreed, Ackbeet, Le fantome de l'opera, Onorem, Surfcuba, Voyajer, Addshore, Stiangk, Paul E T, Huon, Khoikhoi, Kingdon, DenisDiderot, Cybercobra, Nakon, Nick125, SnappingTurtle, Dreadstar, Richard001, Akriasas, Freemarket, Weregerbil, DeFoaBuSe, DMacks, Salamurai, LeoNomis, Sadi Carnot, Pilotguy, Byelf2007, Xezlec, DJIndica, Akubra, Rory096, Bcasterline, Harryboyles, JzG, Richard L. Peterson, RTejedor, AmiDaniel, UberCryxic, Wtwilson3, Zslevi, LWF, Gobonobo, Jaganath, JorisvS, Evan Robidoux, Mgiganteus1, Zarniwoot, Goodnightmush, Jordan M, Ex nihil, SirFozzie, Waggers, MarphyBlack, Caiaffa, Asyndeton, Dan Gluck, BranStark, Iridescent, JMK, Dreftymac, Joseph Solis in Australia, UncleDouggie, Rnb, Hikui87~enwiki, Cain47, Mbenzdabest, Nturton, Civil Engineer III, Cleric12121, Tawkerbot2, Chetvorno, Carborn1, Mustbe, SkyWalker, JForget, Frovingslosh, Ale jrb, Peace love and feminism, Wafulz, Sir Vicious, Asmackey, Dycedarg, Lavateraguy, Van helsing, The ed17, Bad2101, Jayunderscorezero, BeenAroundAWhile, JohnCD, Nunquam Dormio, Harriemkali, Swwright, Wquester, N2e, Melicans, Smallpond, Myasuda, Gregbard, Xana's Servant, Dragon's Blood, Cydebot, Wrwrwr, Beek man, Meznaric, Jack O'Lantern, Peterdjones, Meno25, Gogo Dodo, Islander, DangApricot, NijaMunki, Pascal.Tesson, Hughgr, Benvogel, Michael C Price, Doug Weller, Christian75, DumbBOT, FastLizard4, Waxigloo, Amit Moscovich, FrancoGG, CieloEstrellado, Thijs!bot, Epbr123, Derval Sloan, Koeplinger, Mbell, N5iln, Headbomb, Marek69, Ujm, Second Quantization, Martin Hedegaard, Philippe, CharlotteWebb, Nick Number, MichaelMaggs, Sbandrews, Mentifisto, Austin Maxwell, Cyclonenim, AntiVandalBot, Luna Santin, Widefox, Tkirkman, Eveross, Lontax, Grafnita, Rakniz, Prolog, Gnixon, CStar, TimVickers, Dylan Lake, Casomerville, Danger, Farosdaughter, Tim Shuba, North Shoreman, Yellowdesk, Glennwells, Byrgenwulf, GaaraMsg, Figma, JAnDbot, Leuko, Husond, Superior IQ Genius, MER-C, CosineKitty, Matthew Fennell, Eurobas, IJMacD, Andonic, Dcooper, Hut 8.5, 100110100, Skewwhiffy, Four Dog Night, Acroterion, Magioladitis, Connormah, Mattb112885, Bongwarrior, VoABot II, AtticusX, JamesBWatson, SHCarter, FagChops, Bfiene, Rivertorch, Michele123, Zooloo, Jmartinsson, Thunderhead~enwiki, Couki, Catgut, Indon, ClovisPt, Dirac66, 28421u2232nfenfcenc, Joe hill, Schumi555, Adventurer, Cpl Syx, Robb37, Quantummotion, DerHexer, Chaujie328, Khalid Mahmood, Teardrop onthefire, Guitarspecs, Info D, Seba5618, Gjd001, CiA10386, MartinBot, Arjun01, Rettetast, Mike6271, Fpaiano~enwiki, CommonsDelinker, AlexiusHoratius, Andrej.westermann, Tgeairn, Dinkytown,

J.delanoy, DrKay, Trusilver, Kaesle, Numbo3, NightFalcon90909, Uncle Dick, Maurice Carbonaro, Kevin aylward, 5Q5, StonedChipmunk, Foober, Acalamari, Metaldev, Bot-Schafter, Katalaveno, DarkFalls, McSly, Bustamonkey2003, Ignatzmice, Tarotcards, JayJasper, Gcad92, Detah, LucianLachance, Midnight Madness, NewEnglandYankee, Rwessel, Nin0rz4u 2nv, SJP, MKoltnow, KCinDC, Han Solar de Harmonics, Cmichael, Juliancolton, Cometstyles, MoForce, Chao129, Elenseel, Wfaze, Samlyn.josfyn, Martial75, GrahamHardy, CardinalDan, Sheliak, Spellcast, Signalhead, Pgb23, Zakuragi, MBlue2020, Pleasantville, LokiClock, Lear's Fool, Soliloquial, Philip Trueman, TXiKiBoT, Oshwah, Maximillion Pegasus, SanfordEsq, RyanB88, SCriBu, Nxavar, Sean D Martin, Sankalpdravid, ChooseAnother, Qxz, Someguy1221, Liko81, Bsharvy, Olly150, XeniaKon, Clarince63, Seraphim, Saibod, Fizzackerly, Zolot, Raymondwinn, David in DC, Handsome Pete, Geometry guy, Ilyushka88, Leavage, Krazywrath, V81, Sodicadl, RandomXYZb, Lerdthenerd, Andy Dingley, Enigmaman, Meters, Lindsaiv, Synthebot, Antixt, Falcon8765, Enviroboy, Spinningspark, H1nomaru senshi, The Devil's Advocate, Monty845, AlleborgoBot, Nagy, The Mad Genius, Logan, PGWG, DarthBotto, Vitalikk, Belsazar, Katzmik, EmxBot, Givegains, Kbrose, Mk2rhino, YohanN7, SieBot, Ivan Štambuk, Nibbleboob, WereSpielChequers, Dawn Bard, AdevarTruth, RJaguar3, Hekoshi, Yintan, 4RM0~enwiki, Ujjwol, Bentogoa, Jc-S0CO, JSpung, Arjen Dijksman, Oxymoron83, Antonio Lopez, Henry Delforn (old), Hello71, AnonGuy, Lightmouse, Radzewicz, Hobartimus, Jaquesthehunter, Michael Courtney, Macy, Hatster301, Swegei, Curlymeatball38, Quackbumper, Coldcreation, Zenbullets, StaticGull, Heptarchy of teh Anglo-Saxons, baby, Mygerardromance, Fishnet37222, Stentor7, Mouselb, Randy Kryn, Velvetron, ElectronicsEnthusiast, Darrellpenta, Soporaeternus, Martarius, ClueBot, NickCT, Mod.torrentrealm, Scottstensland, Yeahyeahkickball, The Thing That Should Not Be, EMC125, Zero over zero, Infrasonik, MichaelVernonDavis, Herakles01, Drmies, Cp111, Diafanakrina, Mackafi92, Mrsastrochicken, VandalCruncher, Agge1000, Otolemur crassicaudatus, Ridge Runner, Neverquick, Asdf1990, DragonBot, Djr32, Ondon, Excirial, HounsGut, Welsh-girl-Lowri, Quercus basaseachicensis, Jusdafax, Krackenback, Winston365, Brews ohare, Sukaj, Viduoke, NuclearWarfare, Ice Cold Beer, Arjayay, Terra Xin, PhySusie, Kding, Imalad, The Red, Mikaey, SchreiberBike, Vlatkovedral, Jfioeawfjdls453, Thingg, Russel Mcpigmin, Aitias, Scalhotrod, Versus22, Mafiaparty303, SoxBot III, Apparition11, Mrvanner, Crowsnest, Vanished user uih38riiw4hjlsd, DumZiBoT, Finalnight, CBMIBM, Javafreakin, X41, XLinkBot, Megankerr, Yokabozeez, Arthur chos, Odenluna, Matthewsasse1, Feinoha, Ajcheema, AndreNatas, Paul bunion, WikHead, Loopism, NellieBly, Mifter, JinJian, Truthnlove, Airplaneman, Billcosbyislonelypart2, Mojska, Stephen Poppitt, Willieru18, Tayste, Addbot, Ryan ley, 11341134a, Willking1979, Manuel Trujillo Berges, Kadski, TylerM37, Wareagles18, XTRENCHARD29x, 11341134b, Tcncv, Betterusername, Captaintucker, Robertd514, Fgnievinski, Mjamja, Harrytipper, SunDragon34, Blethering Scot, Ronhjones, PandaSaver, WMdeMuynck, Aboctok, JoshTW, CanadianLinuxUser, Looie496, Cst17, MrOllie, BuffaloBill90, Mitchellsims08, Chzz, AnnaFrance, Favonian, LinkFA-Bot, Adolfman, Brufnus, Barak Sh, AgadaUrbanit, Ehrenkater, Tide rolls, Lightbot, NoEdward, Romaioi, Jan eissfeldt, Teles, Jarble, Csdavis1, Ttasterul, Luckas-bot, Yobot, OrgasGirl, Tohd8BohaithuGh1, TaBOT-zerem, Niout, II MusLiM HyBRiD II, Kan8eDie, Nallimbot, Brougham96, KamikazeBot, Fearingfearitself, Positivetruthintent, IW.HG, Solo Zone, Jackthegrape, Eric-Wester, Magog the Ogre, Armegdon, N1RK4UDSK714, Octavianvs, AnomieBOT, Captain Quirk, Jim1138, IRP, Rnpg1014, Piano non troppo, AdjustShift, Giants27, Materialscientist, Gierens22, Supppersmart, The High Fin Sperm Whale, Citation bot, Bci2, Frankenpuppy, LilHelpa, The Firewall, Joshuafilmer, Rightly, Mollymop, Xqbot, Nxtid, Sionus, Raaziq, Amareto2, Melmann, Capricorn42, Jostylr, Dbroesch, Mark Swiggle, TripLikeIDo, Benvirg89, Sokratesinabasket, Gilo1969, Physprof, Grim23, P99am, Qwertyuio 132, Gap9551, Almabot, Polgo, GrouchoBot, Abce2, Jagbag2, Frosted14, Toofy mcjack34, Richard.decal, Qzd800, Trurle, Omnipaedista, Mind my edits, WilliunWeales, Kesaloma, Charvest, The Spam-a-nata, Dale Ritter, Shipunits, FaTony, Gr33k b0i, Shadowjams, Adrignola, Dingoatscritch, Spakwee, A. di M., Naturelles, Dougofborg, Cigarettizer, ⍰⍰, C.c. hopper, JoshC306, Chjoaygame, GliderMaven, Bboydill, Magnagr, Kroflin, Tobby72, Pepper, Commander zander, Guy82914, PhysicsExplorer, Kenneth Dawson, Colinue, Steve Quinn, N4tur4le, Pratik.mallya, Razataza, Machine Elf 1735, 06twalke, TTGL, Izodman2012, Xenfreak, Iquseruniv, HamburgerRadio, Citation bot 1, Cheryledbernard, Greg HWWOK Shaw, WQUlrich, Brettwats, Pinethicket, I dream of horses, Pink Bull, Tom.Reding, Lithium cyanide, DanielGlazer, Deaddogwalking, FloridaSpaceCowboy, RobinK, Liarliar2009, JeffreyVest, Seattle Jörg, Reconsider the static, Fredkinfollower, Superlions123, GreenReflections, Tjlafave, FoxBot, Chris5858, Anonwhymus, Trappist the monk, Buddy23Lee, 3peasants, Beta Orionis, Train2104, Hickorybark, Creativethought20, Lotje, PorkHeart, Michael9422, Lmp883, Bowlofknowledge, Leesy1106, Doc Quintana, Reaper Eternal, Azatos, SeriousGrinz, Pokemon274, Specs112, Vera.tetrix, Earthandmoon, MicioGeremia, Tbhotch, Jesse V., Sideways713, Dannideak, Factosis, MR87, Borki0, Taylo9487, Updatehelper, Seawolf1111, Onesmoothlefty, Carowinds, Bento00, Beyond My Ken, Andy chase, WildBot, Deadlyops, Phyguy03, EmausBot, John of Reading, Davejohnsan, Orphan Wiki, Bookalign, WikitanvirBot, Mahommed alpac, Dr Aaij, Gfoley4, Roxbreak, Word2need, Beatnik8983, Alamadte, Racerx11, Dickwet89, GoingBatty, Minimac's Clone, NotAnonymous0, Dmblub, KHamsun, Wham Bam Rock II, Solarra, Stevenganzburg, Elee, Tommy2010, Uploadvirus, Wikipelli, Dcirovic, Elitedarklord dragonslyer 3.14159, AsceticRose, JSquish, AlexBG72, White Trillium, Harddk, Checkingfax, Angelsages, NickJRocks95, Fæ, Josve05a, Stanford96, MithrandirAgain, Imperial Monarch, 1howardsr1, Plotfeat, User10 5, Brazmyth, Raggot, Alvindclopez, Dalma112211221122, Wayne Slam, Tolly4bolly, EricWesBrown, Mattedia, Jacksccsi, L Kensington, Qmtead, Lemony123, Final00123, Maschen, Donner60, HCPotter, Scientific29, Notolder, Pat walls1, ChuispastonBot, Roberts Ken, RockMagnetist, TYelliot, Llightex, DJDunsie, DASHBotAV, The beings, Whoop whoop pull up, Isocliff, ClueBot NG, KagakuKyouju, Professormeowington, CocuBot, MelbourneStar, This lousy T-shirt, Satellizer, MC ShAdYzOnE, Baseball Watcher, Sabri Al-Safi, Arespectablecitizen, Jj1236, Braincricket, ScottSteiner, Wikishotaro, Widr, Machdeep, Ciro.santilli, Mikeiysnake, Dorje108, Anupmehra, Theopolisme, MerllwBot, BlooddRose, Helpful Pixie Bot, Novusuna, Olaniyob, Billybobjow, Leo3232, Elochai26, Jubobroff, Ieditpagesincorrectly, Bibcode Bot, Psaup09, Lowercase sigmabot, Saurabhagat, BG19bot, Physics1717171, Brannan.brouse, ThisLaughingGuyRightHere, Happyboy2011, Hashem sfarim, The Mark of the Beast, Northamerica1000, Declan12321, Cyberpower678, BobTheBuilder1997, Yowhatsupdude, Metricopolus, Solomon7968, Mark Arsten, Bigsean0300, Chander, Guythundar, Joydeep, Trevayne08, Roopydoop55, Aranea Mortem, Jamessweeen, F=q(E+v^B), Vagigi, Snow Blizzard, Hipsupful, Laye Mehta, Glacialfox, Winston Trechane, In11Chaudri, Achowat, Bfong2828, PinkShinyRose, Tm14, Lieutenant of Melkor, Penguinstorm300, Pkj61, Williamxu26, Jnracv, Samwalton9, Lbkt, Kisokj, Bakkedal, Cyberbot II, StopTheCrackpots, Callum Inglis, Davidwhite18, Macven, Khazar2, Adwaele, Gdrg22, BuzyBody, BrightStarSky, Dexbot, Webclient101, Garuda0001, William.winkworth, Belief action, Harrycol123, Saehry, Jamesx12345, Josophie, Brirush, Athomeinkobe, Thepalerider2012, JustAMuggle, Reatlas, Joeinwiki, Mmcev106, Darvii, Loganfalco, Everymorning, Jakec, Rod Pierce, Backendgaming, DavidLeighEllis, Geometriccentaur, Rauledc, Eapbar, Ryomaiinsai12345, Pr.malek, LieutenantLatvia, Quadratic formula, Desswarrior, Ray brock, The Herald, Shawny J, DrYusuf786, Bubblynoah, Asherkirschbaum, W. P. Uzer, Cfunkera, SJ Defender, Melquiades Babilonia, Atticus Finch28, Dfranz1012, PhuongAlex, JaconaFrere, 15petedc, AspaasBekkelund, QuantumMatt101, Htp0020, Derenek, Russainbiaed na, Internucleotide, Emmaellix, Renegade469, Nikrulz07, HiYahhFriend, Johntrollston1233, BethNaught, HolLak456, Castielsbloodyface, Trackteur, Black789Green456, Kinetic37, Theskruff, DaleReese1962, Zazzi01, Garfield Garfield, Potatomuncher2000, 3primetime3, 420noscopekills, HMSLavender, The Original Bob, EvilLair, 427454LSX, ChamithN, Suman Chatterjee DHEP, HelloFriendsOfPlanetEarth, Zppix, Audiorew, Trentln1852, CheeseButterfly, Blackbeast75, Justdausualtf, Whijus19, Govindaharihari, Dubsir, Virophage, Lanzdsey, Tetra quark, Isambard Kingdom, Rohin2002, Bloodorange1234, Harsh mahesheka, Skipfortyfour, Username1234567890101112131415161718l920, Camisboss5, WebdriverHead, SamuelFey666, Cnbr15, Jerodlycett, KasparBot, MintyTurtle01, Peter Richard Obama, Sweepy, Pengyulong7, TheDoctor07, Tropicalkitty, Jpskycak, Javathunderman, Seventhorbitday, 420BlazeItPhaggot, Jeffjef, Matthewadinatajapati, Fthatshiit, Zackwright07,

RedExplosiveswiki, Urmomisdumb69, JonahSpars, Eisengetribe13, PlayGatered, Eep03, PANDA12346 and Anonymous: 1776

- **Quantum superposition** *Source:* https://en.wikipedia.org/wiki/Quantum_superposition?oldid=715176262 *Contributors:* Marj Tiefert, Andre Engels, David spector, Stevertigo, Erik Zachte, SebastianHelm, Stevenj, J-Wiki, Reddi, 4lex, Chuunen Baka, Robbot, Fuelbottle, Widsith, Giftlite, DocWatson42, Bradeos Graphon, Curps, Jason Quinn, Mboverload, Tothebarricades.tk, Sonett72, Dcole, Discospinster, Jmayer, El C, Visualerror, Greenleaf~enwiki, PopUpPirate, Keenan Pepper, Burn, Woohookitty, Yurik, Rjwilmsi, John187, Fissile, Sdornan, Jrtayloriv, Wavelength, Retodon8, Gene.arboit, David R. Ingham, Amakuha, Madkour, Dna-webmaster, KnightRider~enwiki, SmackBot, MattieTK, Incnis Mrsi, Eskimbot, Jpvinall, Aksi great, Gilliam, D.328, Regford, Pieter1, DJIndica, T g7, Phancy Physicist, Physis, Clark Mobarry, Dl2000, D Hill, Marysunshine, Myasuda, Peterdjones, Mbell, Marek69, OrenBochman, Nick Number, Spencer, Martinkunev, David Eppstein, Jakecs50, Tgeairn, J.delanoy, Maurice Carbonaro, NewEnglandYankee, Erwinraysparks, Sheliak, VolkovBot, GWheaton, Oshwah, Anonymous Dissident, Graymornings, Voldemore, Likebox, Pasiasty, Nyelvmark, Randy Kryn, Mx3, Imonmywaynow, Blanchardb, Aggel000, Vksgeneric, Kville105125, Mastertek, Teraldthecat, MystBot, Stephen Poppitt, Addbot, Betterusername, Non-dropframe, Chemuser, Dr. Universe, Weekwhom, Fireaxe888, JeremyDanielBenjamin, Zorrobot, Luckas-bot, Yobot, DrTrigon, Examtester, AnomieBOT, Citation bot, Durand QM, LilHelpa, Magnesium, NOrbeck, GrouchoBot, RibotBOT, Waleswatcher, ??, Chjoaygame, FrescoBot, Tangent747, Westwoodct, Radiohead40540057, Mikespedia, Seattle Jörg, Trappist the monk, RjwilmsiBot, John of Reading, Slightsmile, Adamcheasley, Wikipelli, Mz7, Nobelium, Kusername, Wiggles007, Zephyrus Tavvier, Donner60, 31428571J, ClueBot NG, Jasper3838, CocuBot, Hermajesty21, Zefoteus~enwiki, Lonewolf9196, Jubobroff, Wbm1058, Bibcode Bot, DBigXray, BG19bot, Electrical & computer engineer, Alfreema, Mn-imhotep, Mitch H. Waylee, Davidcpearce, BattyBot, PatheticCopyEditor, Stormygirlie, ChrisGualtieri, Frosty, Graphium, AHusain314, RootSword, Ozdarka, M dasd12066, Poloniumll, Serevix, Knife-in-the-drawer, JJMC89, MintyFreshBreath, Ihsanturk, Watchtheworld and Anonymous: 140

- **Bit** *Source:* https://en.wikipedia.org/wiki/Bit?oldid=717623254 *Contributors:* Derek Ross, Uriyan, Bryan Derksen, Tarquin, Stephen Gilbert, Andre Engels, Fritzlein, Christian List, Aldie, PierreAbbat, SimonP, Boleslav Bobcik, Imran, Mjb, Heron, Hirzel, B4hand, Dwheeler, Frecklefoot, Edward, Michael Hardy, Lousyd, Liftarn, SGBailey, Ixfd64, Fruge~enwiki, Anders Feder, Mac, Docu, Basswulf, Andres, Kaihsu, Jonik, Mxn, Iseeaboar, Hashar, Ralesk, Gutza, DJ Clayworth, Jcajacob, Omegatron, Spikey, Vaceituno, Indefatigable, Dbabbitt, Robbot, Fredrik, Schutz, Jmabel, Altenmann, Naddy, Mdrejhon, Centrx, Giftlite, DocWatson42, Harp, Fleminra, Markus Kuhn, Frencheigh, Jorge Stolfi, Siroxo, AlistairMcMillan, VampWillow, Bobblewik, Vadmium, Stevietheman, Bact, Quadell, Rdsmith4, Icairns, Marc Mongenet, Lev, Troels Arvin, Urhixidur, Ukexpat, Andreas Kaufmann, Random account 47, NathanHurst, Guanabot, Smyth, Paul August, Sietse Snel, Art LaPella, Aaronbrick, Longhair, Viriditas, StoatBringer, R. S. Shaw, Johnteslade, SpeedyGonsales, Toh, Boredzo, Towel401, Gsklee, Jumbuck, Karlthegreat, CyberSkull, PoptartKing, PAR, Wanderingstan, Dirac1933, TenOfAllTrades, Duplode, Tariqabjotu, Woohookitty, Shreevatsa, Armando, Marudubshinki, Mandarax, Graham87, Kbdank71, Rjwilmsi, Geimas5~enwiki, Srleffler, Glenn L, Physchim62, E Pluribus Anthony, YurikBot, Sceptre, FrenchIsAwesome, Gunblade~enwiki, Splash, Stephenb, Archelon, Yyy, Wimt, NawlinWiki, Grafen, Nick, Cholmes75, LaraCroft NYC, E rulez, Mikeblas, RL0919, Zwobot, Ospalh, Jeh, Alan Millar, Light current, Lt-wiki-bot, Sharkb, Dspradau, JLaTondre, Rwwww, Dkasak, Groyolo, SmackBot, Monkeyblue, Bomac, KocjoBot~enwiki, Thunderboltz, Eskimbot, Mgreenbe, BiT, Ohnoitsjamie, Tennekis, Rmosler2100, Anwar saadat, TimBentley, MK8, Oli Filth, Jerome Charles Potts, Nbarth, Discharger12, JonHarder, Juandev, VMS Mosaic, SundarBot, Calbaer, BostonMA, Cybercobra, Mwtoews, Demicx, PanBK, Ex nihil, George The Dragon, Vagary, Bobamnertiopsis, Vaughan Pratt, Aubrey Jaffer, Neelix, Chrisahn, NE Ent, Gregbard, Sopoforic, Mblumber, Kallerdis, Hendrib, Dusty relic, Ameliorate!, Omicronpersei8, Epbr123, Shmaltz, Michagal, N5iln, Mojo Hand, Sobreira, Neil916, JustAGal, Philippe, AlefZet, Escarbot, AntiVandalBot, Luna Santin, Widefox, Guy Macon, Opelio, Samsbc12, Ozzieboy, Quintote, Leuko, BrotherE, Bongwarrior, VoABot II, JamesBWatson, Animum, Dan Pelleg, 0612, Holistic~enwiki, MartinBot, Flexdream, R'n'B, Nono64, J.delanoy, Hrollins, Ten-K, NerdyNSK, Александр Сигачёв, VolkovBot, DagnyB, Tesscass, Philip Trueman, Charleca, TXiKiBoT, Oshwah, PaulTanenbaum, RiverStyx23, Jesin, Synthebot, Spinningspark, YordanGeorgiev, Thunderbird2, EmxBot, Neparis, Kbrose, Bill Riojas Mclemore, SieBot, JoeyLJ, Mar(c), Happysailor, Flyer22 Reborn, E.shijir, Harry-, Lightmouse, SimonTrew, Ericjul, BenoniBot~enwiki, OKBot, Paulinho28, Troy 07, ClueBot, Quadstrike, The Thing That Should Not Be, Mild Bill Hiccup, ChandlerMapBot, LeoFrank, Excirial, Jusdafax, NotSarenne, Jiemurat, Thehelpfulone, MpMadhuranga, Aitias, Johnuniq, SoxBot III, DumZiBoT, Williams.daryl, Freakinewirddawg, GSMR, CarsracBot, RTG, AnnaFrance, 5 albert square, Tide rolls, Alfie66, Luckas-bot, Synapses12, Yobot, Synapses13, OrgasGirl, The Earwig, Terryblack, Ayrton Prost, François Melchior, Naderra, AnomieBOT, Wikifane12, 1exec1, Whittlepedia, 9258fahsflkh917fas, Zangar, Citation bot, Kuwaity26, TechControl, Almabot, RibotBOT, Shadowjams, GiacomoV, FrescoBot, Nicolas Perrault III, LucienBOT, GEBStgo, MathFacts, Weetoddid, Big threatening button, MacMed, Pinethicket, Vicenarian, HRoestBot, Brad Polard, MastiBot, TobeBot, Dinamik-bot, Vrenator, Bluefist, Sabisteven, Suffusion of Yellow, Unbitwise, Tbhotch, Marie Poise, DARTH SIDIOUS 2, EmausBot, Lanceallenhall, Wikipelli, BigMattyO, Quondum, Poisock, Jay-Sebastos, ඝම්ඊ විජේසේකර, ChuispastonBot, DASHBotAV, ClueBot NG, Matthiaspaul, Satellizer, HonestIntelligence, Mightymights, Cliffj123, Calabe1992, Wbm1058, Doorknob747, Vagobot, Umais Bin Sajjad, Klilidiplomus, Tagremover, Dschryver, JYBot, Bitso, Audakhan, Frosty, DavidLeighEllis, Comp.arch, Wikiuser13, Ugog Nizdast, Textcheese, Aleks000, Textcheese pro, Ethically Yours, SwaManBra, MarkiPoli, Amortias, Asdfugil, AZ1199 and Anonymous: 312

- **Qubit** *Source:* https://en.wikipedia.org/wiki/Qubit?oldid=717153107 *Contributors:* Damian Yerrick, Derek Ross, Seb, Stevertigo, Hfastedge, Michael Hardy, Oliver Pereira, Tannin, Pde, Ejrh, Looxix~enwiki, Ihcoyc, Stevenj, Cherkash, Smack, Timwi, Reina riemann, ThomasStrohmann~enwiki, Omegatron, Nnh, Rogper~enwiki, Fredrik, Sanders muc, Xjaguar~enwiki, Marc Venot, Giftlite, DocWatson42, DemonThing, CSTAR, Mikko Paananen, Icairns, MementoVivere, Andreas Kaufmann, Blanchette, Pak21, Pietzsche, El C, Kwamikagami, Haxwell, Robotje, Cmdrjameson, .:Ajvol:., Hyperdivision, Riana, AzaToth, UnHoly, Cburnett, Egg, Gmaxwell, Woohookitty, Linas, Henrik, LOL, Isnow, RckmRobot, Snafflekid, Rjwilmsi, Syndicate, FlaBot, M7bot, Chobot, YurikBot, Freiberg, Foxxygirltamara, Odddmonster, Anotherwikipedian, Trigger hippie77, 21655, Caco de vidro, Katieh5584, Snaxe920, Danielsavoiu, Incnis Mrsi, Ccalvin, Vald, DHN-bot~enwiki, Colonies Chris, Scwlong, Frap, Aldaron, Cybercobra, Stephen Bartlett, Soap, Jezabel, ShakingSpirit, Adriatikus, Igoldste, Rhetth, Ripounet, Mct mht, GavinMorley, Gogo Dodo, Zginder, Nielsen~enwiki, Headbomb, Dgies, Jeffthompson, Widefox, Shlomi Hillel, JAnDbot, Deflective, Bongwarrior, Appraiser, Kinston eagle, Tercer, B9 hummingbird hovering, Jamesd9007, Foncea, The Anonymous One, C. Trifle, Maurice Carbonaro, Smite-Meister, Shawn in Montreal, Pdrx, Sigmundur, Barraki, TXiKiBoT, GLPeterson, A4bot, Anaqreon, BlackVegetable, HEAVYMEDLEY, PaulTanenbaum, Seb az86556, Falcon8765, Skippydo, EmanWilm, ClueBot, Azaniewski, Thebigblutch~enwiki, ChrisHodgesUK, Jonverve, Addbot, Atethnekos, Zahd, Mac Dreamstate, LinkFA-Bot, Verbal, SPat, Yobot, AnomieBOT, Materialscientist, Mister fu-ck you, Sahehco, Freddy78, Citation bot 1, AstaBOTh15, I dream of horses, RobinK, ItsZippy, Lotje, RjwilmsiBot, Siddharth.kulk, EmausBot, WikitanvirBot, GoingBatty, RA0808, Jeevenson, Shijjiri, Solomonfromfinland, Prayerfortheworld, Dondervogel 2, L0ngpar1sh, Strafym, Glosser.ca, Tls60, Xto 999, ClueBot NG, Matthiaspaul, Hermajesty21, Chester Markel, Physics is all gnomes, Delusion23, Kcragin, Phchy, Calabe1992, Bibcode Bot, I donotwork, Who.was.phone, DoubleYang, Jimw338, Dexbot, Pintoch, Pidzz, Epicyaseen, Grajasumant, Lagoset, Monkbot, Yikkayaya, Noblesse1Oblige, Philipp Mirzoev, Superblarkoopa22, KM4JWL and Anonymous: 140

- **Qutrit** *Source:* https://en.wikipedia.org/wiki/Qutrit?oldid=673894190 *Contributors:* AugPi, David Latapie, Lumos3, Jaberwocky6669, Woohookitty, LocoBurger, Quale, FlaBot, YurikBot, Bluebot, Colonies Chris, Alaibot, RainbowCrane, Tercer, STBotD, TXiKiBoT, Kbrose, Bassplr19, Addbot, Quondum, Matthiaspaul, ChrisGualtieri, Lagoset and Anonymous: 7
- **1QBit** *Source:* https://en.wikipedia.org/wiki/1QBit?oldid=715241658 *Contributors:* Giraffedata, Anthony Appleyard, Rjwilmsi, Marozols, Frap, My Gussie, Sargdub, Senator2029, Chess, BattyBot and Anonymous: 10
- **Quantum state** *Source:* https://en.wikipedia.org/wiki/Quantum_state?oldid=717848758 *Contributors:* RTC, Michael Hardy, Julesd, Andres, Laussy, Patrick0Moran, Bevo, BenRG, Bkalafut, Rorro, Papadopc, Tea2min, Giftlite, MathKnight, MichaelHaeckel, CSTAR, H Padleckas, Elroch, Mschlindwein, Chris Howard, Freakofnurture, Hidaspal, Slipstream, Bender235, Giraffedata, Geschichte, Alansohn, Cortonin, Dan East, Ott, Woohookitty, Mpatel, Dzordzm, Colin Watson, Rjwilmsi, Mathbot, Margosbot~enwiki, Fresheneesz, Bgwhite, Wavelength, RobotE, Bambaiah, Agent Foxtrot, Hydrargyrum, PoorLeno, Larsobrien, Modify, Sbyrnes321, A13ean, Incnis Mrsi, Ptpare, Jutta234, Physis, Erwin, CapitalR, Petr Matas, BeenAroundAWhile, Mct mht, Phatom87, Dragon's Blood, Waxigloo, Thijs!bot, Colincmr, Headbomb, Second Quantization, Iviney, Eleuther, Bizzon, Magioladitis, Tercer, B. Wolterding, R'n'B, Hans Dunkelberg, Maurice Carbonaro, ARTE, Hulten, Sheliak, VolkovBot, LokiClock, Kinneytj, Thurth, TXiKiBoT, V81, Spinningspark, Kbrose, YohanN7, SieBot, Phe-bot, Jdcanfield, OKBot, Randy Kryn, StewartMH, ClueBot, Alksentrs, EoGuy, Rockfang, SchreiberBike, The-tenth-zdog, TimothyRias, Dragonfi, SilvonenBot, RealityDysfunction, Stephen Poppitt, Addbot, Bob K31416, Luckas-bot, Yobot, JTXSeldeen, AnomieBOT, Götz, Xqbot, Pvkeller, J04n, GrouchoBot, Omnipaedista, Nathanielvirgo, Waleswatcher, WaysToEscape, ??, Chjoaygame, FrescoBot, Freddy78, Steve Quinn, Machine Elf 1735, Oxonienses, RedBot, RobinK, BasvanPelt, Heurisko, Lotje, Eagleclaw6, RjwilmsiBot, Pierluigi.taddei, EmausBot, John of Reading, Gaurav biraris, Solomonfromfinland, Harddk, Josve05a, Zephyrus Tavvier, Maschen, Xronon, ClueBot NG, MelbourneStar, Theopolisme, Helpful Pixie Bot, Bibcode Bot, BG19bot, F=q(E+v^B), Ganitvidya, DrBugKiller, Chetan666, Jochen Burghardt, W. P. Uzer, Noix07, 7Sidz, Monkbot, Pratixit, AliShug, AlterHollow and Anonymous: 75
- **Quantum algorithm** *Source:* https://en.wikipedia.org/wiki/Quantum_algorithm?oldid=717431043 *Contributors:* Charles Matthews, Topbanana, Alan Liefting, Hyperdivision, Ruud Koot, Kbdank71, Rjwilmsi, Wavelength, Ripper234, Dijaster, SmackBot, Stepa, Skizzik, Chris the speller, Mhym, A5b, Mgiganteus1, CRGreathouse, Mudd1, PKT, Headbomb, Skalchemist, Hillgentleman, David Eppstein, Bender2k14, DumZiBoT, Addbot, Zahd, Yobot, TaBOT-zerem, AnomieBOT, Rubinbot, Materialscientist, Citation bot, Citation bot 1, MastiBot, RobinK, RjwilmsiBot, ZéroBot, AManWithNoPlan, Surya Prakash.S.A., Quantum theorist, Helpful Pixie Bot, Bibcode Bot, BG19bot, Jimw338, Toni 001, Dexbot, Comp.arch, Lyoova, Stamptrader, Ajbilan, Lagoset, Melcous, Vmayar, Williamhchuang and Anonymous: 32
- **Quantum algorithm for linear systems of equations** *Source:* https://en.wikipedia.org/wiki/Quantum_algorithm_for_linear_systems_of_equations?oldid=691833761 *Contributors:* Michael Hardy, Aram.harrow, Mild Bill Hiccup, LilHelpa, Orenburg1, John of Reading, Airwoz, Irvings1, Spinquantum, CV9933, Kilionsson, JamesP and Anonymous: 1
- **Quantum programming** *Source:* https://en.wikipedia.org/wiki/Quantum_programming?oldid=697815937 *Contributors:* Jarekadam, Furrykef, Art LaPella, Tritium6, RussBlau, Linas, Doughboy, Rjwilmsi, Elharaty, DVdm, Saintali, Trevor1, Amakuha, SmackBot, JanusDC, DreamOfMirrors, A5b, Physis, JohnCD, Harej bot, Alphachimpbot, Couchpotato99, Gwern, Selinger, Wbrito, Alksentrs, Mild Bill Hiccup, DumZiBoT, Addbot, Jarble, Yobot, HooHooHoo, RobinK, ClueBot NG, BG19bot, Catclock, Cofunctor and Anonymous: 22
- **Quantum error correction** *Source:* https://en.wikipedia.org/wiki/Quantum_error_correction?oldid=717403283 *Contributors:* Michael Hardy, Pnm, Sanders muc, Yelyos, Bobblewik, WpZurp, Dbachmann, Pearle, Lysdexia, RJFJR, Mwilde, CygnusPius, Woohookitty, GregorB, Rjwilmsi, Ikh, SanGatiche, Kerowyn, Smithbrenon, Gene.arboit, Btwied, Oatmeal batman, Cryptonaut, Inkington, Dabacon, Lotte Monz, Pjvpjv, Widefox, Dheerav2, Harbinger of Truth, Wavehunter, Katzmik, SieBot, Trumpsternator, Bender2k14, Justin545, SchreiberBike, Addbot, Phoneused, Queenmomcat, Biezl, Yobot, Baxxterr, Louxiabd, LilHelpa, FrescoBot, JokeySmurf, Citation bot 1, Schiefesfragezeichen, RobinK, John of Reading, Tls60, ChuispastonBot, Woottonjames, Netromdk, BG19bot, Faizan, Lagoset, Doyenheist and Anonymous: 31
- **Quantum circuit** *Source:* https://en.wikipedia.org/wiki/Quantum_circuit?oldid=712123192 *Contributors:* Edward, AugPi, Sanders muc, DavidCary, CSTAR, Creidieki, Tooto, Calton, Oleg Alexandrov, Joriki, Linas, Seidenstud, Dudegalea, Pyroman~enwiki, YurikBot, Wavelength, Dantheox, Disconcision, SmackBot, Mithaca, Takamaxa, CmdrObot, Cydebot, Nick Number, Widefox, MetsBot, David Eppstein, Kenatsun, Skippydo, Bender2k14, SchreiberBike, Addbot, Download, Baxxterr, RobinK, Mathtyke, EmausBot, Hhhippo, David.s.hollman, Helpful Pixie Bot, Bibcode Bot, BG19bot, Anubhab91 and Anonymous: 21
- **Quantum clock** *Source:* https://en.wikipedia.org/wiki/Quantum_clock?oldid=716417175 *Contributors:* Bkell, Pol098, McGeddon, Skizzik, OrangeDog, PiMaster3, Dicklyon, Peterdjones, TAnthony, Dulciana, GermanX, Maurice Carbonaro, Triesault, Francis Flinch, Juandresh, Forbes72, Addbot, Eric Drexler, Redheylin, OlEnglish, Trappist the monk, RjwilmsiBot, Clockbox, MonroeIX, Timetraveler3.14, BG19bot, Dwightboone, Dexbot, Samarth261, Tetra quark and Anonymous: 8
- **Quantum gate** *Source:* https://en.wikipedia.org/wiki/Quantum_gate?oldid=715304070 *Contributors:* Michael Hardy, AugPi, Charles Matthews, Sanders muc, Hadal, Alan Liefting, CSTAR, V79, Cedders, One-dimensional Tangent, Cortonin, Linas, Ruud Koot, Rjwilmsi, Phillip Jordan, Marozols, Vyroglyph, Stepa, Dave Kielpinski, Njerseyguy, BlindWanderer, Samharrison, Vaughan Pratt, Mct mht, Cryptonaut, Jhansonxi, SalvNaut, LokiClock, WereSpielChequers, Bender2k14, Justin545, Addbot, Zahd, LaaknorBot, Verbal, Luckas-bot, Yobot, AnomieBOT, GrouchoBot, Meieram, RobinK, Kodus, Ssposts, Mattedia, Vincent Russo, Wbm1058, Bibcode Bot, Cardinal Direction, W. P. Uzer, Kancer89, M. M. Eshom, Geek3, Www42www and Anonymous: 33
- **Quantum entanglement** *Source:* https://en.wikipedia.org/wiki/Quantum_entanglement?oldid=717748953 *Contributors:* CYD, Mav, Timo Honkasalo, XJaM, Toby Bartels, Roadrunner, FlorianMarquardt, Stevertigo, Michael Hardy, FrankH, Jarekadam, SebastianHelm, CesarB, Looxix~enwiki, Strebe, J-Wiki, Glenn, Vodex, RodC, Charles Matthews, Timwi, Scmarney, Ewout~enwiki, Fuzheado, Gutza, Patrick0Moran, Phys, Thue, Bevo, Nnh, Twang, Phil Boswell, Robbot, Chealer, Sanders muc, Naddy, Rursus, Hadal, Fuelbottle, Diberri, Giftlite, DocWatson42, Fennec, Lethe, No Guru, Dratman, Alison, Zumbo, Andris, Geni, Beland, CSTAR, Sam Hocevar, Lumidek, JohnArmagh, Trevor MacInnis, Thorwald, Mike Rosoft, RossPatterson, Caroline Thompson, Rich Farmbrough, Rhobite, Pjacobi, Luqui, Tony Weeks, Bender235, V79, MisterSheik, El C, Stain, Nickj, Individualno241, Jon the Geek, Tsirel, Passw0rd, Espoo, Mrzaius, DanielVallstrom, Keenan Pepper, Cortonin, Qcomp, Cal 1234, Matthew Mattic, Cgibbard, Linas, RHaworth, ^demon, WadeSimMiser, Pthalo, CharlesC, Milez, DGDanforth, BD2412, Drbogdan, Rjwilmsi, Syndicate, Quiddity, TheRingess, Thangalin, ScottJ, Kaluza81, ManiG, Chobot, Theo Pardilla, DVdm, YurikBot, Wavelength, Borgx, Gene.arboit, Dotancohen, Bboyneko, JocK, Roy Brumback, Mysid, Jess Riedel, C h fleming, Jules.LT, Ninly, Oakwood, RG2, Profero, GrinBot~enwiki, KasugaHuang, KnightRider~enwiki, SmackBot, KocjoBot~enwiki, Xblkx, Kintetsubuffalo, Gilliam, PJTraill, Dave Kielpinski, Jjalexand, Benixau, Dlohcierekim's sock, Incoherent fool, Kostmo, DHN-bot~enwiki, Colonies Chris, Dart evader, Rrburke, Percommode, Mitrius, Metta Bubble, Omgoleus, Chrylis, Xiutwel, Gatoatigrado, Vgnessvg, DJIndica, Ironcito, Bcasterline, ThomYoung, Vgy7ujm, AstroChemist, JorisvS, Phancy Physicist, Paul venter,

Bgirardo, Rnb, Richard75, Quodfui, Skirtner, Crk~enwiki, Gsjaeger, CmdrObot, Juhachi, Mct mht, Phatom87, Meznaric, Gmusser, Ryannurmela, Cryptonaut, Miguel de Servet, Christian75, Ebrahim, Mickproper, Thijs!bot, Klasovsky, Keraunos, Headbomb, Dtgriscom, Peter Deer, Marek69, Second Quantization, Hcobb, Eb.eric, MichaelMaggs, Peashy, Widefox, BMB, Awesomepenguin, IndigoAK200, Bm gub, Superperro, Itistoday, M cuffa, Alphachimpbot, Lfstevens, Qwerty Binary, Deadbeef, MER-C, Lino Mastrodomenico, Grant Gussie, Jimbobl, Lkjt, Andrewthomas10, Darthkurai, SHCarter, Ruibjr, LorenzoB, JaGa, Tercer, Yawe, Rickard Vogelberg, HEL, Gillwill2000, McDoobAU93, C. Trifle, AstroHurricane001, Dani setiawan, AltiusBimm, Maurice Carbonaro, All Is One, Nigholith, Acalamari, RIPSAW1986, Aoosten, NewEnglandYankee, Babedacus, Thelegendary, DorganBot, Lexoka, RJASE1, Sheliak, Hadunsford, Shiggity, Pleasantville, Jamenta, JosephJohnCox, Martin451, Aaport, Jackfork, TBond, Mezzaluna, Costela, Sylviaelse, YohanN7, SieBot, YonaBot, Bravo two one, Ujjwol, Likebox, Janopus, Nanobri, Zylox, JohnSawyer, Hamiltondaniel, Thorncrag, Myrvin, Church, Orangedolphin, WurmWoode, Pseudyx, Agge1000, DragonBot, Justin545, Mihaiam~enwiki, Brews ohare, PhySusie, Hcs42, Gumby55555, DJ Sturm, DumZiBoT, XLinkBot, Ost316, WikHead, Jd027, Stephen Poppitt, Acaeton, Addbot, Out of Phase User, AndrewHarvey4, WMdeMuynck, Cuaxdon, Mac Dreamstate, MrOllie, Ozfilm, Bob K31416, Xev lexx, Rodeo90, Ettrig, Jack who built the house, Drpickem, Yobot, The Vector Kid, Deicool, AnomieBOT, Arjun G. Menon, FiberOptix, Hunnjazal, Citation bot, Durand QM, Northryde, Stsang, Dutch chatty, NOrbeck, Bizso, Omnipaedista, Earlypsychosis, RibotBOT, Drormata, ??, Another disinterested reader, Chjoaygame, FrescoBot, SHAMSAWY, Mewulwe, Citation bot 1, Jonesey95, Schiefesfragezeichen, Lithium cyanide, Trappist the monk, Jordgette, Dc987, MrX, Korepin, RjwilmsiBot, Itamarhason, Navyswimmer96, Harry Audus, Skamecrazy123, EmausBot, John of Reading, Dewritech, GoingBatty, RA0808, Slightsmile, BelaLugosiwasdead, John Cline, Brazmyth, TonyMath, Crochet, Aschwole, Staszek Lem, Iiar, Aturzillo, Loggerjack, Adrian-from-london, Lilrell94, Mystikol, Donner60, HCPotter, Oberones, Conservatismismurder, Socialismismurder, Ontyx, ChuispastonBot, Smarthand, Ferek, JamesRJohnston, Kartasto, Aurelien.desbrieres, FeatherPluma, Isocliff, Maxkingesq, ClueBot NG, Cwmhiraeth, Koornti, Sabri Al-Safi, Marigorringoa, M11101, Madis731, Rezabot, Toddrmcallister, Prasoc, Crazymonkey1123, Theopolisme, Helpful Pixie Bot, Olgasavelieva, Bibcode Bot, BG19bot, Ymblanter, Cthulhu Inc, AvocatoBot, Wdlang, Zedshort, Hamish59, BattyBot, Liam987, La marts boys, RoundEye123, Mogism, Wikiforron, WolfgangAzureus, RicardAnufriev, PC-XT, Paradox the Sneath, WorldWideJuan, Asdfjasdjkfl, Binse, Debouch, Lyuflamb, Comp.arch, Alghenius, Joeletaylor, Ginsuloft, Alexbrandts, DrRNC, W. P. Uzer, Jfizzix, TheLeopardQueen, Mfb, BioticPixels, Antrocent, Monkbot, ChristFollower78, Gronk Oz, The1andOnlyGabe, Garfield Garfield, Iokevins, Stuffff, OdedMe, Huangyc07, Dorianluparu, Prajwalvathreya, Hsjdhdjs, Gilessukkert, Luchaoyang, MichaelE, Jbohnet, Pkwyweds, Paradoxicality94, Larryxyzwiki, DarkAssassin22, Shashaank Venkatesh, Ani Ifeatu and Anonymous: 349

- **Quantum neural network** *Source:* https://en.wikipedia.org/wiki/Quantum_neural_network?oldid=717604416 *Contributors:* Glenn, Charles Matthews, Mtcv, Dimadick, Chris Howard, Alai, Natalya, Woohookitty, BD2412, Gurch, Ansell, Zwobot, SkanderH, Noah Salzman, Dicklyon, Amalas, Cryptonaut, Allmightyduck, Addbot, Yobot, Gricehead, BG19bot, Arlene47, Chenolf, Maria Schuld, Mary Stable, Quinto Simmaco, VaibhavGandhi1, Klogram and Anonymous: 10
- **Quantum t-design** *Source:* https://en.wikipedia.org/wiki/Quantum_t-design?oldid=696559708 *Contributors:* Dratman, Tabletop, CharlesHBennett, Azaghal of Belegost, Tercer, JL-Bot, DFRussia, Yobot, Abaglaen, Theopolisme, Khazar2 and Anonymous: 3
- **Quantum threshold theorem** *Source:* https://en.wikipedia.org/wiki/Quantum_threshold_theorem?oldid=590295022 *Contributors:* Giftlite, MSGJ, D6, Ruud Koot, RDBury, Epbr123, David Eppstein, KathrynLybarger, Addbot, AnomieBOT, TheOtherInsaneMoose, Pcghostlmin, RobinK, Mark viking and Anonymous: 2
- **Quantum bus** *Source:* https://en.wikipedia.org/wiki/Quantum_bus?oldid=671705867 *Contributors:* Bearcat, Connelly, Woohookitty, Rjwilmsi, Ilmari Karonen, Geremia, Headbomb, Dmitri Yuriev, Mm40, MystBot, Addbot, Citation bot 1, Trappist the monk, RjwilmsiBot, Tls60, Bibcode Bot, BattyBot, Monkbot and Anonymous: 5
- **Quantum spin model** *Source:* https://en.wikipedia.org/wiki/Quantum_spin_model?oldid=590708192 *Contributors:* MuffledThud, Freddy78, RockMagnetist and Anonymous: 1
- **Quantum channel** *Source:* https://en.wikipedia.org/wiki/Quantum_channel?oldid=715450641 *Contributors:* Michael Hardy, Grendelkhan, Creidieki, Rich Farmbrough, Sole Soul, Jag123, Passw0rd, Linas, Tabletop, Rjwilmsi, J S Lundeen, Wavelength, Conscious, Zwobot, Jess Riedel, SmackBot, Njerseyguy, Cloudres~enwiki, Colonies Chris, TiCPU, JoeBot, Jafet, CmdrObot, Mct mht, Azaghal of Belegost, Knotwork, Sullivan.t.j, David Eppstein, R'n'B, Warut, Justin545, Lambtron, Addbot, Xp54321, Download, Yobot, Dreamer08, JokeySmurf, Sanpitch, Korepin, Snotbot, Primergrey, ChrisGualtieri, Holmesindiana and Anonymous: 27
- **Quantum depolarizing channel** *Source:* https://en.wikipedia.org/wiki/Quantum_depolarizing_channel?oldid=638045742 *Contributors:* Rjwilmsi, Melchoir, LokiClock, Iohannes Animosus, Addbot, Yobot, Shenchenxu, Bibcode Bot, Brirush and Anonymous: 3
- **Quantum capacity** *Source:* https://en.wikipedia.org/wiki/Quantum_capacity?oldid=655561309 *Contributors:* Bearcat, Sole Soul, Qcomp, Mwilde, Marozols, Bgwhite, Tercer, TutterMouse, AnomieBOT, InsufficientData, RjwilmsiBot, Bibcode Bot, BG19bot and Anonymous: 2
- **Quantum cognition** *Source:* https://en.wikipedia.org/wiki/Quantum_cognition?oldid=717156712 *Contributors:* Dcljr, Dratman, DragonflySixtyseven, Robin klein, Klemen Kocjancic, Chris Howard, Dmol, BD2412, Nihiltres, GünniX, DVdm, Wavelength, Rathfelder, Sadads, Seifip, Racklever, Arnoutf, Aeternus, Caramel01, Gregbard, Headbomb, David Eppstein, Wikimandia, Jbusemey, Hankhuck, Lova Falk, Cnilep, Wing gundam, Martarius, Taketa, Yobot, AnomieBOT, LilHelpa, I dream of horses, Donschrott, John of Reading, Slightsmile, Timetraveler3.14, Jenico465, QIGuy, Saistmp, AndroidScienceGuy, BG19bot, DanversCarew, Gibbja, ChrisGualtieri, Mogism, ?, Cadillac000, KirstenRichards, Qcogn78, Arlene47, 1958andrei, Arnab Way, Delikeva and Anonymous: 26
- **Quantum catalyst** *Source:* https://en.wikipedia.org/wiki/Quantum_catalyst?oldid=685762339 *Contributors:* Rpyle731, Widefox, Strilanc, Yobot, Citation bot and Dexbot
- **Quantum complex network** *Source:* https://en.wikipedia.org/wiki/Quantum_complex_network?oldid=716016620 *Contributors:* Phil Boswell, Bgwhite, Egsan Bacon, !dea4u, WereSpielChequers, Just a guy from the KP, John of Reading, BG19bot, BrunoCoutinho, BrunoGCoutinho and Anonymous: 7
- **Quantum LC circuit** *Source:* https://en.wikipedia.org/wiki/Quantum_LC_circuit?oldid=704223931 *Contributors:* Sj, Rich Farmbrough, Tabletop, Torquil~enwiki, Godzatswing, Bgwhite, SmackBot, Chris the speller, Mets501, Myasuda, Spartaz, Leyo, Baileypalblue, Cerebellum, Spinningspark, Paradoctor, Dahnamics, JL-Bot, Mild Bill Hiccup, PMDrive1061, Timirdatta, Addbot, AnomieBOT, Eumolpo, DSisyphBot, Slow Phil, DrilBot, ArticCynda, Tmvphil, Theopolisme, BG19bot, Faizan and Anonymous: 12
- **Quantum cryptography** *Source:* https://en.wikipedia.org/wiki/Quantum_cryptography?oldid=716460019 *Contributors:* Edward, DniQ, Graeme Bartlett, Fgrosshans, Rjwilmsi, Agrumer, Koavf, Bgwhite, RussBot, Paul Magnussen, Arthur Rubin, Centie, SmackBot, Chris the speller, GVnayR, Epachamo, Salamurai, A5b, Cydebot, Widefox, Danielik~enwiki, R'n'B, Maurice Carbonaro, TXiKiBoT, Billinghurst,

Denisarona, Buchskj, Myrvin, Coinmac, Addbot, ماني, Yobot, Nghtwlkr, KamikazeBot, AnomieBOT, Jim1138, Danno uk, Citation bot, ArthurBot, Xqbot, Eric.cavalcanti, Frosted14, Citation bot 1, Gautier lebon, Kirsim, Jonesey95, Tom.Reding, RjwilmsiBot, WikitanvirBot, Dcirovic, Quelrod, Cf. Hay, Rangoon11, ClamDip, Sarathkris, Ndk.clanbo, ClueBot NG, Feihu Xu, Writepank, CyberknightMK, Cschff, Bibcode Bot, BG19bot, Blaspie55, Qinfy, Khazar2, محسن پورپونه, Summut46, Brianzang, Lagoset, Urbaninformative, Monkbot, AntiqueReader, Hannasnow, Prodx3, Gauntman1, BooBoo314159, Lhfbtit, KasparBot, Ggravier, Aiwlwlttok and Anonymous: 45

- **One-way quantum computer** *Source:* https://en.wikipedia.org/wiki/One-way_quantum_computer?oldid=685690834 *Contributors:* Stone, Jheald, Rjwilmsi, Gadget850, SmackBot, SkanderH, Michaelbusch, Headbomb, Widefox, QuantumEngineer, Justin545, DOI bot, Trisetyarso, Citation bot 1, Jonesey95, GoingBatty, Phchy, Bibcode Bot, BG19bot and Anonymous: 4
- **Kane quantum computer** *Source:* https://en.wikipedia.org/wiki/Kane_quantum_computer?oldid=705978486 *Contributors:* Tim Starling, Dgrant, Angela, Sanders muc, Herbee, Peter bertok, Kevyn, Arminius, ArnoldReinhold, RJFJR, Linas, Ruud Koot, BWDuncan, Widefox, Tyco.skinner, Pdfpdf, Crisfor~enwiki, Addbot, Tassedethe, Lightbot, Finn-Pauls, Yobot, EmausBot, GoingBatty, Lagoset, Gauntman1 and Anonymous: 6
- **Quantum technology** *Source:* https://en.wikipedia.org/wiki/Quantum_technology?oldid=709357440 *Contributors:* GangofOne, SmackBot, BeenAroundAWhile, Quantumpundit, Stickee, Addbot, LaaknorBot, Lightbot, AnomieBOT, Baz.77.243.99.32, LucienBOT, Tom.Reding, Orenburg1, Rickky678, ZéroBot, Tolly4bolly, BG19bot, Virtualerian, DPL bot, Cyberbot II, Nibiko and Anonymous: 10
- **Bennett's laws** *Source:* https://en.wikipedia.org/wiki/Bennett'{}s_laws?oldid=702635001 *Contributors:* Stevertigo, Bearcat, Rpyle731, Malcolma, Trivialist, OlEnglish, Gilderien, Yikkayaya and Anonymous: 1
- **Bistochastic quantum channel** *Source:* https://en.wikipedia.org/wiki/Bistochastic_quantum_channel?oldid=523077494 *Contributors:* Bearcat, Reyk, Njerseyguy, Delusion23 and Anonymous: 1
- **Channel-state duality** *Source:* https://en.wikipedia.org/wiki/Channel-state_duality?oldid=599230818 *Contributors:* Rich Farmbrough, Rjwilmsi, Wavelength, Closedmouth, Mct mht, Addbot, Erik9bot and Anonymous: 1
- **Classical capacity** *Source:* https://en.wikipedia.org/wiki/Classical_capacity?oldid=659052339 *Contributors:* Bearcat, Utcursch, Mwilde, Bgwhite, David Eppstein, Propithecus137, Bibcode Bot, ChrisGualtieri and Anonymous: 3
- **Coherent information** *Source:* https://en.wikipedia.org/wiki/Coherent_information?oldid=556127810 *Contributors:* SebastianHelm, Creidieki, Clarahamster, Jheald, Oleg Alexandrov, Linas, SmackBot, Betacommand, Racklever, Kukini, Mct mht, Daniel Olsen, Ciphers, Delusion23 and Anonymous: 3
- **Entanglement witness** *Source:* https://en.wikipedia.org/wiki/Entanglement_witness?oldid=708497379 *Contributors:* Tea2min, Fgrosshans, Linas, Aram.harrow, Mets501, Mct mht, Sullivan.t.j, Smite-Meister, Melab-1, Yobot, Bibcode Bot, Coolfarmer, 22merlin and Anonymous: 7
- **Greenberger–Horne–Zeilinger state** *Source:* https://en.wikipedia.org/wiki/Greenberger%E2%80%93Horne%E2%80%93Zeilinger_state?oldid=717861422 *Contributors:* Michael Hardy, Pt, Slicky, Linas, Tone, JocK, Jess Riedel, SmackBot, Incnis Mrsi, Planet1537, TenPoundHammer, Ivan.Savov, Vyznev Xnebara, Knotwork, Magioladitis, KConWiki, Gill110951, Marek.zukowski, LokiClock, Rei-bot, Legoktm, Arjen Dijksman, Rumping, Crowsnest, Yobot, AnomieBOT, Götz, EmausBot, Bibcode Bot, Wassermaus, AHusain3141 and Anonymous: 15
- **Holevo's theorem** *Source:* https://en.wikipedia.org/wiki/Holevo'{}s_theorem?oldid=698135862 *Contributors:* Jheald, Linas, Marudubshinki, Bgwhite, Oakwood, CRGreathouse, Daniel Olsen, Appraiser, Atayero, Tokenzero, David Eppstein, Djacobs7, Jenny Lam, Dziewa, Addbot, Yobot, Korepin, Drhumble and Anonymous: 10
- **Joint quantum entropy** *Source:* https://en.wikipedia.org/wiki/Joint_quantum_entropy?oldid=709498839 *Contributors:* Michael Hardy, SebastianHelm, Charles Matthews, Sam Hocevar, Creidieki, Rich Farmbrough, John Vandenberg, Jheald, Linas, Cleared as filed, SmackBot, Bluebot, Mct mht, LokiClock, G.offenhartz, Thehotelambush, Yobot, Helpful Pixie Bot, BG19bot and Anonymous: 1
- **Lieb-Robinson bounds** *Source:* https://en.wikipedia.org/wiki/Lieb-Robinson_bounds?oldid=707309953 *Contributors:* Maury Markowitz, Bgwhite, TLSuda, Incnis Mrsi, Huon, Myasuda, Magioladitis, Wiae, Blurpeace, Thomas.schick, Biscuittin, Miniapolis, Wee Curry Monster, Hasteur, TimothyRias, Dthomsen8, Rankersbo, MatthewVanitas, AnomieBOT, Alvin Seville, BG19bot, PaintedCarpet, Lucie911, SEGSuser, Yikkayaya, KSFT, TimidSings and Anonymous: 4
- **Mutually unbiased bases** *Source:* https://en.wikipedia.org/wiki/Mutually_unbiased_bases?oldid=705613082 *Contributors:* Michael Hardy, Pascal666, DemonThing, Rich Farmbrough, Zaslav, RHaworth, Will Orrick, Rjwilmsi, Marozols, Wavelength, Kreizhn, Yobot, Capricorn42, Mschirm, Marcin.wiesniak, FrescoBot, Skyerise, Trappist the monk, Haaj86, Hsar500, Bibcode Bot, Wimvdam, Qinfy, Stevebrierley, Faizan, Monkbot, Broido and Anonymous: 12
- **No-teleportation theorem** *Source:* https://en.wikipedia.org/wiki/No-teleportation_theorem?oldid=711595267 *Contributors:* Rich Farmbrough, GregorB, Closedmouth, Egsan Bacon, Pwjb, Mct mht, Headbomb, Hweimer, MTCown, Djr32, Pianomikey0, Erik9bot, BG19bot and Anonymous: 12
- **Peres–Horodecki criterion** *Source:* https://en.wikipedia.org/wiki/Peres%E2%80%93Horodecki_criterion?oldid=672460374 *Contributors:* Charles Matthews, Fibonacci, Tea2min, Matthew Mattic, Linas, Stevey7788, Tinissimo, SmackBot, Njerseyguy, Egsan Bacon, Mwtoews, CmdrObot, Mct mht, Tercer, Alsee, LokiClock, Yobot, Omnipaedista, FrescoBot, Mforets, Bibcode Bot, Philodemos, Huangyc07 and Anonymous: 11
- **POVM** *Source:* https://en.wikipedia.org/wiki/POVM?oldid=706186216 *Contributors:* Lethe, CSTAR, Oleg Alexandrov, Linas, BD2412, Salix alba, FlaBot, J S Lundeen, Gaius Cornelius, Grafen, Johnpseudo, Ilmari Karonen, Njerseyguy, Furby100, BWDuncan, CmdrObot, Mct mht, Waxigloo, David Eppstein, Tercer, R'n'B, LordAnubisBOT, Djacobs7, Kreizhn, Belsazar, Jim E. Black, ClueBot, Shai mach, Mild Bill Hiccup, Sun Creator, Iratsu, SchreiberBike, Addbot, ???, WMdeMuynck, Yobot, AnomieBOT, Abaglaen, Thehelpfulbot, FrescoBot, Dewritech, Almacd, Xmlu, Jingsiaosing, Jodosma, DianaFong and Anonymous: 25
- **Schmidt decomposition** *Source:* https://en.wikipedia.org/wiki/Schmidt_decomposition?oldid=714878543 *Contributors:* Charles Matthews, Giftlite, BenFrantzDale, Rich Farmbrough, Bender235, Qcomp, RJFJR, Arvid42, Linas, SmackBot, Bluebot, Mct mht, Mikenorton, S (usurped also), Wiae, Tcamps42, Arjen Dijksman, Beastinwith, Mathmoose, Addbot, E.mubeen, Li3939108, Erik9bot, Foobarnix, Jujutacular, Katherine, Rolancito, Phleg1, Matteorossi90 and Anonymous: 21
- **SCOP formalism** *Source:* https://en.wikipedia.org/wiki/SCOP_formalism?oldid=712452927 *Contributors:* Tony1, RomanSpa, Ninetyone, Wiae, WereSpielChequers, CorenSearchBot, TutterMouse, Yobot, FrescoBot, John of Reading, Tveloz, DanversCarew, Khazar2, ? and Anonymous: 1

- **Superoperator** *Source:* https://en.wikipedia.org/wiki/Superoperator?oldid=715060812 *Contributors:* Eruantalon, Oleg Alexandrov, Linas, Tedder, CambridgeBayWeather, Wknight94, SmackBot, Jambaugh, Myasuda, Mct mht, JonGUK, David Eppstein, Goluckyryan, Addbot, Erik9bot, FrescoBot, IXhdBAH, Bdb1988, Rasim, Darienmorrow and Anonymous: 10
- **Typical subspace** *Source:* https://en.wikipedia.org/wiki/Typical_subspace?oldid=513052334 *Contributors:* Bearcat, Mwilde, Malcolma, Steel1943, SchreiberBike and Anonymous: 1
- **W state** *Source:* https://en.wikipedia.org/wiki/W_state?oldid=718224547 *Contributors:* Qcomp, SmackBot, Bluebot, Sadads, Ivan.Savov, Waxigloo, Marek.zukowski, WereSpielChequers, Erik9bot, FrescoBot, Frietjes, Bibcode Bot, ChrisGualtieri, Equinox and Anonymous: 7
- **Institute for Quantum Computing** *Source:* https://en.wikipedia.org/wiki/Institute_for_Quantum_Computing?oldid=696520439 *Contributors:* Melaen, Mindmatrix, GregorB, Thirty-seven, Mandarax, Spencerk, Welsh, SmackBot, Steam5, Chris the speller, Twas Now, Wafulz, Alaibot, Headbomb, Yewlongbow, The Anomebot2, Tikiwont, Bungimail, Tt801, Hugo999, Peter K Burian, Neworder1, JL-Bot, ImageRemovalBot, Addbot, BrainMarble, Joseph2625, Yobot, Amfleming, BirgitW, Cbiddiscombe, RobinK, JodiSz, Ebun1974, JeanM, JSFarman, Quantumiqc, Bookblack, Shipandreceive and Anonymous: 10

56.10.2 Images

- **File:1QBit_logo.png** *Source:* https://upload.wikimedia.org/wikipedia/en/3/3d/1QBit_logo.png *License:* Fair use *Contributors:* http://www.1QBit.com *Original artist:* ?
- **File:Ambox_important.svg** *Source:* https://upload.wikimedia.org/wikipedia/commons/b/b4/Ambox_important.svg *License:* Public domain *Contributors:* Own work, based off of Image:Ambox scales.svg *Original artist:* Dsmurat (talk · contribs)
- **File:BQP_complexity_class_diagram.svg** *Source:* https://upload.wikimedia.org/wikipedia/commons/1/1d/BQP_complexity_class_diagram.svg *License:* Public domain *Contributors:* Drawn by User:Mike1024 *Original artist:* User Mike1024
- **File:Bloch_Sphere.svg** *Source:* https://upload.wikimedia.org/wikipedia/commons/f/f4/Bloch_Sphere.svg *License:* CC BY-SA 3.0 *Contributors:* Own work *Original artist:* Glosser.ca
- **File:CNOT_gate.svg** *Source:* https://upload.wikimedia.org/wikipedia/commons/4/4e/CNOT_gate.svg *License:* CC BY-SA 3.0 *Contributors:* Created in LaTeX using Q-circuit by the following code: *Original artist:* Self
- **File:Commons-logo.svg** *Source:* https://upload.wikimedia.org/wikipedia/en/4/4a/Commons-logo.svg *License:* CC-BY-SA-3.0 *Contributors:* ? *Original artist:* ?
- **File:Controlled_gate.svg** *Source:* https://upload.wikimedia.org/wikipedia/commons/d/dc/Controlled_gate.svg *License:* CC BY-SA 3.0 *Contributors:* Created in LaTeX using Q-circuit by the following code: *Original artist:* Self
- **File:DFAexample.svg** *Source:* https://upload.wikimedia.org/wikipedia/commons/9/9d/DFAexample.svg *License:* Public domain *Contributors:* Own work *Original artist:* Cepheus
- **File:DWave_128chip.jpg** *Source:* https://upload.wikimedia.org/wikipedia/commons/1/17/DWave_128chip.jpg *License:* CC BY 3.0 *Contributors:* D-Wave Systems, Inc. *Original artist:* D-Wave Systems, Inc.
- **File:Edit-clear.svg** *Source:* https://upload.wikimedia.org/wikipedia/en/f/f2/Edit-clear.svg *License:* Public domain *Contributors:* The *Tango! Desktop Project*. *Original artist:*
  The people from the Tango! project. And according to the meta-data in the file, specifically: "Andreas Nilsson, and Jakub Steiner (although minimally)."
- **File:Emoji_u1f4bb.svg** *Source:* https://upload.wikimedia.org/wikipedia/commons/d/d7/Emoji_u1f4bb.svg *License:* Apache License 2.0 *Contributors:* https://code.google.com/p/noto/ *Original artist:* Google
- **File:Folder_Hexagonal_Icon.svg** *Source:* https://upload.wikimedia.org/wikipedia/en/4/48/Folder_Hexagonal_Icon.svg *License:* Cc-by-sa-3.0 *Contributors:* ? *Original artist:* ?
- **File:Fredkin_gate.svg** *Source:* https://upload.wikimedia.org/wikipedia/commons/c/ca/Fredkin_gate.svg *License:* CC BY-SA 3.0 *Contributors:* Created in LaTeX using Q-circuit by the following code: *Original artist:* Self
- **File:Gnome-searchtool.svg** *Source:* https://upload.wikimedia.org/wikipedia/commons/1/1e/Gnome-searchtool.svg *License:* LGPL *Contributors:* http://ftp.gnome.org/pub/GNOME/sources/gnome-themes-extras/0.9/gnome-themes-extras-0.9.0.tar.gz *Original artist:* David Vignoni
- **File:HAtomOrbitals.png** *Source:* https://upload.wikimedia.org/wikipedia/commons/c/cf/HAtomOrbitals.png *License:* CC-BY-SA-3.0 *Contributors:* ? *Original artist:* ?
- **File:Hadamard_gate.svg** *Source:* https://upload.wikimedia.org/wikipedia/commons/1/1a/Hadamard_gate.svg *License:* CC BY-SA 3.0 *Contributors:* Created in LaTeX by the following code:
  <span class="k">\documentclass</span><span class="na">[11pt]</span><span class="nb">{</span>article<span class="nb">}</span> <span class="k">\input</span><span class="nb">{</span>Qcircuit<span class="nb">}</span> <span class="k">\thispagestyle</span><span class="nb">{</span>empty<span class="nb">}</span> <span class="k">\begin</span><span class="nb">{</span>document<span class="nb">}</span> <span class="k">\begin</span><span class="nb">{</span>align*<span class="nb">}</span> <span class="k">\Qcircuit</span> @C=1em @R=.7em <span class="nb">{</span> <span class="nb">&</span> <span class="k">\gate</span><span class="nb">{</span>H<span class="nb">}</span> <span class="nb">&</span> <span class="k">\qw</span> <span class="nb">}</span> <span class="k">\end</span><span class="nb">{</span>align*<span class="nb">}</span> <span class="k">\end</span><span class="nb">{</span>document<span class="nb">}</span>

  Original artist: Self
- **File:HarmOsziFunktionen.png** *Source:* https://upload.wikimedia.org/wikipedia/commons/9/9e/HarmOsziFunktionen.png *License:* CC BY-SA 3.0 *Contributors:* File:HarmOsziFunktionen.jpg *Original artist:* AllenMcC.
- **File:Hydrogen300.png** *Source:* https://upload.wikimedia.org/wikipedia/commons/a/ad/Hydrogen300.png *License:* Public domain *Contributors:* Own work (Original text: *I created this work entirely by myself.*) *Original artist:* PoorLeno (talk)

- **File:Hydrogen_Density_Plots.png** *Source:* https://upload.wikimedia.org/wikipedia/commons/e/e7/Hydrogen_Density_Plots.png *License:* Public domain *Contributors:* the English language Wikipedia (log).
Original artist: PoorLeno (talk)
- **File:IQC_logo,_updated_2013.png** *Source:* https://upload.wikimedia.org/wikipedia/commons/5/52/IQC_logo%2C_updated_2013.png *License:* Public domain *Contributors:* http://uwaterloo.ca/institute-for-quantum-computing/ *Original artist:* The Institute for Quantum Computing
- **File:Infinite_potential_well.svg** *Source:* https://upload.wikimedia.org/wikipedia/commons/2/27/Infinite_potential_well.svg *License:* Public domain *Contributors:* Created by bdesham in Inkscape. *Original artist:* Benjamin D. Esham (bdesham)
- **File:Internet_map_1024.jpg** *Source:* https://upload.wikimedia.org/wikipedia/commons/d/d2/Internet_map_1024.jpg *License:* CC BY 2.5 *Contributors:* Originally from the English Wikipedia; description page is/was here. *Original artist:* The Opte Project
- **File:Kane_QC.png** *Source:* https://upload.wikimedia.org/wikipedia/commons/1/15/Kane_QC.png *License:* CC-BY-SA-3.0 *Contributors:* Own work *Original artist:* Diagram drawn by Tim Starling
- **File:Laflamme_presents_a_boomerang_to_Hawking,_Institute_for_Quantum_Computing,_21_June_2010.jpg** *Source:* https://upload.wikimedia.org/wikipedia/en/8/8f/Laflamme_presents_a_boomerang_to_Hawking%2C_Institute_for_Quantum_Computing%2C_21_June_2010.jpg *License:* Fair use *Contributors:* **Original publication**: Institute for Quantum Computing Flickr photostream, 23 June 2010

  Immediate http://www.flickr.com/photos/quantumiqc/5012598880/in/set-72157625011199788/ *Original artist:* Institute for Quantum Computing
- **File:Library-logo.svg** *Source:* https://upload.wikimedia.org/wikipedia/commons/5/53/Library-logo.svg *License:* CC0 *Contributors:* Own work *Original artist:* Mononomic
- **File:Max_Planck_(1858-1947).jpg** *Source:* https://upload.wikimedia.org/wikipedia/commons/a/a7/Max_Planck_%281858-1947%29.jpg *License:* Public domain *Contributors:* http://www.sil.si.edu/digitalcollections/hst/scientific-identity/CF/display_results.cfm?alpha_sort=p *Original artist:* Unknown<a href='//www.wikidata.org/wiki/Q4233718' title='wikidata:Q4233718'><img alt='wikidata:Q4233718' src='https://upload.wikimedia.org/wikipedia/commons/thumb/f/ff/Wikidata-logo.svg/20px-Wikidata-logo.svg.png' width='20' height='11' srcset='https://upload.wikimedia.org/wikipedia/commons/thumb/f/ff/Wikidata-logo.svg/30px-Wikidata-logo.svg.png 1.5x, https://upload.wikimedia.org/wikipedia/commons/thumb/f/ff/Wikidata-logo.svg/40px-Wikidata-logo.svg.png 2x' data-file-width='1050' data-file-height='590' /></a>
- **File:NYT_May_4,_1935.jpg** *Source:* https://upload.wikimedia.org/wikipedia/commons/a/a0/NYT_May_4%2C_1935.jpg *License:* Public domain *Contributors:* http://www.ias.edu/articles/physics *Original artist:* New York Times
- **File:People_icon.svg** *Source:* https://upload.wikimedia.org/wikipedia/commons/3/37/People_icon.svg *License:* CC0 *Contributors:* OpenClipart *Original artist:* OpenClipart
- **File:Portal-puzzle.svg** *Source:* https://upload.wikimedia.org/wikipedia/en/f/fd/Portal-puzzle.svg *License:* Public domain *Contributors:* ? *Original artist:* ?
- **File:QHarmonicOscillator.png** *Source:* https://upload.wikimedia.org/wikipedia/commons/b/bb/QHarmonicOscillator.png *License:* CC-BY-SA-3.0 *Contributors:* Own work *Original artist:* en:User:FlorianMarquardt
- **File:Qcircuit_CNOTfromSQRTSWAP.svg** *Source:* https://upload.wikimedia.org/wikipedia/commons/6/65/Qcircuit_CNOTfromSQRTSWAP.svg *License:* CC BY 3.0 *Contributors:* Own work *Original artist:* Geek3
- **File:Qcircuit_CX.svg** *Source:* https://upload.wikimedia.org/wikipedia/commons/6/6d/Qcircuit_CX.svg *License:* CC BY 3.0 *Contributors:* Own work *Original artist:* Geek3
- **File:Qcircuit_CY.svg** *Source:* https://upload.wikimedia.org/wikipedia/commons/9/92/Qcircuit_CY.svg *License:* CC BY 3.0 *Contributors:* Own work *Original artist:* Geek3
- **File:Qcircuit_CZ.svg** *Source:* https://upload.wikimedia.org/wikipedia/commons/b/ba/Qcircuit_CZ.svg *License:* CC BY 3.0 *Contributors:* Own work *Original artist:* Geek3
- **File:Qcircuit_SqrtSwap.svg** *Source:* https://upload.wikimedia.org/wikipedia/commons/f/f7/Qcircuit_SqrtSwap.svg *License:* CC BY 3.0 *Contributors:* Own work *Original artist:* Geek3
- **File:Qm_step_pot_temp.png** *Source:* https://upload.wikimedia.org/wikipedia/commons/8/87/Qm_step_pot_temp.png *License:* Public domain *Contributors:* Own work *Original artist:* F=q(E+v^B)
- **File:Qm_template_pic_4.svg** *Source:* https://upload.wikimedia.org/wikipedia/commons/f/fe/Qm_template_pic_4.svg *License:* CC0 *Contributors:* Own work *Original artist:* Maschen
- **File:QuantumHarmonicOscillatorAnimation.gif** *Source:* https://upload.wikimedia.org/wikipedia/commons/9/90/QuantumHarmonicOscillatorAnimation.gif *License:* CC0 *Contributors:* Own work *Original artist:* Sbyrnes321
- **File:Quantum_circuit_composition.svg** *Source:* https://upload.wikimedia.org/wikipedia/commons/2/2d/Quantum_circuit_composition.svg *License:* CC BY-SA 3.0 *Contributors:* Created in LaTeX using Q-circuit by the following code: *Original artist:* Self
- **File:Quantum_complex_network_vs_classic_complex_network.png** *Source:* https://upload.wikimedia.org/wikipedia/en/c/cc/Quantum_complex_network_vs_classic_complex_network.png *License:* PD *Contributors:*
http://arxiv.org/abs/0907.3283 *Original artist:*
S. Perseguers, M. Lewenstein, A. Acín, J. I. Cirac
- **File:Quantum_computer.svg** *Source:* https://upload.wikimedia.org/wikipedia/commons/5/53/Quantum_computer.svg *License:* CC BY 3.0 *Contributors:* adapted from *Nanocomputers and Swarm Intelligence* (page 157) ISTE, Waldner, JB (2007), ISBN 2746215160. Reproduced with author's authorization *Original artist:* Original reproduction: Jbw2, SVG version: WhiteTimberwolf
- **File:Quantum_error_correction_of_bit_flip_using_three_qubits.svg** *Source:* https://upload.wikimedia.org/wikipedia/commons/8/80/Quantum_error_correction_of_bit_flip_using_three_qubits.svg *License:* CC BY 3.0 *Contributors:* Created in LaTeX using Q-circuit. Source code below. *Original artist:* Self

- **File:Quantum_error_correction_of_phase_flip_using_three_qubits.svg** *Source:* https://upload.wikimedia.org/wikipedia/commons/7/74/Quantum_error_correction_of_phase_flip_using_three_qubits.svg *License:* CC BY 3.0 *Contributors:* Created in LaTeX using Q-circuit. Source code below. *Original artist:* Self
- **File:Quantum_superposition_of_states_and_decoherence.ogv** *Source:* https://upload.wikimedia.org/wikipedia/commons/8/8b/Quantum_superposition_of_states_and_decoherence.ogv *License:* CC BY-SA 3.0 *Contributors:* Own work *Original artist:* Jubobroff J.Bobroff and full list in credits
- **File:Quantum_swapping.png** *Source:* https://upload.wikimedia.org/wikipedia/en/7/79/Quantum_swapping.png *License:* PD *Contributors:*

  http://arxiv.org/pdf/0906.2977v2.pdf *Original artist:*

  M. Cuquet, J. Calsamiglia
- **File:Question_book-new.svg** *Source:* https://upload.wikimedia.org/wikipedia/en/9/99/Question_book-new.svg *License:* Cc-by-sa-3.0 *Contributors:*

  Created from scratch in Adobe Illustrator. Based on Image:Question book.png created by User:Equazcion *Original artist:*

  Tkgd2007
- **File:Question_dropshade.png** *Source:* https://upload.wikimedia.org/wikipedia/commons/d/dd/Question_dropshade.png *License:* Public domain *Contributors:* Image created by JRM *Original artist:* JRM
- **File:Reversible_circuit_composition.svg** *Source:* https://upload.wikimedia.org/wikipedia/commons/3/39/Reversible_circuit_composition.svg *License:* CC BY-SA 3.0 *Contributors:* Created in LaTeX using Q-circuit by the following code: *Original artist:* Self
- **File:Rtd_seq_v3.gif** *Source:* https://upload.wikimedia.org/wikipedia/commons/5/51/Rtd_seq_v3.gif *License:* CC BY 3.0 *Contributors:* Tool:Resonant Tunneling Diode Simulation with NEGF simulator on www.nanoHUB.org. Link: http://nanohub.org/resources/8799 *Original artist:* Saumitra R Mehrotra & Gerhard Klimeck
- **File:SPDC_figure.png** *Source:* https://upload.wikimedia.org/wikipedia/commons/2/2d/SPDC_figure.png *License:* GFDL *Contributors:* Transferred from en.wikipedia.
  Original artist: J-Wiki at en.wikipedia
- **File:Science.jpg** *Source:* https://upload.wikimedia.org/wikipedia/commons/5/54/Science.jpg *License:* Public domain *Contributors:* ? *Original artist:* ?
- **File:Shore_code.svg** *Source:* https://upload.wikimedia.org/wikipedia/commons/a/a9/Shore_code.svg *License:* CC BY-SA 3.0 *Contributors:* Created in LaTeX using Q-circuit. Source code below. *Original artist:* Self
- **File:Solvay_conference_1927.jpg** *Source:* https://upload.wikimedia.org/wikipedia/commons/6/6e/Solvay_conference_1927.jpg *License:* Public domain *Contributors:* http://w3.pppl.gov/ *Original artist:* Benjamin Couprie
- **File:State_discrimination_POVM.png** *Source:* https://upload.wikimedia.org/wikipedia/en/2/20/State_discrimination_POVM.png *License:* Cc-by-sa-3.0 *Contributors:* ? *Original artist:* ?
- **File:State_discrimination_proj.png** *Source:* https://upload.wikimedia.org/wikipedia/en/8/8b/State_discrimination_proj.png *License:* Cc-by-sa-3.0 *Contributors:* ? *Original artist:* ?
- **File:Stylised_Lithium_Atom.svg** *Source:* https://upload.wikimedia.org/wikipedia/commons/e/e1/Stylised_Lithium_Atom.svg *License:* CC-BY-SA-3.0 *Contributors:* based off of Image:Stylised Lithium Atom.png by Halfdan. *Original artist:* SVG by Indolences. Recoloring and ironing out some glitches done by Rainer Klute.
- **File:Swap_gate.svg** *Source:* https://upload.wikimedia.org/wikipedia/commons/e/ea/Swap_gate.svg *License:* CC BY-SA 3.0 *Contributors:* Created in LaTeX using Q-circuit by the following code: *Original artist:* Self
- **File:Symbol_book_class2.svg** *Source:* https://upload.wikimedia.org/wikipedia/commons/8/89/Symbol_book_class2.svg *License:* CC BY-SA 2.5 *Contributors:* Mad by Lokal_Profil by combining: *Original artist:* Lokal_Profil
- **File:Symbol_list_class.svg** *Source:* https://upload.wikimedia.org/wikipedia/en/d/db/Symbol_list_class.svg *License:* Public domain *Contributors:* ? *Original artist:* ?
- **File:Text_document_with_red_question_mark.svg** *Source:* https://upload.wikimedia.org/wikipedia/commons/a/a4/Text_document_with_red_question_mark.svg *License:* Public domain *Contributors:* Created by bdesham with Inkscape; based upon Text-x-generic.svg from the Tango project. *Original artist:* Benjamin D. Esham (bdesham)
- **File:Toffoli_gate.svg** *Source:* https://upload.wikimedia.org/wikipedia/commons/2/26/Toffoli_gate.svg *License:* CC BY-SA 3.0 *Contributors:* Created in LaTeX using Q-circuit by the following code: *Original artist:* Self
- **File:Von_Neumann_entropy_for_bipartite_system_plot.svg** *Source:* https://upload.wikimedia.org/wikipedia/commons/3/3e/Von_Neumann_entropy_for_bipartite_system_plot.svg *License:* CC BY-SA 3.0 *Contributors:* File:Binary entropy plot.svg *Original artist:* User:Alejo2083, User:□□
- **File:Wiki_letter_w.svg** *Source:* https://upload.wikimedia.org/wikipedia/en/6/6c/Wiki_letter_w.svg *License:* Cc-by-sa-3.0 *Contributors:* ? *Original artist:* ?
- **File:Wiki_letter_w_cropped.svg** *Source:* https://upload.wikimedia.org/wikipedia/commons/1/1c/Wiki_letter_w_cropped.svg *License:* CC-BY-SA-3.0 *Contributors:* This file was derived from Wiki letter w.svg: <a href='//commons.wikimedia.org/wiki/File:Wiki_letter_w.svg' class='image'><img alt='Wiki letter w.svg' src='https://upload.wikimedia.org/wikipedia/commons/thumb/6/6c/Wiki_letter_w.svg/50px-Wiki_letter_w.svg.png' width='50' height='50' srcset='https://upload.wikimedia.org/wikipedia/commons/thumb/6/6c/Wiki_letter_w.svg/75px-Wiki_letter_w.svg.png 1.5x, https://upload.wikimedia.org/wikipedia/commons/thumb/6/6c/Wiki_letter_w.svg/100px-Wiki_letter_w.svg.png 2x' data-file-width='44' data-file-height='44' /></a>
  Original artist: Derivative work by Thumperward
- **File:Wikibooks-logo.svg** *Source:* https://upload.wikimedia.org/wikipedia/commons/f/fa/Wikibooks-logo.svg *License:* CC BY-SA 3.0 *Contributors:* Own work *Original artist:* User:Bastique, User:Ramac et al.

- **File:Wikinews-logo.svg** *Source:* https://upload.wikimedia.org/wikipedia/commons/2/24/Wikinews-logo.svg *License:* CC BY-SA 3.0 *Contributors:* This is a cropped version of Image:Wikinews-logo-en.png. *Original artist:* Vectorized by Simon 01:05, 2 August 2006 (UTC) Updated by Time3000 17 April 2007 to use official Wikinews colours and appear correctly on dark backgrounds. Originally uploaded by Simon.
- **File:Wikiquote-logo.svg** *Source:* https://upload.wikimedia.org/wikipedia/commons/f/fa/Wikiquote-logo.svg *License:* Public domain *Contributors:* ? *Original artist:* ?
- **File:Wikisource-logo.svg** *Source:* https://upload.wikimedia.org/wikipedia/commons/4/4c/Wikisource-logo.svg *License:* CC BY-SA 3.0 *Contributors:* Rei-artur *Original artist:* Nicholas Moreau
- **File:Wikiversity-logo-Snorky.svg** *Source:* https://upload.wikimedia.org/wikipedia/commons/1/1b/Wikiversity-logo-en.svg *License:* CC BY-SA 3.0 *Contributors:* Own work *Original artist:* Snorky
- **File:Wiktionary-logo-en.svg** *Source:* https://upload.wikimedia.org/wikipedia/commons/f/f8/Wiktionary-logo-en.svg *License:* Public domain *Contributors:* Vector version of Image:Wiktionary-logo-en.png. *Original artist:* Vectorized by Fvasconcellos (talk · contribs), based on original logo tossed together by Brion Vibber

56.10.3 Content license

- Creative Commons Attribution-Share Alike 3.0

www.ingramcontent.com/pod-product-compliance
Lightning Source LLC
Chambersburg PA
CBHW080405060326
40689CB00019B/4140
* 9 7 8 1 5 3 5 2 9 6 4 0 3 *